During many years' service in the Royal Navy, Peter Bruce experienced extraordinarily rough weather in the Atlantic in winter and two Pacific typhoons, one off Japan and the other off Mexico – where he simultaneously came all too close to both the eye of the storm and the beach.

Now retired from the Navy he is an active cruising and racing yachtsman, and has followed in the footsteps of his famous ocean-racing father, Erroll Bruce, to skipper many crews to victory. Indeed, he is one of the top Corinthian sailors in the world, has twice been in Britain's winning Admiral's Cup team, has competed successfully in many of the Fastnet Races over the past 55 years, and has been guest skipper, helmsman and navigator aboard numerous racing yachts, including being the sighted skipper who led a blind crew to a spectacular win in international competition. Some of his most remarkable results have been achieved in very stormy weather.

Peter's pilotage books continue to prove invaluable bestsellers. He took over the compilation and editing of *Heavy Weather Sailing* from its original author, Adlard Coles, for its fourth edition, and has overseen each of the subsequent three editions.

HEAVY WEATHER SAILING

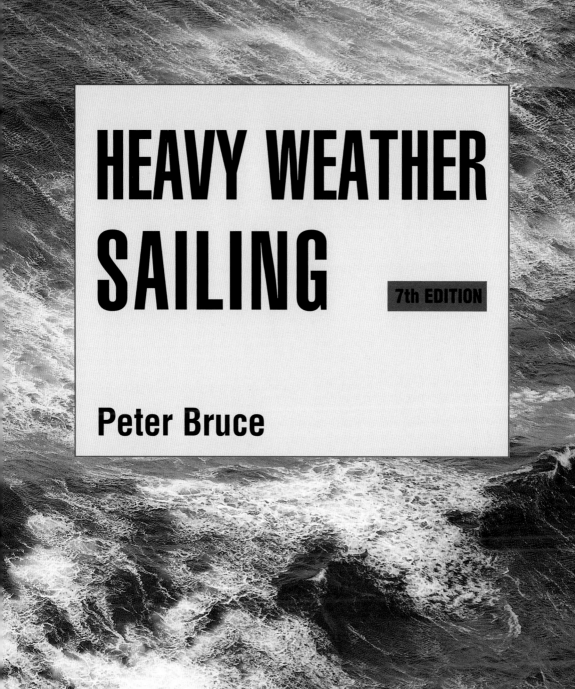

HEAVY WEATHER SAILING

SAILING

7th EDITION

Peter Bruce

Contents

Foreword

by Sir Robin Knox-Johnston

No one in their right mind goes to sea to encounter heavy weather. But those who make longer voyages are likely to experience bad weather at some time because it cannot be avoided all the time. It is in these situations that our seamanship is tested and this is not a test we can afford to fail, so thought and preparation for bad weather are an integral part of the preparation for a voyage offshore or across an ocean.

The preparations start with knowing your boat. Even boats from the same mould will behave differently if their stores and equipment have been placed in different places, and it is getting to understand how your boat behaves in different circumstances that are fundamental to survival in heavy weather. We say that the essence of good seamanship is safety, and safety begins with knowing your boat. The next most important issue is preparation. This applies both to the boat and the crew. Sit inside the boat and imagine it on its side. What might shift at that angle? Well, ensure that it cannot. Can I still find the items I might need quickly? Well, if not, plan where you will put them so you can find them in a hurry.

Crew preparation is paramount. You cannot deal with emergencies unless the crew also know how to respond. Make sure they know where everything is stowed, how to reef at night in a bucking boat and of course, how to set the last resort, the storm sails. Above all, exercise them with man overboard procedures and ensure they know where all the safety equipment is stowed and how to use it.

Many organisations still insist on storm trysails with a separate track on the mast.

Forget it. Very few of us who go solo ocean racing bother with them as they are difficult to set up and hoist. Have the mainsail made with a deep fourth reef which reduces its size to that of the trysail. It does not require all that fumbling on a pitching deck, probably in the dark, putting slides on a track, and is much easier to set. In more than 55 years of sailing I have never owned a trysail but I have always had that fourth reef in my mainsails, and it has been used very effectively and necessarily on a number of occasions.

If bad weather is forecast, charge up the batteries. They will be needed to restart the engine and keep the electronics working. Watch the wind and the waves because that will dictate how you might manage the boat in large breaking waves. One of the worst scenarios is a cross sea, where the waves have built up from one direction and the wind has changed and now other waves are coming from a different angle. This is an especially dire situation because you can get the yacht to lie to one set of waves but the other set, coming in from the beam, will be the one that smashes into the boat. How to deal with that? Well, we all have different experiences and you have to work out what will be best for you and your boat. The ideas recounted in *Heavy Weather Sailing* are likely to provide the answer. When a boat is handled with knowledge and thought she should come through without damage.

When I went around the world in the 9.8m (32ft) *Suhaili*, the only literature in existence that gave an indication of what a storm in the Southern Ocean could be like was that of the Smeetons in *Tzu Hang*. They were pitchpoled in a larger boat. I had to experiment as to how I could hold *Suhaili* so she would not rush down the front of 80-foot (24.3m) waves when the rudder has little effect, and prevent her swinging across the front of the wave when she would have been almost bound to be have been rolled and dismasted. I found that 220m (720ft) of 5cm (2in) circumference rope, paid out as a bight, held *Suhaili*'s stern to the waves and that was when I could get my best sleep because I knew that, as she started her downhill rush, the warp would check her speed before she went out of control. That worked for *Suhaili*, but would not necessarily work for another boat. When I participated in the Velux5oceans race 37 years later the boat, a 60-footer (18.3m), was fast enough to keep ahead of the waves. Well, most of the time!

Heavy Weather Sailing is a classic. It gives examples of handling bad weather from many different experiences in very different yachts. You will find that all the matters I've raised here feature within its pages, including a carefully considered treatise on the subject of whether to use a trysail or a fourth reef. The book cannot tell you how to handle every circumstance you might find yourself in, but it does give you a wealth of advice and examples of how others have managed, that can help you find what is best for you. We often talk about essential reading, but for anyone contemplating a longer voyage, with land and a safe haven over the horizon, then reading other people's experiences is an essential part of preparation. *Heavy Weather Sailing* gives this with great care and relevance.

Preface

Adlard Coles OBE died in 1985. He left behind him a multitude of friends and admirers, many of whom knew him only through his books. Apart from his ability to write vividly and clearly, Adlard was an extraordinary man. In spite of being a diabetic, a quiet and very gentle person with something of a poet's eye, he was incredibly tough, courageous and determined. Thus it was very often that Adlard's *Cohoe* appeared at the top of the lists after a really stormy race. When reading Adlard's enchanting prose one also needs to take into account that he was supremely modest, and his scant reference to some major achievement belies the effort that must have been required. It is clear that Adlard minimised everything, which does him credit. As an example, the wind strengths he gave in his own accounts in the earlier editions of *Heavy Weather Sailing* were manifestly objective and warrant no risk of being accused of exaggeration for narrative effect.

There were three editions of *Heavy Weather Sailing* undertaken by Adlard Coles and this new edition of *Heavy Weather Sailing* is my fourth, and brings the total number of editions to 7 over a span of 50 years. In writing about a subject that most people do their best to avoid, it should be remembered that to have successfully sailed through a particularly violent storm gives a sailor confidence at sea as nothing else will. Adlard Coles lightly referred to the collection of storms that he endured as being like trophies of a big game hunter, but they are educational and character forming too. After a big storm it will be easier to judge how much a boat and crew can endure before they break, and what the warning signs are.

The ethos of this book is to supply the specialist information that will prepare a sailor for heavy weather, and give honest examples of what happened to people and their vessels that have encountered a severe storm. Most space has been given to the specialist information – the expert advice – as this provides a platform of knowledge to enable the reader to be able to glean the maximum from the storm experiences that follow, and the principles to employ when bad weather approaches. These storm experiences have been carefully picked to cover a wide range of predicaments. They tend to relate to unusually high wind strengths because these rare extreme conditions best prove the worth of a particular course of action. They also illustrate how modern heavy weather seamanship has been able to evolve with the benefit of improved knowledge, clothing, design and materials. The improved knowledge is the most important factor, of course, and the contributors of these accounts have freely given of their experience to help others who may follow in their wake.

Over the years the average size of offshore leisure vessels has constantly increased. For example in the first three ARCs 56 per cent of the participants were under 12m (40ft); now the average length of yachts in the ARC is about 13.5m (45ft). This trend is in many ways desirable and welcome, but places more dependence on the ship's equipment being serviceable and therefore the need for maintenance.

Buying a sailing boat can loosely be compared to buying a new house in a mountain region. The house and the newly-built adjoining ones look good, well-constructed, well equipped, comfortable and spacious, but the question that must be asked of someone knowledgeable and responsible, other than sales people, is whether the house is *vulnerable to an avalanche* and whether the site has ever been known to have had one!

A capsize is roughly in the same league as an avalanche: out of the question for much of the time and, even when possible, one would have to be unlucky to have the experience.

It is easy to be persuaded that one will never be out in conditions that would put stability in question, as if one always had the choice.

It seems that little has changed for the good over 40 years regarding stability and incidentally keel security. They should be matters of some concern to all yacht owners.

The 'Expert Advice' part of this new edition has been substantially rewritten, taking new developments into account, whilst continuing to reinforce past practices that have conclusively stood the test of time. The advice is given without any intended commercial interest.

PART ONE

Expert Advice

1 Yacht design and construction for heavy weather

Olin Stephens, edited by Martin Thomas and Peter Bruce

The loss of a vessel at sea is a disaster and especially if crew are lost too. A subsequent enquiry of such a dreadful event will assess how much was due to the boat's design, construction or maintenance and how much to crew error. The failure to right after inversion by some ocean racing yachts in the 1990s was related, at least in part, to design; although the stranding of *Gipsy Moth IV* in 2006 and of *Vestas Wind* in 2014 resulted from human mistakes. Heavy weather has taken its toll of vessels of all shapes, size and design. We should consider the design characteristics of those yachts that best survive the worst that weather can offer. Boat design matters and can be decisive, although once at sea it is the action of the crew that counts.

For a boat to survive a storm it must stay afloat, keep water out of the hull, remain upright or, if it does invert, to do so for only a few moments. Strength of hull and range of positive stability are first requirements. In this chapter we shall try to determine how these essentials can best be refined to provide for the safety and comfort of the offshore crew.

A lifetime around the water has shown me that many types of boat can come through the extremes of weather on long cruises. I think it must have been in 1926 when my brother Rod and I spotted Harry Pigeon's *Islander* lying in New Rochelle harbour, not far from our home. We were quick to borrow a dinghy and greet him so as to inspect the home built 10.4m (34ft) yawl that he had sailed single handed around the world. Neither *Islander*'s light

displacement nor simple vee bottom form had made for survival difficulties. One was most impressed by the simplicity of the construction and equipment: no engine or electrics of any kind, no speedometer or even a patent log. We admired the man who made it all seem so easy. Soon we heard that Alain Gerbault and his *Firebird* were at City Island, so we went there. Although the contrast was in every way disappointing to us, the older, heavier boat had made it through some very bad weather.

I retain a great deal of respect for the work of Dr Claud Worth, the owner during the twenties of several yachts called *Tern*. He was a meticulous student and practitioner of offshore sailing. He advocated moderate beam, plenty of displacement and a long keel as explained in his books, *Yacht Cruising* and *Yacht Navigation and Voyaging*.

This background led me to believe that, if structure and handling are sound, the bigger the boat the better. Of necessity, a larger vessel demands more of the builder and crew as the loads increase geometrically with size. Big sails require strength and skill to control; small sails can be easily manhandled. Similar observations apply to hull, spars, and rigging.

Analytical studies, such as those carried out in the course of the joint United States Yacht Racing Union (USYRU) and the Society of Naval Architects and Marine Engineers (SNAME) study on Safety from Capsizing and by the Wolfson Unit of the University of Southampton, have noted two characteristic conditions of capsize that bear on design.

Yachts should be designed and built to withstand extreme weather, even as severe as in this photograph of the South Atlantic when the wave height was estimated at between 12 and 15m (39 and 49ft), and wind speed between 60 and 80 knots. Photo: Christian Février/Bluegreen

In geometrically similar hulls the righting moment increases in proportion to the fourth power of length while the heeling moment grows only as length cubed. Because of this, small boat designs need more inherent power, meaning beam and displacement, while big yachts with similar proportions need very large rigs. Thus smaller boats should avoid the bottom of this range and the larger boats should avoid the top.

Design displacement is determined primarily by the requirements of strength and stability but also relates to motion and room below for the comfort of the crew. The yacht's total weight must provide for an adequate structure and be able to accommodate the crew stores and equipment. The total weight must also allow for sufficient ballast to ensure the power to carry sails with positive stability. Efficient use of the best materials can give a light hull and rig. With enough ballast, appropriate design can provide stability and so give a lower limit on safe displacement. Though structural materials are not the subject of this review, sound light hulls can be built of many different materials including wood, GRP and aluminium alloy. The high strength, high modulus materials often used as composites, such as carbon fibre, when used with care and experience offer strength and light weight. Steel and concrete are inherently heavier, especially the latter. Boats with light displacement must have light hulls so as to carry a reasonable amount of ballast for the sake of stability. In heavier boats material selection is less critical.

The vertical centre of gravity and hull geometry combine to establish the range of positive stability. A good range, for illustration's sake at least over 120°, will virtually assure that an upturned boat will right herself in conditions that have caused a capsize. Much lower values may ensure the reverse. The centre of gravity, so crucial to stability, will be affected by sails, especially those that are roller furled. This suggests the need for some allowance over a stated minimum. It seems unfortunate that racing influences on the IOR and the IMS have led to wide beam and a shoal body; these aspects can lead to a

These are the force of the wind on the rig and the power of a breaking sea. In the first condition the light structure of a small boat may not necessarily be overloaded by strong winds, but in the second the hull or deck can be smashed by a breaking sea.

As the terms are often used, size and displacement mean about the same thing. The terms 'light' or 'heavy' displacement usually refer to the displacement/length ratio often expressed as tons of displacement divided by the cube of 1 per cent of waterline length in feet. Though extreme, one can accept a range of 500 to 50 in that ratio over a range of 6–24m (20–80ft) in waterline length.

poor range of positive stability. At least the IMS rule favours hulls with a low centre of gravity, a better situation than the IOR that encouraged an unwholesomely high centre of gravity. Ballasted narrow deep hulls of the older International Rule type, like a decked over 12-metre, could go to 180°, representing the full 360° rollover. For beam and hull depth, moderation is the best course. Beam offers initial stability and roominess, but too much of it reduces the range of positive stability and results in quick motion. Depth provides easier motion, headroom, structural continuity and space for some bilge water; all desirable but less conducive to high speed. Heavy ballast contributes to range of stability but also gives quick motion. A moderate ratio of beam to hull depth seems ideal; for instance a beam of not more than three to four times the hull body depth, with the centre of gravity low enough to give a positive stability range of at least 130°. The damage to *Vertue XXXV*, described in earlier editions of *Heavy Weather Sailing*, was caused by a breaking sea which threw her over and down smashing the lee side of her cabin trunk (coach roof), a vulnerable structure, at best, due to structural discontinuity. The *Vertue*'s small size probably did not permit the incorporation of the material needed for greater strength. A similar occurrence was the damage to *Puffin*, one of my own designs and not quite so small, but hit hard at a weak point. *Sayula*'s survival, after a severe knockdown in the Whitbread Race of 1973, with great discomfort but minimal damage, contributes to confidence in the larger boat.

The potential weakness of the coach roof in the smaller boat should not be seen as a condemnation. The coach roof provides headroom. It can also contribute usefully to range of stability by virtue of its volume if the hull is free of water. It is simply a reminder that any structural discontinuity and all corners can be sources of weakness and should be carefully designed and built.

It is clear that the trend to thin keels, narrow at the hull juncture, weakens an already highly loaded spot. High loads in that area cause stress in keel bolts, the keel and the associated hull structure. Whenever a narrow base is used, the structure must be most carefully considered.

The power to carry sail is quite different from stability range. A naval architect evaluates both at small heel angles by measuring the vertical span between the centre of gravity and the metacentre where, at a small heel angle, a vertical line through the centre of buoyancy cuts the heeled centre plane. The product of this height and the tangent (a trigonometrical function) of the heel angle gives the righting arm at small angles, which, multiplied by the displacement, gives the righting moment. The displacement is constant but with increasing heel the righting moment is strongly dependent on hull shape and the ratio of beam-to-hull body depth. A beamy shoal-bodied boat will have great upright metacentric height but without a large heeled righting moment. With increasing heel the righting moment will diminish as the righting arm shrinks and becomes negative. Good proportions between beam and hull depth will hold that factor almost constant up to angles of 35 or 40° while assuring a safe range of positive stability. The first example, the beamy boat, will feel stiff but must be kept upright to use the power of her rig while the deeper boat can benefit from plenty of sail power up to a large heel angle. The beamy, lighter yacht depends greatly on crew weight to minimise heel so as to maintain sail power and speed. Comfort is another characteristic related to beam. Over-generous beam contributes room and space below but tends to quicken the ship's motion and reduce the stability range.

In respect of reducing the ingress of water into the cabin, I should like to refer favourably to the Dorade ventilator. Despite its appearance and the many efforts to do something better it still leads in supplying maximum air and minimum water. Like other vents, the Dorade can admit solid water if fully immersed in a capsize. Preparation for the most extreme conditions should include replacement of the cowl with a deck plate. It is well to avoid companionways and other deck openings that are away from the centreline where they are at increased risk of down-flooding.

Touching briefly on other aspects of safety and comfort we should consider strong, well-located handrails and we should be sure that generous rounding eliminates sharp corners. Galleys should be arranged so that cooks can wedge or strap themselves in place and, if possible, out of the path of spilled hot food. The water supply must be divided between several tanks, each with its individual shut-off valve. This will save the supply in case of leakage or contamination and also helps weight distribution and thus trim. The effect of water surging about within the tank is reduced. Engine exhaust systems may admit water in bad weather, though careful design can minimise that problem.

Rigs must be designed for the high but uncertain loads of heavy weather. It seems evident that many racing rigs lack the strength to stay in place. Improved analytical methods such as finite element design have not replaced basic calculations based on the righting moment and the consequent rigging loads that apply tension at the chain plates and compression in the mast. Most designers use Euler column methods often with assumptions on end fixity and safety factors based on their experience. Such assumptions will vary but they must be generous so as to allow for the unexpectedly severe conditions of heavy weather sailing.

Rig geometry and sail shape seem to be a matter of personal preference. Under severe conditions two independently supported masts can be recommended. Strong storm sails and arrangements to set them quickly and easily are essential to a well-found offshore yacht. The storm sails should not be too large. No more than one third of mainsail area is suggested for the storm trysail and about 5 per cent of forestay length squared for the storm jib. Sail area, relative to stability, can often relate to the home port and cruising grounds, and is usually influenced by comfort more than by safety. Sail can always be shortened but too large a working rig means frequent reefing or sailing at an uncomfortable angle of heel.

The areas of storm sails given above are very close to those defined in the Special Regulations Governing Equipment and Accommodations Standards of World Sailing (formerly ISAF). Although drawn up for racing yachts there is a great deal of good sense in these regulations. I recommend a study and implementation of these regulations to anyone preparing to sail offshore.

On the subject of hull geometry I have stressed the ratio of beam to hull depth. There are other considerations, less vital but still important. Positive and easy steering control is one such. In this day of analytical yacht design there is still no subject more deserving of intensive study than that of balance and steering control. Possibly the lack of understanding explains why there are few subjects that stir greater differences of opinion than the shape of the lateral plane including keel and rudder.

Course stability is often characterised as that condition in which, without the adjustment of the steering mechanism, a boat sailing a given course when diverted by an external force will return to the initial course. This could be a definition of self-steering ability. Many boats can be trimmed to steer themselves under the right conditions but few will do so on all courses and wind strengths. The forces involved and the direction of their application and the tendency of the hull to turn one way or another at different heel angles and speeds form a very complex system. We can accept these difficulties and yet still ask for steering that is light and responsive; this can be hard for the designer to attain.

A long keel is frequently cited as the best solution. Probably it is, if light weather speed is less important than good manners on the helm, and if the length extends well aft. The disadvantage is the great wetted area associated with the long keel. With such a keel, turning is necessarily less abrupt, and second, a large part of the lateral plane is abaft the centre of gravity. Consider the converse with keel area forward, and visualise a sea turning the boat. It is as though the boat were being towed from a point abaft the pivot point so that the further the new course departs from the original, the further the inertial direction departs from the course, thus causing the boat

A typical broach by a modern racing yacht, in this case a Mumm 36. If the balance between spinnaker and mainsail is lost, the boat will heel over and forces may be generated that are more than the rudder can correct. The yacht will adopt the angle shown, and due to the buoyancy of the wide stern the rudder may be partly out of the water, making recovery difficult. Although this is a frequent occurrence with modern racing yachts, and unnerving for those who are not accustomed to it, damage to the yacht or injury to the crew is rare. Photo: PPL

to turn continually further from the intended direction. Conversely if the tow point, the centre of gravity, where the force is applied, is forward of the pivot, the centre of lateral resistance (CLR), then the more the course changes the more the direction of the inertial, or tow, force is directed back toward the original course. I should add that this principle of sailing balance is not universally accepted, though to some it seems evident.

Small wetted area carries with it advantages that have resulted in the almost universal adoption of the short keel and separate rudder. Comparatively it means equal performance with less sail area, especially in light weather, or to windward when speeds are low. Using a short keel the required position of the ballast dictates the location of the keel that further dictates the location of the CLR. This disadvantage can be lessened by locating disposable weights as far forward as possible, permitting the ballast keel to come aft, but such gains are limited and the best available strategy to move the CLR aft seems to be to use a large skeg and rudder. These serve the function of feathers on the arrow. Most new

boats follow this pattern and they can behave well, exhibiting no loss of steering control, the ability to heave to or other good seagoing characteristics.

Other characteristics that seem to contribute to good manners are reasonably balanced, yet buoyant, ends and moderate to light displacement (see Figs 1.1 and 1.2). Both minimise trim change with increasing heel so that the unavoidable changes in the yacht's tendency to alter course occur gradually and the abrupt application of helm is seldom needed. Easy and positive control is valuable in a big sea.

For the sake of an easy and steady helm the pressure of the water on the hull must be evenly distributed and constant over the range of speed and heel. Long lines, minimally rounded, with relatively constant curvature make for constant water velocity, and thus constant pressure, over the hull surface. Any short quick curve in the path of the water implies a quick change in pressure on the hull surface and, very likely, a quick change on the helm. Again, a light displacement hull with moderate beam and rather straight lines in the ends best meets these conditions.

The motion of a yacht in rough water is probably better understood than is balance under sail. It depends a great deal on the weight and the way it is distributed. Weight distribution may be considered in any desired plane, usually in longitudinal and transverse senses. It is measured by the moment of inertia and is usually expressed as the gyradius that relates the moment of inertia to displacement. The former, the moment of inertia, is the sum of the products of all weight elements and the squares of their distances from a chosen axis. The radius of gyration, or gyradius, is given by the square root of the quantity obtained by dividing the moment of inertia by the total mass. It serves as a measure of the yacht's resistance to acceleration around the chosen axis. Thus a large gyradius, either longitudinal or transverse, tends toward easy motion and is desirable in terms of comfort. In passing it might be observed that the need for a very minimum longitudinal gyradius has become an article of faith among racing sailors. One suspects that they are right more often than not. Studies of resistance in waves show that the weight distribution that results in synchronism with wave encounter is bad; otherwise the effect is small.

Weight itself, or more correctly mass, slows acceleration so that the motion of a heavy boat tends to be comfortable. In this calculation the rig, due to its distance from the centre, makes a major contribution. Anyone who has experienced the loss of a mast in rough water will confirm the quickened motion that followed. Thus, by resisting sudden roll, a heavy rig contributes to both comfort and safety. Studies have shown that, by increasing the transverse gyradius, resistance to capsize in a breaking sea, like that of the 1979 Fastnet, is greatly enhanced.

Variations in hull shape are most significant as they relate to displacement and stability. Other effects of shape are worth noting. As mentioned above, there should be balance between the ends. This does not mean anything like true symmetry. My approach was by eye, which spells guesswork, possibly judgement, though today it is easy to check heeled static trim with a computer, a step toward eliminating excessive trim change.

It is well to avoid flat areas in the hull to avoid slamming. Flat areas can easily develop in the ends, especially in a light displacement design where the fore and aft lines become pretty straight. If sections have a moderate U shape, rather than a V, the flat area that occurs where straight lines cross in a surface will be avoided. Even some slight rounding on a long radius extends the period of impact, reducing the tendency to slam. Freeboard is another characteristic on which moderation is a good guide. High sides increase stability range but present a large area exposed to the impact of a breaking sea, while a high point of impact increases the overturning moment. Low freeboard leads to the early flooding of the lee deck with its sheet leads and fittings. Related to freeboard is sheer. It can be argued that this has more to do with appearance than seaworthiness. I think a good sea boat should keep her ends above water without excessive freeboard amidships. Let us agree that the beauty of the Watson and Fife boats of the previous century was also functional.

Cockpits that can hold a great deal of water can be dangerous. It is essential that all cockpits be self-draining through scuppers that should be large. Deep cockpits offer protection and comfort but can have an effect on buoyancy. Different priorities play a part in cockpit dimensions but the smaller cockpit must be the safest in the end.

The conditions we are considering are less than ideal for centerboarders. They have their supporters and I have been responsible for many centreboard designs. I always advised the owners that capsize was possible and that in many cases the stability range was less than I should have liked. Where draft was not too restricted so that the ratio of beam to depth was not too great, and freeboard and deck structures were appropriate, the stability range seemed fully acceptable. Among S&S designed centreboarders, *Sunstone*, ex *Deb*, due to her rather deep hull, seems a good example of a centreboarder suited to heavy weather sailing (see Fig 1.1).

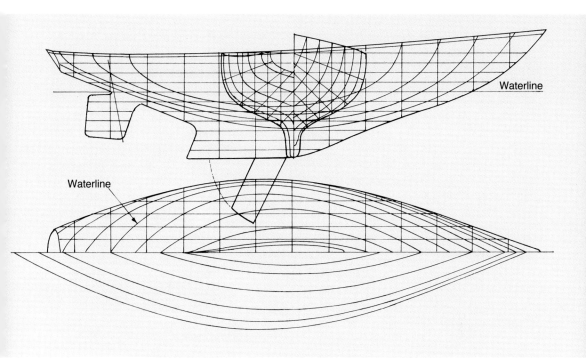

Figure 1.1 *The balanced lines plan of* Sunstone, *previously named* Deb. *Her present owners, Tom and Vicki Jackson, live aboard throughout the year and have achieved outstanding success in RORC races.*

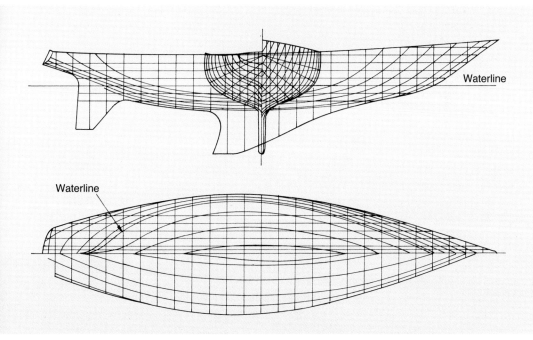

Figure 1.2 *The balanced lines plan of* War Baby, *previously named* Tenacious, *winner of the 1979 Fastnet Race, when owned by Ted Turner. Subsequently she was owned by the late Warren Brown who cruised extensively in her.*

I hope it has been useful to consider in this chapter a number of specific characteristics. While each has an influence on the ultimate ability of a yacht it is always the combination that counts. No individual dimension means too much. Good performance can be reached by different paths and, finally, the good combinations are the ones that work.

When I think of the boat in which I should be happiest in meeting heavy weather I visualise one that is moderate in every way, but just as strong as possible. I should avoid extremes of beam to depth or depth to beam, either very light or very heavy displacement or a very high rig. I should like the ends to be buoyant, but neither very sharp nor full, and neither long nor chopped right off. Though I have stressed resistance to capsize, in my own seagoing experience I have never been worried on that score. I have, however, occasionally been concerned about leaks or the strength of hull or rig. In the end I recommend moderate proportions and lots of strength.

COMMENT

In the 1950s and 1960s yachts were usually built with colossal strength in reserve but nowadays, with better knowledge of stress and materials, and the ever-present quest for better performance, yachts are designed and built with much lighter construction. Olin Stephen's emphasis on the necessity for structural strength, especially in the highly loaded keel attachment area, is a reminder of current instances when an overly-light construction caused disaster.

In 2001 two British lives were lost when an Australian Farr 38 called *Rising Farrster* capsized off the New South Wales coast when her keel broke off. The coroner, John Abernathy, said that 'the primary cause was inadequate hull thickness around the keel washer plates', i.e. the hull was simply not strong enough to support the twisting force of the keel when the yacht heeled over. It emerged that the hull was built to the minimum standard required by Australian law, but not to the thickness stipulated by the designer, Bruce Farr. Subsequently the chairman of the Cruising Yacht Club of Australia's sailing committee advised participants in the Sydney–Hobart Race to 'check the bilge and satisfy themselves that the designed thickness of hull was actually there'. This can usually be achieved quite simply, as will be seen.

Another similar accident occurred in April 2005 when a crewmember died when the keel of his 12.8m (42ft) yacht came off. The building company put out various statements. These included that the builders assumed that the yacht had hit a rock, which was denied by all the crew that had ever sailed her. The survey of the damaged yacht stated that 'the bottom section of the yacht as found did not have sufficient strength in the areas designed to take up the forces generated by the keel due to serious manufacturing defects in the laminates and bonding. The wall thickness was between 12mm and 17mm rather than the 25mm or more that was thought appropriate'. A more recent event was when the Bruce Farr designed Beneteau 40.7 *Cheeki Rafiki* lost her keel while crossing the Atlantic in May 2014 with the loss of all four of her crew. This was attributed to progressive damage caused by repeated grounding over the life of the yacht.

The incidence of keel failure, often with attendant loss of life, is all too common. Indeed the UK's Marine Accident Investigation Branch investigating the *Cheeki Rafiki* tragedy identified 72 keel failures between 1984 and 2013. More details will be found in Chapter 3.

It is not only keels that can fail. For example a well-known class of sport boat of 11.1m (36ft) length called *Django* was being delivered from Fiji to Auckland, in July 2014. When running under storm jib in wind speeds of over 60 knots she suffered severe failure of hull structure surrounding the lower rudder bearing after a broach. The *Django* crew were aware of a similar situation when

Walawala II, a 2011 built epoxy glass Sydney GTS 43, racing from Hong Kong to Vietnam in October 2013, sank in five or ten minutes with a very similar structural failure.

The rescue authorities were alerted by the skipper's satellite phone and *Django* stayed afloat long enough for her crew to be rescued by a New Zealand frigate. Incidentally a satellite phone was also used by *Walawala*'s crew to seek help and found it to be the most effective means of communication at the time.

Yacht designers sometimes mention that boat builders do not build the boat exactly to the one that they have designed. Some yacht builders simply skimp on the number of laminates used in laying up a hull, thereby saving time and considerable cost in labour and material. The inexperienced racing owner is likely to be pleased to find his boat is 'down to weight' or even lighter than expected, as to have a light boat is in a racing man's mantra.

There must come a point when lack of structural stiffness leads to loss of boat speed in addition to the danger of losing the keel, or other structural failure. Keeping weight out of the ends of a yacht is another racing man's mantra, but the ends of a yacht are the most vulnerable to knocks, such as berthing incidents and, with some modern yachts, the ends are not even built to withstand the minor collisions of normal use. As Olin Stephens simply says 'a yacht should be built as strong as possible'.

In the case of light displacement yachts, there is little margin of safety in hull design. Thus the designer's laminate specification should be most strictly adhered to. In 2000 a yacht builder in Britain supplied a 10.6m (35ft) 'one-design' racing yacht in which the hull thickness adjacent to the keel was 30–40 per cent less than some of other yachts in the class. In this case two different builders had built the yachts, but their keels and keel bolts were made by the same keel manufacturer who said that all the keels and keel bolts were virtually identical. The second manufacturer produced yachts which were up to 500kg lighter than the first, and it was evident from the exposed height of the keel bolts that there was less hull thickness at the keel intersection, compared to those of the first manufacturer. The matter came to light when external cracking appeared over the length and width of the keel flange, which defied straightforward remedy. It was apparent that the hull, which was bending significantly under load, did not properly support the keel. The movement was borne out in practical trials, as the saloon table supports happened to be attached to the keel bolts, and thus reflected the keel's lateral movement whenever the yacht tacked.

To assess the depth of the hull at the keel it is necessary only to drill a small diameter hole through to the keel or the keel flange, and measure the depth. Of course the hole needs to be properly filled afterwards, but there is no surer way of knowing the true hull thickness at this vital point. The designer, or the designer's drawings, should give the designed depth of hull adjacent to the keel, and a rough guide is that the hull thickness should be no less than the diameter of the keel bolts.

As a matter of interest to racing yacht owners, the scantily built lighter yachts produced by the second yacht builder were never as fast as those built by the first builder, suggesting that, in this case, gain in hull speed through reduction of weight might have been more than offset by the loss of structural stiffness.

Reference has been made to yacht designers not having the yacht built to their drawings. Equally so owners do not always have the vessel they had envisaged. There is much to be said for owners engaging a trustworthy and experienced surveyor to oversee construction whether a production yacht or 'one off'.

Olin Stephens has passed on but his designs will be long remembered for their strength and admirable sea-keeping qualities, from which much can still be learnt.

2 The stability of yachts in large breaking waves

Andrew Claughton

Causes of capsize

What causes a yacht to capsize? Sailing dinghies and lightly ballasted day sailboats such as a J24 can be laid flat and capsized solely by the pressure of wind in the sails. In larger yachts the nearest equivalent of this is the broach whilst under spinnaker. In a bad broach the mast can be pressed down as far as the water but once the heeling influence of the spinnaker is removed, the yacht recovers to an upright position. Experience shows us that, in flat water, gusts alone cannot capsize a yacht.

Even encountering high and steep waves the story remains the same. The action of wave slope in heeling a dinghy or day sailer may assist the wind in producing a capsize, but a conventional yacht's stability is such that it cannot be capsized by even the combined action of wind and waves, no matter how high or steep.

It is *breaking waves* that cause capsize; if the yacht is caught beam on to breaking waves of sufficient size, then the exaggerated steepness of the breaking wave front, coupled with the impact of the jet-like torrent of the breaking crest, will knock the yacht down to a point where the mast is well immersed. (See photo sequence overleaf). At this point the yacht's fate is decided by its stability characteristics; it will either return to an upright position or carry on to an inverted position, where the boat may remain for some time until another wave disturbs the yacht

sufficiently to flip itself upright. If the wave is high enough or the encounter with it is timed appropriately, then a full 360° roll will occur. This analysis has often been proved correct by the unfortunate experiences of sailors who found themselves at sea in gale conditions, or crossing shoal water.

How big do breaking waves need to be to cause this type of behaviour? Unfortunately the answer is 'not very big'. During the model tests that were carried out to investigate the problem, when the *breaking* wave was 30 per cent of the hull length high, from trough to crest, it could capsize some of the yachts, while waves to a height of 60 per cent of the hull length would comfortably overwhelm all of the boats we tested. Beam is usually close to one third of the waterline and is often used as the criteria. In real terms this means that for a 10m (32.8ft) boat, caught in the wrong place, when the *breaking* wave is 3m (9.8ft) high, this presents a capsize risk, and when the *breaking* wave is 6m (19.7ft) high whatever the boat shape it will capsize. The word breaking is italicised to stress that it is breaking waves that present the danger, big waves in themselves are not a problem.

As shown in the photo sequence, the model tests were done in waves that broke all along their crest at the same time, unlike the waves at sea where short lengths of crest break as the wave systems interact. Once the breaking crest at the point of impact is as wide as the boat is long, then its full effect will be felt.

No combination of hull form or ballasting arrangement can offer a substantial improvement to capsize resistance, though enhancement can be made to the sometimes vital recovery time.
Photo: PPL

How can capsize be avoided?

The simple answer to avoid capsizing is to avoid breaking waves. This does not necessarily mean staying tied to a mooring, but rather in avoiding certain sea areas in wind or tide conditions where breaking seas may be thrown up. For example, to help their small boat fishermen avoid breaking waves, the Norwegian authorities define no-go areas where breaking waves are more likely to occur as part of their weather forecasts.

Taken a step further, even if caught out in extreme conditions of wind and wave, a technique to avoid the breakers can be employed, but on a more local scale. During the 1979 Fastnet Race many yachts were able to keep sailing, and actively pick their way through the waves, avoiding the breaking part of the seas, much as a surfer keeps to the unbroken part of the wave by tracking across its face. Once the boat is to one side of the breaking part of the crest the danger is over

and even delaying the moment of impact until the breaking wave has dissipated some of its energy will reduce the capsize risk. The wave is at its most dangerous at the point of breaking and immediately afterwards. Active sailing also keeps the boat from being caught beam-on to the seas, which is its most vulnerable position. The risk is that a mistake in steering might cause a broach that results in the boat being left beam-on to the waves. This technique does, however, need a strong and competent crew to execute for long periods of time. It is nevertheless a well-established and successful technique for dealing with heavy weather.

As was demonstrated by crews' experiences during the heavy weather races described in Chapters 3, 15, 17 and 22 it is not always possible to avoid capsize situations. Due to crew fatigue, or plain bad luck, a yacht, especially if short-handed, may encounter a capsize or knock down incident. The research carried out in the wake of the 1979 Fastnet Race has been aimed at evaluating what features of hull

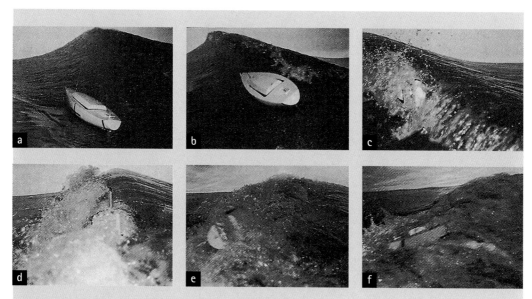

A fin keel parent model under test showing beam-on 360° capsize.

a *Beam-on to a large wave.*
b *Crest begins to break.*
c *90° heel angle (transom visible).*

d *Upside down (keel and rudder pointing to the sky).*
e *Nearly upright again.*
f *Returned to normal!*

design contribute to a safer yacht in survival conditions.

So far I have written in general terms about stability, but we cannot go much further without explaining in more detail the physical mechanisms that keep a sailing yacht the right way up, and how things behave once the mast is below the horizontal.

Fig 2.1 shows a typical righting moment curve; this describes the variation of righting moment as heel angle increases. All of the yacht's weight can be assumed to act vertically down through the centre of gravity, whilst the buoyancy force opposes this through the centre of buoyancy. The righting moment is the torque generated by the increasing misalignment of the yacht's centre of gravity, which remains fixed on the hull centreline – unless the crew sit out – and the centre of buoyancy that shifts to leeward as the yacht heels. Intuitively one can see that in the normal sailing range of up to an angle of say 45°, an adequate righting moment to

resist the heeling moment of the sails can be achieved either by a wide beam, so that the centre of buoyancy shifts outboard more, or by a low centre of gravity, so that it is further away from the centre of buoyancy. Whichever way the designer does it, a yacht has to have an adequate righting moment at 30–40° of heel to carry its sail properly. Some boats are stiff, i.e. the righting moment rises quickly with increasing heel angle, whilst others are more tender, i.e. with a slower rise of righting moment. In the latter case such boats very often require the crew to sit out to produce an adequate righting moment, by shifting the centre of gravity outboard.

At the point of maximum righting moment, the centre of buoyancy is as far to leeward as it is going to get. It then starts to move back to the centre as heel angle increases further. This means that at 90° the righting moment can be quite low, hence the ease with which the broached yacht can be held with its mast close to the water by the flogging spinnaker. A

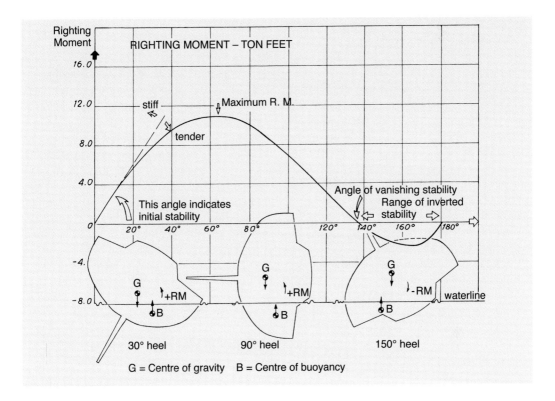

Figure 2.1 *A typical righting moment curve.*

few more degrees past this point and the centre of gravity and centre of buoyancy are in line again, but the wrong way up. This is the angle of vanishing stability (AVS). At this point the boat is balanced in unstable equilibrium like a pencil on its end and can fall either way, i.e. back to upright or to end up floating upside down. At 180° heel – i.e. upside down – the two centres are in line, and this is another stable position unless the boat is fully self-righting. Before the hydrostatic forces can act to turn the boat the right way up some external force must push the boat back past its angle of vanishing stability.

To calculate the righting moment curve for a yacht, the position of the centre of buoyancy is calculated from the hull shape and the position of the centre of gravity is determined by physically inclining the yacht a few degrees and measuring the heeling moment required.

The ability of a yacht to recover from a breaking wave encounter depends on the hull and coach roof shape. This is not only for its

influence on how the breaking wave affects it, but also for its influence on the shape of the stability curve.

The conclusions about capsizing are based on the results of model tests carried out by the Wolfson Unit at Southampton University. The tests were carried out using free running models in a towing tank 60m long x 3.7m wide x 1.8m deep. The breaking waves were generated using computer controlled wave makers, and fans provided a full scale 40 knot wind over the test area. The behaviour of different hull shapes will be described in the context of the models tested at Southampton. The results from these tests were complementary to those obtained from the parallel Sailboat Committee of the Society of Naval Architects and Marine Engineers/ United States Yacht Racing Union study carried out in the USA.

The three basic hulls tested were: a traditional yacht form, a typical 'fin and skeg' yacht, and a derivative of the 'fin and skeg'

15

yacht modified to give it higher freeboard with no coach roof. From these three parent hulls a further six forms were derived, each identical in all respects to its parent with the exception of beam, one narrower and one wider for each type. Models were then constructed from these lines plans to represent 9.75m (32ft) yachts at 1:13 scale. The lines plans of the 9 models are shown in Fig 2.2.

The different characteristics of the hulls allowed individual design features to be evaluated in relation to three aspects of behaviour:

1. Hydrostatic performance, angle of vanishing stability and stiffness.
2. Response to the impact of a breaking wave.
3. Influence on controllability, i.e. how design features can help an active sailing approach in avoiding a capsize.

Beam

The beam variation tests were done on the wide and narrow versions of the fin keel parent hull. The righting moment curves for the three hulls shown in Fig 2.3 are calculated with the centre of gravity at the same distance above the hull bottom and demonstrate the strong influence of beam on stability and stiffness. The widest yacht is the stiffest and has the highest maximum righting moment, but it also has a very large range of inverted stability. By contrast the narrow yacht has good self-righting ability but would be hopelessly tender because of the flatter slope of the early part of the curve.

In the capsize tests both the parent and wide hull forms could be inverted by a breaking wave of height 40 per cent of hull overall

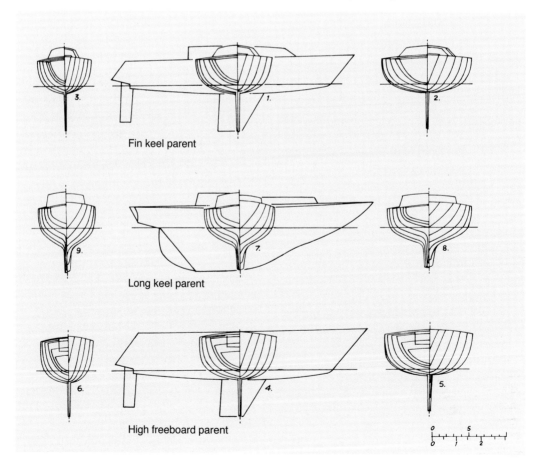

Figure 2.2 *Body plans of standard series yachts. Length overall 9.75m (32ft).*

The Hungarian yacht K&H Banque Matav *knocked over to 66° in the Southern Ocean whilst participating in the Vendee Globe single-handed race. At this angle a yacht may not right herself quickly.* Photo: Nanda Fa/DPPI

length (LOA) whilst the narrow hull form suffered only a 120° knock down followed by recovery. However, a 55 per cent LOA wave caused all the models to execute 360° rolls when caught beam on to the wave. One of the factors influencing the behaviour of the wider beam boats was the immersion of the lee deck edge as the boat was pushed sideways by the breaking crest. This dipping of the side deck appeared to produce a tripping action that the narrow boat was able to avoid.

Running before the seas, the wide hull proved quite difficult to control and did not show any more willingness to surf ahead of the wave than its narrower sisters.

Freeboard

A comparison was made between the behaviour of the low freeboard model with a typical coach roof, and the high freeboard model with a flush deck. Both models exhibited the same propensity to capsize, showing that high freeboard does not increase capsize risk but, once capsized, the yacht with the lower freeboard and coach roof had a greater ability to self-right.

On studying the righting moment curves of the two forms it became apparent that it is the contribution to buoyancy of the coach roof that reduces the area of inverted stability. This is illustrated in Fig 2.4, which shows the righting moment curves for the two hulls. Also of interest is Fig 2.5 where the righting moment curve of the traditional yacht is shown with and without its coach roof, demonstrating how the buoyancy of a coach roof can increase the angle of vanishing stability.

The static stability analysis indicated that a further increase in coach roof size could eliminate the range of inverted stability completely (a concept used with great success in the RNLI lifeboats), thus rendering even a very light and beamy craft self-righting.

Fin or long keel?

One of the most obvious design developments in the last 50 years has been the substantial reduction in the lateral area of the keel. This aspect of design was evaluated not only by comparing the traditional and modern designs but also by fitting extension pieces fore and aft to the fin keel so that the keel area was

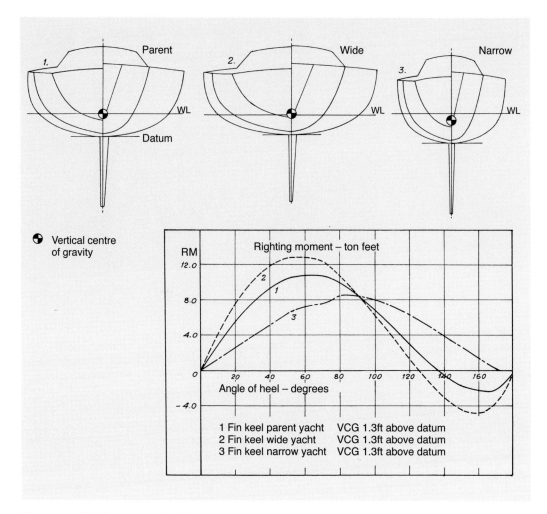

Figure 2.3 *Righting moment for fin keel yacht beam series; the displacement is 4.5 tons.*

approximately trebled, as shown in Fig 2.6. This produced no discernible improvement in capsize resistance, and, more surprisingly, only a marginal improvement in controllability when sailing downwind. A similar result, at least as far as capsize resistance goes, was found when the fin keel and traditional design were compared at the same weight and position of the centre of gravity. Neither design showed a discernible superiority, although of course the traditional design with its narrow beam and larger coach roof had a higher angle of vanishing stability, and therefore recovered more readily from the knockdown.

When it came to down wave controllability, however, the traditional design model was far easier to control and, despite its greater weight, it surfed very readily. The more modern design, by contrast, was hard to keep stern-on to the seas, and once the hull was slightly pushed off course it broached beam-on to the breaking wave, and, in this vulnerable position, was prone to capsize. These tests indicated that lateral area, per se, does not improve capsize resistance, and down wave control is not only influenced by keel area. It was the more balanced ends of the traditional design that helped its controllability as much as the larger lateral area of the keel, because, as a wave approached from behind, the stern was lifted less, and, consequently, the bow was less immersed.

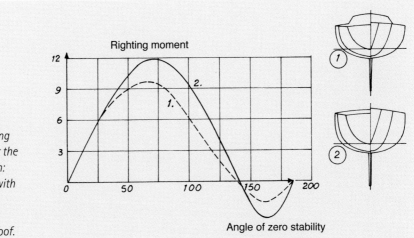

Figure 2.4 *Righting moment curves for the freeboard variation:*
1) fin keel parent with coachroof.
2) high freeboard without coachroof.

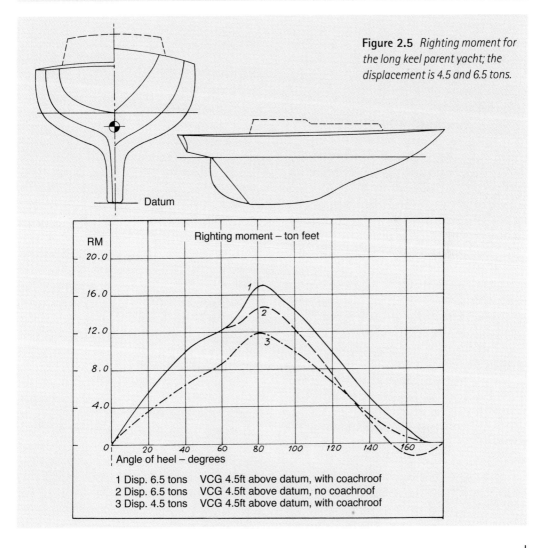

Figure 2.5 *Righting moment for the long keel parent yacht; the displacement is 4.5 and 6.5 tons.*

1 Disp. 6.5 tons   VCG 4.5ft above datum, with coachroof
2 Disp. 6.5 tons   VCG 4.5ft above datum, no coachroof
3 Disp. 4.5 tons   VCG 4.5ft above datum, with coachroof

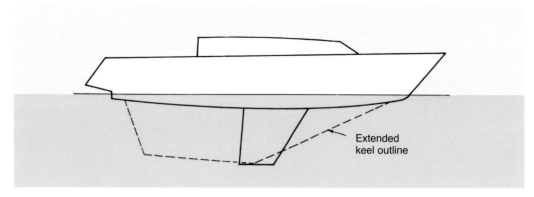

Extended
keel outline

Figure 2.6 *The keel extension.*

The wide-sterned modern design suffers because the passing wave lifts the stern and buries the bow deeply where it can exert a large turning moment on the hull. This will cause the yacht to broach unless the rudder can be quickly used to counter the turning moment.

The different behaviour of the three models – traditional long keel, fin keel, and increased area fin keel – gave a glimpse of the complex interaction of hull design features on controllability when running before large waves. The easy surfing and control of the traditional design model was a surprise. The results, however, should not be extended to a generalised conclusion about all traditional and modern boats. Whilst a lighter hull will be carried forward more readily by an advancing wave, to benefit from the effect of the wave, the hull shape must be such that it can be held on course easily. In strong winds, as opposed to survival conditions, the light wide-stern boats can be propelled to high speed by the sails, and any lack of buoyancy forward is compensated for by the dynamic lift generated by the forward part of the hull. This will keep the bow up and will allow the rudder to control the boat with ease. However, once the driving force of the sails is removed and the boat speed falls – the situation modelled in the tests – it was apparent that balanced ends become an important part of the control equation.

As with many aspects of sailing boat performance it is the complete combination of design characteristics that is important, and herein lies the designer's skill to blend hull shape, keel area and weight successfully into a harmonious whole.

Displacement, vertical centre of gravity and roll inertia

These three parameters differ from those discussed so far because they can be altered fairly easily on existing yachts, whereas the other parameters are fixed at the design stage and cannot be changed so readily.

Increasing the displacement of the fin keel yacht by 60 per cent whilst keeping all other factors constant made very little difference to its propensity to capsize; however, the increased displacement did improve the course keeping qualities of the yacht and resistance to broaching. This result is not unexpected when viewed in the context of static stability, since an increase in displacement increases the righting moment in approximately direct proportion, as shown in Fig 2.5.

Changes in the vertical location of the centre of gravity (VCG) lead to some intriguing results. The effect of large movements of the VCG on the propensity to capsize was surprisingly small; indeed in some cases the high VCG configuration actually offered more resistance to a knockdown. When considering recovery from a capsize, however, the high VCG should be discounted as it greatly increases the range of inverted stability. Again,

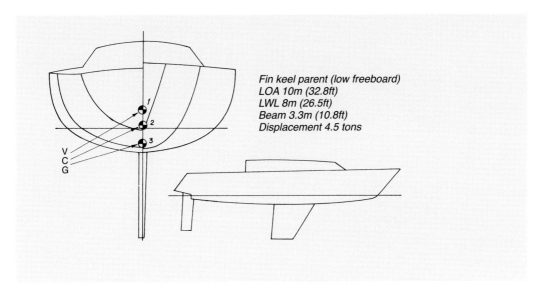

Figure 2.7 *Stability curves of models with centre of gravity (above) and that of the parent model (below).*

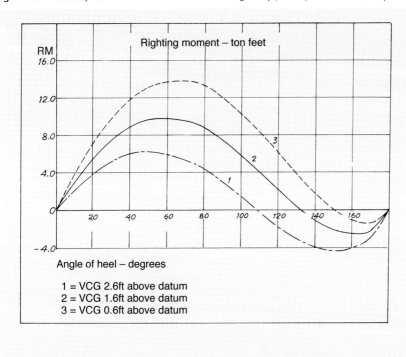

as with increasing displacement, a lower VCG would be beneficial to the control of the craft as it increases stiffness at normal angles of heel. Fig 2.7 demonstrates the influence of the position of the centre of gravity on the shape of the righting moment curve.

Another feature linked to weight and VCG is the roll inertia or radius of gyration. Inertia is increased by moving the component weights of the yacht further from the centre of gravity, and by so doing the yacht is made less easily disturbed by roll inducing forces, in much the same way as a skater can control the speed of a spin by bringing his arms in and out from his

Racing yachts use crew as moveable ballast, but contrary to a fixed keel, crew weight becomes less effective as the angle of heel increases to higher values. Photo: Erwan Quéméré/Bluegreen

body. In a yacht using a heavy mast and keeping the ballast as low as possible, preferably on the end of a deep keel, can induce a high inertia. The capsizing tests do indicate that inertia is one of the important influences on capsize resistance. As a rough guide, increasing the inertia of the boat by 50 per cent increases the wave height needed to cause capsize by 10–15 per cent. This is discernible experimentally but its effect on the overall risk of capsize would not appear to be very great. Beware, however, of increasing inertia by use of heavy spars without a corresponding addition of ballast, otherwise the boats VCG will rise and the angle of vanishing stability will be reduced.

Summary

The model tests and hydrostatic calculations allowed us to evaluate the influence of several basic design parameters on a yacht's ability to resist capsize, or recover from severe breaking wave knockdowns. Fig 2.8 below summarises the results of the tests and calculations. The table describes how the fundamental design parameters influence capsize – and stability – related characteristics.

Two of the strongest influences on the vulnerability to capsize are both differences in form. Firstly, a narrow craft appears to have improved resistance to capsize when beam-on to the seas, being able to slip away from the breaking wave. Also the narrow beam leads to an increase in angle of vanishing stability. Secondly, the full lateral plane and *more balanced ends* of the long keel design make it less liable to broach and capsize in following seas. From the tests it was apparent that those yachts having angles of vanishing stability less than 140° can be left floating upside down for a period after encountering a breaking wave. At the other end of the heel angle range, a high value of initial stability which makes the yacht 'stiff' in sailing terms, does not provide resistance to the capsizing forces of a breaking wave, and it appears that it is the righting moment values in the range 100–130° of heel which determine the hydrostatic resistance to complete inversion and capsize.

The beneficial influences of increased displacement and inertia are also apparent from the tests, but these results highlight the difficulty of designing to minimise capsizability. Many of the design features one might adopt to resist capsize actually mitigate against desirable sailing and living characteristics, which are, after all, the boat's prime function for, hopefully, all of its life. For instance, narrow beam reduces both internal volume and the power to carry sail; high inertia leads to excessive pitching in a seaway, and so on. Finally, even when all the precautions are taken in our models tests, although discernible trends in resistance to capsize have been determined, no hull form or ballasting combination consistently resisted capsize in a breaking wave with a height of 55 per cent of the yachts' length. Moreover all the yachts could be rolled to 130° of heel by an appropriately timed encounter with the 35 per cent LOA high breaking wave. This suggests that alterations in form which improve capsize resistance may be rendered ineffective by a relatively small increase in breaking wave height.

So what is the answer to avoiding capsize? The best and most effective way is to avoid breaking waves by avoiding sea conditions where breaking waves are prone to occur. If caught out in extreme conditions, then by continuing to sail the boat, she can be kept away from the breaking crests, or positioned to surf ahead or clear of them. This avoids the dangerous beam-on condition, and delays the encounter with the breaking crest until much of its energy has been dissipated. As discussed earlier, this strategy requires active rudder control and some skill to carry out. Ultimately the technique may well prove beyond even an experienced racing crew, let alone a short-handed cruising complement. Once the conditions are so severe that the crew are not able to remain on deck then the vessel must look after herself. Unfortunately all yachts have a natural tendency to lie beam on to wind and wave when left to their own devices. This is the most vulnerable position, and it is in

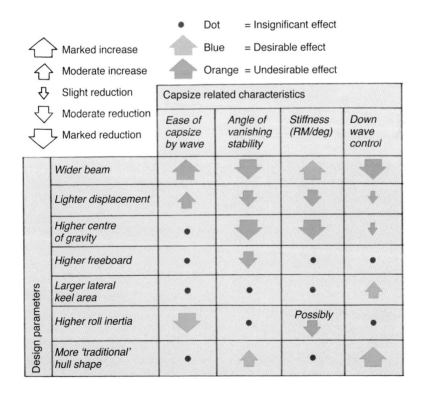

Figure 2.8 *Summary of design influences on capsize.*

this situation that the influences of hull design features on capsize resistance and recovery come into play, realising, of course, that no conventional yacht design can offer complete immunity from capsize under these conditions. Naturally increasing the size of the yacht will decrease the chances of encountering a wave capable of capsizing the boat.

After our tests and calculations examining all these different design features one must admit to a sense of disappointment that no combination of hull form or ballasting arrangement offered a substantial improvement in capsize resistance. Something, say, that would enable her to withstand double her previous capsize breaking wave height.

Regulations

There is now a substantial body of regulatory procedures for the evaluation of conventional yachts. *All* of these are based on the concept of an angle of vanishing stability, which is a measure of how readily a boat may be capsized by wind or wave action.

The angle of vanishing stability represents a fundamental measure of the boat's ability to recover quickly from the impact of a breaking wave, and is the design parameter that determines whether knockdown and recovery, or full capsize results from the impact. The angle of vanishing stability figures strongly in the certification requirements for sail training vessels, and in the safety regulations for offshore racing yachts and the international safety standards for production yachts.

The common factor in all these regulations is:

a) that the Angle of Vanishing Stability is a key factor in a yacht's ability to recover from a knockdown or capsize event,

b) the required AVS can be reduced as the boat gets bigger because the larger the boat the less chance there is that a wave large enough to capsize the boat will be encountered, and

c) the required AVS must be increased as the boat operates in more exposed waters.

The range of positive stability for a vessel fitted with an external ballast keel may be estimated from the following formulae:

$$\text{Estimated range of stability (in degrees)} = 110 + \frac{400}{SV - 10}$$

$$SV = \frac{Beam^2}{BR \times DCB \times \left(\frac{DISPLACED}{VOLUME}\right)^{1/3}}$$

Noting that

Beam = greatest beam measured, excluding rubbing strips, in metres

Ballast Ratio (BR) = weight of ballast in tonnes contained in the keel divided by the full displacement in tonnes

Displaced Volume = the volume of a vessel's displacement, in m³, at the operational draft

Draft of canoe body (DCB) in metres is taken by measuring the maximum draft at the ⅛ of the full beam from the centreline in way of the transverse section at greatest beam

A yacht's AVS can be estimated from the formula above, which is reproduced from the Maritime and Coastguard Agency (MCA) *Rules for Sailing Yachts.*

Examination of the formula shows that beam acts to reduce the range – i.e. reduces the AVS – whilst a high ballast ratio, deeper canoe body, and higher displacement increase the range.

It must be stressed that the formula is only an approximation based on the actual results of inclining tests and calculations on a number of typical sailing yachts. This means two things. Firstly it may over or under estimate the AVS by up to 10–15° in some cases, and secondly it will not work for unusual vessels. Nevertheless it offers a good guide.

That said in the digital age we no longer need rules of thumb to avoid complex calculations. A yacht owner who wants to know what the stability curve for his yacht looks like can easily find out. The three dimensional shape

Yacht capsize and drogue research: the wide fin keel model being held stern-to a breaking wave by a drogue. Notice that the rudder is largely out of the water in the final photograph, so only the drogue can be holding the boat straight at this point.

of the yachts hull is now always available on the designers computer and many yachts have their centre of gravity recorded as part of their handicap racing certificate, e.g. ORCi, or ORCclub. It takes a fraction of a second to compute a stability curve, there is no need to guess, and serious offshore sailors should know how their boat will behave.

The following organisations have published stability standards that are used to assess a yacht's suitability for operation, or eligibility to race.

Offshore Racing Congress Stability Index (http://www.orc.org)

These regulations also contain regulations related to water ballast and canting keel yachts

ISO Standard 12217-2

Maritime and Coastguard Agency (MCA) Rules for Sailing Yachts

Royal Ocean Racing Club (RORC) Safety and Stability Indices (SSI) (http://www.rorc. org/special-regulations/safety-and-stability-indices-ssi.html)

Conclusion

Since this chapter was added to *Heavy Weather Sailing* in 1990 it has become clear that no small yacht can be rendered immune from capsize by clever manipulation of her hull shape. The envelopes of safe operation in terms of matching a required AVS to the size of the boat and area of operation are now much better defined and understood. Also research by the Wolfson Unit has continued, supported by the Royal Ocean Racing Club, to evaluate the influence of a drogue or sea anchor on a yacht's behaviour in breaking waves. This research complemented similar studies in the USA by the late Donald Jordan. These studies showed that use of a *suitable* drogue – regarding which more details will be found in Chapter 7 – deployed from the stern of the yacht, will cause it to lie steadily down wind and wave, so that any breaking wave will see only the transom of the yacht and will not be able to exert any capsizing force. Using an appropriately sized drogue even the lightest, widest fin keel yacht could safely survive the 55 per cent LOA wave with no assistance from the helmsman, whereas, lying beam-on, it would be easily rolled over by the 35 per cent LOA breaking wave. Indeed, it was only our inability to make higher waves in the tank that prevented us from moving further up the safe wave height range. As will be seen from the sequence of photographs below, the yacht moves steadily down wave with little or no disturbance from the foaming crest.

Thus it may well be that the crew's ability to deploy such a drogue is the simplest and most reliable way of substantially reducing the risk of capsize.

Design trends of yachts with regard to heavy weather

3

Peter Bruce

After so many years of evolution it might be thought that the optimum yacht shape would have been established by now but, for one reason or another, this appears not to be the case. New yachts appear continually, none quite like their predecessors. As yacht design progresses, some desirable design features can be left behind as other features evolve. Generally speaking the boat industry gives people exactly what they want: space, grace, comfort, boat speed, lots of electronic aids, effortless handling and shallow draft. However, less obvious features, such as seaworthiness – particularly stability – and structural strength, tend to be taken for granted by the buyer.

Unlike cruising yachts, racing yachts are subject to a handicap rule, which could be used to pressurise designers towards seaworthiness but, through the influence of owners, the handicap rules are predominantly applied to achieve racing equality between competitors. It was not always thus. Up to the mid-1970s, certainly in the United States and United Kingdom, seaworthiness and strength were paramount considerations for racing yachts. Until then yachts had a reputation of looking after their crews when it came on to blow; furthermore it was rare for any yacht to give up a race due to her design or construction, or as a result of gear failure.

As time went by designers tended to create yachts with more beam, which increased their form stability, i.e. stability derived from the shape of the hull. Some designers allowed less weight in the keel. Performance was improved but at the expense of stability at high angles of heel.

The yacht racing International Offshore Rule (IOR) was introduced in the 1960s as a compromise between the rule used in the United States of America and the United Kingdom. This rule required a measure of actual stability, called the inclining test. To obtain a performance rating advantage, some designers used to give their racing yachts low stability from the keel, relying instead upon crew weight on the windward rail. The IOR faded out in the mid-1990s having been replaced by other handicap rules such as the Royal Ocean Racing Club's IRC and the ORC's improvement on the IMS rule, the ORCi, which were more satisfactory from the stability point of view.

Keels became slimmer and of higher aspect ratio i.e. shaped long and thin like a knife, and this made keels more efficient but difficult to attach sufficiently strongly to the hull, whilst also making the boat more vulnerable when the vessel ran aground.

Designs of the 1950s and 1960s

The following comparison illustrates the point on stability. John McDonell describes a storm that *Cavalier* encountered on the return home from the Sydney–Hobart Race in 1963, after coming second. The 9.4m (31ft) yacht was built of wood by Swanson Brothers in Sydney and by modern day standards would probably be

A sister ship to Half Pint, *which is a good example of a strongly built yacht of the 1960s period with good stability, balanced ends and accompanying excellent sea-keeping qualities.*
Photo: Ben Davies/PPL

judged as extremely heavy and lacking some desirable accommodation features. Having suffered no damage after being rolled, she might also be judged as seaworthy and with a strong rig. *Cavalier* appears to have stood up to the storm much as one would expect of her traditional design and John McDonell could have made more complaints than he did. His first criticism was that the cockpit did not drain fast enough, which was true of yachts of that time. The other problem was that in the storm she did not have the speed necessary to keep out of trouble. Modern yachts do have such speed, but usually need to be steered constantly and with some skill. This situation is satisfactory as long as there are sufficient willing and able helmsmen on board. Racing boats, such as those that take part in the Volvo Round the World Race, will have enough such helmsmen, but cruising boats seldom do.

One of the interesting aspects of John McDonell's latter complaint is how different it is from more recent storm reports where the aim is usually to slow down to achieve a 'comfortable speed'. A possible suggestion, which might have improved *Cavalier*'s handling, would have been

to use her engine, although the tactic would only have been effective while the fuel lasted. This would have prevented her from 'stopping dead in the troughs' as her owner described, and would have given water flow over the rudder in the right direction at all times.

Many traditional yachts are renowned for their sea-keeping qualities, especially those yachts designed by Olin Stephens. One of his designs, *Half Pint*, a Swan 36, encountered an Atlantic storm, the outcome of which reaffirms the seaworthiness of this hull. *Half Pint* had left Gibraltar in December 1968 with Christopher Price and his partner on board, heading for The Canary Islands using Hydrovane self-steering. Eleven days later when 40km (25 miles) off Casablanca the wind built up to a good Force 8 and they hove-to under storm jib. Four hours later the wind increased to Force 9 and they ran back to the NE under just the storm jib. Six hours after that the boat broached with her mast into the sea, but righted immediately. With a healthy angle of vanishing stability of 145° this was not surprising. To slow the boat they put out 72m (240ft) warps in a bight and ran under bare pole with the wind now Force

9, 15 or 20° on the port quarter. In the night the boat was knocked down again while being continually swept by green water.

In this example the Swan 36 ran at a comfortable speed using warps whereas *Cavalier* used none. Not being quite so heavy for her size as *Cavalier*, *Half Pint* might have surfed uncontrollably had she not been restrained. Different methods are appropriate for different boats. More importantly the two accounts suggest that there was not much wrong with the seaworthiness qualities of these two yacht designs of the 1960s, which were genuine cruiser-racers. From the 1960s onwards, racing yacht design evolved according to performance considerations. Yachts became progressively lighter and beamier, freeboard increased; fin keels and spade rudders became the norm. They became faster and more exciting to sail and, unfortunately for their second hand value, many became less attractive for cruising.

1979 Fastnet Race

The story of the 1979 Fastnet storm, albeit an exceptionally ferocious storm for summer, put a big question on the stability of yachts designed in that era. In one noted capsize the boat, which had an angle of vanishing stability of 118°, remained inverted for some minutes. It is memorable that at this period keels did not break off, though the same cannot be said for rudders. After rounding the Fastnet, the larger yachts crossed back into the area of the smaller yachts and therefore experienced similar weather and sea conditions. It was the smaller yachts generally that got into trouble and those that had not undertaken the full season's offshore racing.

The author was navigator aboard the 11.8m (39ft) *Eclipse*, owned by Jeremy Rogers, and in the British Admirals Cup Team, along with *Morning Cloud* and *Blizzard*. *Eclipse* won class two and was second overall behind Ted Turner's 18.3m (61ft) *Tenacious*. *Eclipse* was also the top Admiral's Cup yacht in the Fastnet Race and top Admiral's Cup overall.

From the author's standpoint it seemed that the Force 10 of the 1979 Fastnet had been about as strong as the storm experienced aboard *Rapparee* in the Fastnet of 1961. That race followed a succession of heavy weather Fastnet Races, but the cross sea of the 1979 race made steering to keep the boat out of trouble significantly more difficult. There were few breakages and no casualties in the 1961 Fastnet, making it seem that the lighter and less stable yachts of 1979 were less able to cope.

The stormy Fastnet of 1979 came after a long series of light weather Fastnet Races, particularly that of 1977, which might have given rise to false expectations. It was clear that a whole lot of yachts took part in the 1979 Fastnet that had not taken part in any other RORC offshore race that year and it was mainly these that got into trouble, suggesting that yacht racing, like many events requiring specialised skills, needs progressive and regular practice.

There was a spate of failed rudders, all made of carbon fibre by one manufacturer, who had not quite mastered the construction process. The advantage of a carbon rudder was that it was markedly lighter, thereby reducing the boat's overall weight. It also rendered the stern more buoyant thus giving a more advantageous reading in the inclining test, with consequent better handicap.

In *Eclipse* we noticed the wind becoming lighter, perhaps down to 40 knots, as we approached the Fastnet Rock and, after rounding, even considered increasing our sail area, but not for long. A terrific squall hit us from the north-west shortly afterwards whereupon we dropped the three-slabbed mainsail and continued through the night under storm jib alone.

Analysis of the competitor's barometer readings enabled the meteorologist Alan Watts to explain variations in the storm conditions as 'cyclones within a cyclone'. He suggested that the area's overall isobaric chart showing a deep low pressure system might have had small cells of lower pressure within. This theory might account for the apparent most severe conditions in the area of the Labadie Bank.

A memory of 1979 is the failure of the Met Office to forecast the storm, not that it would have made much difference even if it had, as most of the fleet were well out into the Celtic Sea. The depression was known about before the start of the race but it deepened rapidly just as it approached the United Kingdom making it much more potent. The first shipping forecast to mention a gale (SW 5–6 increasing 6–8) came at 1750 on 13 August, by which time the actual wind speed was a good Force 8 and rising. Long after the storm was through the shipping forecast was still giving out Force 10, as if the Met Office was trying to make up for being caught out. The effect was for some participants to believe that a secondary storm was on the way and unnecessarily abandon their vessels.

The report on the 1979 Fastnet Race did not give any strong pointers on best tactics to employ but a number of recommendations were given, all but one of which appear to have become part of current methodology. The recommendation not firmly acted upon was that regarding stability.

1984 Vasco da Gama Race

After all the tremendous publicity that anything to do with the 1979 Fastnet Race had generated, many people felt that the lessons must surely have been learned. However, on 26 April 1984 an unforecast storm brought havoc to the 29 entries in the Durban to East London Vasco da Gama Race. Winds of at least 60 knots over a period of 6 hours blowing in the opposite direction to the Agulhas Current created seas which caused three yachts to sink and the Lavranos 2-tonner *Sensation* to be wrecked on the coast. One of the yachts that sank, *Rubicon*, was lost without trace. Three yachts experienced 360° rolls. For example, in the case of *Spiffero*, a Dufour 34, the 360° roll dismasted the boat, and the deck-stowed liferaft, the engine and battery became detached from their mountings. The liferaft was lost and when the wreckage had been cleared away the yacht was rolled through 360° for a second time.

The official report, which there is no reason

to doubt, said that the yachts were competently crewed and that safety regulations had been properly applied. The question remained whether performance yachts are sufficiently optimised for extreme weather.

1987 The Great British and French October storm

In October 1987, a short-lived but unusually fierce storm with winds of over 100 knots caused massive destruction to buildings and woodland in both France and England. This storm was accurately forecast in France but not properly forecast, even denied, in England. Two of four yachts caught out in this storm survived without being inverted, a Contessa 32 and a Hallberg Rassy 42. Another yacht with shallow draft but a conservative hull type survived a 360° capsize, and the fourth and more performance oriented design, with a comparatively low range of stability, was rolled through 360° and after colliding heavily with the rescue ship was abandoned and was never found. Both of the latter yachts were lying a'hull. No lives were lost. It so happened that the largest yacht with a low range of stability came off worst, but it would be wrong to draw firm conclusions from such a small sample.

1991 Japan–Guam Race

No further offshore races were to run into serious trouble until 1991, when the matter of stability, coupled now with the strength of racing yacht structure, raised its head again. The Japan–Guam Race tragedy did not receive much publicity in the western world, yet 14 yachtsmen lost their lives. I am grateful to Barry Deakin from the Wolfson Unit who, in 1992, wrote the following description:

THE JAPAN–GUAM YACHT RACE took place in December 1991. Nine yachts crossed the start line in wintry conditions, heading for Guam over 1,300 nautical miles to the south.

Ocean racing yachts tend to have a good stock of people to helm them.
Photo: PPL

On the afternoon of the following day, the wind was 30 knots with waves up to 6m (19.7ft). At 1540 a crewmember, who was not wearing a harness, was lost overboard from the yacht *Marine Marine*, a Yokoyama 39, while trying to untangle a running backstay. He was not found.

At midday on 28 December a female crew-member of *Marine Marine*, incapacitated by severe seasickness, was transferred to a patrol boat that had attended to assist with the search.

Twenty four hours later, with the rough conditions persisting, *Marine Marine's* engine was started but a rope was around the propeller and the engine stalled. A tow was requested from a second patrol boat which made five unsuccessful attempts to pass a line to the yacht. That evening one of the crew became aware that the rolling motion of the yacht felt unusual and transfer of the crew to the patrol boat was requested. It was decided, however, that it would be too dangerous in the dark and rough conditions. The crew put on lifejackets and a liferaft was prepared.

At around 0530 on 30 December the keel parted from the hull, which rolled upside down and filled rapidly with water. One crewmember escaped through the hatch on his second attempt, finding it difficult to dive through it with the lifejacket on, and was joined a little later by two others. The incident was not seen by the patrol boat which had lost visual and radio contact with the yacht, although the empty liferaft was found at 0700. At 1020 an aircraft, which had joined the search, located the yacht with one surviving crewmember. There was a hole in the hull roughly the same size as the root of the keel. A transverse frame was seen to have remained intact inside the hull. Seven members of the crew were drowned: four of their bodies were found inside the yacht.

Whilst the crew of *Marine Marine* were beginning to worry about the motion of their yacht, *Taka*, a Liberty 47 about 230 nautical miles to the south, was capsized by a breaking wave whilst sailing under storm jib in a quartering wind of 32 knots. The maximum wave height in that area was in excess of 6m

The loss of Exide Challenger's *keel in the 1997 Vendee Globe Race led to an epic Southern Ocean rescue. To optimise performance, modern keels have become extremely narrow and thin at the root, and require very careful design and construction. Even then they are vulnerable to running aground.* Photo: 92 Wing RAAF Edinburgh

(20ft). The yacht remained upside down and after more than half an hour, the four crew inside the yacht made their way out through the hatch. Their EPIRB, which did not appear to be functioning correctly, was lost at this time. They found that one of the three crew on watch had drowned. After a further 15 minutes the yacht rolled upright. The upper washboard was lost and, as the yacht was half submerged, water continued to flow in. The mast was broken and the bilge pump tangled with ropes. The liferaft was inflated but capsized soon after with the loss of some of the gear. The six remaining crew boarded the raft and drifted. Despite the mobilisation of 11 patrol boats and 52 aircraft, the raft was not found until 25 January, when it was spotted by a British cargo vessel. Only one crewmember remained alive, the others having died between the 10 and 16 January.

The Nippon Offshore Racing Club wasted no time in forming a research committee to investigate the casualties. The man overboard was caused by human error, demonstrating the value of safety harnesses and lines, but the keel failure and the inability of *Taka* to return upright after a capsize suggested design deficiencies. Two lines of investigation were followed. In the first, the detailed arrangement of *Marine Marine*'s keel attachment and local GRP structure was studied from drawings, and calculations were carried out to assess the strength. It is not clear from the report on the investigation whether the keel was attached to a fair canoe body or a laminated stub, but detailed drawings of the local laminate configurations and the attachment of transverse floors show features that might be considered bad practice.

Disturbingly, the report suggests that the hull failed in shear around the outline of the keel and at the keel bolt washers, probably as a result of fatigue, implying that other well-used yachts may lose their keels. The hull's shell had become detached from the transverse frame. The yacht was built in 1983 and had competed in many offshore races. She had run aground five years before the failure and required some repair to the hull-keel joint but details of the damage were not included in the report. The authors assumed that delamination between the shell and the frame may have occurred at that time and gone unnoticed by the repairers.

The figures suggest an inadequacy either in the structural design or in the assumptions used to calculate the keel loadings.

In the other avenue of research the capsize of *Taka* prompted the Japanese to investigate her range of stability, and a figure of 114° was derived, marginally below average for the fleet.

The effects of flooding of the yacht were investigated, and it was concluded that, when upside down, the stability gradually reduces as the amount of flooding increases. Thus the yacht remained inverted for a considerable time despite some flooding, but after the main hatch was opened the rate of flooding increased and the yacht righted herself, albeit in a seriously swamped condition.

A range of stability of 114° was insufficient for a yacht of this size undertaking an offshore passage. The yacht would not comply with the UK Department of Transport's Code of Practice for commercial sailing vessels that requires a minimum range of 125°.

Some items covered by the ORC Special Regulations were also inadequate. For example, washboards must be secured to the boat, but those on *Taka* were swept away. Bilge pumping arrangements on *Taka* were inadequate because one pump was disabled.

It is important to note that neither *Marine Marine* nor *Taka* were anything other than typical offshore racing yachts, and the Force 7 to 8 conditions in which they failed were not particularly extreme.

It was unfortunate that the lessons learned since the Fastnet disaster had not changed design trends significantly.

1993 Sydney–Hobart Race

Another test of racing yacht seaworthiness came in the windy and rough Sydney–Hobart Race of 1993. After a brief period of tail winds on leaving Sydney, most yachts were on the wind for three and a half days in gale or storm force winds. The 2 knot south-going current met the north-going wind, causing steep breaking seas. Hulls delaminated, yachts sank, yachts were dismasted, yachts lost their keels, and the skipper of one yacht spent five and a half hours in the water before being rescued. The New Zealand yacht *Swuzzlebubble VIII*, a Davidson 40, when under storm jib and trysail was rolled through 360° by a breaking wave, dismasted, damaged and swamped. Her doughty crew, by the way, cleared away the mast wreckage, put a No 3 genoa out as a sea anchor whilst bailing, managed to start the engine and put into harbour unaided. Another yacht, a Farr 40, was doing 7.2 knots in 46 knots of wind when she fell off a wave. Next moment the starboard side of the main bulkhead, to which the chainplates were attached, appeared through the deck and then disappeared over the side, complete with mast and rigging. There were no casualties in spite of all this. One of the smaller class winners, and third overall, was the twenty year old S&S 34 *Marara*, a close relation of *Half Pint*.

Some instructive comments came from the winners and losers. Winners commented on strong crew teamwork, on the need for strongly built boats and the necessity of having three slabs in the main rather than 'the two sailmakers try to persuade you to have'. Storm trysails proved their worth as well. Comments made by those not so lucky were that the average modern racing yacht is more suited to inshore 'round the buoys' racing. The IMS handicap rule was encouraging light, shallow rocker craft which were very difficult to steer and would slam badly in a sea. Keels were not strongly enough attached, rigs were too light and cockpits gave little protection in severe conditions. It was said by some that their modern racing yachts were also impossible to slow down.

1998 Sydney–Hobart Race

Conditions were yet more severe in the 1998 Sydney–Hobart Race and, sadly, there was loss of life. After the race had started a low formed suddenly in the Bass Strait, bringing winds of hurricane strength for a period of 10 hours from a westerly direction. At Wilson's Promontory, at the north end of the Bass Strait, average wind was 79 knots, gusting 92 knots, a phenomenal strength for summer time and rather more than had been predicted. The south-going coastal current had been running strongly, but by the Bass Strait it had largely dissipated and its influence was probably small. Only yachts that were close to the Australian shore might have been affected.

Six people died, 55 people were rescued and out of a total of 115, six yachts were rolled and seven yachts were abandoned, some of which sank due to structural failure. One of these was the 1942-built 16m (52ft) wooden cutter *Winston Churchill*. When she was thrown into a trough, a common cause of structural damage in storms, it seems that her hull was opened up as part of her port side bulwark was torn off. Help was not at hand and three of her crew were lost from her liferafts. Two others died aboard the Farr 40 *Business Post Naiad*, built in 1984, which capsized twice. On the first occasion the yacht was doing 4 knots under bare pole when a massive breaking wave rolled her over, breaking the mast and causing major structural damage. Harnesses held the crewmen on deck and, after the mast had been secured, the yacht set off under power for shelter at Gabo Island. Some hours later another large breaking wave turned the boat over and she remained upside down for a period of four or five minutes. Whilst the boat was inverted the owner-skipper suffered a fatal heart attack, and a crewman on deck was drowned through being unable to detach his safety harness in the same circumstances, probably, as when *Taka* capsized in the Japan–Guam Race of 1991.

Finally the helmsman was lost overboard from the Reichel/Pugh 43 *Sword of Orion*, built in 1993, when she was rolled through 360° as she headed back to Sydney after retiring from the race. As the yacht rolled, force of water broke the stanchion to which the boom had been lashed. The freed boom smashed the wheel and swept the helmsman over the side, parting his safety harness. With the mast gone and the engine off its mountings, rescue was impossible. Moreover all her ring frames had been broken and the deck to keel joint had split between the cockpit and the stern. After 12 hours the remaining crew were taken off.

Other yachts rolled and dismasted were the Young designed 12m (39.3ft) *VC Offshore Stand Aside*, built in 1990, the Bashford Howison 41 *B52*, built in 1995, which remained inverted for three or four minutes, and the Tartan 40, *Midnight Special*, built in 1995, which was rolled twice and stayed afloat just long enough for the crew to be rescued by helicopter. The Swan 44 *Loki* was rolled and had her cabin windows broken, and the sturdy Cole 43, *Solo Globe Challenger*, ex *Rangatira* and built in 1984, a renowned seaboat, was rolled to 135° which caused loss of her mast and a skylight hatch to break, allowing flood water to render inoperable all the essential electrics. Most of the crew were injured and were taken off, one with a broken leg, leaving just three to bring the boat in.

The 19.5m (65ft) *Team Jaguar*, after losing her mast, was struck by a breaking wave that submerged the boat to the companionway and brought her to a near vertical angle. All her deck beams were sprung.

There is always something to be learnt from those who *did* complete the race successfully and accounts follow from the skippers of the winners of the three major classes. Firstly that of Ed Psaltis, skipper of the overall IMS winner *AFR Midnight Rambler*. She was tenth to finish, beating numerous larger yachts. Shortly after the race he commented:

THE 10.53M (35FT) *AFR MIDNIGHT RAMBLER* is of exotic GRP construction. There was no sign of hull/rig, keel joint damage although we put her through a horrible pounding. The fin keel is of lead, with no bulb, and she has no internal ballast. The angle of positive stability is 123°. In

The 10.7m (35ft) AFR Midnight Rambler, *built in 1995, making steady progress at the height of the storm. She went on to win the IMS Class overall.* Photo: Richard Bennett/PPL

addition to worldwide experience, the crew of seven had 50 Sydney–Hobarts between them.

During the eight hours when the breeze was 70 to 80 knots with very big waves, we just had the storm jib up. We were overpowered at times but mostly the helm felt good with just enough weather helm. Attempts were made to set a trysail but it created too much weather helm.

We had two important defensive weapons: speed and acceleration. Our usual speed was 7 knots and after a bad knockdown or confrontation with a big wave the speed would quickly accelerate up to this speed again due to the modern lightweight design. Having speed and manoeuvrability was essential to steer through the big and confused seas. We were able to position ourselves best for each wave as it came, or steer around it. Otherwise the boat would have been a sitting duck.

During the storm we changed to a 'survival' watch system and had only two on deck at one time. One sat on the rail facing the storm, sheltering the helmsman from the bullet-like spray and called 'wave' when a big one came. The helmsman altered course to bring the bow into the wave, then pulled away sharply on the top of the wave and back onto the normal course. No helmsman should stay on watch for more than an hour in extreme conditions for, if concentration lapses, the outcome will be devastating.

I would never recommend a yacht to turn and run with the weather. Much better keep going into the wind and seas at about 60° apparent. Most boats that had severe trouble had retired and were running with the storm.

A second account comes from Alex Whitworth, owner and skipper of the *Berrimilla*, a Brolga 33, designed by Professor Peter Joubert in 1969. She finished first overall in the Performance Handicap System division out of over 45 yachts, and had the

The stricken VC Offshore Stand Aside *with part of her coachroof ripped off.*
Photo: PPL

disadvantage of having to weather the storm in the night. The Brolga 33 is somewhat similar to an S&S 34, with deep vee-shaped underwater sections, pronounced tumblehome and long overhangs. She is described by her owner as very strong and very stable with a range of stability of 136°. She came through the storm undamaged though, he says, the hull took a real beating.

During the storm the same watchkeeping regime was adopted as *AFR Midnight Rambler,* i.e. two on deck, and changing every hour. Steering was made difficult by darkness and was mostly done by feel. The crew had 15 Sydney–Hobarts between them.

WE SAILED THROUGH THE STORM with just the trysail because I felt that we would have been seriously overpowered with the storm jib as well and she was handling all but the biggest breakers with no dramas. The trysail

was sheeted to the spinnaker turning blocks on each quarter. We were sailing at around 60–70° apparent, averaging about 4 knots. It was generally possible to set the boat up for each wave, or avoid it, but the occasional breaker was either going too fast or coming from further abeam. On about ten occasions the boat was caught by one of these bigger breakers. She would be carried down the wave front at about an 80° angle of heel (i.e. on her beam-ends) on a wild surf, with the wave breaking right across the boat and filling the cockpit. A technique that evolved during this situation was to put the helm over to push the bow down the wave as the boat was being carried bodily sideways. In this way the sideways motion was converted into some forward motion and lessened the tripping effect of the keel. I am convinced that this technique helped us to avoid the worst effects of the breakers that did get us.

The boat is so stable that, once in the trough, she immediately stood upright, gathered speed and went on sailing, though on one occasion the boat was turned though 180°. With just the trysail up we could not tack so had to gybe which we felt was particularly hazardous. A wave breaking over the boat would fill the cockpit entirely and the storm boards were very necessary to keep water out of the cabin. The four cockpit drains are just about on the waterline when the cockpit is full and it takes an age to empty.

Modestly, Alex Whitworth says that he suspects that *Berrimilla* was behind the worst of the storm and was quite lucky not to get rolled. The morning after the storm they saw a helicopter that was looking for *B52* which had been rolled in their area. Incidentally Professor Peter Joubert, who designed *Berrimilla*, was in the race in a larger but similar very stable design. His 12.9m (43ft) *Kingurra*, with six tons in her keel, got almost totally inverted by an enormous breaking wave but she righted herself 'in about five seconds'.

The winner of the 12 yacht CHS division by some 12 hours, was *Aera*, a Swan 46. The skipper said:

AT MIDDAY ON THE 27 DECEMBER the storm hit with the wind building rapidly up to 60 knots from the west and by this time *Aera* was under only her storm jib.

As the waves built up to a maximum of 10m (32.8ft) it became clear that it would not be safe to maintain the rhumb line so we bore off some 30–50°, bringing the true wind angle to 110–130°. The wind continued to build and was too much even for the storm jib, so we peeled to the storm staysail maintaining our course and 10–11 knots.

The wind strengthened to 70 knots for a period of two hours with gusts to 75 or 80 knots. Fifteen per cent of the surface was breaking and the wind was blowing the top off every wave. As a result there were long streaks of

A satellite photograph of the storm taken at 1615 on 27 December 1998.

wind-blown water joining one crest to the next. The sea looked as if it was covered in a layer of smoke. Wavelength was about 100m (328ft) and the waves were not long-crested as one might expect, but diamond-shaped. During this period we suffered three or four small knockdowns, not more than 45°, and the cockpit filled seven or eight times. We kept a full watch of six on deck throughout, the most vulnerable person being the helmsman who was washed up against the pushpit a couple of times when a wave filled the cockpit.

In the next couple of hours the wind abated to 50 knots and we were able to set the storm trysail in addition to the storm staysail, and alter our course by 20–30° towards the rhumb line. However, at about 1700 cloud cover became complete, we had sheeting rain and the wind built up to 65 knots. We were forced to drop the trysail and bear away to the old course. By now wavelength had increased to 150–200m (492–656ft).

In the 2008/9 Vendee Globe Race, Jean le Cam's VM Materiaux *capsized 200nm west of Cape Horn.* Photo: PPL

Though we had been heading southeast at about the same speed as the low-pressure system we considered this safer than trying to turn back. However, the system was soon to move quickly towards the south allowing us to resume the rhumb line course and set more sail. By morning the storm was over. Our biggest problem had been our auto-inflating lifejackets that inflated when solid water came on board (see Chapter 9).

We have heard that if a big enough wave breaks at a critical moment catching a yacht beam on, she will capsize whatever her stability, but what happens afterwards is also critical. Will the boat come back up again in about five seconds as Peter Joubert's *Kingurra* did, or will she remain inverted for four or five minutes? Had *Business Post Naiad* recovered from her inversion as quickly as *Kingurra*, at least one life might not have been lost.

After the race it remained questionable whether racing yachts in more extreme form are 'capable of withstanding heavy storms and are prepared to meet serious emergencies without the expectation of outside assistance', the supposed criteria for a Category 1 offshore race.

Other possible lessons that emerged from the race were:

1. The need for smaller storm sails in hurricane strength winds (see Chapter 17).
2. Too many accessories attached to lifebuoys.
3. Insufficient knowledge of safety gear throughout crew.
4. Lack of effective radio communications from dismasted yachts.

The race review recorded that the best trim under which yachts handled the conditions was emphatically 'eased off the wind up to 15°'.

Giovanni Soldini's dismasted Open 60 after capsizing 380nm from Land's End on a record breaking attempt. Photo: PPL

Stability requirements and assessment

I am again grateful to Barry Deakin of the Wolfson Unit for his thoughts.

TRADITIONALLY, small cruising yachts had a range of stability of at least 150° and would therefore always return to upright if capsized. Such a stability range requirement is generally considered by modern designers to be unnecessarily conservative, and is certainly not readily achievable with a modern hull form. In general, traditional forms with narrow beam and a deep hull were more resistant to capsize, but breaking wave height in relation to boat size is the overriding factor. Larger yachts are therefore safer in a given sea state, since they are less likely to encounter a breaking wave of sufficient size to cause capsize. This fact has led to proposals for stability requirements that vary with size (see Fig 3.1).

There is no doubt that there are many yachts which are vulnerable to being inverted by breaking waves, and some of them are also unlikely to return to the upright, despite being in storm conditions where further large waves will be encountered.

It is unfortunate that those characteristics that have an adverse effect on safety in survival situations make the yacht fast, spacious and comfortable in favourable conditions.

An alarming illustration of the dangers of approximate assessments is given by a comparison of the stability curves for two examples of the same class of 8.7m (28.5ft) production cruising yacht (see Fig 3.2). The yacht with a range of 127° has a conventional rig as designed. The other with a range of only 96° has a mast furling mainsail and roller furling headsail fitted. The additional weight aloft on this yacht has reduced its range by 31°. The way to identify such effects

Thierry Dubois clinging onto his capsized yacht which, by virtue of her extreme beam, is stable when inverted. Only by venting air from inside will she right herself. Photo: AFP/PPL

accurately is with an inclining experiment and a conventional stability calculation.

Thus, there are two aspects to stability assessment: the range needs to be determined properly, and there needs to be a sufficiently conservative minimum requirement. If an approximate method must be used an increased factor of safety should be introduced, for example by increasing the minimum requirement.

The Recreational Craft Directive (RCD) specifies essential safety requirements for designers and builders of yachts, which have been mandatory since 1998. An international working group (WG 22) published the international standard, ISO 12217, giving details of how the requirements should be assessed, which is subject to continuous review. In order to obtain a consensus it was necessary to incorporate the views of the industry representatives from many countries, and the standard inevitably represents a compromise. The stability is judged to be adequate for a particular design category if the 'STIX' numeral is adequate. This numeral is derived from the length, adjusted by a number of factors incorporating other characteristics of the yacht, including stability. A particularly poor characteristic will lower the numeral slightly, and may be offset by some other positive characteristic, but the compromise is such that the STIX number doesn't really provide realistic information for buyers on the capabilities of the yachts.

Clearly *Taka*'s stability range of 114° was not enough for an ocean storm if a yacht is to right herself quickly in the event of a total capsize. Compromise is allowable as vessels get bigger and Barry Deakin's figures in Fig 3.1 are worthy of note. He adds that the approximate methods of establishing the range of stability are acceptable for more stable craft but the more elaborate and accurate methods are necessary for craft in the lower range. This will include most racing boats.

Not only will a yacht's stability be significantly reduced by furling sails (Fig 3.2), but equally for radar, radar reflectors, spinnaker poles which fold up the mast, and

Figure 3.1 *A chart put together by Barry Deakin of the Wolfson Unit at Southampton from information obtained by the Royal Yachting Association and the Royal Ocean Racing Club. The diagonal line represents the minimum requirements for commercial yachts such as used for charter or sail training which are certificated for unrestricted operation, as required by the UK Maritime and Coastguard Agency (MCA).*

The triangles represent a large proportion of modern production yachts and the graph shows the preponderance of yachts below the line, as are the preponderance of yachts that have got into trouble.

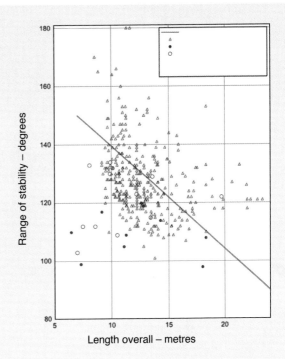

mast steps. Even just loading up a yacht with food, and equipment which is stowed above the waterline (e.g. outboard motors, liferafts), will have the same effect to a lesser degree. The problem is not confined to smaller yachts. There are a few super-yachts that can only set their sails in gentle conditions due to heavy top hamper combined with shallow draft.

It was notable that *Taka* self-righted after 45 minutes. A yacht should eventually self-right if she floods, and the effect of free surface water is to accelerate the process. Once righted there will usually be enough fore and aft structure to break up the free surface and discourage the yacht from inverting immediately, though several tons of water will need to be pumped out.

The less lucky participants in the Vendée Globe Challenge single-handed race of 1996/97 showed that there was still a rash of keel and stability weakness around the racing circuits. Far from bringing good ideas in for the cruising sailor this race seemed, up until then, to be breeding unsafe yachts. At least the Vendée Globe type of yachts are now

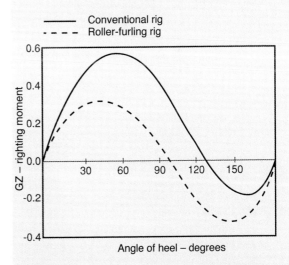

Figure 3.2 *A dramatic illustration of how a small yacht's range of positive stability can drop with modifications to the rig.*

designed, like multihulls, with capsize in mind, e.g. with escape hatches fitted in the stern. It would have been preferable for them to have sufficient stability to right themselves quickly. One well-known case was Thierry Dubois' Open 60 *Amnesty International* which, in the 1996/7 Vendée Globe Race, remained firmly capsized in spite of large waves and the flooding of one of her stabilising water tanks. The designer said that the boat had flooded as much as she was going to, and for the boat to right herself it would have been necessary to vent off air through a seacock to bring more water inside. That Isabelle Autissier capsized in the South Pacific in February 1999, whilst taking part in the Around Alone race, and abandoned her yacht after being unable to right her, suggests no progress was then being made in the realm of single-handed competition yacht design.

The stability characteristics and, in particular, the angle of vanishing stability is information that can and should be obtained before a yacht is purchased for ocean voyaging. This information should include the effect of modifications such as furling sails, radar and other mast hamper, and also increasing displacement by the addition of fuel drums and motor bicycles on the upper deck and large quantities of stores and equipment down below. With this information one will have a good guide as to how stable a boat really is. In certain cases racing boats have acquired adequate or even abundant stability through using a bulb on the end of a high aspect keel but such yachts have an unsuitably large draft should they ever be considered for cruising.

Other yachts have not righted themselves, as might be expected, when the keel has broken off. High aspect ratio keels, by virtue of their extra depth and smaller cross-sectional area, need considerable extra support. It is not so easy to tell at a glance how likely it is that such a keel will break off, though a surveyor is likely to give good advice. There is little to be lost in performance, or any other characteristic, by increasing the factor of safety in this region and this is most easily done at the design stage.

Cape Town–Rio Race (South Atlantic Race), January 2014

The Cape Town to Rio Race, called the South Atlantic Race when not going to Rio, has been held since 1971. In 2014 the largest boat was the Volvo 70 called *Maserati* and amongst the smallest was a Sunfast 32. It is usually a downwind and undemanding race, which is not to say that the entries were not well-scrutineered, but a well-forecast depression hit the 36-strong fleet soon after the start. The wind strength was reported as 52 knots and the wave height 6m (19.7ft). *Billie*, a Bavaria 54, lost a man overboard when the boat was dismasted who, sadly, died after his recovery. The remaining four in her crew were seriously injured and were taken off by a naval frigate. *Black Cat*, a Didi 38, a plywood sloop designed by Dudley Dix who was on board, lost her rudder, followed later by suffering a complete roll when lying a'hull. It transpired that the rudder had probably been strained before the race. *Isla* had an electrical fire. Ten yachts gave up the race, which was notable for what might have happened, rather than what did, quite bad enough though that was. The race gave another reminder that even modern yachts which comply with all regulations are vulnerable to losing their masts, rudders and crew overboard as well as being rolled.

Cheeki Rafiki, May 2014

The strong and experienced crew of the Beneteau 40.7 *Cheeki Rafiki* reported taking on water on their way back to the UK after a regatta in Antigua in which she had won her class, and stated that they were going to divert to the Azores. Contact was lost in the early hours of 16 May 2014 and locator beacons were activated later that day. A US Navy helicopter crew discovered the wreckage about 1,600km (1,000 miles) east of Massachusetts after a protracted search for the missing crew. The US Coast Guard said at the start of the

A Beneteau 40.7, showing the deep narrow keel. Note the contrast with the much older design behind. Photo: Peter Bruce

search winds were blowing at more than 40 knots and seas reached up to 4.5m (15ft).

A US Navy boat crew was deployed after the helicopter sighting and found the upturned flooded yacht on 23 May with her keel missing. There was no sign of the crew, and the liferaft was still in its stowage.

The capsize of *Cheeki Rafiki*, and the desperate search for survivors, made headlines. The Beneteau 40.7 is a well-known class designed and built by reputable companies and has a typical modern deep high aspect ratio keel. Without the boat to study one can only speculate that, after *Cheeki Rafiki*'s six recorded groundings in the United Kingdom well before her capsize in the Atlantic, there were structural issues with the hull. Pat Shaughnessy, President of Bruce Farr, the designer, commented:

IN REVIEW OF the high resolution pictures of the hull bottom, taken by the passing freighter, it appears as though the forward centreline keel bolts failed in tension, which may be consistent with a grounding incident. It appears as though the internal structure and local hull shell then failed in way of the pairs of central keel bolts in broaching. The keel, the hull shell, the internal structure, bolts, washer plates, and nuts, appears to have separated from the remainder of the hull. The remainder of the aft centreline bolts also appear to have failed in tension, and are surrounded in rust stains which might indicate previous damage. All of these observations are only that, observations and some potential theory.

Regarding the following Marine Accident Investigation Branch (MAIB) report he said that at no stage were the designers asked to comment though they would have been very willing to help. The report came to the same conclusions, i.e. the keel and its securing arrangements were progressively damaged as a result of groundings over the life of the boat and the keel probably became detached in stormy conditions in consequence. Beneteau say that, in the case of a 40.7, it is necessary to remove the keel after a heavy grounding to establish whether the bond has failed between the hull and the internal shell and this had not been done with *Cheeki Rafiki*. Four other Beneteau 40.7s had been identified where the bond had failed. It was postulated that there might have been additional groundings to the ones reported but certainly not in the Antigua Regatta in which the boat had participated before the accident. The report drew attention, but provided no solution, to the problem of having a liferaft and EPIRB in a useful position for both when a vessel is upright and when inverted. As an aside it should be mentioned that, when leakage was apparent, the skipper was reluctant to divert to Bermuda as he had no appropriate chart.

The lesson learnt is that every grounding needs to be taken very seriously and thoroughly investigated by a surveyor with appropriate knowledge.

It is so easy to be wise after the event, but one should add that having charts of possible ports to go to en route in an ocean crossing is important not just for when there is a boat malfunction but also for when a crewperson is injured, ill or has an urgent family or business problem. Had *Cheeki Rafiki* berthed in Bermuda, perhaps mainly to take on fuel, there might have been a different outcome.

The MAIB had compiled a list of 72 yacht keel failures between 1984 and October 2013, a figure that demonstrates that keel engineering remains an issue.

2014 *Vestas Wind*

On 29 November 2014 the 20m (65ft) Volvo Round the World Race yacht *Vestas Wind* went aground in the dark at a speed of 19 knots on the remote Indian Ocean reef known as the Cargados Carajos shoals, which had not shown up on the zoom setting of the chart plotter. Fortunately no one was injured nor did the yacht break up in the subsequent pounding and she was eventually salvaged. After hitting the shore the boat turned round so the bows were pointing to seaward. Although the rudders and keel bulb came off and the stern was badly damaged, the remarkable thing was that the keel remained in place – all credit to those who put together the specification.

Additional questionable design features

Apart from lack of stability and insufficient strength at the intersection of hull and keel, other features which buyers should be wary of are: flat sections in the bow area that can cause severe slamming in a sea way, the mainsheet being located just forward of the steering position which can destroy the steering console in a gybe, hatches that open only as far as their hinges allow which fail under more pressure, brass seacocks which de-zincify and shatter, insufficient strength at the rudder skeg, large Perspex (acrylic) windows which can break too easily, weak coachroof structures that fail when the boat is thrown into a wave trough, open centreboard casings which can flood the boat, weak cockpit locker lids which can break leaving a gaping hole into which water can stream, weak steering arrangements that fail in stormy weather, 'high tech' but unproven composite hull construction, off-centre hatchways which can allow the hull to flood in a broach, weak and unsecurable washboards which fail when a boat is pooped or float off when a boat is inverted, objects that rely on gravity to stay put, such as engines, batteries, anchors, fuel and fresh water tanks, and exhaust pipes which are not sufficiently well designed to stop water flooding back to the engine in bad weather, and exhaust pipes on the stern that allow exhaust smoke to flow forward into the cockpit or cabin. Many racing yachts, these days, have large shallow open cockpits with little protection from the elements, insufficient lockers, and uncomfortable accommodation. There are still a few yachts about with fragile rigs though, in this instance, the rule has encouraged a seamanlike design.

Twin rudders are often used for modern yachts, the rudders being offset from the centreline and angled outwards. Rudder damage can very occasionally occur with this configuration owing to the keel no longer giving protection, and if one rudder is damaged the alternative one is usually only effective on one tack. High-aspect ratio single rudders of racing boats may fail as a result of having insufficiently large bearings beneath the cockpit floor and the hull.

Structurally, a rudder supported by a skeg should be stronger than a blade, thus there is a valid argument for using a skeg in the case of boats intended primarily for cruising. Not only is the skeg-hung rudder better supported but also it is much less likely to stall. It is not sufficient just to have a skeg; the skeg must be built to withstand the most extreme loads that the rudder can give. An illustration was given by the owner of one of many yachts that encountered a bad Atlantic storm. Most of the yachts put into the Azores after the storm and quite a number of them were hauled up on the slipway with broken rudders; skeg-hung rudders being about equal in number to the blade type. The wry comment was that in some boats the whole skeg had been torn off, leaving a hole in the hull, a disadvantageous situation compared to the blades.

Straight or plumb bows are another characteristic of modern yachts. The elegant overhanging bow causes a rapid increase of buoyancy when the bow dips and discourages 'submarining', the straight bow does not.

Conclusion

One must appreciate that designers and builders are bound to try to give cruising yachts the sparkling performance characteristics of a racing boat if this is what their customers want. Thus every would-be buyer of an ocean cruising yacht needs to be careful that he or she has a boat truly designed and built for the job – allowing for the extras they have in mind. Compliance with RCD regulations may not guarantee a yacht's fitness in design for extremely bad weather.

Would-be buyers of racing yachts have to be equally careful. The quest for performance and excitement has, in some cases, been at the expense of acceptable stability, sea-keeping qualities and strength. Moreover, in a fresh wind, the design might possibly be beyond the ability of an enthusiastic 'amateur' crew to control.

The implications for the prudent ocean cruising yachtsman might simply be to purchase a strong, stable proven design of vessel, unrelated to the current racing breeds and influenced by the sensible design characteristics given in Chapter 1 by the late Olin Stephens, the past-master-designer of seaworthy yachts. Such thinking should produce a sensible craft.

There is another argument worthy of consideration. If offshore or ocean racing crews are in need of help from the rescue services every time it blows more than Force 8, there will come a time when governments will decide that yachtsmen are not able to manage their own affairs properly. The authorities could take control of leisure craft safety regulations by creating all kinds of expensive and unsympathetic new legislation, to the detriment of all.

We must hope that improvement of yacht design will continue, but not at the expense of good stability, adequately supported keels and similar less obvious but important design features for heavy weather. Onus should always be on racing rule-makers to give precedence to seaworthy characteristics over equality of boat speed. International working groups should insist on higher standards of stability regardless of understandable but unacceptable commercial pressure to leave the vital matter of stability at the current standard.

It is clear that heavy weather does not have much influence upon yacht design. In the UK the Maritime and Coastguard Agency has control only over commercial and training craft and stipulates appropriate standards. Leisure craft designers do not need to comply and rarely do so, being more influenced by market pressures.

4 Spars and rigging considerations

Matthew Sheahan and Harry James

Coastal-hopping in heavy weather conditions is one thing, long distance blue water cruising quite another. When the going gets tough many miles from land, self-sufficiency and confidence in the boat and her equipment are essential requirements.

As the primary driving force aboard the boat, the rig is fundamental to the crew's well being in more ways than one. Lose the rig and there is a risk of having to cope with more than just the initial loss of motive power. Communications can be made inoperable and a longer passage time will put the food, water and fuel supply in question. Depending on the type of craft, the motion of the boat may change completely as well, especially in bigger seas, and can make life very uncomfortable.

Prevention is always better than cure, and although it is never possible to guarantee the security of a yacht's rig, there are several ways of minimising the risk. It is this approach that will be looked at first in this chapter and then what to do if the worst does happen. But first a brief explanation of some of the most common types of rigs and what sets them apart from each other.

Rig configurations

Although there are many historical reasons for the development of the wide variety of rigs in evidence today, the main reason for the differences are due to practicalities of handling a given sail area. Modern day furling devices and reefing systems have done much to nudge up the size of sail plans that can be easily handled by, say, a crew of two. As boats get bigger, the configuration of the rig starts to play an important part in the manageability of the sail plan.

For boats of up to around 12m (40ft) LOA, 'Bermudan Sloop' rigs are by far the most popular as they are simple and easy to manage. However, above 12m the cutter rig comes into its own. With this configuration, a staysail is set from an inner forestay either instead of, or in conjunction with, the primary headsail. Breaking down the foretriangle area into two sails does make life easier for trimming, tacking and changing headsails. The configuration is particularly popular for coping with heavy weather when just the staysail and a deep reefed mainsail can be used.

Since the advent of modern sail handling systems, ketch and yawl rigs have become less popular. Yet they still have their place in reducing the total sail area into manageable sizes, especially on boats of 16m (52ft) LOA and above. Furthermore, having two masts means that there is at least the possibility of a spare mast, albeit smaller, in the event of losing the main mast. However, this will not always be the case, especially if a triatic stay – running from the top of the main mast to the top of the mizzen – is fitted. Having a mizzen mast can also provide a well balanced heavy weather rig configuration too, where a staysail can be set on the main mast and a mizzen sail set aft.

In the 1981–2 Whitbread Round the World Race, Ceramco New Zealand, *skippered by the late Sir Peter Blake, lost her mast 241km (150 miles) north of Ascension Island when the port lower intermediate rod shroud broke where it had been bent around the lower spreader. The 15m (50ft) top section was recovered and lashed to the 3m (11ft) stump using a breadboard as a baseplate. The destination of Cape Town was 3,951km (2,455 miles) away, but it was necessary to sail over 1,609km (1,000 miles) more to stay in favourable winds. During the passage,* Ceramco's *crew achieved one day's run of 383km (238 miles).* Photo: PPL

Schooner rigs, where the forward-most mast is the shorter, offer similar advantages to ketches and yawls, where the total sail area is divided up into smaller individual areas. Again, this allows more options when it comes to balancing up the sail plan for heavy weather sailing on a given point of sail. And once more, in the event of losing one mast, there is at least a chance that there will be another still standing.

Although less popular, there are the unstayed mast configurations that should be mentioned too. These are cat rigs with their single large mainsails, swing rigs with their rotating mast and boom fixed unit, and junk rigs.

Whilst providing several solutions to some of the potential problems and shortcomings of conventionally rigged spars, such configurations do have weaknesses of their own, particularly for the long distance sailor.

Having no rigging does mean that the spar is more likely to flex and, depending on the spar's material is therefore more susceptible to fatigue in certain areas. Most builders for these types of spars are well aware of the problems and it is true to say that this is less of an issue with carbon masts than those built in alloy. Nevertheless, while compression is the biggest problem for stayed spars, fatigue through flexing is the unstayed rig's biggest enemy. Lack of rigging also makes it more difficult to go aloft, especially while under way. A blessed excuse perhaps, but take time to consider how you would cope in such an event, before it happens for real.

Perhaps the most important factor to bear in mind, though, is that of setting storm sails. Few unstayed masts have attachments for inner forestays onto which storm jibs can be

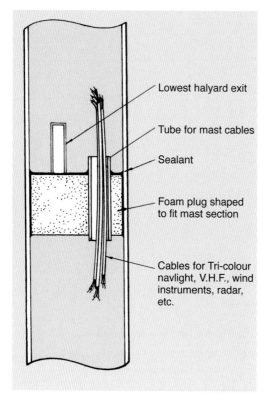

Lowest halyard exit

Tube for mast cables

Sealant

Foam plug shaped
to fit mast section

Cables for Tri-colour
navlight, V.H.F., wind
instruments, radar,
etc.

Figure 4.1 *An example of a means by which a keel-stepped mast can be made to drain on deck rather than in the accommodation area.*

hanked and some mast/mainsail arrangements have problems in fitting a trysail track. Such considerations must be borne in mind before heading off over the horizon.

A seaworthy spar?

The biggest dilemma for many designers and prospective owners is whether to opt for a deck-stepped or keel-stepped mast. There is a continuing debate as to which is the most suitable for long distance cruising; there are advantages and disadvantages on either side. From a structural and spar design point of view, a keel-stepped mast should always be lighter, yet no less secure, than the same rig stepped on deck. Keel stepped masts derive a large part of their security by the fact that they are 'built in' – as engineers would say – being

supported at the mast heel and at the deck.

To use the same engineering terminology, deck-stepped masts on the other hand are 'pin jointed' structures. In other words, without the rigging, a deck-stepped mast would fall over straight away. A keel-stepped mast would not – at least not so easily!

When it comes to designing the mast section, a deck-stepped mast should always be constructed from a stiffer mast section – one having higher moments of inertia in the technical jargon – compared to the keel stepped alternative. Heavier masts can have a considerable effect on the stability and motion of the boat, as well as her performance, and although this may not be a key issue in some cases, it is nonetheless an important consideration.

Keel-stepped masts do have their disadvantages, though. The most common is water leakage down the inside of the mast into the boat. This can be avoided by fitting a dam inside the mast near the lowest halyard exit in order to let the water run out (Fig 4.1). A dam between the mast and deck collar can also be fitted using Spartite that will give the mast proper all-round support and reduce the water ingress. A boat with a deck-stepped mast does not suffer this problem. In the event of being dismasted, the bury section (the section below decks) of keel-stepped masts can sometimes cause damage below decks too, especially if the heel comes away from the mast step. This can happen if the boat is rolled or knocked down.

Although this type of damage is rare, a recent case in the Southern Ocean contributed to the loss of the boat as a watertight bulkhead was damaged. So preventative measures are important. They are simple too. Fastening the mast heel down to the mast step either by through bolting, or by attaching a rigging screw strop to a hull attachment is usually sufficient.

But what about the rest of the rig? What should be looked for or specified in a set of spars that will be fit for bad weather? Spreader roots, gooseneck attachments, shroud tangs and masthead units are the main areas to focus

With only the top section of the mast lost, after some sorting out, it may be possible to still use a reefed mainsail. Spinnakers flying free up the mast can usually be recovered by sailing or motoring dead downwind.
Photo: David Harding

on. Although they all perform separate tasks, they do tend to fall into three categories: cast aluminium units, fabricated aluminium fittings and fabricated stainless steel fittings.

Cast alloy fittings are popular among production spar manufacturers as they are cheaper to produce in numbers and simple to fit to the spars, requiring only a few rivets or machine screws to fasten them. Although fine for normal coastal and occasional offshore sailing, castings like these can present more of a problem for longer distance sailors for a number of reasons.

Aluminium castings are brittle when compared to alloy or steel fabrications, and consequently do not fare well if they receive sharp blows. In the case of a gooseneck, a crash gybe transferring high shock loads along the

boom, could be enough to damage a casting irreparably, where it might simply bend or distort a fabricated unit. Cast fittings do not like being distorted either. A spreader set at an incorrect angle can, when loaded, distort a casting to the extent that it fails completely. Again, a fabrication may be more tolerant of such misalignments.

It has to be said that there are different views on this subject. One justification in favour of simple screw or rivet secured castings, is that they are usually a stock item for the spar builder. As a result they can be easily sent almost anywhere in the world and can often be fitted without specialist tools. The balance that needs to be struck when considering which system to go for is between the likelihood of failure, against the difficulty of repair.

Figure 4.2 *Worn sheave at the outboard end of a boom. These sheaves take heavy loads and deserve regular inspection. Any worn or failed sheaves will cause severe friction with added difficulty in heavy weather and damage the ropes.*

Figure 4.3 *A slight bend indicates an over-compressed spreader which could fail altogether, with simultaneous rig failure.*

Figure 4.4 *The shroud wire and swage are not in alignment. In this case the bottom of the mast hole has to be filed down just enough allowing the body of the swage to align with the wire correctly.*
Photos: Harry James

In this respect there is one type of fitting that is not suitable for those travelling further afield. Spreader root castings welded to the mast wall itself should be avoided where possible. Not only are they more susceptible to failure, for the reasons above, and often reduce the strength of the mast wall locally but, should they be damaged, it is often difficult to repair the mast as the fitting cannot be removed easily. Indeed, any arrangement where the spreader transmits its thrust to the mast wall rather than to a through bar is to be avoided.

On the other hand, welding masthead units and sheave cages into a tube is not only acceptable, but also desirable for a robust spar, so long as the work is carried out properly. To achieve full strength, most types of aluminium alloy need to be heat treated from a 'soft state' to a 'hard state'. Subsequent welding heats up local areas of the mast section, usually in critical points, and lower the mechanical properties of the alloy back towards the soft state.

The optimum procedure is to perform all welding tasks such as tapering, attaching masthead units, forestay attachments and sheave cages, while the tube is in its soft state. Once complete, the tube is then heat treated to achieve its full strength. As far as finish is concerned, anodising is technically the best means of protecting a mast against corrosion and is normally the most cost effective too for boats of up to around 18m (60ft) LOA.

Painted spars are the next best thing for larger boats, as there are few anodising tanks that can cope with the size and length of large yacht masts. Furthermore, many people consider a paint finish to be prettier.

Paint finishes have improved significantly, and can offer good protection for an alloy spar so long as the surface is not damaged, but maintaining a perfect, scratch-free mast is a near impossibility. Although scratches and flaking paint are unlikely to cause structural problems themselves, one must keep an eye on any unusual signs that may indicate more serious corrosion beneath.

Figure 4.5 *The Pull/Pushpit Guardwire attachment lug when subjected to unfair load. To avoid losing all the advantage of a guard wire, an additional lashing of Dyneema core (3mm diameter) can be fitted between the guard wire fitting and around the pull/pushpit leg.*

Figure 4.6 *Right: The spacers for this chain plate are in place but the effect of no spacers will cause an uneven point load and wear at one end of the clevis pin and can also put an unfair load on the split pin, both of which can lead to a rigging failure.*
Photos: Harry James

Staying the rig

There are few statistics to prove it, but most spar manufacturers would agree that setting aside poor maintenance and set up, fatigue and rigging failure are among the common reasons for dismastings aboard cruising boats. Fatigue cycles, where the fitting is effectively work hardened through repeated flexing, usually start as a result of poor articulation. This is particularly true of the shroud attachments to the mast where the less articulation that is present, the greater the risk of fatigue and subsequent failure (Fig 4.4). As is so often the case, all it takes is one inexpensive fitting to break to cause far more serious and costly damage to the mast.

So how is it possible to be sure that attachments are suitable? As a rule of thumb, pin and eye attachments are structurally the best as there is a greater chance of the eye articulating (i.e. rocking) on the pin to accommodate different angles. Fittings designed as ball and sockets – often referred to as stemball systems – have greater friction between their surfaces and are less likely to articulate. The result is fatigue cycles somewhere else in the fitting, usually some way down the stem of a swaged fitting or at the point where the wire exits the end fitting.

T-terminals and similar devices may well be suitable for many applications, but it has to be borne in mind that they will articulate less and need to be replaced on a more regular basis. The big problem is that, apart from the considerable expense of x-raying the terminals, there are no visual indications of how far the fatigue problem has progressed.

Another factor to consider is that few masts remain rigid in one place. Indeed, if they did, high shock loads would be transferred throughout the boat. Instead, masts do move in the boat and the rigging should be able to accommodate the full range of movement. But what is an acceptable amount and how should a mast best be stayed?

The wide range of basic configurations,

plus the added combinations of the variety of multiple spreader arrangements makes this area a difficult one to define precisely. If it was not for considerations of sheeting the headsail the wider the chain plate base the better. But as a small sheeting angle is essential for good windward performance, a narrow chain plate base has to be offset by an increase in the number of spreaders up the mast. Larger craft often require discontinuous rigging once three or more sets of spreaders are used.

Generally most boats are adequately stayed in the athwartships plane. It is achieving sufficient fore and aft support that causes most problems. Beating into a heavy seaway with a deep-reefed mainsail can be one of the most punishing situations for a mast. High shock loads transferred through the rigging, as the boat pitches and slams through each wave, can cause the mast to pump fore and aft. A deep-reefed mainsail can make the situation worse as the sail tries to pull the middle of the mast aft. Unless checked, this can cause a full inversion of the mast, i.e. when the middle of the spar bows aft. Under these conditions, masts can and do fail due to the high compression loads, especially when the boat drops off a wave. To prevent this it is important to stop the mast from moving too much in the fore and aft plane. Checkstays and running backstays, prevent the mast from moving too far forward. Forward lowers or a babystay can help to prevent the mast moving aft, but the small angles where the stays meet the mast mean that an inner forestay should also be included for a belt and braces approach.

The inner forestay, as with the running backstays and check stays, need not be permanent features and can be stowed by the mast in normal conditions. But for anyone considering trips where they may encounter heavy conditions, such stays are a must, especially on masthead-rigged boats.

With the wide popularity of furling headsail systems, it is advisable to make provision for an emergency forestay. Although generally reliable, furling units can fail and to be left with no headsails is inadvisable. Furthermore, even if the furling system works perfectly,

when reefed heavily the shape of the remaining scrap of sail is too full and positioned too high up the forestay to act as a sensible storm jib. Setting a flat storm sail, low down will drive the boat better and reduce the heeling providing a much more comfortable ride.

In most cases, an emergency forestay can be easily fitted to existing masts as well as new ones. A tang fitting positioned on the forward face of the mast, just below the main forestay fitting, making sure it can articulate in as many planes as possible, and a tack fitting on deck are usually all that is required.

One popular concern of long distance sailors is whether rod rigging should be chosen rather than the more conventional 1x19 wire. Although rod rigged systems are generally more expensive than their equivalent in wire, the decision will usually depend upon ease of maintenance.

Conventional stainless steel wire is commonly available around the world and is easy to work with. Swaging tools are found in most popular ports and sailing areas, but for those travelling much further afield, bolted cone and socket type (or swageless) fitting terminals require just a hacksaw and spanners to fit them. A further advantage is that these types of terminations can easily be re-made if any local damage to the wire is found or suspected. In addition extended versions of these fittings that fit the swageless sockets are available should you have to reuse your existing wire in an emergency.

Rod rigging on the other hand, requires specialist tools to make the terminations and can be more prone to fatigue with few outward signs especially if not serviced and greased on a regular basis. Rod rigging does have advantages, though. For a given diameter, rod stretches less than wire. This means that a mast can be secured more efficiently in the boat with less deflection of the mast itself, and that weight aloft can also be reduced, improving the performance and motion of the boat.

On large cruisers and super yachts, composite fibre cable rigging, such as Carbon, Polybenzoxazole (PBO), Kevlar, Dyneema, are all proving themselves extremely strong and reliable. Most importantly they have a weight saving advantage of over 50 per cent plus compared to conventional rod or wire rigging, and in some cases it is the only option for the ever increasing size of yachts. The disadvantage is the cost and, depending on the types of fibres and their construction, the necessity for the cables to be periodically tested or in some cases completely replaced depending upon age rather than usage. Determined by construction, the outer sheathing or cover also may require regular inspection for chafe, splits or cracks that could allow water to leak in and damage the fibre. The developments on composite rigging are ongoing and one day will be used universally, as in the days of yore.

Shortening sail

While highly practical, affordable and best of all simple, roller reefing systems for main or genoa do have a few drawbacks that should be considered. Headsail furling gears are generally easier to get at than those used for in-mast mainsail furling and present less of a problem in the event of a failure. Furling mainsail systems can snag with the sail jammed in the section and refusing to come in or out which, in the teeth of a gale could be very awkward. Even if the system is to be trusted completely, provision should be made for some other means of storm mainsail that doesn't rely on the furling device, such as a trysail track.

Unlike slab reefing systems or boom furling systems, where the weight is lowered each time a reef is taken in, vertical furling systems mean that the sail weight remains at the same height above the waterline. Keeping weight high up means that there is no stability improvement as the sail plan is reduced. This can lead to a slow heavy motion due to the inertia of a heavier spar with a furled up sail inside it. Furthermore, with furling headsails, the increased windage of a rolled up headsail over a bare forestay is much greater. Another significant drawback is that if the sail cannot be fully furled, the only way to get it down is to open it out fully before lowering it. This may not be feasible or desirable in severe conditions.

In-boom furling systems offer some advantages over their in-mast equivalents, especially when it comes to reducing weight aloft, but the problems of an even furl and the distance of the luff back from the aft face of the mast can cause problems.

Slab reefing is a practical and reliable method of reefing. The comforting thought is that in the worst case, there is a better chance that the sail can be lowered, although this is still by no means guaranteed, especially if a headboard car or batten sliders are fitted. Fully battened and semi/fully battened mainsail systems make the reefing process simpler to manage, especially if lazyjacks are fitted, which exercise some control over the mainsail as it is lowered. The sail also stows more easily on top of the boom.

Single line reefing systems, where the tack and the clew of the reefed mainsail are controlled by a single line, are also very popular and allow a mainsail to be reefed quickly and without having to leave the cockpit. However, one of the potential drawbacks with any control line led back to the cockpit is friction. In order to make the system work as smoothly as possible it is very important to ensure that the reef lines or halyards are kept as free from abrupt turns around lead blocks wherever possible.

Checking and maintaining the rig

How often the rig should be checked will depend entirely on the type of sailing undertaken. While every sailor should keep an eye on the rig all the time, there are practical limits. At the very minimum, weekend, home-based sailors should check their masts at the beginning and end of every season, with the mast being taken out of the boat for a thorough check at least every three years. At the other end of the scale, checking the mast and rigging while on passage should be a daily event. Whatever type of sailing engaged upon, the potential causes of damage or failure are more likely to be as a result of chafe, fatigue or corrosion, than they are from the effects of overloading. In most cases tell-tale signs of problems can be identified visually, while the mast is in situ, which is just as well as x-raying the mast and fittings would in most cases be impractical, extremely expensive, and sometimes inconclusive.

Aluminium alloy used for most spars has a high natural resistance to corrosion resulting from the formation of the tough impervious oxide film on the surface of the aluminium when exposed to air. This oxide film, which is grey in colour, is self-repairing. So if removed by chafing or scratching, it will protect the aluminium from further corrosion, provided no dissimilar metals are in contact with the aluminium to cause electrolytic corrosion. However, any substantial corrosion at the base of the mast and at deck level should be treated seriously, as these are high load areas for the mast. In these areas, dents in the mast

wall can be a problem too and could cause the mast to buckle. This type of damage is not easy to repair without specialist tools and help.

Cracks are a particularly common starting point for mast or rigging failures and can be remedied so long as they are caught before they have had a chance to propagate too far. The areas to look at are wherever there is an exit or hole in the mast wall – especially if it is rectangular, for example, around halyard exits and where mast fittings penetrate the mast wall. Drilling a small hole at the end of the crack can, in most cases stop the crack from travelling further, but it will only be a temporary measure and will need more elaborate attention as soon as possible.

Ensuring that all fastenings are secure is perhaps an obvious check, but one that is often overlooked, as is the free running of sheaves

In the 1992–3 British Steel Global Challenge a number of bottlescrews cracked, and aboard British Steel II the mast was lost after the forestay bottlescrew failed on the leg between Rio and Auckland. A jury-rig was made using the boom and spinnaker pole, staysail sheets and reefing lines but, having been refuelled by a P&O tanker, she was able to complete much of the leg under power.
Photo: PPL

A rain squall struck contenders for the British Admiral's Cup Team seconds after the start of a selection trial race, dismasting the Yeoman 25. Her mast failed in compression as a result of the mainsail luff rope pulling out of the track, which allowed the mast to bend forward out of control until it broke. Photo: Peter Bruce

which, if jammed can cause premature chafe and failure of halyards and control lines. If the mast is keel-stepped, another area that is frequently ignored is the deck level chock arrangement. The chocks should be so secured in place that the mast is prevented from moving at all.

While there are ways in which rigging terminations can be checked using electrical methods, a few simple checks can often reveal potential problems. Looking for broken strands or corrosion within the wire is the most obvious. Elongated eyes or bent pins are an indication of overloading and should be replaced. Alignment of rigging is another important check as a stay or shroud that is distorted may fail from fatigue. As has already been mentioned, poor articulation is also very important and a common cause of fatigue-related rigging failures. All standing rigging attachments should have some degree of articulation in as many planes as possible. Another simple but essential check is to make sure that the standing rigging is secured to the spreader ends.

Heavy weather procedures under way

Preparation in all areas of the boat is the key to riding out heavy weather conditions, and nowhere is it more important than with the rig. As with many other dramas at sea, all too often a catastrophic event is the culmination of several otherwise controllable or avoidable incidents. Be prepared. Ensure that the trysail will fit in its track by hoisting it, preferably without having to climb above deck level. Have enough sail ties ready to strap down the mainsail if it has to be lowered altogether, and ensure that there is a secure means of lashing the boom to the deck to prevent it being hurled about the cockpit. Life will be difficult enough with the boom in the cockpit instead of overhead, without the further complication of the spar sliding from one side of the boat to the other as the boat rolls in big seas. Just as important is to make sure that all the heavy weather sails are tried out, not just when tied up to the pontoon or swinging at a mooring, but then underway and preferably when it's blowing. Anticipation is important too, as it is far easier and safer to throw out a reef in calm waters than it is to put a reef in when the weather has deteriorated. Anticipating the weather is particularly important if furling sails are used. A furled headsail can present considerable windage in gale conditions, to say nothing of the weight aloft. If the forecast is for heavy conditions, it may be prudent to take the sail down altogether and this means unfurling it completely – the last thing to be doing in 40 knots of wind. This also goes for furling mainsails. Although there is no additional windage when the main is furled, in extreme weather it may be sensible to lower the mainsail to reduce the centre of gravity.

When the worst happens

Mast failures are frequently a result of rigging failures and in many cases, quick thinking can save the day – just. A shroud failure, be it a wire or terminal problem, often results in losing the mast. But if the helmsman is quick enough, and it is safe to do so, a smart tack with the jib left cleated will cause the boat to heave-to and allow the mast to be jury-rigged. In some situations it may not be possible to spend much time in this position, but at least there is time to think about how the mast can best be supported. If a halyard is used to replace a shroud, bear in mind that the angle at the masthead will be very small as the halyard won't be held out by the spreaders, thus using a jockey pole or spinnaker pole just above deck level as an outrigger may help to increase the angle at the masthead and will much improve the support of the spar.

The use of Dyneema ropes for halyards is an advantage as they are significantly lighter than any wire-to-rope or polyester halyards, have extremely high strength in comparison and hardly stretch. This will not only be beneficial during normal sailing because stretch affects the set of the sail, but will also reduce wear on the sheaves and internal wear on the mast. Furthermore if there is trouble with a stay Dyneema will provide good backup.

A forestay or backstay failure is less likely to result in an instant dismasting, but is still a serious problem and should be dealt with quickly. In this case the most important thing to do is to turn either down wind or upwind, to take the load onto the intact stay, and then rig temporary support using a spare spinnaker or genoa halyard. If the backstay fails upwind, don't over react. Leave the mainsheet cleated as the leech of the mainsail will help to support the mast. In many cases, be it shroud or stay that fails, it is important not to be too quick to lower the sails, especially if there is a big sea running, as the sails can often help to stabilise the motion of the boat and prevent the mast from panting. However, if the rigging failure happens in flat water and is simply a result of overstressing, dropping the sails without delay may be the best option.

If the worst does happen and the mast falls over the side of the boat, there are two golden rules – get the spar away from the hull and don't start the engine until you are absolutely sure that rigging cannot foul the propeller. Hull damage is a major consideration in the case of a dismasting, as is the issue of remaining safe on deck and not getting dragged overboard by tangled rigging. Extreme care, yet swift action is required. Cut the rig free to protect the boat, but do remember that the more that can be salvaged the better the chances are of setting up a jury rig. Sometimes it is not possible to save any of the rig so it is a good idea to have thought about how such a rig might be arranged with just the boom and the spinnaker poles.

Spares and tools

The ideal tool kit is one that provides tools to deal with every component aboard. Taken to a conclusion this is impractical and a compromise has to be reached. Basic tools should include drills, knives, hacksaws, screwdrivers, spanners, grips and wrenches which are usually considered essential for all kinds of shipboard tasks. Tools that are needed specifically for the rig might include the following:

Rigging tools
- Rigging cutters (e.g. Felco) if 1x19 wire rigging is used. (Note that only an HT grade hacksaw blades, an angle grinder or a hydraulic cutter will cut rod rigging.)
- Club hammer
- Pipe wrench
- Extra large adjustable wrench and a length of hollow pipe to fit over it
- Sharp cold chisel
- Marlin spike
- Long tape measure
- Rivet gun
- Hacksaw

Spares
- Clevis pins
- Split pins
- Shackles
- Nuts & bolts
- Screws, machine and self tapping
- Blocks
- Toggles
- Rigging terminals, swage and swageless
- A length of wire, longer than the longest stay aboard and no less than the biggest diameter – or extended swageless fittings to match
- Bulldog clamps
- Mast and boom sleeving kit
- Rivets
- Tef Gel – Zinc Chromate paste (or other insulating material)
- Seizing wire
- Tape
- Rope and cordage
- Hacksaw blades
- Whipping twine
- Palm and needles
- Splicing needles

5 Storm sails

Peter Bruce and Richard Clifford

Sailing offshore requires small strong sails to cope with extreme wind conditions. On some cruising boats no sail can sensibly be set once the wind has reached storm force whilst other yachts have so much power that they can keep sailing in surprisingly heavy weather. As yachts get bigger they usually become more able to carry sail but their crews will not necessarily be any stronger, so the larger yacht may need more mechanical aids. In winds of gale force or more the most useful sail will be a storm jib and possibly a trysail. Yachts racing under World Sailing's (formerly ISAF) offshore special regulations, and this means virtually every racing yacht in the world, are required to carry both a storm jib – which must be possible to set independently of the headfoil – and, in races of extended duration, a trysail. However, big cruising yachts these days often rely on a fourth reef in the mainsail rather than a trysail, which may be rather big and heavy for their crew to manage. Indeed, some current high latitude sailors, such as Skip Novak, advocate a deep-reefed mainsail rather than a trysail. A fourth slab is easy enough for a sailmaker to insert into a mainsail, but may be somewhat difficult to use in the circumstances it may be required. It is often impractical to convert the boom to take a fourth reef line system therefore the first reefing lines will have to be detached and re-secured at the fourth slab, a tiresome task that preferably needs to be done in daylight and before the storm is manifest. If there is no permanent fourth line, a wise skipper will re-reeve the first reef line as the fourth as soon as the third reef

is taken in. It is important to insert a permanent continuous loop messenger line between the third and fourth clew cringles otherwise it will be necessary to lower the mainsail to insert the reef line, as *Eclipse* had to do for the third slab in the 1979 Fastnet. Another problem may be that the stack of mainsail sliders above the gooseneck may be too deep for the fourth reef luff cringle to reach the staghorn, and to climb up to the top slider and take it out of the mast gate may not seem wise in a wild sea. Like everything else, anyone who chooses to rely on a fourth slab must be sure to try it out before it is needed in earnest.

If it is still possible to carry sail at all in gale or storm conditions the combination of storm jib and trysail or heavily reefed mainsail enables progress to be made to windward, but if the wind is abaft the beam then the storm jib alone is often satisfactory.

Storm jibs

Long ago, before furling foresails became the norm, cruising yachts carried a separate storm jib, along with other sizes of headsail, which were hanked onto the forestay, though this arrangement is now very rare. It is wise to have a storm jib as, by the time the furled sail has reached the size of a storm jib, the sail will have become baggy and unable to form an efficient windward shape (see page 268). The poor sail shape is more apparent for, say, a 150 per cent overlap genoa than

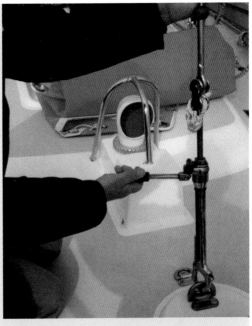

A storm jib set up on a temporary inner forestay. A ratchet lever system is used to tension the inner forestay. Photo: John Clothier

for a 100 per cent genoa, which furls up with fewer rolls and may still be efficient down to half size. The unfurled part of an overlapping genoa is also likely to be quite high up the forestay, thus increasing the heeling moment, and in extreme conditions it is liable to become stretched or damaged. However, if running downwind, the shape of the sail does not matter so a well-furled foresail is a reasonable option. Racing yachts are required to carry a storm jib of no more than defined dimensions[1]. In practice a sail made to the specified maximum size may be too large for gale or storm conditions, and it may be wise to carry an even smaller storm jib, called a spitfire jib, as just one size of storm jib cannot be expected to suit a very wide range of wind speeds of, say, between 35 and 60

knots. An additional advantage of a spitfire jib is that, given two spinnaker poles, it may be 'twinned' with the storm jib when running dead downwind in heavy weather.

The balance of the storm sails should also be taken into account when deciding the position for the storm jib, and this will depend upon the rig and hull shape of individual yachts. In some cases a storm jib on the forestay makes the vessel carry a lot of lee helm without a mainsail or trysail set, and there are common instances of yachts where the storm jib removable inner stay has been set so far back that the normal sheet leads are too wide, and do not allow the yacht to point.

The weight of cloth used for a storm jib should be similar to that used for an offshore cruising mainsail and certainly heavier than a

---

[1] The World Sailing regulations state that the maximum area of the storm jib should be 5 per cent of the height of the fore triangle squared (12) and it must not exceed 65 per cent of the height of the fore triangle.

This sail is carried on a Naiad 39. It has a 2:1 purchase on the halyard to ensure that the luff is really tight and a 'torsional stay' luff rope that does not twist so it can be rolled up with a furler. The arrangement is suitable for a storm jib of any size and the tack should be positioned on the centreline near to but clear of the furled headsail where there is sufficient strength in the deck to take the vertical load.
Photo: Peter Bruce

weights, but it should not be forgotten that the correct weight and material of cloth is more important than colour. The World Sailing special regulations sensibly prohibit the use of aromatic polyamides or carbon for either storm jibs because they can fail catastrophically, whilst Spectra and Dyneema are acceptable.

When considering how best to hoist the storm jib, it might be thought that it could replace the furling foresail on the headfoil, but, in most circumstances the unfurling, lowering and replacing of head sail would be both difficult and dangerous. Hoisting a storm jib loose-luffed can be unsatisfactory due to the difficulty of obtaining a straight enough luff, plus the difficulty of hoisting the jib in windy conditions with the likelihood of a wrap around the mast or spreaders. One way round this problem is to have the storm jib on a ratchet furler, allowing the jib to be hoisted when furled. The luff tension problem can be overcome by using a two part non-stretch halyard and the luff rope should be a 'torsional stay' which will not twist, allowing the sail to be used as any furling headsail (see left).

Another quite common solution is to have a dedicated inner stay, and to hoist a hanked storm jib on this using a spare halyard, but this stay must be attached to the mast from as near to the main forestay as possible without causing chafe to the furled headsail, otherwise runners may be required. Attachment of a storm jib over the tightly furled headsail is yet another possible solution and devices using this system are available on the market. Of these, the most popular are those using a sleeve over the furled genoa, connected with hanks, which forms a good aerofoil shape. Another option is a double sail set over the furled genoa, with the two sides held together by wind pressure, and the sheets attached to both clews. This set up is quite easy to hoist, and sets well, but chafe damage is likely to occur at the metal attachment points unless replaced with tape straps. If this sail is allowed to 'inflate', i.e. the clews come apart so one side is no longer folded over the other as can happen when going downwind, the sail becomes extremely hard to control. Another disadvantage is that

normal headsail with abundant strength at the clew to prevent damage when flogging. Edges should be taped, and not just turned over and stitched. Some sailmakers add non-adjustable leech and foot lines within the tapes to add strength. The sail should be cut so that the clew is well off the deck, and usually a tack pendant – a strop made of wire, Dyneema or similar low stretch material 60–100cm (2–3ft) long – is added to keep the sail above green water on deck. Consideration should also be given to using a high visibility coloured fabric or the addition of a highly visible patch (e.g. in day-glo orange, pink or yellow) to both sides of the sail. Cloth manufacturers now make orange fabric in a wider range of

Given two poles, setting two headsails with no mainsail can be the most comfortable method of sailing downwind in heavy weather for many boats. The boat will probably roll less if the sails are hoisted on separate headfoils. A trysail sheeted aft may also reduce rolling. Photo: PPL

the doubled sail is very difficult to re-bag on board. Although seemingly suitable, both these systems have critics from amongst those that have used them in earnest.

Other arrangements using a storm jib with the furled genoa often lead to chafe. For example, most cruising yachts use a stretchy 'braid on braid' spinnaker halyard to hoist the storm jib, and the vertical movement of the storm jib halyard acting on the furled headsail and other hard points, such as those caused by parrel beads, will sooner or later cause chafe. Though chafe is obviously most undesirable in the furling headsail, the damage can be patched by making a localised repair which initially may only affect the sun strip.

Cutter and slutter rigged yachts have the option of setting the storm jib on the inner forestay. Alternatively, if a small furling staysail is used, in some cases it will furl down adequately for use as a storm jib, especially if it is made from material with a low stretch character. As already stated, siting is critical when sloops with furling headsails are using an inner stay onto which the storm jib can be

hanked. The inner forestay should be easy to fit and, when not in use, it should be capable of being moved out of the way. The inner stay must also be sufficiently clear of the forestay so that it is possible to operate the furling sail with the inner forestay in position, and located so the hanks of the storm jib cannot chafe the furled sail. The top of the stay should be designed to articulate at the mast to allow free movement between the stowed and working position, and must be attached at a point that is below and clear of the furling gear to prevent interferences. Experience has shown that the bottom end of the inner forestay should have free movement too when in use, either with toggles or with a clip. There are various levers and systems on the market that can be used to tension the inner stay, which include a wheel-operated rigging screw and a Highfield lever.

Once the inner stay is set up, it may seem necessary to roll the furling headsail before tacking or gybing, but this may only be required when short tacking. The inner stay can also be used for twin headsail running and as a backup should the main forestay fail. It is common

61

practice to passage-make with the inner forestay set up for additional security. When not in use the inner stay must be kept clear of the mast, spreaders and running rigging. It can, for example, be secured on a pad eye on the coachroof with both ends of the tensioning device held firmly. Yachts with in-line spreaders allow the inner forestay to be stowed on the toe rail between the cap shroud and the forward lower shroud provided the chosen location is clear of the genoa. Other yachts have a cleat mounted on the leading edge of one of the lower spreaders. The arrangement takes up excess wire and stops it flogging against the rig.

Ideally a separate halyard should be used for the storm jib, and this halyard needs to lead clear of the furling gear at the top of the mast. It should either leave the mast just below the attachment point for the inner forestay, or run from a sheave at the truck down to a fairlead below the attachment point for the top of the inner forestay. Halyards which are not often used need to be carefully protected against chafe. The spinnaker pole topping lift, if made of low stretch rope, can sometimes double as the storm jib halyard.

The correct sheeting position for the storm jib should be established and marked in calm conditions, and a narrow sheeting angle is desirable in high-pointing yachts. This is also helpful when heaving-to, and allows motor sailing to take place close to the direction of the wind. Accordingly Rod Stephens, working in conjunction with his brother, Olin, who used to design very close-winded yachts, specified dedicated leads for a storm jib that gave a very narrow sheeting angle. Such careful arrangements are not often found these days, but the J46 *Cielita* (see Chapters 15 and 26) with her storm jib set on an inner forestay did have inboard sheet leads configured for the narrow sheeting angle of the storm jib with which the storm jib worked significantly well.

As already stated a tack line is advantageous to raise the tack clear of breaking seas and improve forward visibility, and if fitted, it may be useful to have a hank, snap shackle, or even just a lashing in the tack cringle to attach to the forestay in order to stop the sail pulling away from the stay and stressing the lowest hank. In some cases the storm jib may have its own sheets and its own cars, but if the sheets are permanently attached to the storm jib two people may need to go forward to set it – one to hank on, and the other to run the sheets. Unless the storm jib sheets have been meticulously coiled and lashed they can come out of the bag snarled up, and it may be found easier to have two sheets permanently set up with the cars positioned, so that the sheets can be secured to the clew after the sail is hanked on. If using non-furling headsails, the sheets from the previous sail can often be used, and in some yachts the storm jib tack strop is arranged so that the sheeting position of the smaller genoas is the same as for the storm jib, avoiding the need to move the cars.

The storm jib needs to be stored in its bag together with all of its shackles, strops and blocks in a reasonably accessible stowage, and brought out from time to time for examination and for exercise in setting. The storm jib hanks tend to become solid if not looked after, and the good seaman will lubricate them periodically to ensure that they can open freely whenever needed.

When it becomes apparent that the storm jib will be required, the first action is to prepare the inner forestay and ensure it is appropriately tensioned and clear of any running rigging that may be flapping around the mast. The storm jib halyard will require a winch, which may mean clearing the winch that is normally occupied by the halyard for the furling headsail. The storm jib must then be taken forward in its bag, and the bag attached to the inner forestay using a hank or karabiner fitted to the bag. Pre-rigged sheets can save a lot of work in difficult conditions.

After the sheets have been attached, the foresail should be furled, and then the storm jib hoisted and sheeted in as quickly as possible, preferably with a bit of windward sheet tension to control the flog, preserve the clew, and to ensure that the sheet bowline does not shake itself undone. Just how much sheet tension should be used is boat specific, and is learned by trial and error.

The Elliot 50, Venture II, *going well to windward under a Dacron storm jib, secured with softsail hanks around a textile inner stay. The deep-reefed mainsail has been set commendably flat.*
Photo: Carlo Borlenghi/DPPI

It may be necessary to ease the sheets of the furling sail, or to secure them well forward to prevent them either catching on the storm jib as it is hoisted or chafing when the storm jib sheet is eased. Likely causes of chafe include the hanks of the storm jib or inner stay rubbing on the furled headsail, and the sheets of the furled headsail rubbing on the storm jib which may need to be temporarily re-routed. The sheets of the furled headsail or even a small area of foresail can be useful to contain the storm jib as it is lowered. Some ocean sailors tack their boat before lowering a hanked storm jib, leaving the jib sheeted as before the tack. In this hove-to situation, foredeck motion is easier and the sail will not flog.

A properly configured storm jib which can be set separately from the furling headsail is absolutely essential if windward progress in heavy weather is to be possible.

Trysails

The trysail is a triangular sail, which is attached to the mast but set loose-footed, and can be sheeted independently of the main boom. The traditional use of a trysail is to replace the mainsail in heavy weather in order to balance the storm jib and improve the ability of the yacht to sail to windward. It has secondary uses such as to replace the mainsail if it has been damaged or blown out or if the boom or gooseneck has broken. An example of this use of a trysail was when Hugh Clay in *Aratapu,* having broken his gooseneck, sailed under trysail for most of the passage from Tasmania to Chile. The World Sailing regulations require yachts racing in Categories 0–2 (Trans-Ocean in offshore or large unprotected areas where a high degree of self-sufficiency is required) to carry one storm trysail, and it specifies the maximum size and some aspects of sail construction[2].

---

[2] The racing rules state the trysail is to be capable of being sheeted independently of the boom and of an area not greater than 17.5 per cent mainsail luff length x mainsail foot length. There should be neither headboard nor battens. The yacht's sail number and letter(s) shall be placed on both sides of the trysail in as large a size as is practicable. Aromatic polyamides, carbon fibres and other high modulus fibres shall not be used in the trysail.

A trysail must be strong, and should be made from a fabric that is easy to handle and the same weight as the mainsail, preferably using a high visibility colour. The major consideration in construction is strength at the three corners, and in particular at the clew due to the narrow angle at the aft end of the sail which is a high-stress area made weaker by the insertion of a cringle eye to take the sheets. All three corners thus need reinforcement patching, backed up with webbing straps, and the eyes need to be fitted using a hydraulic press. The sail can be leech cut, with the seams parallel to the leech to maintain continuity of strength along the most highly loaded edge of the sail, or cross cut with the seams perpendicular to the leech, giving less stretch. If slides are used on the luff the top and bottom slides should be aluminium or stainless steel, whilst the others can be plastic – but all should be attached to the sail with webbing rather than the weaker plastic shackles often used on mainsails. If lacing or parrel beads are used, care should be taken to avoid snagging points on the mast.

One of the many comments coming out of the Sydney–Hobart Race storm in 1998 was that skippers thought that their trysails were too big. Tim Trafford thought the same as he was closing the coast of Chile on passage from Easter Island in 1998. While sailing the 16.8m (55ft) yacht *Ardevora* he was caught in a northerly storm with a strong northerly current running while on the edge of soundings, and refrained from setting his trysail as he thought it was too big for those conditions, using instead a sea anchor which, incidentally, proved to be too small.

The issue of size must therefore be considered carefully and one might even consider carrying two trysails; one made close to the World Sailing maximum recommended size to substitute for the main in case of damage, and the other made much smaller for use as a storm trysail in very severe conditions. An alternative might appear to be to add reef points on the larger trysail, but to attempt to reef such a sail in severe conditions would be adding another operational hazard, so this is not practical.

Sheets can be permanently bent to the sail using a single line, halved at the clew. Although one sheet may be sufficient, as tacking is unlikely under trysail, two will provide better control. The lead should be judged from the cut of the sail, and a block fitted to the appropriate point on deck. Sheeting to the end of the boom is another possibility when the boom is not damaged, but the downward angle of the leech from the mast to the clew is likely to be very flat, and therefore an inefficient carrier of the combined weight of boom, mainsail and perhaps 50 litres of water, so the boom would need support from a topping lift or possibly a solid vang. An inadvertent gybe involving the boom in storm conditions can be disastrous, for example the binnacle can be picked up and damaged or the boom mainsheet fitting can fail. But with just the two sheets in use without the boom, inadvertent gybes are not usually a big problem as the sail just flops over. When sailing downwind the clew of the trysail sheeted to the boom and held by a foreguy can be more efficient and more convenient than using double sheets and no boom, but it is even better to set twin headsails. When sheeting without using the boom, a block on the quarter or the spinnaker sheet block will be suitable. Yachts with a limited number of winches may need to lead the sheet across to a windward winch. As with setting the storm jib, a little practice in light weather will determine the best arrangement, and prove invaluable when the sail has to be set in anger.

Small yachts may have only one mainsail halyard and a topping lift, in which case transferring the halyard needs to be done with care due to the risk of losing the shackle, of allowing the halyard to fly loose, or of allowing the halyard to wrap around a mast fitting. A safety line from a cleat to the thimble on the halyard is a wise precaution, as is seizing the shackle – which should have a captive pin – to the halyard. A spare main halyard will make the transfer a bit easier, and if the topping lift is made of a sufficiently low stretch material it can double as the spare halyard, although this does assume that either a solid kicker is fitted, or that the boom will be lashed to the coach roof

If this yacht needed to come on the wind, she would need to change to a smaller headsail, to avoid becoming uncontrollable. Photo: Erwan Quéméré/Bluegreen

or deck when the trysail is set. Ideally a set of boom gallows should be fitted which will allow the boom to be firmly secured when the main is lowered, and can accommodate solid kicking straps and spray hoods, making the task of changing sails aft of the mast safer and easier.

Another consideration is that the halyard from the masthead down to the head of the trysail is liable to flog tiresomely against the mast when the trysail is hoisted. Changing the halyard tension simply alters the frequency, and in storm conditions it is obviously impractical to get up there and secure it. A remedy is to add a long reinforced tape fitted to the head of the trysail with slides at appropriate intervals, long enough to reach to about half a metre from the halyard sheave. The tape must be carefully fed untwisted into the mast luff slot before hoisting, and flaked and tied before stowing.

The tack of the trysail needs to be fitted with a tack line that should be attached to a strong point below the boom, and be long enough for the trysail to set above the handed and bundled mainsail. Finding a suitable securing point may require some thought on yachts with aft-led halyards, because if the tack is secured directly to the gooseneck it may foul and chafe the stowed mainsail; moreover consideration should be taken for the possibility that the gooseneck has broken.

If a yacht has lazy jacks, before taking the trysail out of its bag, it will help if they are cleared away by leading them forward and passed around a convenient cleat on either side of the mast.

There are several different systems for hoisting a trysail. When Bermuda rigged yachts had wooden masts many had two tracks, one for the mainsail and the other for the trysail. A system of lacing the luff of the trysail to the mast is not feasible on most masts because the lacing can snag on a mast fitting. Some yachts had a very short secondary track with a junction and gate system so that once above the top slides of the handed mainsail the secondary track joined the main track. Today, with the predominance of aluminium masts, a second track can sometimes be fitted alongside the main track, though a problem may occur if the track obstructs the cars of full length battens when the mainsail is let out. Ideally the track should lead down to near deck level to enable the bagged trysail to be put at the foot of the mast with its tack made fast, and all the slides in the track ready to hoist at short notice. Both Willy Ker and Michael Thoyts, two experienced single-handed ocean sailors, habitually used to sail with their trysail at the base of the mast, all ready for the moment it was required, but this had potential disadvantages with the risk of chafe from non-slip deck paint and the possibility of loss or damage through the sail living in such an exposed stowage.

Those with in-mast reefing may consider that they do not require a separate sail as they can reef the main until it is very small, provided that it is made sufficiently strong in the clew area. Though in-mast reefing is becoming more reliable, the consequences of the mechanism jamming or breaking should be considered. Such is the ease of working in-mast furling it is tempting to adopt it and there are those who have sailed successfully with it for years. Best quality manufacturers are desirable but even then there is a chance of calamitous failure, as Sir Ben Ainslie found on his honeymoon. In-boom reefing has the disadvantage of requiring a very precise boom angle to obtain a satisfactory reef, and allows the unattached luff of the mainsail to spread uncontrollably over the deck if the halyard is let go in emergency, such as in a squall.

The trysail should be the easiest sail on the boat to set but, perversely, it is often the most difficult. If no second track is fitted it may be necessary to drop a tightly reefed and bundled main out of the only track, to secure it and then to fit the trysail slides into the track – a difficult task in conditions in which a trysail might normally be set – and consequently one which needs to be tackled early, as it may be the only means (in conjunction with a storm jib) to make to windward, perhaps off a lee shore.

Those owners who have a gate on the track above the bundled mainsail may find operation difficult due to the height of the gate off the deck, and in most cases the gate is located part way up the stowed stack of slides, resulting in some or all of the mainsail slides having to be removed before the trysail slides can be inserted. This operation may be unworkable with a fully battened mainsail. With a boltrope system, once the mainsail has been lowered it is easier to insert the boltrope of the trysail and hoist the sail, but lowering a mainsail without sliders can be hard to control, even with several strong crew. All in all, the best system is to use where possible a long second independent trysail track fitted for sliders.

In most modern yachts the most convenient method of securing the boom when not in use is to set it up tight on the topping lift or rod kicker, and sheet it in hard, although this will cause most windage. In the days of long heavy booms the answer was either to secure the boom firmly in the gallows, or lower the end of the boom to the quarter and secure it well; but lowering to the quarter may be difficult on yachts with rod-kickers, fixed windscreens, or spray hoods. The end of the boom lying on the deck is also an obstacle for green water breaking across the deck, and if the boat is tacked and the boom is up to windward it is yet more unsatisfactory. In the Sydney–Hobart Race of 1998 a helmsman was tragically swept overboard and lost when the stanchion, to which the boom was lashed, carried away. Unless a boom crutch is used, the preferred method is to have the boom hoisted and held firm with two preventers, or the mainsheet and one preventer, as using the mainsheet alone allows too much movement. It needs to be remembered to set the boom lower than the foot of the trysail, and to set the leeward trysail sheet on the correct side of the topping lift.

As it has been known for a knockdown wave to blast a hole through the flaked mainsail, it is vitally important to have the main as tightly furled as possible, preferably using spare line to wrap the sail with a lashing every 30cm (1 foot) in order to present a minimised target. Yachts fitted with stack packs allow the mainsail to be tidily zipped up

A fully-crewed racing yacht powering to windward under well-configured storm jib and trysail.
Photo: Mark Pepper/PPL

and out of harm's way. Whatever solution is adopted, care must always be taken to prevent any chafe, which could hole or damage either mainsail or trysail.

Some yachts will heave-to best under trysail rather than mainsail and storm jib, through not forereaching at such speed as to nullify the slick, whilst other yachts will heave-to best under storm jib alone.

David Cowper used a trysail successfully when rounding Cape Horn on his second single-handed round-the-world passage in *Ocean Bound* when he went to windward in a series of storms up to Force 11, which had been blowing for a week. He put up his orange trysail, finding that the motion of the boat was easier, and any shipped water was quickly shed. However, in over 320,000km (200,000 miles) largely in the higher latitudes, he only used his trysail twice. In many ocean miles Willy Ker has also only used his trysail twice though some cruising skippers use their trysails frequently in milder conditions (Force 6–8), when comfort is more important than speed. In the 1979 Fastnet Race storm 12 yachts in the fleet of 303 used a trysail, and in the Sydney–Hobart Race in 1998, out of 115 entries 47 yachts used their trysail, though most thought their trysail too large for the Force 12 conditions. *Berrimilla* was an exception: her trysail was not too big and, although she was knocked down a few times, all the solid water tended to go below the sail with just froth going into the sail, and the boat behaved exceptionally well. Some believe that, when sailing off the wind, it is better to sheet in the trysail hard to avoid giving dirty air to the jib, others have found that sheeting the trysail in hard when using twin headsails cuts down rolling noticeably.

There are offshore cruising yachtsmen who prefer to carry a spare mainsail and a small storm trysail. Some sailmakers, for example in New Zealand, place mainsail reefing points in such a way that the boom lifts higher with every reef (for example 45cm (18in) per reef for an 11m (36ft) yacht), to make it less likely that the boom will dip into the sea. The main boom foreguy or preventer led from the top of the kicking strap sometimes leads to boom breakage in the open ocean, so the foreguy should be led forward from the end of the boom if there is any chance that the end of the boom can drag in the sea when heeled. As access to the end of the boom is difficult and dangerous in wild conditions, a short length of rope from the end of the boom should be permanently rigged under the boom to ensure that a properly led foreguy can be made available when required.

Although the rig and crew capability will differ widely, all offshore yachts must be capable of handling extremely bad weather, so skippers must have appropriate sails and rig. This will generally mean carrying a storm jib and either a trysail or the means to cope without one. These sails not only serve in extremely bad weather, but also act as back up in the event of some failure of the working rig. Careful thought should put be into how they are rigged both for efficient and trouble free operation, and then exactly how they can be set most practically with a minimal crew in storm conditions. It is important that storm sails should be exercised from time to time in normal conditions and regularly serviced.

6 Preparations for heavy weather

Peter Bruce

After ships of his US Pacific fleet were seriously damaged or sunk in Typhoon Cobra on 18 December 1944 with the loss of 790 officers and men, the letter that Fleet Admiral Nimitz wrote to the fleet ended in the following comment: 'The time for taking all measures for a ship's safety is while able to do so. Nothing is more dangerous than for a seaman to be grudging in taking precautions lest they turn out to have been unnecessary. Safety at sea, for a thousand years, has depended upon exactly the opposite philosophy.'

Whilst some heavy weather is almost the inevitable lot of the ocean voyager, the majority of coastal sailors will, by the exercise of discretion and by good planning, be in a position to avoid it most of the time. But meteorology is not an exact science, so there is always a chance of being caught out in a blow at sea. However carefully one has studied the weather and listened to the weather forecasts, one can find oneself caught out in a storm anytime and anywhere, sometimes with little warning.

If this does happen, the aim should be to come through the experience safely, without damage, independently of outside assistance and in as much comfort and good humour as the circumstances permit.

To achieve this aim, the wise skipper will make contingency plans and will practise for heavy weather either in harbour or in calm weather, knowing that he should expect no more than simple tasks to be undertaken by his crew when it comes on to blow. For storms can creep up insidiously on the crew of a vessel at sea: in a sailing boat, this often happens via a period of exhilaration as wind and wave exceed normal expectations. Later the time comes when crews show a gradually decreasing tendency to make any additional effort, save that of attending to necessary reductions of sail, adjusting to discomfort or reconciling themselves to seasickness.

A crew's energy and resources are best reserved for matters that cannot have been anticipated. A skipper with no inner doubts about the fitness of his vessel and equipment will find it easier to inspire his crew to make the special effort that may be needed in a storm. This chapter is written without a particular level of weather severity in mind, but rather in acknowledgement of the fact that an unexpected encounter with heavy weather may occur at any time.

In-harbour preparations

One can neither buy safety nor guarantee survival, but one can buy equipment that in practised hands can improve safety. Predominately it is a crew's skill that will mostly affect the outcome in an emergency. Preparations that can assist a boat at sea in anticipation of heavy weather are included at the end of this chapter. It is suggested that, where relevant, a note of these preparations is copied and kept on board.

Safety equipment comes in many forms and will vary according to the intended extent of the voyage. As mentioned by the late Olin Stephens in Chapter 1, a useful list of seaman-like measures to cope with eventualities in bad weather is provided by the World Sailing's (formerly ISAF) Offshore Special Regulations. These regulations are compulsory for yachts in offshore races worldwide, and are the basis for the World Cruising Club and similar organisations' own regulations. They are being increasingly applied for yacht rallies. The regulations cover mono- and multi-hulls in a range of categories appropriate to the degree of exposure and self-sufficiency expected. Cruising boat owners will do well to study them, as they represent much common sense and have been distilled from years of experience. As already said, if a skipper is to face bad weather with confidence, he or she needs to do more than just buy and fit the safety equipment that conscience dictates or which merely complies with regulations. Skipper and crew must know how to use the safety equipment through test and practice in calm conditions.

In addition to the demands of regulations there are many sensible other actions which should be taken in harbour in anticipation of bad weather. It is normal to ensure that the crew have good foul weather gear and sea boots but in storm conditions inside layers soon become damp as high wind drives moisture ever inwards. One or two 'dry suits' on board will keep the wearers snug in any conditions and can be a tremendous asset, especially in a cold climate. At least one pair of goggles or simple safety glasses should be available for looking to windward in extreme wind strengths and the installation of active and passive Automatic Identification System (AIS) will reliably alert shipping when wave returns mask small radar echoes.

Deep bowls, some use stainless-steel dog bowls, should be available to eat from when motion is severe and a well-ordered yacht has a specially constructed stowage in the galley for such bowls. Roll down curtains in clear spray hood quality plastic can be set up on each side of the companionway and secured at the bottom. These curtains prevent water going sideways into the boat and make a tremendous contribution to keeping the interior dry, either in stormy weather or when it is raining in a following wind.

Several items on deck may benefit from consideration for when it comes on to blow, including the absolutely secure stowage of the liferaft, the robustness of the spray hood and the strength and completeness of the guard rails. Davit-hung dinghies may become a serious problem in big seas as, if the dinghy fills, the load can break the davits. A strong waterproof cover may help, but better is to deflate the dinghy and store it below, or if it cannot be deflated, a system to firmly secure it upside-down on deck.

Storm sails tend not to be used very often and, after use, are sometimes returned to their bags with little thought for the future. It is wise, therefore to wash and check the storm sails for weak or broken stitching and sticky or seized hanks before the start of every season.

It has to be said that few new boats are fit for heavy weather on delivery, particularly production boats, and the best time to arrange modification is before the vessel is built. Apart from the need for inherent structural strength, serious offshore owners will often want to make numerous improvements. For example: bolts may have to replace screws in places, and penny washers changed for proper backing pieces for deck fittings. Some fuel tanks do not have access hatches so cannot receive a periodic clean, essential to remove sediment which can be stirred up in bouncy conditions, leading to stoppage of the engine. The companionway latch must be operable from outside and inside. A seaman-like location and sound securing arrangement for the liferaft has to be established, bearing in mind that about half the yachts using the popular location on the coach roof lose their liferaft early on in their first storm often from fastenings which had appeared to be adequate. Anchor-well lids may need fastenings. Cleats, from which a drag or drogue device might be deployed, may need substantial reinforcement.

A well-prepared and strongly built vessel should be able to withstand any breaking sea, but caught beam-on to waves such as these, there will be a high chance of capsize. A yacht with good stability will tend to right herself in seconds whereas a yacht with poor stability may not right herself for many minutes. Photo: Safehaven Marine

A separate trysail mast track might be added, running down to near deck level, allowing the trysail to remain bagged at the foot of the mast ready for instant use. Arrangements may be necessary to allow the setting of a storm jib, mainsails may need more reefing points, and so on.

Lee cloths will probably have to be changed for ones of appropriate size, strength and design bearing in mind that there are a large number of cases where injury has occurred when a person has come out of their bunk through inadequate design. Some serious sailors also fit two sets of webbing straps in their bunks, the upper one to go round the chest and the lower one to go round the thighs. This arrangement, akin to a car seat belt, gives increased protection from falling when sea conditions are really severe.

The necessary outlay to bring a production yacht to an ocean-going standard may be considerable.

In addition to safety equipment, the owner, or skipper, of a vessel will need to keep on top of defects in the vessel and her equipment. In calm weather, adaptable humans quickly reconcile themselves to such things as small leaks, quirky navigation lights, a seized hull valve, a defective pump, a worn main halliard sheave and so on. Such shortcomings can assume enormous proportions in rough weather, creating a crisis out of something previously regarded as a trivial problem. Recording faults in a 'defect book' is a helpful means of assessing priorities when the opportunity for maintenance occurs.

As well as dealing with commonplace failures, another potentially weak area lies with standby equipment. For example when the main GPS fails, will the batteries for the standby handheld GPS be charged, and will it work? Likewise, the reserve bilge pump, the emergency navigation lights, and so on.

When planning a vessel's chart portfolio and chart plotter software before a voyage, consideration should be given to ensuring that there is adequate information in the event of being blown off course, or of having to find and enter an unfamiliar port of refuge under

A yacht caught on a lee shore will be fortunate to end up on a beach rather than rocks. Photo: PPL

the stress of bad weather. The anguish of being forced into an area of shoal waters for which one has no information will be memorable. A tablet computer, or even a smart phone with suitable area coverage is now commonly used as back up for the chart plotter. A good and up-to-date pilot book often has sufficient charted detail on its port and harbour plans, including lights and buoyage information, to enable a safe entry to be attempted.

In May 2014 when the crew of *Cheeki Rafiki* found the boat was leaking, they would have put into Bermuda if only they had a suitably large-scale chart on board. This would have saved their lives.

Practising for dire situations

A good heavy weather principle is to hope for the best and prepare for the worst. For example, Chay Blyth used to prepare himself on a flat calm day by staging the onset of a fictitious gale and work through his sail wardrobe from full sail to storm sails.

Another method is to plan and practise for dire circumstances. Such action can have a negative effect on less experienced crew, so give notice, i.e. 'Tomorrow morning at 10am, we will do safety drills'! Among the worst of all dire situations which should be considered are: loss of steering capability; one or more members of the crew falling overboard; fire; or the need to abandon ship.

Loss of steering

A storm tests most features of a vessel and inevitably the steering gear is one such. When the boat's steering mechanism fails, as opposed to losing the rudder stock or blade, there is usually something that can be done, but the situation is much eased if the matter has been thought through beforehand. Most yachts have provision for the loss of steering due to tiller failure, or breakage of the steering cable or quadrant, and such arrangements should be tried out to assess the ease with which they can be operated. In one case, for example, a long reverse acting tiller was provided for a 17.4m (57ft) aft cockpit yacht. In June 2000, a few days out from Bermuda on an Atlantic crossing, it was needed after the failure of the wheel steering cable. One steering cable had been tightened earlier but not the other, which may have caused the failure. When a larger quarter wave than usual pushed the stern round, the helmsman made a firm correction movement on the wheel and part of the steering pedestal structure failed. The emergency arrangement worked well, especially because the boat was well balanced, but the fact that the helmsman had no nearby compass in close view made things difficult. Luckily the split backstay was near enough to give support to the helmsman as the boat rolled in the ocean seaway.

Troubadour, a 13.7m (45ft) cutter, lost her hand steering capability when the rusty quadrant failed. This was due to sea water leaking over a long period from the steering pedestal, causing corrosion to the quadrant underneath but, happily, the autopilot steering ram could still be used. In some cases the length of the emergency tiller is constrained by the hull structure, necessitating tackles to be rigged to give the necessary leverage, which can be considerable in heavy weather. Some owners take the precaution of drilling a hole at the top end of the rudder blade towards the trailing edge that allows a rope to be passed through. Then, by putting overhand knots on the rope either side of the hole and leading the ropes to the most suitably placed winches via leading blocks if necessary, again a degree of control is possible. This provision is best made with a metal, or any very strong and solid, rudder.

On odd occasions yacht rudders have jammed when a rope has been caught between the blade and the hull. Racy fin rudders are most prone, and it is good practice to fit a deflector, mounted to prevent a rope entering the leading edge which also stops weed collecting. In the 1979 Fastnet a yacht's rudder jammed when one of the warps she was towing overtook the yacht on a breaking wave and then became stuck in the gap. Precipitate action is likely to aggravate the situation, so setting a drag

device may be the first step to take in rough weather. When and if sea conditions permit it may be advantageous to have someone go over the side to inspect and, maybe, clear the problem. Some owners like to carry breathing apparatus but, if not, as a minimum every vessel should be equipped with a wetsuit top, a face mask and fins.

Unless using wind-vane self-steering gear, having its own auxiliary rudder (e.g. Hydrovane) the loss of the whole rudder blade is altogether a more difficult eventuality. The rudder blade or stock can fail without warning, whereupon the boat is usually uncontrollable. A 10m (33ft) yacht drifted onto a lee shore off California with loss of one crewman in March 2013 after her rudder broke and her crew failed to find a method of steering her in the prevailing heavy sea. They had successfully steered her on a trial using sail trim in 10 knots of wind with her rudder still in place and in sheltered waters, but when the rudder broke in the open ocean the conditions were much more severe. Alternative methods of steering are best proved for the worst case scenario.

A happier story came from Andrew Wilkes when the rudder broke off his Swan 44 *King of Hearts* in April 2004, some 500nm short of Mar del Plata. Showing the kind of foresight with which Admiral Nimitz would no doubt approve, he had ordered a jury rudder to go with his Monitor self-steering gear. It wasn't easy

Andrew Wilkes' yacht King of Hearts' *broken rudder stock, seen after the boat was lifted out at Mal de Plata.* Photo: Andrew Wilkes

to fit in a seaway but, when accomplished, it could just cope with a sea state commensurate with Force 5. Any more than that and he had to leave the boat to lie a'hull which he had to do for 30 hours. A similar story was that of Brian and Anne Lowrie who somehow lost their rudder and half the skeg in their Hallberg Rassy 42 on their way from Fiji to New Zealand in October 2004. Their Windpilot self-steering gear gave them crude control and they were able to reach Whangerei unaided.

Attempts to steer most modern yachts without a rudder by trimming the sails can seem just laughable at first, but with patience there can be some ability to make to windward by partially backing the jib and playing the mainsheet. Angles further off the wind can usually be obtained when very little mainsail is set. To obtain better control in all directions the first option usually employed is to try a flat board fastened onto one end of the spinnaker pole, which is then secured on the stern halfway down the pole. The arrangement can work on smaller craft, especially those with low sterns, so owners of craft that happen to have this feature will do well to manufacture and trial a blade rather than, perhaps, have to carve up the saloon table in dire weather. At the same time the fulcrum point and its reinforcement should be considered. In many other cases the pole and flat board arrangement simply will not work because the pole is not long enough, or the load is too heavy at higher wind strengths. Another method that can be used in more severe conditions is the employment of a drogue. The drogue is attached to two long sheets to form a bridle and thence to leading blocks either at the beam or on the quarter, whichever works best, and then to the most conveniently placed winches. It may well pay to weight the drogue to keep it submerged but, if the drogue is not weighted, the optimum length of the sheets may depend upon the existing wave length, and it will be advantageous to have the drogues pulling hardest as the boat is going down the face of a wave. The yacht *Scarlet Oyster*, an Oyster 48, lost her rudder in the Middle Sea Race of 2014 and managed to broad reach in Force 8

conditions with a drogue on the quarter and the jib set on the opposite side to the drogue. A small part of the mainsail was hoisted when it was necessary to bring the boat on a closer course to the wind.

The size of drogue is not absolutely critical but a parachute sea anchor has far too much drag, and a drogue normally used on a lifebuoy has far too little. An alternative to a drogue is to secure ropes to the spinnaker pole at its ends and drag it at right angles to the path of the vessel. By altering the length of one line some measure of control can usually be achieved.

All these contrivances constitute rather desperate remedies and, even with carefully balanced sails, only allow limited control at much reduced speed. Thus the prudent owner carries out a rudder survey for cracks or rust stains when the boat is out of the water and he will remove the rudder for closer inspection if these are apparent. After unshipping the rudder it will be possible to detect crevice corrosion at the stock, or the start of separation of the two halves of the rudder where the stock enters the blade. Any signs of these problems should be thoroughly dealt with straight away. Checks should be made inside the boat for excessive play, loose nuts, and stranding of the steering cable. Rudders can be heavily stressed if allowed to slam over to full deflection, for example when going astern at speed, which may bring about failure at a later moment. It is important that rudders have some limiting device to prevent the rudder being damaged, and it should be remembered that a rudder will be less efficient after 35° of travel, though the load on the whole steering system will increase, so there is no necessity for the rudder to be allowed to turn further. The limiting device is usually in the form of stops which ideally should have some cushioning capability.

Some larger vessels have hydraulic steering, and failures usually occur as a result of chafe of hoses, use of an incorrect replacement hose or the wrong hydraulic fluid. Accordingly spare hoses and spare hydraulic fluid should be held on board if a ready source is not available. For ocean crossings, if steering cables are used, spares should be carried.

A Swan 82 competing in the Sydney–Hobart Race. Preparations for heavy weather are a winning factor in offshore races and most boats are made ready with meticulous care.
Photo: Carlo Borlenghi/DPPI

Loss of steering capability is a major upset and is quite common, especially in heavy weather, so it behoves the owner to keep an ear open for problems with others in the class, and to have considered all the options in the event of a failure.

Crew overboard

In incidents involving a fatality where the lifeboat has been called out, a crewmember over the side is the most common cause. There are four phases involved when someone is lost overboard: location, attachment, recovery on board and treatment.

Location is much assisted by someone being nominated solely to keep the casualty in sight. This will not always be possible in big seas, so it is of equally urgent priority to practise recording the vessel's position, both with appropriate navigational aids and such buoyant objects as may be available. In a real situation, in addition to the measures taken on board, outside help should be summoned without delay.

Even a strobe light may be difficult to see in high seas and impossible in fog and it may not be possible to hear the whistle normally attached to lifejackets. Much better is a personal AIS, activated when the lifejacket inflates. This system provides position information to all vessels fitted with an AIS chart plotter.

Two different methods for the retrieval of man overboard are in favour – the 'quick-stop' and the 'reach-tack-reach' method. Instinctive adoption of the 'quick stop' method resulted in an entirely satisfactory result in the author's 7m (23ft) yacht *Scarlet Runner* in 1973, when surfing downwind in Force 6 under spinnaker in an English Channel race. Immediately after the man was lost the yacht, which had no engine, was turned into wind as the spinnaker was dropped. The sail backed across the fore triangle and was successfully gathered in as the boat beat back under mainsail to the man in the water. He was hauled in from the lee side at a point just aft of the shrouds. The 'quick stop' method has the advantage of keeping

the casualty close by, which can be a great comfort, particularly to the casualty.

The other method, taught by the Royal Yachting Association for many years, involves going onto a reach, followed by a tack and a reach back to the victim.

There was Force 6 westerly blowing against a spring tide on 13 July 2014, when racing to windward off Ventnor, Isle of Wight in Michael Hough's 16m (52ft) *Chloe*. The yacht was well heeled and going well in the rough sea when the skipper slipped over the side and was left swimming in the wake. Visibility was good.

A horseshoe lifebuoy was thrown, and the reach-tack-reach method was adopted for the recovery. It was necessary to bear off more than the helmsman expected on the first reach to avoid making too much to windward. The headsail was lowered before the tack and, after that, again the helmsman had to be encouraged to bear away to a broader reach on a course, some 100m (328ft) to leeward of the casualty. From about 150m short of this point, the approach course was judged to bring the yacht from a reach to more and more onto the wind, so the yacht stopped just as the man overboard was alongside, by now holding onto the lifebuoy. The engine was started to assist keeping station though, as it turned out, it was hardly needed. With no headsail to cause noise and leeway, several strong young men in the racing crew and the low freeboard of a Spirit of Tradition yacht all helped in bringing the unharmed casualty back on board beside the shrouds. On this occasion the reach-tack-reach method had also worked well.

At first it may be found that an effort may be necessary to persuade a crew to exercise a man overboard drill, but thereafter it will almost certainly be perceived as an important evolution, worthy of practice and discussion. It could also be mentioned that the quick and seamanlike retrieval of some suitable object from the sea, without the use of the engine – as propellers so often catch a rope in a crisis – provides a source of deserved satisfaction within a crew. Equally important is to prove by practical trial that the equipment intended for quick deployment, such as a horseshoe lifebuoy with a flashing light attached to it by a lanyard, can be used effectively in stressful circumstances. Experience, supported by trials in the United States, showed that, at the first attempt, a tangle with a consequent time delay is likely.

Every boat should have at least one means of recovering a casualty back on board. A stern bathing ladder is not the answer in a seaway. In particular, couples that sail on their own together should consider and practice coping with the situation where the stronger and heavier partner has fallen over the side. The Seattle Sailing Foundation was inspired to study this aspect of the man overboard problem by some understandable but heart-breaking local tragedies. In one case a man, an experienced sailor, went overboard on a blustery day from the foredeck of his yacht. His wife, his sole crew who was not experienced, just steered straight, which was what she had always been told to do, until she struck the beach some time later. Her husband was never found. In another case, a skipper was lost and drowned even after being brought alongside, due to difficulties in hoisting him on board.

There is some very good equipment available to aid the recovery of a man overboard. At the same time one should be aware that there might be a tendency these days to place too much reliance on technology so it is best only to buy items that have withstood the stringency of thorough testing.

Prevention is better than cure and, in addition to non-slip surfaces and footgear, the value of a well-designed safety harness and tether line, built to the standard World Sailing specification and adjusted so that one will not slip out, cannot be overestimated. Foredeck crews are most exposed, but they tend to be nimble and aware of the hazard, whereas those not used to being on deck in rough weather can be equally at risk. Less obvious moments of exposure, but ones that have claimed lives, are those when crews unclip their safety harness lines to go below or have not yet clipped on when coming on deck. It is good practice to pass the clip up for the on-watch crew to clip on before progressing to the cockpit and vice versa. With a double tether lines, well positioned strong points, jackstays and practice, it should be possible to avoid ever being unclipped when on deck. It is worth mentioning that the harness should be clipped on to prevent a person falling over the side rather than merely preventing the person from being separated from the craft having done so. In this case a person will be held over the side by the safety harness facing forward, a position that may not allow the person to breathe when the vessel is moving due to the build up of water flow. A safety harness secured at the back will solve the problem and such lifejackets are becoming available. Otherwise a ready knife is a solution.

Roger Taylor, who has cruised in the Arctic single-handed in a 7.2m (24ft) yacht and in another yet smaller, does not use a jackstay as it has too much spring. He manages with strategically placed 10mm U bolts around the deck to attach his safety harness double tether. He is not alone in distrusting jackstay lines and some owners of larger yachts fit permanent jackstay lines made of tensioned non-stretch rope along both sides of the coachroof with a single line on the foredeck. This enables a short safety line to be used tethered inboard and much reduces the chances of somebody going over the side.

In spite of more general use of safety harnesses, there still remains a chance of losing someone overboard. Two more common examples are when gentlemen are relieving themselves over the side, and when crewmen are struck on the head by the boom in an unexpected gybe. Chances of survival for unconscious victims are increased when a lifejacket with automatic inflation is being worn.

The experience of man who went overboard from the yacht *Hayley's Dream* in the 1989 Fastnet showed that it is necessary to use a crutch strap to prevent the lifejacket riding up over the casualty's head. He said that, without a crutch strap, the buoyant lifejacket was not giving him the support he needed. As the lifejacket rode higher his head came ever lower. Another crew overboard case, which occurred in the 1989–90 Whitbread Round the World Race, draws attention to the value of a spray guard to prevent the casualty drowning from inhaled spray. In stormy weather the layer above the sea surface is more water than air so, without a spray hood, the casualty can drown even with a lifejacket. All such features can be achieved when the lifejacket is combined with a safety harness, an arrangement that would appear to optimise safety and convenience.

In concluding this subject, it should be remembered that drowning, rather than hypothermia, is the predominant cause of loss of life in man overboard incidents.

Fire

A catastrophic fire occurred aboard a 16.5m (55ft) yacht, owned by Jonathan and Gabrielle Lyne, on the night of Friday 13 December 2013 when anchored off South Island, New Zealand. The couple were soon driven into abandoning their yacht, and were left virtually naked with only the dinghy and the grab bag. The yacht sank, and it was fortunate that the dinghy was in the water and they were close to habitation. Had they not been close to the shore when the fire occurred and had been unable to put it out, the consequences could have been much worse. They thought that the liferaft would not have provided an escape route as it would have been drawn in to the boat by the rush of air feeding the fire.

Fortunately fires at sea are rare but if one does occur in stormy conditions, as well it can, the fire is yet more difficult to deal with. The confined space of a yacht will rapidly fill with smoke and will probably have to be abandoned immediately, with the possibility that there is no access to the radio, the liferaft or the flares. Smoke alarms give early warning of a fire and thus give more time to deal with it. They should be located in all appropriate spaces, including the bilge, if electrical equipment is located there.

Electrical fires can occur in rough weather due to ingress of salt water or by a yacht's movement creating a short circuit. Good design and construction will obviate most problems but the owner must ensure that his boat can stand extreme angles of heel and heavy shock without the possibility of a short circuit being created. If an electrical fire does occur, switching off power will help the situation if the problem is down-current from the switch. However, many fires occur at the main power leads near the battery and these cannot be isolated by breakers or fuses. It is essential that neither the batteries move nor should anything be able to move onto them. For example there is a case where a fuel tank became loose and shifted the battery, which caused the main supply to short, thus causing a disastrous fire.

World Sailing (formerly ISAF) offshore special regulations require racing yachts to carry two fire extinguishers 'readily accessible in suitable and different parts of the yacht'. For trans-oceanic vessels three dry powder extinguishers of 2kg including one extinguisher or system suitable for dealing with a fire in a machinery space are required, plus a fire blanket adjacent to the cooker. Dry powder extinguishers should be turned and shaken every month to prevent the powder compacting. In my own experience of a fire in a yacht at sea, having four robust buckets in a deck locker proved invaluable, and it was the sea water in the buckets that put out the fire, not the fire extinguishers. Reaching the seat of an engine compartment fire can be difficult, as it was in this situation, and encourages the installation of an automatic extinguisher. In the case just described an injection point for an extinguisher could have saved the hazardous necessity of lifting the engine box to reach the seat of the fire.

Capsize

The importance of a stable, strong and watertight hull has been referred to in earlier chapters of this book. The need for these features is particularly important in the dire situation of a capsize. To be prepared for total inversion, one should try to imagine

Yachts burn well once the fire gets established. Photo: PPL

one's vessel being placed upside-down in the sea, with ventilator plugs in place. Thus orientated, a well-designed and soundly built craft should have minimal leaks, even through the companionway or the cockpit lockers. Arrangements must be made for the washboards not to drop out when a yacht turns over. Ballast must be glassed in, or otherwise properly secured, heavy items such as anchors, especially that extra heavy emergency anchor deep in the bilge, need locating chocks with adequate lashings. The engine, the galley stove, the deep freeze, batteries, gas cylinders, and tanks should be installed with total inversion in mind. If yachts, when new, had to be subject to an inversion test with full tanks not all would come through unscathed.

Alex Whitworth, who has had his boat rolled twice, says, 'Months before you even think of leaving the dock, spend a quiet hour sitting in the boat on a calm day with a notepad and imagine the boat inverted. Scary but you must. Is it watertight with everything closed and are the stormboards strong enough? Those little plastic dorade vents will gush water – can you block them? What will end up on the new floor if it isn't tied down or latched into a cupboard? Shelves become useless and gravity becomes your enemy – flying toolboxes are lethal as are icebox lids and anything made of glass. Under bunk stowage must have lids that can be fixed or screwed down and the nav table lid needs to be tied closed. That's just a start. Chances are, any inversion will only last a few seconds, but that could be enough to spoil your day rather severely. And there will be a wave out there that could do it – there always is. If you are unlucky enough to meet it, you may be very glad you prepared the boat. We were, and even though we got some of it wrong what we did was enough to allow us to keep going.'

It might be thought that floorboards do not come in to the category of items that should be secured, on the grounds that access to the bilges can often be useful and perhaps essential in the event of being holed. Compromise may be the best solution. One might leave the floorboard giving access to the strum box unsecured whilst other floorboards are screwed down with a minimum number of fastenings that can be rapidly removed in an emergency, or for cleaning.

Securing heavy items properly is half the battle; the other half entails educating the crew to conform to the time-honoured mariner's practice of 'securing for sea'. Adequate locker space and proper stowage are necessary to give this prescription a chance but, even so, it will be found that stowing and securing all loose gear before leaving harbour, and keeping a vessel tidy thereafter, does not come naturally to most mortals. Unexpected events at sea can be so confounding that it does not always need capsize to prove the wisdom of an orderly ship.

If a yacht is rolled by a breaking wave through 360° the mast is often broken due to rig failure. It may be unrealistic to strengthen the rig so much as to make such failure impossible but as most yachts are designed for 'ordinary' sailing, a degree of beefing up may be wise for ocean-going sailors.

Whilst on the subject of capsize it should be mentioned that a safety harness line should have a clip at both ends so that, in the event of a prolonged inversion or a vessel foundering (see *Waikikamukau*, Chapter 16) crewmen have a means of releasing themselves within immediate reach.

A sinking vessel

Our final worst situation is that moment when a liferaft will shortly be the only craft left that can float, and the moment has come to pull the inflation cord. An example of such a situation took place in a Force 9 gale a mile off Salcombe in August 1985. The 9.1m (30ft) sloop *Fidget*, built of mahogany on oak by Camper & Nicholson in 1939, fell about 6m (20ft) off the back of a wave in a very large cross-sea. She opened up and sank in about 30 seconds. The skipper, Simon Wilkinson, who habitually keeps a knife in his foul weather jacket pocket, had just only enough time to cut the liferaft and uninflated tender free from their lashings before *Fidget* foundered, and

the crew were left swimming. There was an interval before the inflation cord, which was still attached to the yacht, came taut, but the liferaft inflated. Simon Wilkinson thinks that he and his crew might well have drowned if they had not been wearing lifejackets.

Should a vessel sink far from help, the best chance of being found lies with an emergency indicator beacon (EPIRB). This is an automatic radio transmission device that, when activated, transmits a coded message giving the vessel's GPS position and identity on 406 MHz via satellite to ground stations and to the nearest rescue coordination centre (MRCC). It has worldwide coverage and is not prone to spurious activation. The kind of event that *Fidget*'s crew experienced is not one likely to have been practised, though courses of instruction in survival exist and are rated as good value, in addition to books on the subject. That the vessel's liferaft will operate has to be taken on trust. However, an opportunity to learn about one's liferaft occurs at the time of its periodic inspection, when it will have to be inflated anyway. To witness an inflation, it is best to make an appointment with the servicing agent, who should be one authorised by the manufacturer, for an 'opening day'. Inflation in the garden in the company of the crew is entertaining, but will certainly lead to extra cost. For example, the gas bottle is not used for test inflation but is merely weighed and inspected, and replacement bottles are expensive to recharge and retest. Besides, it is quite easy to damage the fabric of a partially deflated liferaft when in transit back to the servicing agent. Nonetheless, it is possible for an owner to inflate the liferaft without using the gas bottle, and those who can trust their own judgement and know the technique for repacking do speak highly of carrying out their own annual inspection.

The merit of having additional items to supplement the liferaft's safety equipment pack will depend very much upon the circumstances. However, the concept of a grab bag, or calamity-bag, located at a suitable position and filled with suitable sundry items deserves recognition. For example, a

No explanation is known for why Wizard *sank. It is surmised that her saildrive membrane might have broken catastrophically.* Photo: PPL

waterproof VHF radio, dry clothing, space blankets, extra flares, food, water, writing materials, passports, money and crew medicines may one day reward the foresight involved. *Fidget*'s crew, for example, were not to know they had been spotted, and would have been glad to have had some drinking water during the interval of forty minutes before they were picked up. Also they were short of flares, one being faulty, and the others having been used immediately.

Sea preparations for imminent bad weather

A skipper should delegate various tasks within his crew to spread the load, and to take care of the situation if he himself were to be incapacitated or lost overboard. This means an organisational structure has to be formed, and though some people may go sailing to escape such duress, there is a clear need for it in times of crisis.

Likewise it is always desirable to establish and maintain a watch routine so that a crew can rest properly when off watch. With an experienced crew the watch keeping routine may need no adjustment with the onset of bad weather. On the other hand a less experienced and less well-prepared crew may find some members opting out through seasickness while others become involved in one drama followed by another, leading to whole-crew exhaustion. This can be a recipe for disaster, as people tend not to make good decisions when they are cold, wet, anxious and tired.

Quite often the situation, bad though it may be, does not require the whole watch on deck. Two people or even one person on deck may be enough to ensure the safety of the boat whilst conditions are stable. Others on watch may best stay down below where it should be more warm and dry. Depending on the severity of the conditions, it may be necessary for the person or people on deck to change over every hour or less.

It is suggested that all craft likely to be in the open sea could benefit from an owner's check-off list covering actions to be taken in the face of an impending storm. Such measures will depend very much on the circumstances, such as the experience of the crew, the type of craft and her distance from base. The following list may be helpful to some, whilst others may think of the suggestions given here as being standard procedure before going to sea:

1 Issue seasick pills. Consider revision of watch keeping system.
2 Charge batteries. On stopping engine, close all valves that could allow water to flood back to the engine or engine compartment e.g. engine ventilation space supply and exhaust.
3 Prepare sailplan for heavy weather. Remove any removable furled headsails and stow below. Remaining rolled headsails should be tightly furled and wrapped with a spare halyard if available. Set up inner forestay for storm jib, if appropriate. Consider preparation of trysail for hoisting. Lead lazy jacks forward. Consider removal of mainsail and stowage below deck. With a view to minimise windage remove cockpit dodgers, which have enough area to end for end a yacht in a storm, and stow or lash up bimini. Items normally stowed on deck, such as fender boards and fuel cans, should be stowed below. Any item that has to remain on deck should be firmly secured.
4 Aim to change to storm canvas in good time.
5 Check windows and hatches are tightly closed. Fit or have ready ventilator cover plates. Attach hatchway and window storm screens. If appropriate put a stopper, such as cork or plasticine, in the hawse pipe.
6 Move storm sails, buckets, warps or other drag devices, to a handy position, bearing in mind that it may be difficult and dangerous to open cockpit lockers during a storm.
7 At large angles of heel it may be necessary to close the heads sea cocks to prevent flooding. Experience may show that other cocks need to be closed during bad weather, not that there are many boats still around with this handicap. If shutting such sea cocks could cause catastrophic results, an appropriate notice should be displayed. For example, a sign saying 'engine cooling water cock closed' taped over the engine starter.
8 Plot position and, if a survival situation is anticipated, report this and intended movements to coastguards or shore authority. Put a dry towel, or absorbent material, within reach of the chart table. Start recording frequent barometer readings, or better still refer regularly to a barograph.
9 Check security of batteries and other heavy weights stowed below, such as anchors, toolboxes and cans. Use additional lashings as necessary.
10 Plan for much colder conditions. Put on appropriate clothing, such as thermal underwear, sea boots, gloves, etc. Dry suits are remarkably good in gale conditions.
11 Pack a 'grab-bag'. In addition, spare clothing, bedding, matches, lavatory paper, bread, etc should be sealed within clear heavy-duty polythene bags.
12 Pump bilges. Check pump handles are attached to the boat and the whereabouts of spares.
13 Put washboards into position, and secure their fastening arrangements so they cannot lift out should the boat invert.
14 Firmly secure latches of cockpit locker lids.
15 Check cockpit and anchor well drains are free. If narrow it may be helpful to blow through with an inflatable dinghy air pump or sink drain clearer.
16 Check deck items, such as the spinnaker pole, anchor, anchor well lid, and liferaft are properly secured. Winch handles should not be left loose, and a spare should be kept below decks.
17 Check halyards are not twisted and the free ends of the lines on deck are stowed, so

that they are not likely to go overboard and foul the propeller. Lead spare halyards etc clear of mast to reduce noise.

18 Check navigation lights and AIS are working; hoist radar reflector.

19 Deflate an inflatable and stow below decks. Bring a towed dinghy inboard and stow securely upside down. Either put a strong well-secured waterproof cover on davit-slung dinghies or remove and stow on deck.

20 Consider renewing torch batteries and changing cooking gas cylinder.

21 Make up thermos flasks of soup and coffee. Make sandwiches and place in a watertight container.

22 Ensure that the crew have a good hot meal.

23 Secure and stow loose items below, especially in the galley area. If containers made of glass have been brought on board – and much better not – they must either be packed away with great care or ditched. Put bagged sails at strategic points to break the falls of the crew.

24 Instruct crewmembers to put on their safety harnesses and lifejackets. Ensure that they are adjusted to fit snugly over storm clothing so that the wearer cannot slip out. Also ensure that the crew are familiar with the operating features and strap design so that they may be donned rapidly without assistance, if need be, in violent motion and darkness. Safety harnesses and lifejackets should usually be worn during the period of the storm, notwithstanding the discomfort when resting.

25 If running under mainsail, rig a heavy-duty main boom preventer from the end of the boom to avoid accidental gybes. Ideally this should be rigged round a hefty leading block forward and led back to the cockpit.

26 Consider rigging a rope lattice within the cockpit to give greater security to its occupants.

27 Brief the crew on what to expect. Remind them of the importance of being hooked on to something really strong when on deck, of maintaining a good look-out especially to windward, and the whereabouts of goggles, sharp knife, flares, grab-bag, liferaft, etc.

28 Check rigging cutters. Ensure there is a lanyard on them.

29 Tape up all lockers without positive locking arrangements.

30 Check the liferaft is properly secure but otherwise free to launch, i.e. not locked up.

The well-prepared vessel, applying Admiral Nimitz's doctrine, is much more likely to come through a gruelling storm with only minor problems. Yet storms can be a tremendous test of endurance, and despite very careful preparation, much may depend upon the cool judgement, courage, physical fitness and tenacity of the skipper and crew.

7 The use of drag devices in heavy weather

Peter Bruce

When it really comes on to blow it is safer to lie with the bow or stern into wind and wave, rather than beam on. The choice of heavy weather tactics has been increased by the availability on the market of a large number of drag devices, the generic term for objects used over the bow or stern to hold a vessel end on and slow her down. The requirement to reduce speed is seldom if ever necessary for strongly manned racing yachts such as those taking part in round the world races. On the other hand, for lightly-crewed cruising yachts, slowing down can be a matter of urgency due to stormy weather and a crew's need to rest. Some experienced sailors, especially those with larger boats, have never felt the need to deploy drag devices, preferring traditional tactics. They are concerned by the heavy forces involved and the attachments point which could be torn off, especially those used for drogues. Smaller and lighter yachts are most likely to benefit from a drag device but, given a yacht with adequate cleats, larger yachts may be glad of one at some juncture.

Drag devices fall into two categories: sea anchors in the form of *parachutes* streamed over the bow on a long line intended to hold the boat head-to-wind with a low rate of drift, and *drogues* trailed over the stern designed to slow a boat down to a comfortable speed, to keep the boat's stern into the sea or to act as an emergency steering device. At one time the term 'sea anchor' could mean 'a drogue' and vice versa but now they are coming to be thought of as different devices which are used in a different way.

Once a parachute sea anchor has been successfully deployed in severe weather, the boat should need little further attention and the crew can go below. Except in the case of the series drogue, it is usually necessary to continue to steer when using a drogue but, in some combinations of hull and drogue, again the boat can be left to look after herself. A degree of skill and some specialised seamanship is necessary as heavy loads are involved, especially in the case of larger parachutes.

There is a significant report by the Wolfson Unit for Marine Technology, University of Southampton, UK, published in 1988, which gives the results of tank tests of parachutes and drogues. The report is particularly interesting, as in the ocean no one wave is exactly similar to another, so comparisons are not always valid. In the tank tests an exactly repeatable breaking wave equivalent to 5.85m (19.2ft) in height was created in a wind of 40 knots. As we have seen, a breaking wave with a height equal to or more than the beam of the boat is highly likely to capsize it. A number of 'typical hull shape' yacht models, equivalent to 10m (33ft) overall in length, were used in conjunction with two sizes of parachute and two types of drogue. Drogues underwent trials both individually and in series.

The Wolfson Unit's results demonstrated that, without assistance from a drogue, the models drifted broadside on to the breaking wave and were invariably capsized, sometimes

Deployment of a parachute sea anchor. The deployment bag can be seen in the foreground with the parachute beyond, which will fully open out when the load comes on.
Photo: Peter Bruce

by the breaking wave of 3.3m (11ft), which preceded the main one. What was surprising was that the parachutes did not prevent yachts in the tank from being capsized. The sudden heavy force of the breaking wave caused the parachute line to stretch and then, after the wave had passed, the yacht would be carried forward by the elasticity in the line. Her momentum would take the boat past her original position, allow the line to go slack and cause the parachute to collapse, especially if the parachute had been pulled to, or near, the surface. The yacht would then turn beam-on to the direction of the waves and, before the parachute had redeployed itself and the slack in the line had been taken up, she would be capsized by the 3.3m (11ft) wave which followed the main one. The US Coast Guard, in a report of May 1987, came to the same conclusion that the parachute rode, when rigged directly from the bow, can go slack at times, leaving the vessel to yaw away from the wind and wave direction, and thus be liable to be rolled by a breaking wave. The recommendation was to use a drogue, particularly a series drogue. There is a notable instance of this occurrence at sea, notably *Freya*, a long-keeled 14m (46ft) Stan Huntingdon-designed sloop that was rolled whilst lying to a 5.5m (18ft) parachute sea anchor off New Zealand in November 1998. In Deborah Schutz's account of the ketch *Prisana II*

lying for over 48 hours in Force 12 winds to a parachute sea anchor in July 1996 (see Chapter 20), she describes how the rode became slack from time to time, probably through yawing in the huge swell, but never long enough, it would seem, to be vulnerable to a beam sea. Exposed as *Prisana II* was for about 48 hours, the boat probably would have been rolled if the setup had allowed it. Possibly the ketch rig may have helped keep the boat sufficiently head to wind.

Both the Wolfson and the US Coast Guard report suggested that drogues are more likely to be of benefit, particularly the series drogue. Provided there was tension in the drogue line when the breaking wave struck, and the yacht model was roughly stern on to the breaking wave, she would invariably *not* capsize. Additionally, use of a drogue made it much easier for the rudder to hold the stern into the sea.

In summary, the Wolfson Unit trial results and the US Coast Guard report favoured drogues rather than parachute sea anchors, and series drogues rather than individual drogues. Of course no tank test can exactly reproduce conditions at sea and the findings regarding parachutes seldom seem to be borne out in practice.

Lin and Larry Pardey, a vastly experienced and knowledgeable sailing couple, use a parachute sea anchor with a bridle or pendant line to angle a yacht some 50° from the waves,

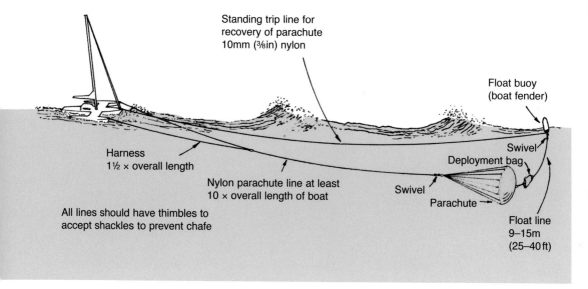

Standing trip line for
recovery of parachute
10mm (⅜in) nylon

Float buoy
(boat fender)

Swivel

Deployment bag

Harness
1½ × overall length

Nylon parachute line at least
10 × overall length of boat

Swivel

Parachute

All lines should have thimbles to
accept shackles to prevent chafe

Float line
9–15m
(25–40 ft)

Figure 7.1 *Sea anchor as used by the Casanovas for their trimaran* Tortuga Too.

an ingenious refinement upon the basic system. The effect of the slick, caused by the hull being dragged half sideways through the water, is to stop waves breaking to windward, thereby removing the risk of capsize. In addition the arrangement improves comfort considerably.

The need for evaluation

To reconcile theoretical and practical assumptions from an impartial standpoint and learn the techniques for the deployment of drag devices, sea trials were undertaken to evaluate practically purpose-built sea anchor type parachutes, cheaper and smaller 'Bu-Ord' parachutes, makeshift alternatives and other commonly used drogues. Trials were initially undertaken in calm weather before working up to heavier weather, using well-known types of cruising boat. These were a Najad 391, a Maxi 1100, a Rustler 36, a Hallberg Rassy 36, a Warrior 35, and a Contessa 33.

The trials in the open sea were undertaken in Force 6 to 7, thus were in conditions below which drag devices would normally be used out of necessity. It was observed that, when using the parachute anchor, the behaviour of the yachts was surprisingly consistent

through the wind range experienced, giving some reason to believe that conduct would be similar at higher wind speeds.

Parachute sea anchors

In later chapters the advantages and disadvantages of tactics dealing with heavy weather are covered in detail and one of these is the use of a sea anchor. Parachute sea anchors have little 'give', as if they were in hydraulic lock, and act in much the same manner as lying-to a mooring. There is something to be said, too, for presenting the bow into the wind and waves during a storm, as a boat is designed to take water flow from ahead.

Properly conceived parachute sea anchor systems have certain advantages, and appear to some sailors to be the ultimate solution and main line of defence (see Fig 7.1).

The parachute

At one time the only parachutes obtainable were those designed for aerial purposes. A good example is the Bu-Ord parachute – the name originates from *Bureau of Ordnance* – which are surplus American military stores designed

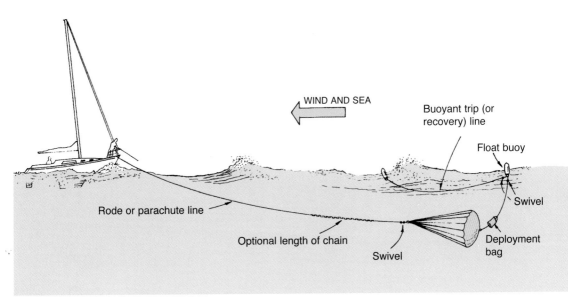

Figure 7.2 *Normal parachute anchor arrangement for a monohull.*

to pull air-dropped loads out of the backs of aircraft. These can work comparatively well for small craft and can be obtained cheaply via the internet. For years fishermen in the USA have used Bu-Ord parachutes, sometimes several in series, for lying to at night in bad weather rather than return to harbour. The Bu-Ord parachutes may be cheap but they may not always be fit for sea use, though some last for years. Purpose-built parachutes designed for use as a sea anchor are manufactured in several sizes and are more likely to be effective and reliable.

On the one hand too large a parachute is not advisable, as the larger the parachute the larger the loads and the greater the handling problems. On the other hand too small a parachute will not hold the boat into the wind. The US SAILING's *Recommendations for Offshore Sailing* specifies a parachute diameter of 35 per cent of overall length. The UK trials showed that long-keeled yachts tend to need larger parachutes than fin-keeled yachts because some long-keeled yachts can take up a very stable broadside-on attitude.

Some manufacturers offer less conventional forms of parachute such as the cruciform, and there are other makeshift options. For example the author's brother, in his Hallberg Rassy 29, successfully lay bows-to an Atlantic storm in 1998 using a square-shaped builder's hoisting bag of low cost, said to be strong enough to lift a ton of sand.

It is more convenient if parachutes are contained in a deployment bag, a fabric container that enables the parachute to open after it has been launched, rather than loose on deck when the wind can hamper operations.

Foredeck work

Some sailors prepare their sea anchor by attaching the gear to guardrail stanchions with cable ties before going to sea, but most will not want to risk damage and deterioration through berthing incidents, neglect or ultra-violet light. Thus sea anchors may require foredeck work at some stage and, if this work is left too late as a storm builds, it can become difficult and dangerous. For example when Robin and Maggi Ansell set off in *Orca* 16.8m (55ft) in March 1997 through the Great Barrier Reef bound for Alaska, they decided to deploy their new sea anchor in the early stages of Cyclone Justin. Even though the deployment of their sea anchor had been rehearsed, after two hours of struggle the difficulties with the chafe guard had still not been resolved. Maggi

Left: Preparing a parachute sea anchor for deployment. Right: The parachute sea anchor has been pulled from the deployment bag. Note the float buoy in the form of a white fender. The red recovery buoy lies beyond. Photos: Peter Bruce

Ansell said that later, only with superhuman effort, had Robin Ansell detached 3m (10ft) of 13mm (half-inch) chain from the stern anchor, crawled forward again and attached it to the end of the parachute line. Motion of the yacht was very severe and, when the load came on the chain, his ankle was caught between it and the toe rail and he was lucky to get away with just severe bruising.

It will be useful to pass the parachute line though the stem fitting at the first indication of a possible storm rather than wait for the moment when it is decided to deploy the parachute. Normally an anchor at the stem fitting should be removed, to prevent chafe, though for some skippers this will be standard procedure when crossing an ocean to keep the weight out of the bow.

Load

In addition to possible handling difficulties, the loads exerted by parachute sea anchors on their attachment points in heavy weather can be tremendous. Cleats, their fastenings, backing pieces and adjacent structure need to be up to the job. The Wolfson Laboratory decreed that these should be strong enough to carry 80 per cent of the weight of the boat. An illustration of the sort of loads created is given by an account of a 12.2m (40ft) yacht, lying to a 5.5m (18ft) parachute in a North Sea gale of some 45 knots, with the parachute line attached to the windlass. When the first heavy load came the windlass was torn out of the deck, taking with it the bow roller and most of the stem fitting. For some yachts, the legs of the bridle can be led from the end of the chain to the port and starboard alloy toe rails which, when running the length of the boat, allow the load to be spread accordingly (see photo on page 91). When cleats are judged to be not strong enough on their own, additional lines can be used to spread the load to other cleats, to the primary winches, or even by taking a line round the stern. A wooden mast might be considered, but the consequence of an alloy or carbon mast being crushed is a risk not worth taking. Stem fabrications, being designed with ground anchors in mind, are usually the appropriate lead for the parachute line to pass through, but the drop nose pin intended to prevent the anchor chain jumping out may need strengthening. Closed fairleads are usually entirely acceptable as an alternative.

Thus before a parachute is used, the means of securing the rode safely must be addressed.

The rode (or parachute line)

Because the parachute is effectively a fixed object, the long rope line used for holding the sea anchor – which is usually called a 'rode' in the USA, and increasingly in UK – must have considerable elasticity notwithstanding the disconcerting results of the tank tests described on page 84. Only good quality nylon will do. Nylon braid rope (equivalent to multiplait) is best, as this is the most elastic type and is torsionally stable. Hawser-laid nylon rope can put twists in the rigging lines as the load increases and decreases, which will reduce the parachute's efficiency. Ropes other than nylon are designed not to stretch. For example polyester or Dyneema are quite unsuitable.

The rode should have the same breaking strain as is appropriate for the main anchor because the line needs to stretch but not to break, even if subject to minor chafe. It should have stainless thimbles at both ends, as knots, particularly bowlines, will weaken it. Recommendations of rode length vary between 120m (394ft), ten times boat length with a minimum of 91m

(300ft) or a minimum of twenty times the expected wave height. This requirement could lead to huge lengths of line to cope with, for example, in the 12.2m (40ft) wave heights of the Auckland–Tonga storm of June 1994. There is a disparity in the recommendations, but the need is for the rode to be long enough to stretch enough to accommodate the varying force of the waves, and thick enough to take the maximum credible load.

There is a good case for putting a length of chain at one or other end of the parachute line, or halfway along it. This helps to reduce peak loading, helps the parachute to stay well immersed, clear of flotsam and wave effects, and may allow the use of less line. In the trials, when there was no large swell, use of chain seemed to make little difference, but the weight of the chain, which does make the task of recovery more onerous, should lessen the chance of the rode going slack and therefore decrease the likelihood of the vessel becoming beam-on to the seas. It may be significant that *Freya* did not have a length of chain in the rode when she was rolled.

An unprotected rode line led through the stem fitting will rapidly chafe through.
Photo: Peter Bruce

A length of parachute line can be heavy to handle. For example, a 136.5m (448ft) parachute line of 16mm (⅝in) eight-strand weighs 28kg (62lb) dry, and 39kg (86lb) when wet. In addition to the parachute deployment bag, a purpose-built 'parachute line deployment bag', into which the line is stuffed rather than coiled, is recommended to avoid tangles and to save time which might otherwise be spent in flaking out the line.

Nylon absorbs over four times as much water as polyester and, if the line is allowed to dry out after use without being thoroughly washed in fresh water, salt crystals will damage the fibres. Ice crystals will have a similar effect.

Chafe

If no proper provision is made for chafe, the whole expensive and elaborate parachute anchor system can be lost. A bare rope, led through a normal stem head fitting, is almost bound to chafe through in a matter of hours. Anchors over the bow, boomkin stays or foul leads around the forestay will have the same effect. On the basis that one may spend a number of days lying to the parachute, a length of chain leading through the stem fitting is a sure way to give adequate long term protection but one should make a provision for emergency release as chain cannot be cut quickly. In the USA, double lined fire hose is also often used for protection of ropes against chafe, but chain is undoubtedly superior. If plastic hose is to be used, it should be inserted over the line before the thimbles are spliced at each end, and small holes to take lashing line should be drilled near the ends. Do not cut the tube lengthwise as the split in the tube tends to work towards the point of contact. The practice of parcelling the line with cloth, as is often used for warps, will be better than nothing but may not last long.

The float

Parachutes above 3.7m (12ft) diameter need a float line, and float secured to the apex of the parachute to ensure that the parachute takes up a suitable depth and not, under zero load, take up a position on the end of the parachute line directly underneath the vessel. If this happens, the effort needed for recovery is tremendous and likely to defeat many crews. In several instances the line was cut and the parachute lost rather than make the daunting effort to haul it all in. Fenders, conveniently, can be used as floats, and the bigger the better as it is nice to be able to spot where the parachute is lying. The float line should be of a length to keep the parachute at a depth of 10–15m (33–49ft), clear of wave effects. Parachutes do tend to come to the surface when the load is especially heavy and Larry Pardey says that he takes comfort from seeing the parachute at work and has never experienced any difficulties due to the parachute being at the surface. A swivel should be placed at the float end of the float line. If a length of chain is used at the parachute end of the parachute line, a single fender may not provide enough buoyancy.

Trip or recovery line

In addition to the float line, another 30–45m (100–150ft) of 5mm (³⁄₁₆in) soft buoyant line with a swivel can be used between the float and the recovery buoy for all but small parachutes. By motoring up to the recovery buoy and bringing the buoy aboard with a boat hook, a large parachute can be collapsed and more easily recovered (see Fig 7.3). Trip lines permanently led back to the boat have been tried but can often become tangled up in the parachute. They are seldom employed more than once but if one perseveres one may acquire the knack, and thus have the advantage of easier recovery. The technique for a 'standing' trip line, is to keep just the right amount of weight on the trip line rather than allow it to become too slack. The standing trip line is recommended in a current, such as the Agulhas or the Gulf Stream, when unusual effects, such as downgoing eddies, may require that the parachute be tripped as a matter of urgency.

Left: A length of 10mm (⅜in) chain enclosed by a length of polythene hose will neither chafe, nor create noise. With this arrangement the load is taken by two legs, secured to the alloy toe rail on each side. Photo: Peter Bruce

Above: Each leg can be shackled to the alloy toe rail. The bolts holding the toe rail pass through the hull-to-deck joint, giving good strength, but can be further backed up to spread the load. Photo: Peter Bruce

Below: Once a parachute sea anchor is deployed it is in virtual hydraulic lock. Photo: Richard Clifford

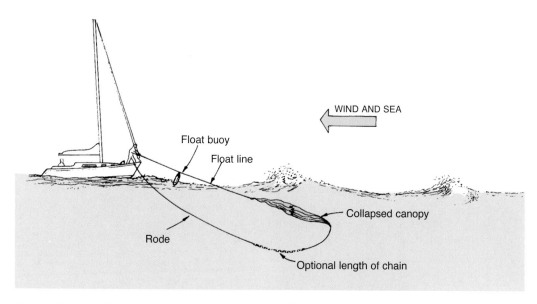

Figure 7.3 *(above) Recovering the parachute.*

Figure 7.4 *(right) Hove-to Pardey-style with triple-reefed main and 3m (9ft) diameter parachute anchor made of coarse-weave nylon stretchable fabric, which allows the water to sieve through under strain. Both boat and parachute anchor should be on the wave crest at the same time.*

Swivels and Shackles

Parachutes can rotate in use and therefore a swivel is recommended by manufacturers, which should be able to cope when the parachute becomes heavily loaded. When considering the size of the swivel, it must be recognised as a frequent point of failure and needs to be of high quality with a greater breaking load than that of the parachute line. The same applies to shackles used to attach the parts of the system when, like the swivel, one can safely verge to the oversize. All shackle pins should be seized.

Riding sail

A few yachts tend to lie nearly head to wind on a parachute sea anchor, but most tend to yaw about, adding to discomfort and risk of capsize. If a yacht yaws about in strong winds

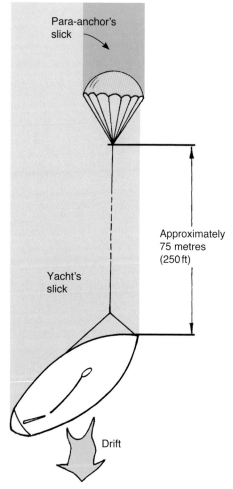

at a mooring, possibly because the mast and/ or hull generate lift, then she will probably yaw on a parachute sea anchor. The amount of yawing will also depend on where a yacht has a lot of windage, for example a furled headsail will increase the amount of windage forward and will increase the yaw.

Yachts with two masts should be able to set a suitably small amount of mizzen to reduce yaw. Sloops will need some kind of riding sail rigged on the backstay and a storm jib set on the backstay tends to be too large. A triple faced sail such as a Delta sail or FinDelta, obtainable via the internet, probably works best. Motoring slowly astern may also achieve the desired effect.

The Pardey method of deployment

Normal practice is to deploy the parachute straight over the bow, but there is an option to rig a parachute – the Pardeys use a Bu-Ord – with a deep-reefed mainsail or trysail set, so that the boat lies at a 50° angle to wind and wave. The advantage of the arrangement is that the boat does not swing continuously through the wind, but stays at a more comfortable fixed angle, much like being hove-to. In addition, the slick formed by the drift of the boat and the parachute reduces the likelihood of waves breaking to weather (see Fig 7.4). It is said that the Bu-Ord parachute is most suitable for the Pardey method of deployment, as it is more porous and therefore capable of taking a shock load.

A snatch block is used at the bow to accommodate the angled parachute line. Then a bridle, or pendant line is taken from another block snatched onto the parachute line and led aft to a cockpit winch. When the bridle is tensioned (and it may be necessary to veer some parachute line simultaneously to give enough slack to position the bridle block) the boat can be made to slew round to an angle that gives neither ahead nor astern movement.

Some yachts may need their stem fabrication adapted to take the bow snatch block so the parachute line will clear obstructions. Larry Pardey likes to adjust the length of the

A triple faced sail, sometimes known as a Delta sail, keeps the bow into the wind and reduces yawing. The Delta sail is not related to the Delta drogue. Photo: Sandy Bruce

parachute line so the yacht and the parachute crest the waves at the same time.

Accounts, where the Pardey method has been used, show that there is a huge weight on the bridle line when using the technique and some deck fittings may not be up to it. The loads for yachts above 12.2m (40ft) are massive and may preclude the use of the Pardey method altogether. In some cases larger yachts naturally take up a good angle to the seas on a parachute in which case the main objective has been achieved without the need for a bridle line. It has been found that the fin-keeled yachts are prone to tack over the lines in less than Force 7 and it seems that the longer and deeper the keel the better when using the Pardey method of deployment.

Deploying the sea anchor

The first step in deploying the sea anchor is to lay out the parachute with all its accompanying gear on deck. This task is made much easier when deployment bags are used for rode and parachute and also if undertaken before rough seas develop. Before putting the parachute over the side the boat should be left to drift with sails lowered. The parachute should be thrown over in its deployment bag on the windward side, clear of the keel and rudder, followed by the floats and float lines. The rode should be paid out as the boat drifts, and it is sensible to snub the rode at an early stage so that the opening of the parachute can be witnessed.

Riding to a sea anchor

The parachute sea anchor provides a remarkably secure mooring but there are records of rudder damage whilst lying to a sea anchor, for example the account of *Prisana II* (Chapter 20). Lashing the helm with heavy shock cord, rather than rope, may help.

Once set up correctly the parachute needs no tending and therefore should allow the crew to go below. This is a welcome situation though, in extreme weather conditions, the hull will take a tremendous battering and the movement of the boat can be severely uncomfortable. As the rode stretches and contracts, heavy, quick rolling, yawing and pitching will take place much as happens when at an exposed anchorage. Maximum drift rate is likely to be about 1.5 knots.

The boat, rode and parachute are vulnerable to other craft when a parachute is deployed. Yachts without AIS should use VHF radio to give a Sécurité message periodically, with position and circumstances.

Recovery of the parachute

Small parachutes that do not need float trip lines and can be recovered by winching in the parachute line until a shroud line can be grabbed. Large parachutes are recovered by motoring gently into the wind, gathering in the line until most of it is on deck, then heading for the recovery buoy, picking this up and using the tripping line to haul in the collapsed parachute. It can be heavy work requiring precise steering. A system of hand signals is advisable to assist the person on the helm, who may not be able to see the direction and tension of the line. During the recovery process in rough conditions there is an evident risk of losing crew overboard, or catching the line round the propeller. Even in moderate conditions the task is tricky, and when the wet parachute is finally back on board it can inflate and be difficult to manage. Some not-so-young cruising couples, sailing on their own in yachts of over 12.2m (40ft) would probably find the recovery evolution difficult in any conditions. Nevertheless practised and experienced short-handed sailors do manage parachutes in severe weather.

Conclusions following sea trials of parachute sea anchors

There have been many accounts of successful deployments of parachute sea anchor, but lingering doubt exists regarding their performance in an ocean seaway with big breaking waves. It seems clear that parachute sea anchors are one of the safer means of coping with heavy weather, provided the boat remains adequately facing into the waves when the rode goes slack. Efforts must be made to ensure this happens. Large parachutes are not easy to recover by small crews and it does need to be remembered they are not a comfortable answer unless rigged Pardey style, a technique that seems to best apply for the Pardey's size and type of boat.

Deborah Schutz's account of the successful use of a parachute in a severe storm (Chapter 20) is evidence that yachts using a parachute can weather ultimate conditions and without active participation from their crew which, for cruising couples of retirement age or with young children, is most desirable. A further welcome benefit of a parachute sea anchor, compared to running with a storm, is that the storm blows through more quickly.

When the direction of wind and sea are markedly different, a yacht will lie to the wind

A parachute sea anchor rigged 'Pardey-style'. Photo: Peter Bruce

Recovering the parachute after a practice deployment in sheltered waters. Note that the anchor has been removed from the stem stowage to avoid chafe. Photo: Peter Bruce

If the parachute is recovered without using the float line, pulling on just one shroud line will empty the parachute. The yellow object is the deployment bag. Photo: Peter Bruce

Left: Recovering a parachute single-handed can be a frustrating process. Right: Two strong men make the business of parachute recovery easier. Photos: Peter Bruce

rather than to the sea and therefore will be vulnerable to beam seas. Sea anchors may, and quite often do, become lost or tangled. They can impose heftier loads than their deck fastenings or their structures are able to take. Thus one needs to allow for circumstances when it will not be possible to use the sea anchor by treating it as one of several options. Overall success is more certain with fully committed investment, preparation, good seamanship, timely deployment and practice.

If the decision is made to carry a parachute, purchasers are well-advised to ensure the parachute, the rode, the swivel and joining shackles are large and strong enough for the job, to ensure their vessel has strong enough fittings to take the considerable load, to make proper provision for chafe and to try the parachute out for the first time in easy conditions.

Inserting a length of chain between the rode and the Para-Anchors Mk 2 drogue.
Photo: Peter Bruce

Drogues

Trailing objects astern to control speed and improve steering is an old and well-known tactic in heavy weather. Drogues are the purpose-made alternative to improvisation and have several other uses. For example, they have been successfully used as emergency steering devices and as devices for promoting directional stability when entering narrow harbours or crossing bars in a swell.

When running before a growing ocean storm the speed generated by a vessel down the fronts of the waves can often be elating. A wise skipper will recognise this to be a time for precautionary action. As wind and wave build up not only does the load on the steering increase but also sponginess of the helm through aeration of the sea. In extreme conditions, on the top of a breaking wave, water flow past the rudder may be reversed, leading to loss of control and the high probability of broaching. The first step will be to reduce sail but, after that, use of a drogue of some sort may be needed to bring the boat down to a comfortable speed as well as maintaining the boat's course.

Slowing the boat down and pointing the stern directly into the sea may result in more waves breaking over the stern than would otherwise occur and may even lead to regular pooping. Accordingly aft-facing structures need to be strongly built and, especially for craft with a stern cockpit, the crew on deck to be well secured.

Trailing the vessel's anchor and chain over the stern is said to be effective. The weight of the anchor and chain takes the arrangement below surface effects and the downward angle creates good drag. There are two disadvantages, one being an encounter with shallow water, and the other, recovery.

The drogue line

The established method when employing a drogue is to use a line of between 80–100 metres (262–330ft), usually with a weight and drag-producing device on the end. Yet more line will be necessary to span great ocean wavelengths. It is preferable to secure the drogue line to a bridle, so that the load is split between attachment points on each quarter of the boat, allowing adjustment of the course to the most desirable angle to the waves. The arrangement is set up by tying a rolling hitch to a point at least a boat length outboard, and securing the bridle line to the opposite stern cleat to the main line. After fastening it, the bridle line is eased out, to middle the two lengths of the 'V' at an angle of 30°, or staggered as necessary. There are some disadvantages in using a bridle. It is neither easy to adjust the length of the drogue line nor adjust the nip, i.e. the first point where the rope is twisted around a cleat and where it will tend to chafe. Also, the rolling hitch may be so taut it may need to be cut out when the arrangement is brought back on board and dismantled.

An essential feature of a drogue system is that the line should remain taut and as evenly loaded as possible. If the line goes slack, shock loads on the vessel are likely, and the vessel becomes vulnerable to lying beam on to the sea and being rolled. To prevent this, experimentation with the line length to bring the drogue into the optimum position relative to the waves may be necessary.

The best way of ensuring a consistent load may be to have a very long line with sufficient weight on the end of the drogue line to keep the drogue away from the worst of surface effects i.e. if the drogue is deep enough it will neither come out of the water nor be much affected by the orbital motion within a wave. An alternative, better but more complicated method, is to deploy two drogues in series, so that if one drogue is carried forward by a breaking wave, the other will still provide a braking force.

The sinker

The Wolfson report recommends a sinker weight between 20 and 30kgs (44–68lbs) so that the drogue will operate at between 10 and 15m (33–50ft) below the surface. Sinkers are awkward objects to manage, and make the task of recovery more difficult, though they do at least have another use as an 'angel' or 'chum'. A suitable length of anchor chain or small anchor is often used as an alternative to ordinary sinkers, and diving weights are

suitable too. In moderate conditions, should the drag of the drogue slow the boat down too much, a little headsail or engine power may improve the situation. Some drogue users find that weighted drogues pull the stern down and that their drogues work well with no sinker at all, and are consequently easier to recover.

The load on the drogue line can be heavy but rather less than that of the parachute. The Wolfson trials showed a peak load of 3.8 tonnes on the drogue line for a 10m (33ft) yacht when struck by a breaking wave. Such loads mean care must be taken that the line has an adequately strong fastening point and a suitable fairlead. A cockpit primary winch is the obvious attachment point so long as it is strong enough, and plastic pipe or other anti-chafe may be necessary at the fairlead.

Towing trials

With the aim of finding a suitable drogue to slow a vessel to a comfortable speed when running before a storm, it was desirable to establish by empirical means the drogue's effectiveness solely at creating drag. It was also desirable to compare commercially available products with makeshift arrangements improvised from whatever happens to be available. For example to compare the performance of a relatively expensive drogue with a used motorcar tyre.

A towing trial was undertaken using a Najad 391 under power, as one can roughly equate the situation when motoring to running under bare pole. A fixed engine speed short of maximum was chosen, and the hull speed measured by the boat's log with the various drogues on tow. The line was 136.5m (448ft) of 16mm (⅝in) eight strand.

The trials

All the commercially available drogues tested provided a good measure of drag, bringing speed down from 6.6 to about 4–5 knots. Some veered or writhed about, and some twisted suggesting that a good quality swivel should be used.

Using a small headsail as a drogue

A No 3 jib, measuring 11.6 x 11 x 4m (38 x 36 x 13ft), was chosen to establish whether satisfactory drag could be achieved with items normally found on board. If a sail joined by pieces of rope from its three corners was to open out like a parachute, one might expect some hefty pulling power. Using rigging lines of about 1.2m (4ft) the sail *did not* open, but when longer rigging lines were used – a 4.6m (15ft) line from the head and two 7.6m (25ft) lines from the tack and the clew (to balance the sail round the centre of effort), drag was more than adequate, suggesting that a storm jib might be the best size of sail to use as a drogue.

Many will prefer to use a proper drogue from a deployment bag rather than use their expensive sails for a purpose for which they were not designed. However, given long enough and carefully balanced rigging lines, a small sail will work as a drogue and a large sail will work as a parachute sea anchor.

More ad hoc arrangements and warps

A home-made cone worked as well as the commercial drogues but the drogue line on its own only achieved a 5 per cent reduction in drag, and with a motor car tyre attached only 11 per cent. At one time, just trailing warps alone was considered a primary storm tactic. The author's father, Erroll Bruce, in the 9m (30ft) *Samuel Pepys*, successfully ran before hurricane strength winds off Bermuda in May 1950 trailing warps. When Robin Knox-Johnston sailed alone round the world in 1969 (the first to do so non-stop and single-handed) he used a long warp in the form of a bight in severe weather. Incidentally for directional stability he used to set his storm jib sheeted amidships, and the canoe-sterned *Suhaili*, 9.5m (32ft) hull length, was so well balanced that, with the tiller lashed, he could retire to his bunk.

The deeper the line is immersed the more even and effective the drag will be. Miles Smeeton, the veteran world-girdler of the 1960s, once remarked that the 110m (360ft)

hawser he was streaming astern did not seem to be making much difference, and that he could occasionally see a big bight of the rope being carried forward on the crest of a wave in storms. Incidentally he later advocates for his own 14m (46ft) boat *Tzu Hang* that some form of drogue should be attached to the line, but he never got round to doing it.

A long enough length of line will produce the same drag as a drogue but the difficulty is that so much rope may be needed that there is insufficient space to stow it and recovering it may be an all-day task. However, Peter Cook used two 91m (300ft) warps to good effect on the 14.4m (48ft) cutter *RED* in February 2004 (Chapter 23). Geoffrey Francis survived a full blown typhoon in 1938 in his new 17m (56ft) ketch *Ma-On-Shan* on passage from Hong Kong to Singapore. He deployed about 300m (1,000ft) of hairy rope astern along with tractor vaporising oil, of which he had an unusually large supply. After the typhoon was through it did take him all day to recover the line.

It makes no noticeable difference to the drag whether the line was towed straight or in a bight, and there are arguments for both. By allowing the line to stream straight behind, it has a better chance of bridging the whole wavelength and therefore may produce a steadier pull. By using it in a bight there is a chance it may discourage waves breaking astern, it is easier to recover and less likely to be lost. Peter Cook believes that a warp in a bight is more likely to surface. The choice should probably depend upon the length of the line and the wavelength of the seas.

Long, wet ropes are awkward and heavy to handle so it may be desirable for larger vessels to install a reel on deck from which the rope can be deployed either for a drogue or a sea anchor. A power driven reel would be ideal. Smaller vessels can best use another 'deployment bag'. This bag contains the entire length of line, has a hole in the centre at the bottom, and can be put in the water, enabling the line to run out without fouling anything. The deployment bag should be prevented from being carried down the line, as it can seriously upset the operation of the drogue. Whether using a reel or a bag, multiplait line is the least prone to tangle.

The handling difficulties and the expense of very long lines make a case for using a good drogue, or drogues in series, in conjunction with a suitable length of line.

The Series Drogue

The Series Drogue is an unconventional drag device of growing popularity. It has a large number of cones spread over a long length of line rather than one or two large cones (see Fig 7.5). The optimum number of cones and the amount of weight on the end of the line relate to the displacement of the vessel.

Unlike other drogues the Series Drogue does not require someone on the helm. Another important feature is that its pull is proportional to the accelerating force of a wave, so the load on the Series Drogue builds up progressively, but more quickly than it does with a single cone. Therefore it is more likely to avert a roll resulting from a breaking wave coming at an awkward angle i.e. not coming from directly stern. In addition there are no violent tugs as can happen with a single drogue, which could cause failure at the attachment point. Users stress the gentleness of the action of a Series Drogue, despite the heavy loads that occur.

Recovery is tricky with a windlass and hard work without. When using a windlass, it may

be necessary to fold each individual cone to prevent part of the cone being trapped by the adjoining turn of line, which causes the cone to be torn as it comes away from the barrel. Putting a line and float, or a floating standing trip line, at the weighted end of the Series Drogue might be an aid to recovery though there is a risk that the recovery line will become entangled with the drogue with the outcome that neither work. Use of a helper line to winch the drogue line in length by length is the accepted method of recovery, with some variations on this theme.

The Series Drogue used for the trials was owned and constructed by Professor Noel Dilly. He used it off the Azores, deployed from his Twister in Force 10, and was deeply impressed by the beneficial effects of its steady pull. He is not alone. For example, Tony and Coryn Gooch have used a Series Drogue most successfully on their worldwide cruises to high latitudes in *Taonui*, both in bad weather and to rest. *Taonui* is long-keeled and holds her course admirably at 1.5 knots with the Series Drogue deployed. Tony Gooch says wait until the wind drops to below 20 knots before attempting recovery and that using an engine to go astern can help.

Another remarkable high latitude sailor, Roger Taylor in *Mingming*, a 6.3m (21ft) Corribee

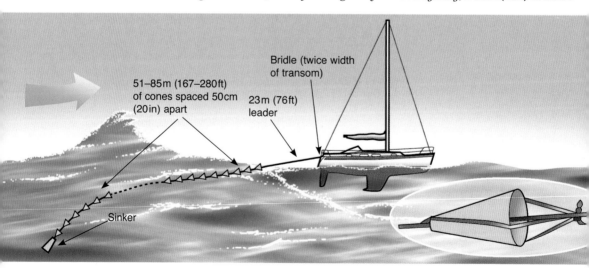

Figure 7.5 *The Series Drogue is an increasingly popular drag device which was invented by the late Donald Jordan after the 1979 Fastnet Race. It uses a multitude of cones attached to a weighted non-stretch line streamed astern.*

Left: Part of a Series Drogue showing the droguelets. Right: Deploying a Series Drogue.
Photos: Peter Bruce

which is an extraordinarily small yacht for ocean passages, has used his Series Drogue to good effect in Arctic waters, as did Paul Kirby in his 14m (46ft) Seafarer centre-cockpit yawl *Midnight Sun* off Stewart Island in March 2012, to the south of New Zealand in winds that peaked at 80 knots.

A vessel using a Series Drogue might be thought vulnerable to breaking waves from astern but experienced users say that the more worrying waves are those that come from an angle, though pooping should be allowed for. Some users claim that the Series Drogue causes a moderating effect to the approaching waves.

All users say that, though not the most convenient of drogues to recover, nor to stow, the Series Drogue is superbly effective.

The Bu-Ord

Using the 3m (10ft) Bu-Ord parachute as a drogue produced the most dramatic drag in the trial results. The yacht's propeller was unable to cope with the parachute at the rpm set and cavitated severely. It was necessary to reduce rpm by 30 per cent to avoid cavitation when a speed of only 1.2 knots was achieved, indicating very high resistance. Without a float and recovery line attached to the apex,

the unloaded parachute will sink, and then becomes seriously hard work to recover. The Bu-Ord provides so much drag that steerage way cannot be maintained so is best used as a parachute sea anchor for small monohulls, multihulls or RIBs.

Cone drogues

Cone or sleeve drogues are available in chandlers, or are easy to make. These are the shapes that gave early sea anchors a bad name by being too small, but in the sizes available, perhaps if weighted, they seem to be no less effective than other drogues. Two were tested, one proprietary type with a 61cm (24in) diameter mouth and 10cm (4in) exit hole, and another of 76cm (30in) diameter and 7.6cm (3in) exit which was home-made in two layers of parachute nylon. They were tried both singly and in series with 15.2m (50ft) between them and were weighted with chain. The results of drag trials were impressive, both as a single drogue and when two were set up in series. The latter arrangement can be expected to give especially good results in a seaway as a single drogue is bound to be disadvantaged by wave effects.

A heavy-duty sewing machine was needed to make the homemade drogue.

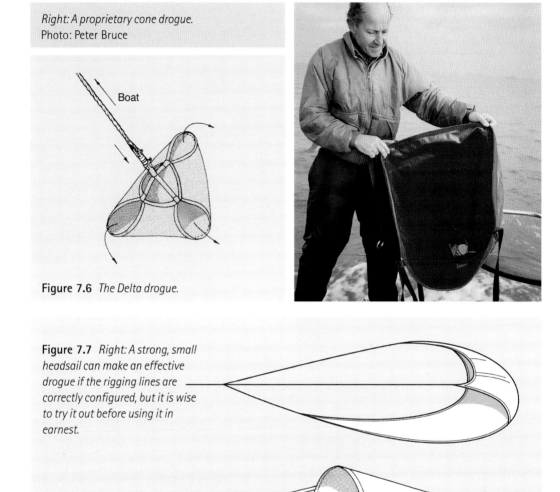

Right: A proprietary cone drogue.
Photo: Peter Bruce

Boat

Figure 7.6 *The Delta drogue.*

Figure 7.7 *Right: A strong, small headsail can make an effective drogue if the rigging lines are correctly configured, but it is wise to try it out before using it in earnest.*

Figure 7.8 *The cone drogue is very efficient except when collapsed by the forward motion of a breaking wave.*

The car tyre

The tyre seemed to produce a modest but useful amount of drag. For example it doubled the amount of drag given by the line on its own. It had been expected that the tyre might porpoise or just skid along the surface, but there was no sign of this in calm conditions, though instances have been reliably reported in a seaway. A car tyre is an awkward, large object to stow and can mark paintwork. One should drill drain holes in the side of the tyre or remember to sponge out the inside after use. Some will find a dual purpose for a car tyre, for example a tyre makes a good fender for slimy walls, as it does not rotate.

Recovering drogues by hand is extremely hard work, especially when weighted.
Photo: Peter Bruce

Recovery

When the drogue is weighted, hand recovery is heavy work and a single person might need to allow an hour or more for the task. In one recovery in the open sea the line had to be let go when an especially heavy load came on it, a reminder that it is advisable to keep the bitter end secured. In boats under 11m (37ft) it is usually easiest to recover the drogue using a primary sheet winch. In larger craft it may be easier to recover the drogue over the bow using a power-driven capstan if there is no other power winch.

Conclusions following sea trials of drogues

The commercially-made drogues tested were all strong, compact, easily handled, and gave an effective amount of drag, though probably few small craft owners will wish to find space for solid-built drogues.

Except for the series drogue, yachts using a drogue may be able to maintain only a downwind course using vane steering, an auto helm or hand-steering. A weighted drogue will probably perform best in a seaway.

Small parachutes, such as Bu-Ords, have been used over the stern of multihulls as drogues as well as over the bow as parachute sea anchors. Monohulls will find the drag of a parachute too much to retain steerageway. At the other end of the scale a single weighted line, similar to the line used in the trials, will provide insufficient drag for most purposes. Makeshift devices such as car tyres do not give much drag and can be the least trusted to stay submerged. Sails and warps can be used with reservation or if nothing else is available.

If choosing between a parachute sea anchor and a drogue, the pros and cons of each will be argued for some time. All craft are safer end-on to the waves, so any drag device, be it rigged over the bow or stern, which holds a vessel end-on firmly into the waves for the duration of a storm, is highly advantageous. Currently popular amongst high latitude ocean voyagers is, again, the Series Drogue, but there are advocates for all the other options.

One thing for sure is that drag devices are useful appliances to have on board and widen the skipper's options when a tempest comes to call.

8 The meteorology of heavy weather

Richard Ebling

This is written for the benefit of sailors not meteorologists and therefore many of the finer points have been simplified or glossed over.

These days, with the vast amount of weather information that is available to the sailor, in theory there is no need to be caught out, but no meteorologist can truthfully put his hand on his heart and always guarantee 100 per cent satisfaction for 24 hour forecast products, let alone those that look ahead for the best part of a week.

This chapter covers:
1. Obtaining weather data offshore.
2. The variation of wind strength with height above sea level and how wind strength is reported.
3. The development of secondary lows and how they can be forecast.
4. The phenomenon of explosive deepening of weather systems.
5. Winds generated by high pressure.
6. Zones of convergence or divergence of winds.
7. Tropical revolving storms.
8. Thunderstorms and tornadoes.

Obtaining data offshore

Most ports have easy access to internet services either via the marina's wifi or via a mobile connection. Once at sea it was necessary at one time to receive actual and 24-hour forecast coded charts by Morse, which then required the plotting an isobaric chart by hand. Then came radiofax which provided charts for up to six days ahead either using a dedicated receiver/printer, or latterly, a laptop plugged into the AF output from the ship's radio. Now of course the laptop can be connected to a satellite phone over large swathes of the ocean.

My own choice on the internet is www.weatheronline.co.uk then on the left-hand side of the screen under the heading 'Weather Maps' select 'Expert Charts'. The weather for virtually the whole globe is available for up to 16 days ahead. The importance of using a large scale must be emphasised, especially for longer voyages. Don't just look at the area where you are going to be over the next 16 days but consider what is happening at that time over a larger area in order to anticipate what might be lurking over the horizon on day 17. The website www.weatheronline.co.uk also provides ready access to GRIB files and radar and satellite imaging.

Strong winds

Outside the tropics, the two commonest causes of heavy weather associated with depressions, are either the development of a secondary low thereby causing the isobars to be squeezed closer together, or the straightforward unexpected deepening of an existing low centre.

With reports in this book from many sources it may be appropriate to comment on wind profiles. Although friction reduces wind

Height in feet above the surface																	
10	20	30	33	40	50	60	70	80	90	100	120	140	160	180	200	250	300
Factor over the sea																	
0.89	0.95	0.99	1.00	1.02	1.04	1.06	1.08	1.09	1.11	1.12	1.14	1.16	1.17	1.18	1.20	1.22	1.25
Factor over the land																	
0.74	0.88	0.98	1.00	1.05	1.11	1.16	1.21	1.25	1.29	1.32	1.38	1.44	1.48	1.53	1.57	1.66	1.74

Variation of windspeed with height relative to 10m (33ft).

blowing over the sea to about 80 per cent of the wind speed above the boundary or friction layer, and friction overland reduces the wind to about 40 per cent; in the scale of winds reported by masthead anemometers there are further factors that are worth looking at, especially when you bear in mind that weather forecasts are all based on the height of a standard (land based) anemometer – 10m (33ft) above ground level; a height derived from calibrations of the Beaufort scale at various mast heights aboard HMS *Worcester* in the 1890s.

For example if the forecast is for 30 knots (Force 7), with an anemometer 15m (50ft) above the waterline, the expected mean speed should be around 30 x 1.04 = 31.2 knots and on a 49m (160ft) lighthouse such as the Fastnet 30 x 1.48 = 44.4 knots could be recorded: a good Force 9! I said 'recorded' as reported wind speed observations on meteorological broadcasts *should* always be corrected for both altitude and exposure. They are in the UK, but may not always be elsewhere, especially in some of the more remote corners of the globe.

It is also perhaps worth remembering the 'weight of the air'. In 24 knots the wind exerts a pressure of 11kg/m^2 (2.3lb/ft^2), but a little under half as fast again, a wind of 34 knots, will exert 22kg/m^2 (4.6lb/ft^2), whilst at 48 knots it exerts 44kg/m^2 (9.6lb/ft^2) (doubling the wind speed means 4 times the pressure); so that even for sails of equal area the 'heeling factor' in a given wind relates very much to the height of the sail's centre of pressure.

Increased height of the centre of pressure means increased wind speed and therefore heeling moment is increased by the wind force multiplied by the increased height.

To avoid confusion, unless otherwise stated, all diagrams and meteorological theories refer to the northern hemisphere i.e. cyclonic flow is anticlockwise, and anticyclonic flow is clockwise. If you do find the look of weather charts confusing as you cross the equator, a tip is to pick up the chart by the bottom edge and hold against a strong light, a sunlit window for example. This has the effect of reversing references to north/south but keeps east/west the same, once more giving a familiar look to the shape of the frontal systems.

Secondary lows

Without access to weather charts, trying to identify conditions leading to the development of a secondary low is next to impossible, as both surface and 'upper air charts' are needed. These can now be obtained from an onboard weather fax receiver, or from the www.weatheronline.co.uk site. Using the default 'GFS' Model, under the 'parameters' and 'pressure' the 'Thickness 500–1,000hPa chart' is a useful tool (the hecto Pascal or hPa is the correct SI unit for barometric pressure with 1hPa = 1mb, which older sailors will recognise). This thickness chart shows the surface pressure in blue or red depending on whether the pressure is above or below 1,013hPa. The height of the 500hPa surface is in black and colour is used to denote the thickness i.e. the vertical distance between the level at which the pressure is 1,000hPa and the level at which the pressure is 500hPa, this is known as the thickness of the lower half of the atmosphere, the lower half being below 5,500m (18,000ft) or so which, after all, is where most weather is found.

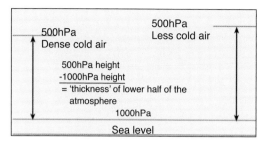

Figure 8.1 *Variation of pressure with height due to variation in temperature.*

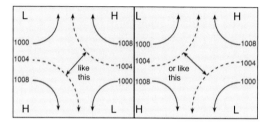

Figure 8.2 *Where should the missing isobars be drawn?*

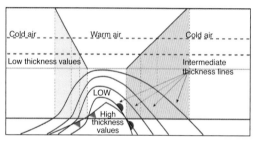

Figure 8.3 *Plan view of met chart with thickness lines. How 3-D information is displayed on 2-D meteorological charts.*

Cold air is denser than warm air, therefore if the thickness value is low the air is cold, and if the thickness value is high then the air is warm (see Fig 8.1).

Many charts will have some lines omitted for clarity. If we take a surface chart with isobars, which is probably the most familiar, filling in many of the missing isobars will be reasonably obvious, but in some cases it won't be possible. Fig 8.2 illustrates possible flow across a col. (Because low and high pressure systems can be thought of as valleys and mountain peaks, some geographic terms are used such as ridge or trough. A col or saddle point is a high valley between two

mountains, which at the same time is a ridge between the lower ground on either side of the mountains.)

The clarity of your chart will of course depend on the screen size/printer used, but this 'thickness' chart will have no fronts marked. However, once the concept of what you are looking at is understood, it should not present too much of a puzzle. Just as tightly drawn depth contours on a marine chart (a steep gradient) denote rapid shoaling, so does the closeness of the 'thickness' lines represent and increasing thermal contrast.

Fronts or, more correctly, frontal zones are areas of change, where either cold air is being replaced by warmer air or vice versa. Whereas warm sectors, with their relatively uniform contents, contain few thickness lines, in frontal zones the greater the contrast in temperature, the closer the thickness lines will be, and the steeper will be the 'thermal gradient'. At a warm front, cold air is replaced by warmer less dense air and so the thickness values will rise, falling again at the cold front as the warm air is replaced by cold air once more.

Forecasting development of secondary lows

In an ideal world the surface and upper air features should be closely related as in Fig 8.4, but unfortunately this is not always the case. Sometimes the thickness lines are bunched along the warm front, or along the cold, and some times even crossing into the warm sector. Secondary lows tend to form where the thickness lines are bunched together.

In Fig 8.5a the thickness lines are bunching where they run nearly parallel to the cold front for a considerable distance. On the surface the cold front may well be trailing with little if any gradient across it i.e. very few isobars crossing the front. In conditions such as these the distance from the point of development of a secondary low – as a cold front wave – from the point of occlusion is likely to be in the region of 1,200–1,500 nautical miles, with the new low moving generally in a direction parallel to the thickness lines or the isobars

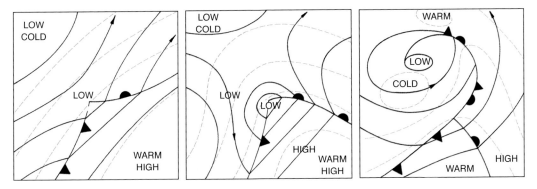

Figure 8.4 *Three stages in the development from a frontal wave to an occluded frontal system showing the relationship between isobars, fronts and thickness lines.*

within the warm sector. This is a common way in which secondary depressions form.

In Fig 8.5b the secondary low develops as a warm front wave. The bunching of the thickness lines in this case is seen to be just ahead of the warm front with a distinct ridging over the warm sector, with the resulting depression moving along the thickness lines. Compare with Fig 8.5d where the bunching is nearer to the triple point.

The development of a secondary low – as a triple point low (Fig 8.5c) – is perhaps the most common. In this case the thickness lines will no longer be parallel to the cold front. Some will cross the warm sector, whilst the rest will turn pole-wards (north) just before they reach the occlusion. Again in this case the movement of the secondary low will be in the general direction of the thickness lines or isobars within the warm sector.

In Fig 8.5d as in 8.5c some thickness lines cross the warm sector, and bunching is seen to be closer to the triple point than in 8.5b. This case is the least likely development.

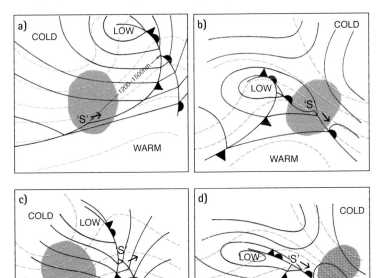

Figure 8.5

Thickness patterns associated with the development of secondary lows and their direction of movement.

a) Secondary low development as a wave on the cold front.

b) Secondary low on a warm front.

c) Secondary low developing west of the triple point.

d) Least common case of a secondary low developing east of the triple point.

In all cases the driving force behind any development of a secondary low is a strong thermal contrast, which is shown on a chart by the bunching of the thickness lines.

The following questions should be asked:

1. Is the strongest thermal contrast along and parallel to the cold front? If so, watch out for cold front waves.
2. Is the strongest thermal contrast along and parallel to the warm front? If so, watch out for warm front waves.
3. Is the strongest thermal contrast across rather than along the front? If so, expect triple point low to develop.

Explosive deepening

Development of weather systems is normally fairly well forecast. So if depressions do suddenly deepen unexpectedly, more often than not it is a case of explosive deepening (which is defined as deepening at over 24hPa (mb) in a day). This usually happens during the winter months, and nearly always occurs over the oceans, with the western North Atlantic being one of the world's more common areas. However, explosive deepening can occur at any time, even in mid summer, especially if the tail end of any ex-tropical revolving storm is involved.

If the signs leading up to one of these events have slipped though the professional forecasters' net, it is very unlikely that the yachtsman will have any additional information to guide him, except that of a steadily falling barometer. With no other information to go on, a good rule is that falls of 10hPa (mb) in 3 hours will be followed by a gale (Force 8). Whilst the falls may not be particularly swift, to the rear of the depression the pressure rise may indeed be rapid. (In the October 1987 storm, the barometer at Hurn Airport fell some 33hPa (mb) in 18 hours at an average of 5.5hPa (mb)/3hr or 1.8hPa (mb)/hr, but later the barometer rose 50hPa (mb) in 15 hours! Peaking at 12.2hPa (mb) in the hour 0400–0500 UTC. Rises of over 10hPa (mb) in one hour covered an area from Lyme Bay and the Isle of Wight to Reading.)

Initially the strongest winds may very well be contained within the warm sector, but there may well be a sting in the tail. Once the explosive deepening gets underway, storm or even hurricane force winds (Force 10–12) can occur over a comma-shaped arc (seen shaded in Fig 8.6) in the cold air behind the cold front, as cold dry air from high in the atmosphere is dragged down and swept into the circulation. A narrow jet, tens rather than hundreds of miles across begins to descend and dry out; then passing through the snow and ice particles

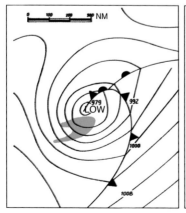

Figure 8.6 *Comma-shaped arc of enhanced wind due to the intrusion of subsided air.*

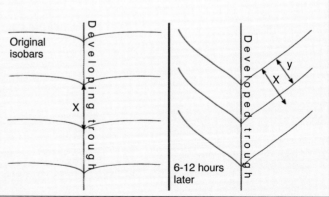

Figure 8.7 *Isobar spacing along a developing trough may remain constant in spite of closer isobars and strengthening winds. Y = tighter gradient, therefore increased wind speed compared with X.*

contained within the cloud mass, cools further as these crystals evaporate. Now being cooler the jet is denser and descends even more quickly, eventually hitting the surface. The dryness of this entrained air will result in an area with clear skies, as reported during the 1979 Fastnet.

However, just because the wind speed is increasing it does not necessarily mean that the associated fronts will also speed up. Pressure falling along a trough line (Fig 8.7a) such as a cold front will sharpen the trough, tightening the pressure gradient each side of the front without affecting the gradient measured along the front.

The distance apart of the isobars measured along the trough – in this case a measurement of 'x' units remains constant even though the distance apart of the isobars 'y' has now decreased. Very rapid post-frontal pressure rises will of course also have the same net result.

Lee lows

Depressions can also be caused by high ground. For example during an Indian Ocean storm in 1984, see page 30, marked troughing occurred on the lee of the Drakensberg mountains. Examination of the chart will show a 'hole in the isobars' or wide space in an apparently regular circulation about the main depression, and it is within this empty space that a lee low may form.

As air is forced to rise over a range of mountains, in general the curve of the isobars becomes more anticyclonic. Likewise on the leeward side of the high ground with descending flow the isobars become more cyclonic. As well as marked troughing to the lee of mountains, lee depressions can also develop. In the same way water flowing past an obstruction will form eddies which break away to be carried in the stream.

Often the only evidence for drawing a discrete circulation around these centres is gleaned from satellite analysis. In the mid 1950s, with an anticyclone over Greenland and northerly winds over the UK, charts would be drawn with perhaps very little in the

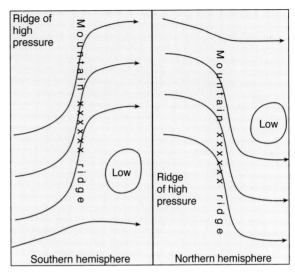

Figure 8.8 *Development of a lee low as an eddy due to the distortion of isobars crossing high ground.*

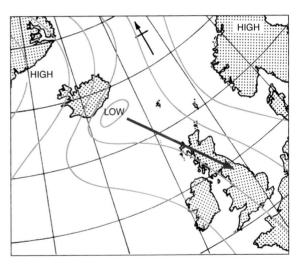

Figure 8.9 *Polar low developing as a lee low before breaking away to be carried southwards across Scotland and possibly eastern England.*

way of isobars, due to lack of observations, to suggest a lee low to the south-east of Iceland. It was perhaps only with the arrival of unexpected prolonged snow in Scotland that we became aware that one of these eddies had broken away from its source and been carried along embedded within the flow, arriving as a polar low.

High pressure generated winds

Unexpected strong winds may also be caused by anticyclones that fail to move away as expected, with little if any indication from an on board barometer.

The reluctance of an area of high pressure to move on was evident in the 1994 Queen's Birthday Storm (Chapter 19) when some 80 yachts were caught out in a storm as they sailed together from New Zealand to winter in the tropical Pacific islands. Again the closest isobars (and strongest winds) were in the quadrant squashed against the anticyclone centred over or close to New Zealand.

Anticyclone winds

The wind circulating around a centre is acted upon by centrifugal forces acting away from the centre. In an anticyclone the pressure gradient force acts outwards as well, so that around an anticyclone both forces act in the same direction. Around a low the pressure gradient acts towards the centre, in other words the centrifugal force is acting against the pressure gradient, reducing its strength (Fig 8.10). Thus around an anticyclone winds are stronger for a given isobar spacing than around a depression.

Figure 8.10 *Forces acting on air under cyclonic and anticyclonic motion.*

Convergence/divergence

When winds meet, either spiralling into a depression or perhaps when a sea breeze blowing inland meets the land breeze, the air has to go somewhere. If the convergence is at the surface the air obviously cannot sink, so it must rise. Convergence also occurs when moving air is slowed down. Obviously air that is rising will expand and cool, and if the air is cooled sufficiently any moisture will condense into clouds. In the same way divergence at the surface can only be satisfied if the air aloft is subsiding – in which case the air will be compressed, warmed, and any moisture particles will evaporate.

With north-east trades in the northern hemisphere blowing towards the south-east trades of the south there must be a front and a line of convergence separating these two flows. It was once thought that there was convergence along the entire length of this intertropical convergence zone (ITCZ), but it is now accepted that the actual convergence occurs only here and there. Nevertheless the ITCZ is a breeding area for tropical storms although they may not develop precisely on the ITCZ.

The bright clouds associated with the ITCZ can be seen over the central Pacific close to the Equator, from Colombia to the north Brazil coast, over the east Atlantic, the Gulf of Guinea and Africa again close to the Equator. Rather more activity is visible over the Indian Ocean and to the northeast of Australia, before dying again over the west Pacific. This shows a series of convergence areas rather than the continuous belt that had been once thought to exist.

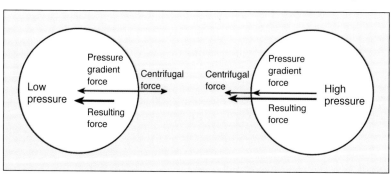

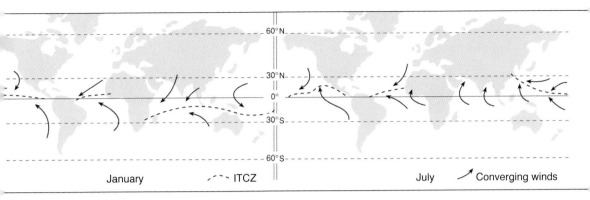

Figure 8.11 *Trade winds converging towards the equator in January and July.*

Figure 8.12 *Photo montage of several satellite pictures. In these the coldest (highest) clouds are brightest.*

Tropical revolving storms

1. Charts displaying tracks of tropical revolving storms (TRS), Fig 8.14, show that formation does not normally occur within 5° north or south of the Equator, nor in the South Atlantic. In March 2004 the first ever reported TRS in the South Atlantic was observed off the Brazilian coast. Whilst we can be pretty sure that it is the first since satellite observation started in 1966, prior to that lack of reports cannot be taken to mean that they never had occurred. This TRS called NoName #1, which was responsible for three deaths and for 2,000 people being rendered homeless, will present a challenge to research, as sea surface temperatures were only around 24°C, and may only be resolved by running repeated mathematical simulations.

2. High water vapour content is required. In order to supply both the water vapour and a sufficient source of heat for convection, sea temperature in excess of 26°C (79°F) is considered essential, allowing the air to contain typically 20–25g of water per 1kg of air (2 per cent of the air will in fact be water vapour!). Thus the warmer the more likely, and the greater depth of warm water the more likely as well; since rough surface conditions will churn up the sea, mixing the warm surface waters

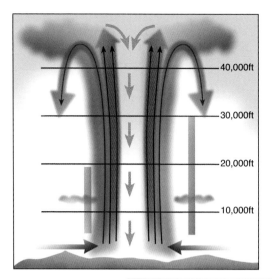

Figure 8.13 *In a fully developed TRS, the rising air and the cloud generated by its furious ascent will be rather like a factory chimney with the condensing water vapour replacing the bricks and stones, and with the descending central core generating the clear eye of the storm. The base of this 'chimney' may be obscured by low cloud or may start a little above the surface, projecting through various layers of cloud; there may be other convective cloud cells embedded within the larger circulation. These embedded convective clouds might well contain active thunderstorms that would be considered severe in their own right.*

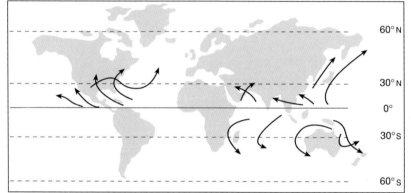

Figure 8.14 *Typical tracks of tropical revolving storms.*

with the deeper colder layers and in so doing can 'kill off' the potential storm. As the moist air within the circulation rises, expands and cools, condensation takes place, releasing large amounts of energy in the form of latent heat.

3. The released latent heat needs to be contained within the vertical column of the circulation and therefore TRS need to be well away from the influence of any jet streams.

4. Eventually a small amount of the rising air at the top of the system turns inwards and sinks. This dry air is then responsible for the clear eye of the storm.

The initial track of a TRS is mainly westwards, typically at 10 to 15 knots, with a slight pole-wards component (Fig 8.14), steered by the

tropospheric flow. Somewhere between 20° and 30° away from the equator, depending on the position of the high pressure belt, the track usually curves increasingly pole-ward at 20 to 30 knots. As the system leaves the tropical circulation, steering will be governed by the westerly winds of the mid-latitude troposphere.

Not that all TRS do as expected, for example Cyclone Justin moved just 180nm in 9 days (3–12 March). With dew points and sea temperatures in the mid to high twenties Justin's slow movement can only have been due to lack of any steering flow throughout the height of the cyclone until around the 12th, when Justin headed north-east towards New Guinea for 3 or 4 days before returning to hit the coast near Cairns and then travel south down the coast towards Mackay.

Tropical revolving storms

Area and local name	Jan	Feb	Mar	Apr	May	Jun	Jul	Aug	Sep	Oct	Nov	Dec	Average No per year	Average of over F11 per year
N Atlantic, W Indies (hurricane)					?	--	--	====	====	====	--	?	10	5
NE Pacific (hurricane)					?	--	====	====	====	--	?		15	7
NW Pacific (typhoon)				?	--	--	====	====	====	--	--	?	25–30	15–20
N Indian Ocean, Bay of Bengal (cyclone)			?	--	====	====	--	--	--	====	====	?	2–5	1–2
N Indian Ocean Arabian Sea (cyclone)			?	--	====	--			?	--	====	?	1–2	1
S Indian Ocean W of 80°E (cyclone)	====	====	==-	--	?					?	--		5–7	2
Australia W, NW, N and Queensland coast (cyclone)	====	====	==-	--						?	--		2–3	1
Fiji, Samoa, New Zealand (N Island) (cyclone)	====	====	====	--	?					?	--		7	2

-- main season ==== period of greatest activity   ? period affected if season is early/late

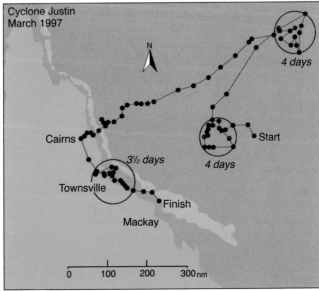

Figure 8.15 *Cyclone Justin's unusually erratic track over some 20 days.*

The notorious Hurricane Katrina that caused so much damage to New Orleans near its peak strength on 28 August 2005. Maximum sustained wind was 280km/h (175mph). Minimum barometric pressure was 902hPa (mb). Note the clearly formed eye in the centre of the swirling cloud mass. Later in the year came Hurricane Rita with maximum wind strength of 290km/h /180mph, and a lowest central pressure of 895hPa (mb).

The moral of this is that although tropical storms *should* curve away from the equator, in reality they are very unpredictable and a close eye on the barometer is required. Within the tropics the diurnal variation of pressure (the atmospheric tide) of perhaps up to 3hPa (mb) may mask early warning of approaching systems. It is normal for tendencies of +/– 0.5hPa (mb)/hour to occur around 0100 and 0700 and 1900 local time.

In a fully developed TRS the rising air and the cloud generated by its furious ascent will be rather like a factory chimney with the condensing water vapour replacing the bricks. The descending central core generates the clear eye of the storm. The base of this 'chimney' may be obscured by low cloud or may start a little above the surface, projecting through various layers of cloud. There may well be other convective cloud cells embedded within the larger circulation and these embedded convective clouds might well contain active thunderstorms that would be considered severe in their own right.

Thunderstorms

On a smaller scale to tropical revolving storms, convective processes also fuel thunderstorms. What is needed is 'conditionally unstable air', allowing a parcel of saturated air to be buoyant and rise, when an adjacent parcel of dry air does not. Indeed were the parcel of dry air to be lifted it would sink again to its starting point. In the lowest 3,000m (10,000ft) of the atmosphere dry air cools with height at around 3°C (5.4°F)/305m (1,000ft), and at about half that rate if the air is saturated, due to the release of latent heat as moisture is condensed out. The trigger to start this movement could be heating from below, or cooling from above, or ascent as air is forced to rise over high ground in the case of air mass storms, or is forced to rise as a front approaches. Convergence near a front can give rise to some of the severest storms, but another requirement for severe storms is a marked change of wind velocity with height, which tilts the updraught.

The updraught is almost self-perpetuating as it is fuelled by the latent heat released by condensation. The small 'cloud' droplets that originally form have a slow drop speed, and will easily be carried up in the strong updraughts giving them the chance of growing larger.

Since within a cloud 'the higher the colder': at around –20°C (–4°F) ice crystals develop. Higher in the cloud as temperatures get even lower, more and more of the updraught consists of ice rather than water, until temperatures reach –40°C/°F by which time the cloud consists only of ice crystals.

As the droplets/ice particles grow they become heavier, and because the updraught is no longer vertical, falling ice/water will leave the saturated updraught and fall into drier air – where evaporation takes place. The latent heat required for this cools the adjacent air – generating negative buoyancy and hence the downdraught. Not only is the downdraught due to the coldness (density) of the air, but the falling precipitation also drags air down with it due to friction.

When this downdraught hits the surface it rapidly spreads out as a cold pool, giving rise not only to a rapid or even violent increase in wind speed, but changes in direction. As the cold pool and its 'gust front' undercut the surrounding air so conditions become ripe for development of a new up-current of air. In storms with many updraughts, the falling ice/water may enter another updraught and so be carried upwards once more giving the opportunity for further growth (this process can be repeated many times). For example, examination of large hail stones will show

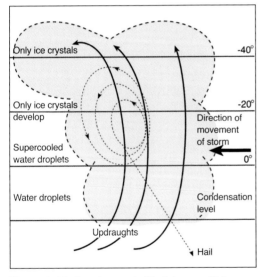

Figure 8.16 *Development of hailstones within a cumulonimbus cloud.*

many 'shells', as layers have progressively built up.

A thunderstorm can also be considered as a very efficient electrical generator even though the exact electrical mechanism is not known. Fields of 100 kV/m to 400 kV/m develop within the storm, a positive charge at the top, a negative charge towards the bottom of the cloud and an induced positive area on the ground immediately below the cloud. It may well have been this 'build up' under the cloud that affected Bill Cooper aboard his steel ketch just before she was struck by lightning (see Chapter 16).

Once a critical field strength has been generated (1,000,000 kV/m) a lightning discharge takes place, temporarily neutralising the field, but build-up is immediately recommenced as long as the cell is still active. The lightning stroke can be cloud to cloud, either within the same cloud or to an adjacent cloud; or cloud to ground, ground in this case being either land or sea.

A ground stroke (land or sea) is initiated by a 'stepped leader'. This is a surge of electrons that move downwards at about 50m (164ft) per microsecond, and after a pause of about 50 microseconds, a second step takes place, this sequence being repeated until the leader

Below: A thunderstorm over East Falkland viewed from Pebble Island. Although the main storm was 48–64km (30–40 miles) to the east, on flying some 80.4km (50 miles) south-east to Goose Green, the last 24km (15 miles) were through hail. Note the effect of the stronger southerly wind towards the top of the cloud, producing the typical anvil head.
Photo: Richard Ebling

A fleet of yachts at the Grenada Sailing Festival seem to be in the path of a squall. Photo: Onne van der Wal/Bluegreen

Right: Waterspout off Guadeloupe Island. Photo: Christian Février/Bluegreen

reaches the ground. A charge will then move rapidly upwards along the path taken by the leader. After about 0.01 second another stroke occurs. (Up to 30 or 40 strokes have been observed in the same channel.) Cloud to cloud strokes also consist of a stepped leader and a return stroke.

Whilst the strength and direction of local winds generated by air being drawn into a thunderstorm will be a combination of both the in-flowing air and the pre-existing wind, the cold downdraught wind will be blowing out from the storm, arriving as a chilly squall with a sudden increase in speed and change of direction, undercutting the surrounding air in the same manner as a cold front.

Tornadoes and waterspouts

Strong updraughts are also needed for tornadoes. This time the updraught is also rotating, initially at an altitude somewhere between 3,000m (10,000ft) and 6,000m (20,000ft). As the rotation increases, the local pressure gradient across the rotating core, and the local centrifugal force about the core, come into balance, and the system is now called a

meso-cyclone. By this time most if not all of the flow is drawn in at its lower end, and this in turn extends the rotating core lower and lower until it reaches the surface.

Near the surface, however, friction prevents the balance between the local centrifugal force and the local pressure gradient, and so air streams in towards the centre. The funnel cloud that extends from the cloud base is mainly condensation caused by the decreasing pressure but if it extends to near the surface, spray will be swept up over the sea and dust and debris will be swept up over land.

Strong or violent tornadoes are thankfully only found over land, when theoretically a maximum speed of 313 knots is possible. Weak tornadoes may also form beneath the rapidly growing cloud that develops over a gust front – perhaps around the fringe of a thunderstorm where funnel clouds and waterspouts may occasionally be seen.

In conclusion, if professional forecasters are not 100 per cent accurate, then amateurs with fewer facilities are unlikely to do better. Nevertheless, if information is available, it is good to have the knowledge to be able to interpret such information correctly, and very satisfying too.

9 Waves

Professor Sheldon Bacon

Introduction

A yacht is far from land, becalmed on a glassy sea; and then the wind appears. What now happens to the surface of the sea? If the wind were a perfectly steady and uniform airflow and the sea surface were perfectly flat and smooth there would be no waves generated. The friction between air and sea would drive a current in the sea, but some irregularity in the wind is needed to disturb an initially smooth sea surface to begin to generate waves.

The real wind is gusty, blustery and turbulent; there is an atmospheric boundary layer about 100 metres (328ft) high above the sea surface within which the air flow is directly affected by the presence of the sea surface, which induces turbulence on scales from millimetres to tens of metres (also, the air/sea temperature difference can induce circulation in the wind to over a kilometre above the surface). The turbulence is carried along by the overall flow of the wind, and it is this turbulence which starts up the wave motion on the sea. This is the initial phase of wave growth, and it is relatively slow.

Once there are some waves present, a very rapid (in fact exponential) phase of wave growth takes place: the more waves there are, the rougher is the sea surface, so the more turbulence is generated in the wind, which produces still more waves, and so on. However, this process cannot continue forever. For any given wind speed, low or high, a state of saturation is reached when energy input to the waves by the wind is balanced by dissipation of energy from the wavefield, either by waves travelling out of the generation region, or by breaking. The exponential growth phase does not tail off to the steady state, however; it gets carried away and for a short time, energy is pumped into the waves which the waves cannot hold. This is called overshoot, and it can be dangerous for yachts because the wave field will have to lose energy by wave breaking at a greater rate than during the saturation phase.

Ultimately, the sea state reaches a steady state which will not change until the wind changes its speed and/or direction. If the wind should increase further, the waves will continue to grow; if it decreases, dissipation will remove more energy than the new lower wind speed is injecting, and the waves will become lower. If there is a change in direction, potentially the most dangerous possibility in extreme conditions, a new sea will develop on top of the declining old one resulting in a cross-sea, and it will develop rapidly since the sea is already rough and the wind turbulent.

With the passing of a wave, water particles travel in nearly circular paths. At the surface, the diameter of the circles is the crest-to-trough height of the wave. At the top of the crest, the water is travelling straight forwards; at the bottom of the trough, straight back. At some point on the front and rear faces of the

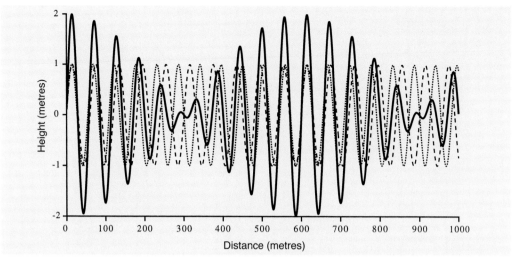

Figure 9.1 *This is a demonstration of the formation of wave groups by the addition of similar waves. In this example there are two basic waves, one of length 54m (177ft) crest-to-crest (dotted) and the other 60m (197ft) crest-to-crest (dashed); they are both 2m (7ft) high crest-to-trough. The height of the resulting wave (solid line) varies between 4m (13ft) crest-to-trough and zero. It is made of waves at the average length of the two basic waves 57m (187ft) wrapped in an envelope whose length depends on the difference between the basic waves: the smaller the difference, the longer the groups made by the envelope.*

wave, the water travels straight up and straight down. The water is also in motion below the surface, to a depth which depends on the length of the wave. Consider, for example, a 20-metre (66ft) long wave: at 5 metres (16.4ft) depth (25 per cent of the wavelength), the particle speeds are 20 per cent of their surface values and at 20 metres depth (one wavelength), only 0.1 per cent. This becomes very important in regions of shoal water: if there is sea bed in the way at a depth where the wave is trying to influence water motion, the wave can feel the bottom.

There is a unique connection between the length, period and speed of a wave, which can take any height, but for any one length of wave, there is only one possible speed and one possible period. Long waves travel faster than short waves (in deep water), so if many waves all of different lengths are produced in one place, which occurs during a storm, the longer waves which are generated will travel out of the area of the storm faster than the shorter ones. This is the origin of swell: fast-moving, long waves which may arrive in advance of an approaching storm. Wave shape changes as the wave becomes steeper: long, low swell

waves are rounded and vertically symmetrical (sinusoidal), but as steepness increases they become asymmetrical: more peaked at the crest and flat in the trough (trochoidal).

If two waves of similar lengths are added, another important phenomenon arises, that of wave grouping. If the crest of one coincides with the crest of the other (or a trough with a trough), the resulting height is the sum of the two, but if a crest coincides with a trough, the two waves cancel. The single wave resulting from the addition of two looks different: there is now an envelope around the short-wave basic wave train which groups the individual waves into 'packets'. This is illustrated in Fig 9.1 which shows two waves of the same height but slightly (10 per cent) different lengths added. Now the two waves travel at different speeds according to their lengths: the longer one faster than the shorter. This will cause the envelope to travel forwards as the crests and troughs move in and out of phase, so that the envelope has a forwards velocity of its own called the group velocity. This is related to the difference in speed between the two waves, so the envelope can move quite slowly forwards while within each resultant group, the individual waves rise at the back, move forwards through the group and finally disappear at the front of the group. This can be seen happening within ships' wakes, for example.

Some of the basics of wave growth, propagation and decay have been presented. The following sections consider wave height prediction, global wave climate and extreme waves.

Wave prediction

Here is a recipe for a reasonably accurate wave height prediction. If a quick estimate is required, skip parts (1) to (5) below and go straight to (6), which will at worst result in an over-estimate.

Wave height depends (amongst other things) on wind speed, fetch (distance upwind to 'where the wind starts' – either the coast or the far side of an approaching weather system) and duration (length of time the wind has been blowing). If the wind blows at the same speed in the same direction for long enough, the waves will stop growing and will have become fully developed; so we proceed to treat three cases: the growing fetch-limited sea, the growing duration-limited sea, and the fully-developed sea.

Accordingly, there are three decision graphs for deciding which case applies, and three prediction graphs for providing the estimate of wave height for the relevant case. This is how they work.

1. First establish your 'case': decide on the wind speed (in knots), fetch (in nautical miles) and duration (in hours). Call these values W, F and D. Fig 9.2 shows limiting duration as a function of wind speed and fetch, and it provides the answer to the first question: is the case duration-limited or fetch-limited? Find what duration on Fig 9.2 corresponds to W and F. If D is greater than this value, the case is fetch-limited, so go to (2) below. If D is less than this value, the case is duration-limited, so go to (3) below.

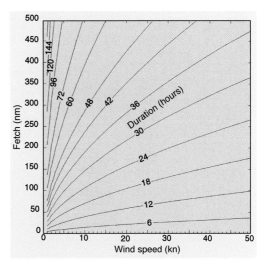

Figure 9.2 *First decision graph. Given a known situation described by wind speed, fetch and duration, use this graph to decide whether the case is fetch-limited or duration-limited.*

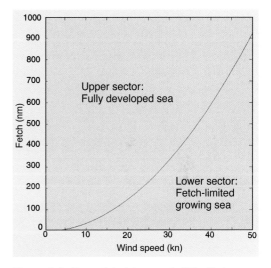

Figure 9.3 *Second decision graph. If the first decision graph has shown that fetch-limiting is relevant, use this graph to decide whether the sea is really fetch-limited or actually fully developed.*

2. Is the case really fetch-limited, or is the sea fully-developed? Turn to Fig 9.3. Find what sector of the plot wind speed W and fetch F fall into. If the sea is a fetch-limited and growing, go to (4) below. If the sea is fully-developed, go to (6).

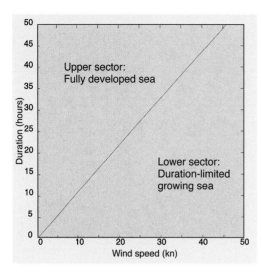

Figure 9.4 *Third decision graph. If the first decision graph has shown that duration-limiting is relevant, use this graph to decide whether the sea is really duration-limited or actually fully developed.*

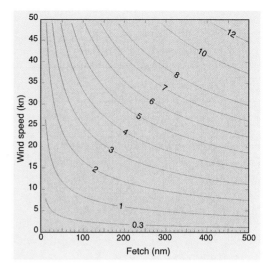

Figure 9.5 *First prediction graph. The decision graphs have led to the conclusion that the sea is fetch-limited and growing. Use this graph to predict wave height (Hs, metres) given fetch and wind speed.*

3. Is the case really duration-limited, or is the sea fully-developed? Turn to Fig 9.4. Find what sector of the plot wind speed W and duration D fall into. If the sea is duration-limited and growing, go to (5) below. If the sea is fully-developed, go to (6).

4. Fetch-limited growing sea: use Fig 9.5 to predict wave height for fetch F and wind speed W.

5. Duration-limited growing sea: use Fig 9.6 to predict wave height for duration D and wind speed W.

6. Fully-developed sea: use Fig 9.7 to predict wave height for wind speed W.

Here is a worked example. Say you are in the North Atlantic, 483km (300 miles) from the east coast of America, and you anticipate 25 knots of wind from the west to last for 24 hours. The limiting duration from Fig 9.2 is 36 hours. Our case (24 hours) is less than this, so proceed to Fig 9.4, from which we see that 25 knots for 24 hours is in the duration-limited growing sea sector. Finally looking

at Fig 9.6, we get a wave height of about 4 metres for our case.

Of course this is not the full story. Rates of decay are less easy to compute, if weather is easing. Shallow water effects come into play when the water depth is less than half the wave length. For waves of 5–10 second period (typical open-ocean values), meaning 50–150 metre (164–492ft) wavelength, water depths of 25–75 metres (82–246ft) and less will begin to affect the behaviour of the waves. They will become steeper until eventually they break, usually in the very shallow water near a beach called the surf zone, but in very severe weather (very high/long waves), they can break over offshore banks. Waves can also be made steeper or less steep by running into or away from a current. This is commonly seen in coastal waters over tidal cycles, but is also relevant for strong offshore currents like the Gulf Stream or the Kuroshio, which are notorious for their steep confused seas whenever the waves run against the current. Swell, which will increase the average wave height just by being around, also slightly increases the growth rate of waves in the presence of wind.

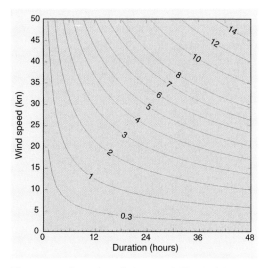

Figure 9.6 *Second prediction graph. The decision graphs have led to the conclusion that the sea is duration-limited and growing. Use this graph to predict wave height (Hs, metres) given duration and wind speed.*

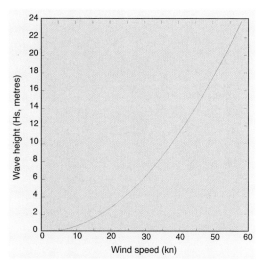

Figure 9.7 *Third prediction graph. The decision graphs have led to the conclusion that the sea is fully developed. Use this graph to predict wave height (Hs, metres) given wind speed.*

A global tour

This section will describe the global wave climate as measured between 2010 and 2014 by the European Space Agency's CryoSat-2 satellite. The instrument used is the Radar Altimeter, which, from a height of 700km (435 miles), is able to measure the sea surface wave height to an accuracy of a centimetre or so, comparable to the best surface-based (ships and buoys) instruments.

Shown in Figs 9.8–9.15 are global, seasonal, significant wave heights, in metres. Significant wave height is a scientific measure close to what an observer would estimate visually, and is denoted by the abbreviation Hs. The four seasons are defined as: December–January–February (northern hemisphere winter, and southern summer); March–April–May (northern spring, southern autumn); June–July–August (northern summer, southern winter); and September–October–November (northern autumn, southern spring). Figs 9.8–9.11 show averages, and Figs 9.12–9.15 show maxima, where 'maximum' means the highest Hs recorded over the measurement period of 2010–14. The distributions of the averages are

smooth because they contain a large number of measurements. In contrast, the distributions of maxima appear less regular, because they are essentially registering the response of waves to individual, severe weather systems, the imprints of which remain discernible. For any location and any season, the measured maximum Hs is roughly double the average.

Ocean surface waves are caused by winds, so to interpret these figures, we require a picture of global atmospheric pressure. Low pressure occurs at the equator (the Doldrums), high pressure about 30° north and south latitude (the 'Horse Latitudes'), low pressure about 60° north and south latitude (Sub-Polar Lows), and finally the polar highs. Strong winds blow between these alternating belts of high and low pressure, their direction deflected by the rotation of the Earth, and are well known: the Trade Winds between the equator and 30° (NE trades in the northern hemisphere, SE in the southern); between 30° and 60°, the northern hemisphere south-westerlies and the southern hemisphere north-westerlies (the Roaring Forties); and between 60° and the pole, south-easterlies off the Antarctic, and north-easterlies off the Arctic. How do the waves conform to this scheme?

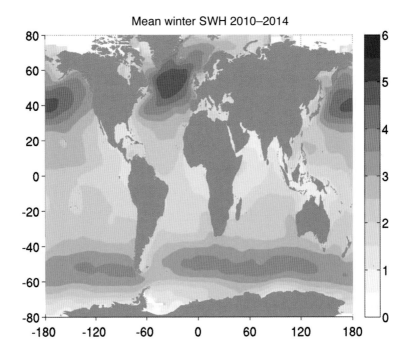

Figure 9.8 *Global mean for December–January–February significant wave height (metres).*

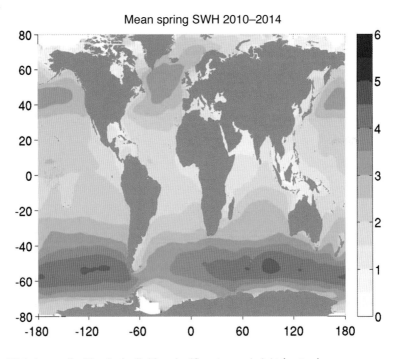

Figure 9.9 *Global mean for March–April–May significant wave height (metres).*

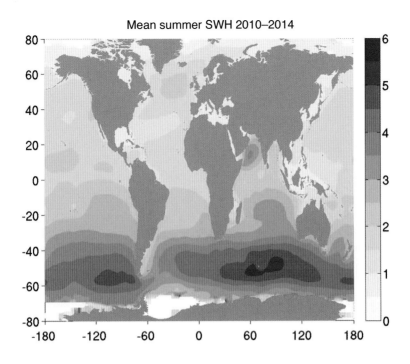

Figure 9.10 *Global mean for June–July–August significant wave height (metres).*

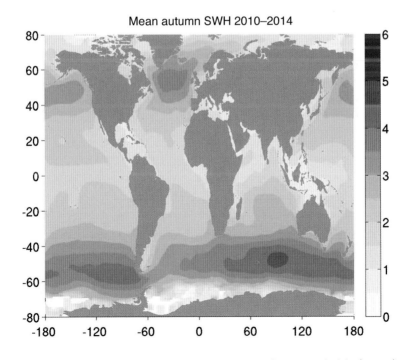

Figure 9.11 *Global mean for September–October–November significant wave height (metres).*

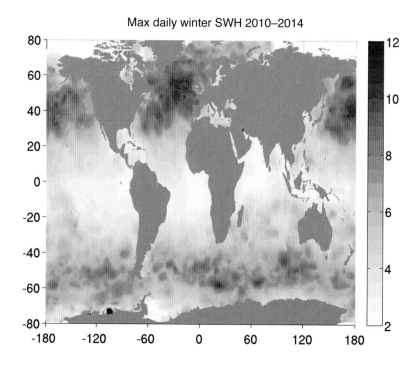

Figure 9.12 *Global maximum (December–January–February) significant wave height (metres).*

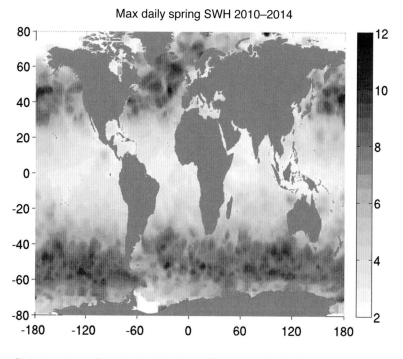

Figure 9.13 *Global maximum (March–April–May) significant wave height (metres).*

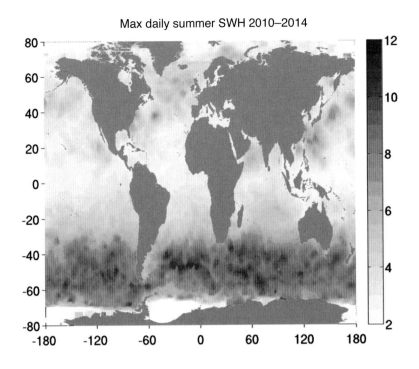

Figure 9.14 *Global maximum (June–July–August) significant wave height (metres).*

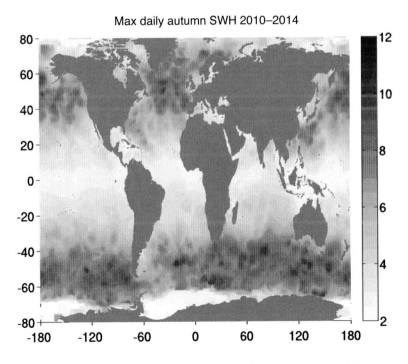

Figure 9.15 *Global maximum (September–October–November) significant wave height (metres).*

There are some obvious features in these figures. The northern winter appears as rough seas in the North Atlantic and North Pacific from about 35°N in both oceans and continues up past Iceland in the Atlantic. Average wave heights in the northern deep ocean winter are in excess of 5 metres (16.4ft), with hardly a trace left in the summer. The southern winter appears as a great belt of rough seas extending from about 35°S to close to the Antarctic continent in about 65–70°S. In great contrast to the northern hemisphere however, in the southern summer, the seas don't reduce nearly so much: from over 5 metres (16.4ft) to 3–4 metres (10–13ft). In further contrast, the equatorial Atlantic and Pacific are relatively placid much of the time. The calms under the Horse Latitudes show up clearly in the North Atlantic, less clearly in the North Pacific, and not at all obviously in the southern hemisphere, where the seasonal advance and retreat of the Roaring Forties sends waves northwards beyond 20°S.

Plainly there is much more to the story beyond the simple 'banded' model, and the most significant missing ingredient is land. Land soaks up and gives out heat much faster than the sea, both on timescales of a day and of a year. Where there is no (or little) land, the sea has a moderating effect on the wind regime, so that the degree of variation between summer and winter is smoothed out. This applies in the Southern Ocean wind belt (the Roaring Forties). The great land masses of the northern hemisphere cause the reverse to happen: changes between seasons are amplified, particularly in that the northern summer is a lot calmer than the southern summer.

Land has other effects on the sea. The figures show the effect of sheltering. Enclosed seas are much calmer on average than the open ocean: look at the Caribbean, the Mediterranean, the Baltic, the seas of the East Indies, and others. As well as the generally short fetch in enclosed seas, they get little or no swell, and the presence of swell promotes wave growth (as well as contributing to the total wave height). There are shadow zones 'behind' Iceland, the Hawaiian Islands, New Zealand, and, very noticeably, east of southern Argentina over a thick slice of the South Atlantic.

Probably the most significant large-scale effect of land on conditions at sea is the monsoon (the word 'monsoon' derives from the Arabic for season). In the northern summer, the Asian land mass heats up, creating an enormous low pressure area centred near the Himalayas. Winds blow around it anticlockwise, and it affects most of Asia, from the equatorial Indian Ocean, past the China Sea to the seas around Japan. In the northern winter, everything reverses: the cold generates a continental high (this centred over Mongolia), the winds blow clockwise, etc. On the figures, the clearest trace of the

View of a small freshwater loch in Uig, Isle of Lewis, on 8 October 1995. The fetch was 183m (600ft) and the wind was south to south-west, gusting 61–78 knots. Photo: Murray Macleod

The Swan 82 Nikata *pounds her way through big waves in the Bass Strait.*
Photo: Carlo Borlenghi/DPPI

waves caused by monsoon winds is in the northern summer in the Arabian Sea, where the south-west monsoon is strong.

Extreme waves

It's useful to think about three sorts of extreme (meaning very high) waves. Firstly, those which crop up in the normal course of events, which we'll call 'normal extremes'; secondly, those caused by rather unusual circumstances which we understand, in principle, and we'll call 'unusual extremes'; and thirdly, those which we might truly call 'freaks', whose existence is shadowy, related through rather terrifying anecdotes but (as yet) not conclusively described or explained scientifically. We'll consider them in order.

Normal extremes

Time is an important factor when thinking about extremes proper. Referring back to Figs 9.8 to 9.11, remember that they show monthly averages. In any ordinary month, there is likely to be a day that is double the average. Now, thinking about individual waves rather than averages: for a given Hs, in any three hour period the most likely highest individual wave will be about twice Hs. The longer you look, the higher the likely highest wave. Engineers like

to use the 50-year return height as an offshore design parameter. This means the highest Hs seen on average once in fifty years. In an enclosed or semi-enclosed sea like the North Sea, this might be 6 or 8 metres (20 or 26ft). In the open ocean the 50-year return value of Hs is over 20 metres (65.6ft) for the North Atlantic, when the highest individual wave might be over 40 metres (131ft). Extremes, and waves intermediate in height between average and extreme, and waves lower than average, can all occur for a given Hs because of the shifting relationship between all the different component waves of different lengths in any sea state, and all these 'ordinary' statistics are quite well measured and well understood.

Unusual extremes

Very large waves can result from well-understood combinations of conditions, and some examples follow.

The Agulhas Current region off South Africa seems to be unique both in its reputation for high, steep waves and deep troughs ('holes') in damaging and sinking ships, and in the combination of oceanographic, meteorological and even orographic features which combine to produce those conditions. There are the long east-going waves propagating out of the Roaring Forties; they run into the strong Agulhas Current itself (similar in strength and

127

Waves reaching about 18m (60ft) were experienced in the Southern Ocean. Les Powles found that his self-steering gear worked even in extreme wind speeds. Photo: Les Powles

character to the Gulf Stream and Kuroshio, reaching up to 4 or 5 knots) running south-west and west on the east and south coasts of South Africa; coastal lows (see Chapter 7) influenced by the presence of the Karoo plateau (over 1,000m/3,281ft high) and the Drakensberg (over 3,000m/9,843ft high) can add more strong winds; and the physical effects of wave trapping and focusing caused by meanders and rings in the Agulhas, on scales of many tens or hundreds of miles add further to the confusion.

Tropical revolving storms (typhoons and hurricanes) cause localised wave conditions rather different from the background average. They originate up to about 30° away from the equator, and if they move more than about 40° from the equator, they turn into 'ordinary' extra-tropical depressions. For example, the West Indies and North Atlantic have about 9 per year; the North-west Pacific, including the South China Sea, gets about 30 per year. The worst of the strong winds (above Force 8) and resulting high seas tend to be confined to a radius of about 100nm of the centre of the storm. Individual waves have been observed under such weather systems in the North-west Pacific, east of Japan, of around 20m (65.6ft) height.

Within this class of examples, we might also consider tsunamis. The Japanese word *tsunami* was borrowed to replace 'tidal wave' (they have no connection with tides), and it refers to very

long (and hence very fast) waves produced by marine geological activity: volcanic eruptions, undersea earthquakes, and the like. Tsunami wavelengths are around 100nm, with 10 to 20 minutes between crests; they travel at speeds of hundreds of knots. Some particularly notable examples are the waves produced by the Lisbon earthquake of 1704 and the explosion of Krakatoa in 1883. In the latter case we know that the waves crossed the Pacific Ocean in 12 hours, travelling at 300 knots. More recently, the 2004 Indian Ocean tsunami, caused by the Sumatra-Andaman subsea earthquake, was of enormous destructive power. Even so, the open-ocean tsunami wave height was less than 1 metre. It was when the waves came ashore that they reached heights of over 20m (65.6ft) in places. These waves are hardly noticeable in the open ocean. They acquire their destructive power by steepening and increasing height as they run into shallow water.

Freak waves

We also sometimes hear of 'rogue' or 'freak' waves. These are well-used terms in the popular press and in broadcast media, and it is worth wondering, whenever the term is employed, whether what is *really* meant is simply 'very large' waves. It is also worth emphasising that, in the strict sense employed here, freak waves

These 8m (26ft) waves were found about 1.6nm off the city of Bayona in north-west Spain. They were breaking where the seabed shelves to between 100 to 30m (328–98ft) depth and could possibly capsize a craft of 24m (80ft). Photo: Hugo Montgomery-Swan

are very, very rare. For this reason, once we exclude the classes of extreme waves described previously, little remains: anecdotal evidence, scary stories and damaged ships. This does not mean that we're dismissing freak waves, because the anecdotes have a persuasive consistency. However, because they are so rare, they are seldom encountered. The 'Draupner Wave', measured from the Norwegian oil rig of that name in 1995, remains the 'poster child' for these rare events, with a crest-to-trough height

of 26 metres (85ft). A second example emerged from measurements made in 1988 in the Sea of Japan, called the 'Yura Wave', named after the Japanese fishing port, of over 10 metres (32.8ft) height, crest-to-trough. These are true 'freaks' in the sense discussed here: individual, very high waves which stand out clearly from the lower 'background' sea state. Oceanographers are still at an early stage in developing theories to explain how, where and when they might appear, but for now, explanations are speculative.

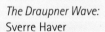

The Draupner Wave:
Sverre Haver

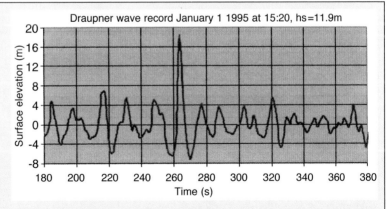

The Draupner oil rig platform is located between the southern tip of Norway and Scotland in the North Sea. On 1 January 1995 the effect of two lows combined to bring strong northerly winds that brought about a significant wave height of 11.9m (39ft). Within this overall pattern a wave of maximum height 15m (49ft) might be expected, but the possible freak wave shown here had a height of nearly 26m (85ft). This may be compared to the maximum significant wave height in the Fastnet storm of 1979 of 7.8m (25ft) and those of the English Channel in 1987.

10 Seasickness

Dr Ed Reeves

Almost anyone who has put to sea will have encountered seasickness, either as a sufferer or a witness. Perhaps a well-planned sea passage with a strong crew became more arduous as the number of healthy crewmembers gradually reduced; or a day sail with a non-sailing guest whose initial joie de vivre was overtaken by the quiet yawning and loss of colour that typically precedes the onset of nausea.

It is no surprise that the word 'nausea' itself derives from the Greek word *nausia* meaning ship-sickness, for seasickness dates back as long as man has travelled by water. The complex human balance organ (the vestibular system of the inner ear) evolved over billions of years to cope with humans as self-propelled animals. This balance system has not yet had the time to adapt further to the relatively recent arrival of other forms of propulsion such as boats, cars and space travel. Seasickness is the commonest form of motion sickness, a major nuisance to recreational sailors and even more so to occupational seafarers.

The role of the vestibular system in seasickness was first suspected in the late 1800s when it was noted that people suffering from deafness at an early age were largely immune to seasickness. Conversely anyone with normal hearing is susceptible given the relevant conditions, to which end it is reported that nearly 100 per cent of liferaft occupants get seasick. The oft-heard claim that 'I never get seasick' might be more cautiously worded 'I have never yet been exposed to conditions that made me seasick.'

History reveals some surprising sufferers, not least Admiral Lord Nelson who, just a year before the Battle of Trafalgar, wrote: 'I am ill every time it blows hard and nothing but my enthusiastic love for the profession keeps me one hour at sea.' Charles Darwin was troubled by recurrent bouts of seasickness on his voyage on HMS *Beagle*. Whilst they both achieved great feats despite their illness, the Duke of Medina Sidonia, who commanded the Spanish Armada in 1588, was plagued by sickness which in all likelihood hampered his ability to lead effectively.

Of course there is wide variation in susceptibility to seasickness, some of which is predictable and some not. In practice, around one third of people will suffer to a sufficient degree that they like to take precautions prior to sailing, and most of them (but not all) will 'get their sea-legs' after a few days. Young children under the age of two years are immune, while from the age of two to twelve years children are the most likely to feel sick. Women, especially during pregnancy and menstruation, are more prone than men to become ill during a voyage, and Asian races are also more at risk of seasickness than non-Asian races. If you are thinking of taking a pet on a cruise, remember that animals share a very similar vestibular system and are also vulnerable to seasickness.

There has been much research into the cause of and treatments for seasickness, leading to a range of ways to try to ameliorate its effects. The mere fact that a range of strategies is required probably gives the clue that no single

cure has been found. However, to have the best chance of warding off seasickness it makes sense to develop an understanding of how and why it occurs.

Nausea and vomiting serve a protective purpose for humans – by removing unwanted contents from the stomach. This mechanism provides a defence against the ingestion of poisons, or foods that have gone off. In other words nausea and vomiting are normal and important physiological processes. The control centre for the process of vomiting is an area in the brainstem known as the vomiting centre.

The vomiting centre can be triggered by a wide variety of different stimuli. For example, when a poison is detected in the blood stream or the gut, messages are sent to the vomiting centre, which then activates the vomiting response. These messages are transferred to the vomiting centre by the release of 'neurotransmitters' such as histamine or acetylcholine. The vomiting centre can also be triggered by other stimuli such as pain, fear, smells and most importantly, for our purposes, by the imbalance associated with motion sickness.

Balance is achieved by the brain interpreting information from three main sources: eyes, muscles and joints, and the vestibular organs in the inner ear. When there is a mismatch between the information that the brain is receiving from these sources it results in a feeling of imbalance. This is sometimes referred to as the 'sensory conflict theory'. So for example, sitting in the cockpit, feeling cold and wet and perhaps slightly anxious,

the vomiting centre is primed. All it now takes is messages from the eyes (staring at the cockpit floor) to conflict with messages from the vestibular organ in the ears (which are detecting the three dimensional rolling and pitching of the yacht) and the vomiting centre is triggered. The result is inevitable.

Prevention

Thorough preparation goes a long way to preventing seasickness. The first aim is to reduce the factors that lower the threshold for seasickness, including: tiredness; dehydration; getting cold and wet; fear and anxiety; smells; lack of mental stimulation; reading from screens, charts or almanacs.

It pays to be well rested and nourished prior to and during a voyage (remembering here the role of establishing a watch system to ensure everyone aboard remains rested). Whilst alcohol and food excess are best avoided, a light meal of mixed carbohydrates and protein may reduce the tendency to seasickness. Eating and drinking small amounts frequently is a helpful strategy and so it is a good idea to have readily available snacks and water bottles. For snacks, saltines (author's favoured choice being Ritz

High speeds in heavy seas induce violent, irregular, impact motion in the boat, further exaggerating the effects of the sea state. Simply slowing the boat or changing its orientation to the sea will often achieve a surprisingly large increase in comfort. Photo: Safehaven Marine

biscuits) and ginger (of which more later) both have their supporters. Hot meals are important for crew morale and nourishment, but planning for easy meals avoids prolonged time in the galley and smells that can be nauseating to those struggling with seasickness.

An essential part of preparation is choosing appropriate clothing. Being warm and dry increases resistance to the effects of seasickness and avoids the need to change from cold and wet clothing if nausea should develop. The three common enemies of a safe and happy passage, namely cold, fatigue and seasickness, will each make the other two worse. Cold and fatigue will exacerbate the nausea.

Fear and anxiety affect seasickness which perhaps explains why the inexperienced are afflicted more than old salts. Apprehension dulled by alcohol is a bad combination. If novice sailors have confidence in the skipper and are given a specific simple task as their own, then much misery can be alleviated.

Time spent focused on reading, navigating or staring at electronic screens risks aggravating seasickness. The eyes will be sending a message to the brain of a relative lack of movement, while the vestibular organ will be detecting movement. Good preparatory passage planning

enables this to be minimised for seasick-prone navigators. By contrast, closing one's eyes removes one of the confusing signals and can help prevent the onset of nausea.

Keeping the mind active distracts the higher centres of the brain from the sensory mismatch that lies at the root of seasickness. Skippers, who carry the ultimate responsibility for the boat, are often less seasick than the crew. Conversation, singing, word games, 'I spy' all have good anecdotal track records. The classic prevention strategy is to take the helm. This combines having a sense of control with the need to concentrate and to look at the horizon, and can have a dramatic effect on preventing or relieving seasickness. When looking at the horizon, the messages from eyes and vestibular organs are less in conflict, and so this in itself can be an effective strategy.

'Getting your sea-legs' is an expression that describes a process called habituation or adaptation. Repeated and increasing exposure to the motion of a boat provides the opportunity for the brain to adapt its response to sensory conflict. Unfortunately, 'sea-legs' are quickly lost again if exposure to boat motion ceases (medical justification for more sailing being good for your health?!).

There are of course multiple reasons for early reduction in sail area as wind increases, not least of which is the improvement of a yacht's motion and the resulting beneficial effect on seasickness. Another technique, to reduce the amount of movement that the confused brain is struggling to interpret, is to seek the spot on the boat with least motion i.e. near the keel. Lying supine (face upwards) on the cabin floor above the keel, with eyes closed, has much going for it.

Non-drug treatment

Ginger has a good reputation for alleviation of nausea. There is evidence of its effectiveness such as a trial involving eighty Danish Naval Cadets who were given either one gram of ginger or a placebo. The cadets given ginger suffered significantly less vomiting and sweating than the placebo group. Another study found ginger to be more effective at reducing motion sickness than the drug diphenhydramine when participants were put in a rotating chair. To paint a fuller picture, it must also be mentioned that some other studies have been less conclusive about the benefits of ginger. However, ginger is readily available and can be easily consumed. Choosing a dose is imprecise but around half a gram of dried ginger seems to be the consensus, taken about half an hour before setting sail. In practical terms quarter to half a teaspoon of dried ginger mixed with a cup of hot or cold water makes a good drink, or better still use about an inch of peeled and chopped fresh ginger root. Ginger capsules, candied ginger, ginger biscuits (5 or 6 biscuits) or ginger ale are other easy forms of ginger that can be kept in the yacht's stores.

Another popular non-drug treatment is applying pressure at the Nei Guan (P6) acupressure point. This is located three fingerbreadths above the wrist (on the same side as the palm of the hand) between the two prominent tendons. Most chemists sell a product called 'Sea-Band' which comprises a pair of elastic wristbands with plastic studs that apply pressure at the correct point. Whilst

Ginger, in various forms, is the most popular non-drug remedy for seasickness.

clear evidence of their effectiveness in reducing motion sickness is lacking, they certainly have many supporters who swear by them. There have been studies which demonstrate a reduction in nausea and vomiting in post-operative and chemotherapy patients using acupuncture.

Electronic wristbands purport to work by a similar mechanism by sending a variable electric current into the wrist at the Nei Guan acupoint.

Drug treatment

A visit to the pharmacy for motion sickness pills can be a confusing experience. Confronted by an array of options it is all too easy to go for the best branding, rather than making an educated decision on what to buy. Forearmed with a little knowledge, a somewhat more rational choice can be made. The drugs Phenergan, Avomine, Sominex and promethazine are for example all the same... but be warned, in the US Sominex is the market name for a different drug, diphenhydramine (which in the UK is sold as Nytol). Confused?

Rule one in choosing drug treatments is therefore to look for the name of the active ingredient rather than the trade name.

It is much more effective to prevent seasickness by taking medication in advance

Generic (drug) name	Brand names	Usual adult dose	When to start taking medication
Anticholineric			
* Hyoscine hydrobromide	Kwells Kwells Kids Joy-rides Scopoderm patch	300mcg every 6 hours (maximum 3 doses in 24 hours) Patch releases 1mg over 72 hours	20–30mins before travel Note: tablets chewed or sucked
Anti-histamines (listed in order of least to most sedating)			
Cyclizine	Marzine (USA) Marezine (USA)	50mg three times daily	1–2 hours before travel
Meclizine	Dramamine less drowsy (USA) Bonine (USA)	25mg four times daily	1 hour before travel
* Cinnarizine	Stugeron	30mg (2 tablets) before travel then 15mg every 8 hours as required	2 hours before travel
Dimenhydrinate	Dramamine (USA)	50–100mg four times daily	½–1 hour before travel
Diphenhydramine	Benadryl (USA)	Not marketed in UK for motion sickness	
* Promethazine	Phenergan Avomine Sominex	25mg every 8 hours as required (also available in some countries as a rectal suppository)	Night before travel

Beware of different brand names in different countries.

* = commonly used treatments in UK.

of travelling, than to wait for the symptoms to start and then try to treat seasickness. To this end one should carefully read the instructions to see how long prior to a voyage the medication should be taken, as this ranges from 20 minutes

A well-stocked first aid kit has a variety of anti-seasickness drugs.

before travelling (e.g. hyoscine) to the night before (e.g. promethazine). The commonest error when taking drugs for seasickness is to take them too late.

Many of the drugs used for seasickness also have a place in the market as over the counter sleeping pills. Whilst this might be useful for children on a long passage, it is certainly not a great deal of help for the night watch-keeper. In fact, the choice of drug treatment is a delicate balance between effectiveness at preventing nausea and sickness versus side effects. Other common side effects include dry mouth and blurred vision, and in rare circumstances hallucinations and confusion.

In order to make some logical decisions about which medication to use, it is useful to divide the available drugs into two groups according to how they work (which of the previously mentioned 'neurotransmitters' they predominantly block).

Hyoscine (sold in the UK as Kwells and Joy-rides) sits in a group on its own, being an anticholinergic (anti-acetylcholine) drug. It is probably the most effective drug available and works quickly, but its use tends to be limited by side effects. It does come in a popular patch preparation, called Scopoderm, which is available on prescription. The patch is placed on the skin behind the ear and slowly releases hyoscine in to the blood stream through the skin, thereby minimising the side effects. Each patch lasts for 72 hours. Care needs to be taken to wash your hands carefully after handling the patch, as inadvertently getting hyoscine in your eyes will cause pupil dilatation and inability to focus the eye.

All the other commonly used drugs belong to a group of old style (1st generation) anti-histamine medications. These differ from the newer (2nd and 3rd generation) anti-histamine medications, which are commonly used for hayfever and allergies, in that they can cross the blood-brain barrier and hence gain access to the vomiting centre. How people respond to different anti-histamines is somewhat unpredictable but loosely speaking as they

get stronger they cause more drowsiness. The standard mid-strength anti-histamine is cinnarizine (Stugeron) which for many people offers an effective balance between reducing the symptoms of seasickness and dealing with unwanted side effects. At the strongest end of the scale is promethazine which is useful for sufferers who don't mind sleeping through it all.

It is of note that MCA Merchant Shipping Notice 1768, which sets out the regulations for medical stores on coded vessels, lists cinnarizine and hyoscine as the required tablets for motion sickness, and promethazine injection as the treatment for severe motion sickness.

One way of counteracting the drowsiness that many remedies cause is to take pseudoephedrine (available over the counter as Sudafed) in a dose of 15–30mg every 4–6 hours, in combination with for example promethazine.

Due to the variable effects that drugs for motion sickness can have on different people it is sensible to 'test drive' your planned remedy on dry land prior to using it in earnest in rough seas. It should be remembered that these are potentially powerful drugs, and you should

A Jeanneau Sun Liberty 34 close reaching off Les Sables d'Olonne in fresh conditions with as much sail as can be carried. The motion in such conditions can be testing. Much could be done to ameliorate its effects. Heaving-to or reducing sail would help. Perhaps the skipper was seasick and finding it difficult to manage his boat efficiently. Most of us cruise for enjoyment not unnecessary discomfort. Notice the reefed genoa beginning to 'bag up'. Photo: Christian Février/Bluegreen

consult the pharmacist particularly if you have other medical problems such as glaucoma, high blood pressure, heart disease, epilepsy or prostate trouble.

Managing a seasick crew

It is usually quite clear to all on board when a crewmember is falling foul of seasickness. There is the uncharacteristic quietness, rapidly followed by skin pallor or even the dreaded 'green tinge'. Questioning might elicit a degree of dismissive bravado. At this stage the situation may be redeemable by putting into action some of the strategies covered so far, but perhaps the most important is to remember the safety aspect. Judgement can often by impaired and the body weakened by seasickness – a lurch to the leeward rail to vomit can become risky, so ensuring that the victim is wearing a harness and clipped on is particularly important.

At this stage involving the crewmember in some form of activity helps provide welcome distraction for the brain. Helming seems to work particularly well, probably due to the combination of looking at the horizon and concentration on the motion of the boat. A similar effect is seen in cars: how often do you hear of a car driver feeling travel-sick? When not on deck the sufferer should be helped to find a good berth in which to rest, away from the pitching movement of the bow or stern so as near amidships as possible. They should be encouraged, or helped, to get out of cold wet clothes and into a warm sleeping bag. Lying with eyes closed to reduce the conflicting visual messages, and wedged in to a snug bunk (lee cloths and bags or cushions to help reduce them from rolling around) is the optimal position. Strictly no reading as this will surely aggravate their symptoms. A bucket should be provided in case of vomiting, and regularly emptied to avoid others having to deal with a cabin smelling of vomit, which is certain to tip other vulnerable crew over the edge.

In terms of medication, anything that requires swallowing will probably no longer

work. The fastest acting drug is hyoscine (Kwells) and it is works best to chew the tablet and then let the chewed tablet sit under your tongue or against the inside of your cheek. This allows it to get absorbed through the lining of your mouth, bypassing the stomach. The same can be tried with cinnarizine (Stugeron) although it may take longer to work. Scopoderm patches also get absorbed directly in to the blood stream, but again take a few hours to work.

For many these simple actions will allow the nausea to subside. For some a quick vomit will provide a good period of relief. For a significant minority, however, the misery of seasickness is profound. The saying that 'at first you fear that you might die, and then you fear that you might not' captures how unpleasant the sensation can be. Sufferers at this more severe end of the spectrum become a danger to themselves, and need firm direction to avoid falling in to a state of hypothermia and dehydration. It is particularly important to ensure that they have adequate water to replace that lost through vomiting.

Better still than water are oral rehydration solutions (such as Dioralyte) which are readily available in all chemists. These balanced solutions provide an isotonic fluid that is easily absorbed by the stomach and replaces essential lost chemicals (particularly sodium) as well as fluid. They come in the form of tablets or sachets to mix with a specified volume of water. Taking small amounts regularly tends to work best. Since the adoption of the widespread use of oral rehydration therapy (ORT) in the 1980s many millions of lives have been saved from diarrheal illnesses such as cholera, particularly in developing countries. ORT forms one of the mainstays of treatment for gastroenteritis in any setting, and on a yacht is invaluable at preventing a crewmember with seasickness from becoming weak and dehydrated.

Fortunately making landfall usually leads to rapid and full recovery. A very small minority of unlucky people will develop 'mal de debarquement' or 'disembarkation sickness' in which a persistent sensation of motion is felt even once ashore.

11 Taking refuge in heavy weather

Peter Bruce and Richard Clifford

The old cry 'any port in a storm' is questionable from a seaman's point of view. Whilst the thought of being in port may sound attractive when being bashed around at sea during a gale, remaining at sea, or even putting to sea, may be both the safest and most comfortable option. It is probably true to say that more small craft come to harm in bad weather when in harbour, rather than at sea.

Alternatively a yacht may be in an unsatisfactory position with the wind already howling, and there may be a need to find a more secure location or even 'hurricane hole'. Deciding whether to stay put, or go to sea in the hope of finding better shelter, can be a difficult choice which will depend on local circumstances, the type of vessel and the strength of the crew.

In this chapter it is assumed that the yacht has suitable gear and deck fittings for anchoring, lying to a mooring or lying alongside and these much-debated matters will not be covered here in detail. However, it bears repeating that when taking refuge in storm conditions, there are no substitutes for good quality ground tackle, strong, carefully designed stem fittings and strong deck cleats. Whether at sea or in port, chafe and other yachts probably present the greatest hazards. Another general point is that heavy weather can be a test of communications between the steering positions and foredeck. All methods should depend upon hand or torch signals rather than voice messages, which are the first to fail when it comes on to blow, even with someone at the mast to relay messages.

When there is a forecast of bad weather or the weather deteriorates, the decision needs to be made whether to ride out the storm at sea, or to run for shelter. As with moving berth, much will depend on the strength of the crew and the ability of the yacht, the expectation of the duration and strength of the storm and the proximity to land. A look at the chart will show whether there is a suitable port that is within reach in the conditions. Staying at sea can often be uncomfortable but the safest option, using one of the tactics described elsewhere. Occasionally it is better to leave shelter and deliberately go to sea. The 10m South African yacht *Gypsy Girl* went to sea on hearing that Hurricane Ivan was approaching Grenada in 2004. Whilst Ivan caused havoc ashore, the crew had an uncomfortable few days at sea, but they had plenty of sea room and suffered no damage. Factors such as having to be in a particular place at a particular time, for example to catch a flight, must remain secondary. The safety of crew and yacht should be pre-eminent at all times.

When selecting a refuge, the primary consideration should be shelter from the seas, protection from the wind generally being a secondary consideration. Richard Clifford once spent 2½ days at anchor on the west side of the causeway joining Tarifa Island to the shore in a strong Levanter easterly (50–60 knots) and, although the wind was too powerful to

The 10m (33ft) Gypsy Girl.
Photo: Morten, Yacht *Blaartur*

of the port should be studied, especially if there is a bar, or such depth that could cause breakers. Allowance should be made for poor visibility, which is to be expected in storm conditions, and every detail noted to make the entrance easier to find. The chances are that others will have heard the same forecast and it may be most advantageous to find out in advance by telephone or radio if there is room in the harbour, whether the conditions in the harbour approaches are acceptable and where to berth. It is often useful to make a list of marks and courses, or draw a chartlet beforehand, as the situation is unlikely to allow detailed consultation of pilot books or charts during entry.

Though preparations are important, there may be times when, for safety reasons, planning for the options on arrival may be all that is possible or sensible until shelter is gained. A good start is to put life jackets on. Just in case things do not turn out quite as expected, preparations should include ensuring that the anchor is at immediate readiness for letting go, even if first choice is to go alongside or pick up a mooring. If the plan is to anchor, it is wise to prepare the second anchor and other anchoring devices such as anti-snubbing gear in advance. Clearly, if it is intended to go alongside, then lines and fenders need to be made ready.

Once at anchor with storm or hurricane force winds in prospect, decks should be cleared of gear that will fly around, cause extra windage, or be lost overboard. This could include dinghies, windsurfers, horseshoe lifebelts, sails, biminis, spray hoods, cockpit dodgers and so on. Mast stowed spinnaker poles and booms are best stowed at deck level. In strong winds a furled headsail is prone to unroll and a flogging headsail makes a fearful noise as it tears itself to pieces. If it is thought that the furled sail may be needed at short notice it may be better secured by wrapping it with the sheets and spare halyards. Otherwise it may be best to take it off, fold it and stow it below. A furled sail causes considerable windage and tends to induce sheering and this will be twice as much for yachts with a

risk launching the dinghy, the sea was flat calm. Contrastingly, in hilly areas gusts can make life unpleasant and possibly dangerous on the *lee side* of high land. For example at the mountainous Island of Rum in the Scottish Islands, if the wind is Force 7 from the west, on the west side of the island there might be gusts of 40 knots, whilst on the east side at Loch Scresort there may be gusts of 60 knots. This effect can also occur off high volcanic tropical islands particularly when the trade winds are strong. So, given the choice, it is generally better to find shelter behind low-lying land.

Another situation is when a vessel has to shelter in the lee of land where it is too deep or difficult to anchor and the vessel has to be kept in place with the use of the engine. If the bow keeps blowing off once the speed drops, it may be found that the boat may lie most comfortably *stern* to wind.

Particularly for an unfamiliar harbour, preparation is the key to making a safe entry in adverse conditions. The offshore geography

At lunchtime on 5 July 2003 a Hallberg Rassy 42 tried to enter Victoria Harbour, Dunbar, on the east Scottish coast, under power on passage from Anstruther. It was an hour before low water when there was possibly only 0.8m (2.6ft) in the harbour. There was a 2m (6ft) swell running from the north, and this was rounding the harbour mouth and running up the entrance. The yacht struck the bottom in the harbour entrance, and was driven by the surge up to Castle cliff to the right of the entrance. Both crew were rescued by hauling them up the cliff face. The yacht was a total loss.
Photos: Alastair Punton

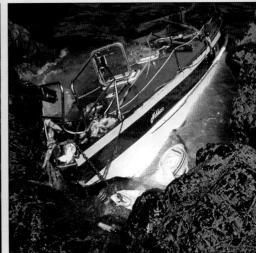

slutter double headsail system. Even with sails removed headfoils create windage and may start flying in the wind whatever tension is set up on the backstay. If the rig is prone to heavy vibration it will put the rigging fittings at risk, so it is worth providing a strop with a halyard and temporary downhaul to midway up the foil. This can be tensioned aft to the mast to dampen any vibration. When headfoils have been allowed to vibrate then it is wise to check the deck and masthead fittings after the storm has passed.

It will probably also be necessary to run a watch keeping system for the duration of the storm. Once safely in port it should not be forgotten to let next of kin and the coastguard know where the vessel is, if appropriate.

Anchoring

Anchoring is usually the best course of action, should space and holding conditions permit, as the boat is free to swing into the wind and there is no need to rely on the integrity of some unknown mooring.

A single anchor may be thought insufficient to provide the required holding power in strong conditions and two anchors are often considered advantageous in heavy weather, though trials using strain gauges suggest the load is only evenly divided momentarily, the rest of the time the load is either on one or the other. Thus the holding power is not doubled and having two anchors out may just give a false sense of security. Using two anchors off the bow with about 45° separation will help limit the tendency for the yacht to sheer about with the consequent risk of breaking the anchor out of the seabed, bearing in mind that a yacht sailing about her anchors in bad weather is employing much the same tactic that is used when trying to break out a stubborn anchor from the seabed. However, two anchors at 45° will not double the holding power.

A New Zealander, Peter Smith, who designed the Rocna anchor, has done his own research on anchoring theory and practice using all kinds of anchor. His methods have been self-tried in remote parts of the world such as Patagonia, South Georgia, the Falklands and the Antarctic and he has brought some new thinking into the technique of using modern anchors with their improved holding capability. He points out that when a yacht is anchored in 40–50 knots of wind the cable is continuously bar taut and thus, in such extreme conditions, it is the weight and area of the anchor that counts while the benefit of the catenary is mostly lost except in very deep water. Consequently, he maintains, light strong cable with a liberal scope is what should be used, in conjunction with an anchor in one size larger or more than that advocated for the boat. He does not recommend an angel aka chum, sentinel or kellet as he believes that it does not help to form a catenary much when the anchor chain is taut.

Traditionally offshore cruising yachts carry three anchors and associated gear and some even carry four. A contemporary interpretation is to have one modern heavier-than-standard anchor plus a good length of high tensile chain with another similar anchor as a back-up in case of accidentally losing the first. A third anchor might be an aluminium kedge anchor for a lunchtime stop.

Using two anchors in *tandem* on the same length of chain will give greater holding power when the system is set up and working correctly and may seem desirable in extreme weather. Yacht owners using the tandem method say they feel bolted to the seabed, though the arrangement works best in a strong wind coming from a single direction. The assembly is complex, takes time to deploy and recover and there are pitfalls for the unwary. The front anchor (tandem anchor) chain must not be attached so that it could topple the second (primary) anchor and thereby negate the primary anchor's value. For example the hole designed for the anchor buoy line in the upper front of the stock of the primary anchor may be unsuitable. If there is not an appropriate hole in the primary anchor, the chain for the tandem anchor can be attached to the chain of the primary anchor though this is not the neatest configuration. Ideally one should dive over the set up to ensure that the components are correctly deployed.

When using anchors in tandem the scope should be increased to ensure that the primary anchor is not subjected to enough vertical pull to break it out. When two anchors are laid without a dual anchor weighing system, the great weight of metal of a larger boat's gear can make recovery of the second anchor difficult. If the tandem method is used, it is important that the distance between the anchors is less than the depth of water so that, by the time the first anchor is housed at the stem fitting, the second anchor will have broken out of the seabed. A line attached between the two anchors before anchoring can be used for hoisting the second anchor and some windlasses have a winch barrel that can be operated separately from the gypsy, which will make weighing the second anchor easier.

If it is thought necessary to take out an anchor from a small vessel by dinghy under oars, or outboard motor in gale or storm conditions, it is hard and dangerous work, even when using a robust solid dinghy. Notwithstanding favourable conditions it is seldom practical for larger yachts unless a lightweight aluminium anchor is used. When taking out an anchor, the anchor and its chain should be put into the dinghy with a long line attached to the yacht, so the chain is paid out from the dinghy not the yacht. It may be preferable to lay additional anchors from the yacht by letting out more scope on the main anchor and motoring over to the drop position for the new anchor. When this has been accomplished the anchor cables should be adjusted to spread the weight appropriately.

The amount of chain required depends on the depth, bottom and available room to swing. Rope or line has its place as an anti-snubbing line and, in a suitable size, as an extension to the primary anchor rode but rope is unsuitable in rocky anchorages or when coral is present because of chafe. Few yachts carry sufficient chain to allow full scope on more than one anchor so it is likely that the second anchor will be on a combination of chain and rope. If the second anchor is modern there will be

only a small loss in holding power, though consideration should be given to chafe both from the seabed and at the stem fabrication or fairlead. Another thought is that yachts with a short length of chain with the rest being rope tend to swing about more, take up extra space and are a worry to the more conservative at anchor. In shallow water, say around 5m (16.4ft), one should have at least five times the depth and in gale or storm conditions up to eight times the depth, as chain does not allow much damping action before becoming bar taut. This results in heavy snatch loads in the chain and a good anti-snubbing device is essential in these conditions. One, or even two, snub lines attached to the chain just short of the seabed can work well provided they are led through adequately strong and chafe-free bow rollers or fairleads. Hawser-laid line with stretch such as nylon is best and in a diameter that would be used as an anchor rode. The addition of a rubber shock absorber may also ease snubbing or, failing that, simply placing a fender under the line will also help. The snub line needs to be attached to the anchor chain with either a chain hook or a rolling hitch. Though a rolling hitch will almost certainly have to be cut off after use, it is the more reliable of the two methods, as chain hooks may become detached when the load is slack. To obtain a fair lead it is usually preferable to rig the anti-snub line, or lines, through the stem head fitting, using reinforced plastic pipe to reduce chafe.

Laying out more chain i.e. increasing the scope, will increase holding power more than anything else and, if the chain is not taut, will help damp swooping movements as it is difficult to drag chain round an arc on the seabed. A good supply of nylon snubbing line is necessary as, when it has been decided to veer more cable, the old snubbing lines will need to be tied to the cable and new ones inserted. In addition, the snubbing lines become shorter every time they are cut to remove the solid rolling hitch. One should bear in mind that snubbing lines may suffer chafe on the seabed when more cable is veered out.

At the Cape Verde Islands Richard Clifford in his 10.7m (35ft) yacht had ten times the depth during a vicious 50-knot blow and still broke the 14mm anti-snubbing line. When anchoring on coral and using a rope extension, it may be worth putting a small fender or float at the join between rope and chain to float the rope clear of the abrasive coral.

One option that reduces shearing around when anchored, particularly in shallower waters of sand, shingle or mud, is to employ the anchor chain snubber as above but to continue feeding out chain overboard so that a considerable bight is formed in a heap on the seabed. This drag weight will reduce the snatching load on the anchor and provide a resistance to sideways movement.

It is easy to underestimate the forces and the amount of movement, should a sea develop. Consequently it is important to use a pin or a similar contrivance to ensure that the cable cannot jump out of the stemhead fitting as the yacht sheers and dips her bows to the seas. Stemhead fittings have even been known to break off in extreme conditions so it is wise to examine the stemhead fabrication to judge whether it needs to be beefed up and whether the working surfaces need to be made more fair. Another consideration is whether the pin is of sufficient diameter to withstand being bent when subject to the full load of the windlass. This happens after the anchor has been stowed and pinned when it is felt necessary to take up the slack in the chain to stop it slapping about. The pin can become so distorted that it cannot easily be removed, resulting in a delay at the anchorage, which may be no fun on a cold, wet, windy night. A good alternative is a rachet operated strap with stainless steel fittings that will hold the anchor firmly when back in its stowage. Smaller yachts will be able to use a short strop from the stemhead fabrication to a shackle attached to a small hole drilled in the stock at a handy position, with perhaps a snap hook at the anchor end of the strop for convenience.

Anchoring fore and aft in storm conditions is inadvisable. In particular, if the wind changes and blows strongly on the beam, this will put considerably more weight onto the chain and deck fittings and may trip one or both anchors. It is much better to let the boat face the wind, except when it is necessary to face an ocean swell coming from a different direction than the wind. In this case comfort may dictate anchoring fore and aft but then a contingency escape plan is necessary.

In wind-against-tide conditions a nasty chop may develop within an anchorage; moreover if the tidal stream is sufficiently strong, the yacht may lie across the wind. This may not place undue extra force on the anchor (or anchors) but it will be necessary to watch the anchor carefully through the turn of the tide to ensure that it resets properly. Of course neighbouring vessels may lie differently and should also be kept under observation.

The nature of some seabeds may warrant special consideration. For example, there are areas of Australia which cannot be visited without an Admiralty type anchor with the flukes ground off to a very sharp point. In some areas of Tasmania it is necessary to know that the anchor must be left to sink through silt for fifteen minutes before it will reach the good holding of the clay bottom. Anchoring in coral is a subject in itself but should be thought about before the first night in an atoll. Much can be learnt by looking at local yachts and asking around.

Once it is believed that the anchor is holding, transits should be chosen and regular checks made to ensure that the anchor is still firmly set. Transits that will remain distinguishable in unexpected weather and in darkness are best. The 'anchor watch' facility fitted to many GPS sets can be used for this purpose. If sea clutter allows, radar can also be useful both day and night, to take bearings and distances off as well as detecting other vessels dragging, hopefully in sufficient time to take avoiding action.

Once the anchor has started dragging and will not reset it should be hoisted to check if it has caught a clump of weed or other encumbrances before laying it once again. Otherwise the best remedy to prevent dragging is to let out more scope of anchor line. Running the engine ahead will take some of the weight off the anchor and reduce sheering about but

Yachts anchored at Dundas Harbour, Devon Island (74° 32' N 82° 25' W). The main wind strength was averaging 40 knots, with katabatic gusts of 60 knots. The photo was taken from Suilven, *an Oyster 47, lying in 10m (32.8ft) depth. She had a 33kg Rocna anchor out on 70m (230ft) scope of ⅜ chain with a snubber of 25mm Nylon approx 10m (32.8ft) long. Anchor cables were bar taut much of the time. Other yachts dragged, but neither of the yachts with* Suilven's *type of anchor did.*
Photo: John Andrews

it is necessary to keep the bow into the wind while running the engine, which requires considerable concentration and will be very tiring if required all night. In wild weather laying out a second anchor from the dinghy may be unacceptably hazardous, but may be possible from the yacht.

Steps taken before bad weather is apparent reduce the chances of dragging in the first place. Ensure, when positioning the anchor that it is well dug in by motoring astern, is on a generous scope and that account is taken of any expected change in wind or tide direction. As in the case of tandem anchors, if possible, it is worth diving on the anchor to ensure that it is properly dug in. There is a case for painting anchors in a striking colour so they can best be seen on the seabed but to do so properly is an elaborate process. When anchored in the tropics on poor holding ground, consideration can be given to intentionally wrapping the anchor chain around a large coral head though this action may have conservation implications these days.

Shock loads caused by snubbing or sheering are the most common causes of anchors breaking out so anti-snubbing measures and an appropriate scope are clearly important. If the yacht has a tendency to sail around her anchor it is often helpful to encourage her to remain on one tack, either by lashing the helm to one side, or leading the anchor rode slightly off centre, even from a bridle. Another scheme is to set a Delta jib, or the like, made for the purpose on the backstay whilst ketches and yawls should ensure that the mizzen sail can be deeply reefed and hauled in tight when at anchor.

The most dangerous aspects of anchoring in strong winds are other yachts dragging and debris flying around the anchorage. Both dangers seem to be more prevalent at night. So

143

when selecting the anchoring spot, be aware of these hazards and also of the fact that different yachts will respond differently to the conditions. Given the choice, there is clearly an advantage in being the windward yacht and it may be worth choosing a point close to yachts of similar design. What seems to be a reasonable distance apart in daylight becomes too close when careering around in the dark. It is obviously seamanlike to have an anchor light turned on at night in case other yachts choose to manoeuvre and, as it is difficult to judge distance from a masthead anchor light particularly in a crowded anchorage, cabin lights or a solar light should be used as well.

There are parts of the world where a yacht can fit snugly into a tight anchorage with rocks, ice or mangrove on three sides. As well as lying to one or more anchors it may be necessary to take lines ashore. It is debatable whether to go bows or stern in. Stern in is easiest from the point of view of handling anchors but, should the vessel drag, the rudder will probably be the first point to touch. Tying lines to old or dead trees should be avoided. In February 2006 the 16.8m (56ft) yacht *Toucan* pulled down such a tree at Puerto Maxwell in Chile, albeit in 50- or 60-knot winds, and grounded on her rudder, fortunately without much harm. Using chain or slinging strops around rocks will prevent chafe and fenders should be used to float lines clear of rocks or coral.

If the seabed is sand or mud, deliberately running the vessel aground can be considered in severe conditions, particularly to be clear of other vessels. Allowance may need to be made for the tide and storm surge. On one occasion *Shamaal*, Richard Clifford's yacht, ran ashore and experienced 100-knot winds without damage. If it is necessary to back up the anchor, mangrove swamps provide good shelter in tropical revolving storms and have plenty to tie up to. When it is considered that the yacht has been made snug, it might be thought that it will be safer for her crew to be ashore. If conditions have already deteriorated this temptation should be resisted, as the dinghy trip may be rather more hazardous than remaining on board.

Some people will always believe that one should stay with the vessel.

A final thought on anchoring procedures is that, in certain circumstances, it may be necessary to slip the anchor and chain in a hurry. Provision should be made to do so by securing the bitter end of the anchor chain in the anchor locker with line which can be easily detached or cut in emergency. Examples are when a neighbouring vessel is dragging down onto one in a storm, or when an iceberg has grounded over one's anchor and it is necessary to leave when another smaller iceberg is bearing down. The chain can be buoyed with a fender.

Lying to a mooring

Having endured bad weather at sea, using a mooring with known good credentials can be a great relief. But to go onto a strange mooring, particularly when cruising away from Western Europe, is potentially disastrous. People often say 'it looks a big mooring buoy, so it must be strong enough for big vessels!' In many parts of the world, diving to survey an unfamiliar mooring should be considered obligatory. This option may not be feasible when entering a strange harbour in bad weather. A dive may reveal that the condition of many apparently serviceable moorings in developing countries is quite horrifying. The sinker is often a lump of concrete with a riser line of dubious worth. Rarely is a swivel attached to it, so the riser is often heavily twisted. If the riser is made of rope it will, of course, chafe. Furthermore, concrete is not a good material for a mooring sinker, as it needs to be very large to overcome its relatively low density.

In many parts of Western Europe, where visitors' moorings are provided and anchoring is either prohibited or strongly discouraged, taking a mooring may be the only option. Such moorings are likely to be in the prime location so that there is no space to anchor safely and it is reasonable to assume that they will have been at least moderately well maintained. If possible, make enquiries to ensure that the selected mooring is of suitable

Boats at moorings in a Force 12 storm at Ringhaddy Sound, N Ireland at 1430 on 16 January 1984. Three yachts broke free from their moorings and went ashore, six inflatable dinghies came adrift, danced up the beach and over the hill. Photo: Sir Dennis Faulkner

strength. Assuming that harbour authorities describe the mooring as sound and there is only a ring on the top, the biggest problem of securing to it will be chafe. It is worth carrying a short length of chain for these circumstances; otherwise some form of protection against chafe will be required. In Europe most visitors' buoys are provided with a rope riding strop, but even in Europe it is wise to check the rope and back it up if thought necessary.

When picking up a mooring singlehanded in a blow it will be easier to lead a picking up line from the bow to the stern and approach the buoy *stern* first. Another useful technique when having difficulty attaching a line to the ring of a mooring buoy is to lasso the mooring with a large loop of wet rope (dry rope tends to float or slide off the mooring buoy). Once the lasso has sunk below the mooring: the boat will be secured and the proper mooring line can be set up at leisure. Do not leave the temporary lasso rope as an extra line to the mooring – it may chafe on the chain, twist and be difficult to remove or foul the main line.

There are proprietary devices that can be of significant assistance such as the Swiftie and various sorts of pick up hooks, often of Swedish design.

When riding out bad weather on a mooring it is prudent to have the yacht's main anchor ready to let go at short notice should the mooring part or begin to drag. In some cases it may be appropriate to drop the anchor underfoot with a tripping line.

Lying alongside

Going alongside in a gale or storm is fraught with problems. A wall with a lee may provide the necessary shelter, but will the wind push the vessel off on the final approach? Is there space? Can lines be attached ashore or onto the pontoon or wall, before being blown off? Is there anyone with sufficient experience on the wall to take lines? If it is a lee wall or pontoon, is it safe to come alongside? Are there waves, which will bounce the boat around at the wrong moment? Even more than when manoeuvring in an anchorage, bold and decisive boat handling will be necessary. The decision may not be perfectly correct but indecision is more likely to cause embarrassment and possibly damage to other vessels involved.

Once alongside problems may not end. The greatest danger associated with lying alongside in gale or storm conditions is probably the consequence of a change of wind direction which might lead to the yacht being crushed against the wall or pontoon, either by the force of wind and waves, or as a result of the weight of boats that may have moored outboard. There is also the potential hazard of vessels that may have broken free from other parts of the harbour. Clearly it is preferable to seek a berth in which the yacht will be blown off, rather than on to the wall or pontoon. If this is not possible, it may be necessary to find a way of holding the yacht off. This could involve stringing lines across a harbour or to the windward side of a finger berth in a marina,

or laying an anchor to windward to hold the yacht off. It also should be appreciated that pontoons in marinas are not always as sturdy as they look. Some will remember the chaos in Concarneau marina after the severe storm of October 1987 when pontoons were broken up into fragments. The ideal solution is probably to four-point moor so that the yacht is held in a cocoon of lines and cannot make contact with either the pontoons or harbour walls. This is the mooring system often used for yachts wintering in exposed locations such as the west coast of Scotland.

Ample fendering is crucial if there is any chance that the yacht will lie against a wall or pontoon. In strong winds the weight of a yacht may be sufficient to burst her fenders. However, the biggest danger is generally associated with fenders popping out either through riding up or becoming trapped as the yacht moves around in her berth. It may be worth attaching the fenders to the wall or pontoon to ensure that the yacht is protected

The photo below shows the 13m (43ft) yacht Ocean Grace *(Dr John Sharp) sheltering alongside a jetty at Kópasker in northeast Iceland on 2 September 2002 following extreme bad weather on the previous night. The crew had to wait until afternoon before it was safe to land and take this photograph. The boat had been secured with every rope available – happily there was plenty on board – and the anchor had been dropped underfoot in case the ropes failed. Warps were adjusted to come taut simultaneously, and were well wrapped with anti-chafe material. There was not much more than a metre's range of tide at Kópasker but the ropes had to be carefully adjusted to allow for the swell.* Photo: Dr Sarah Watson

Above and below: The views forward and aft from Ocean Grace *taken before the storm. Both the yacht's deck and the adjacent part of the quay had been cleared of anything that might fly. As the storm developed, the wind increased from the south-east, blowing the boat onto the large tyres attached to the quay wall, compounded by a significant sea. At this point* Ocean Grace's *fender boards took some heavy punishment and were of great value in preventing serious damage to the topsides. The strongest winds, Force 9 or 10, occurred as the barometer began to rise from a low of 968hPa (mb), after falling by 32hPa (mb) in ten hours. By this time the wind had veered around to the west and* Ocean Grace *was being blown off the quay, held by her numerous lines and strong deck fittings. It was a wild, noisy and uncomfortable night, shared with a large paddling of eider ducks that had come into the harbour the previous evening to shelter. When inspecting the lines in the night, the anchor watch wore safety harnesses, and they could feel and hear waves coming over the outer breakwater. By morning the decks were covered in debris but, apart from the tail end of the burgee in tatters and the new fender boards now looking well used, the boat and her lines were unharmed; all credit to her skipper and crew. Photos: Dr Sarah Watson*

from protrusions, no matter how the yacht moves. If lying against a rough wall, then fender boards or a plank are essential.

It is crucial to minimise chafe on mooring lines used to secure the yacht and time should be spent in working out the leads. Account should be taken of the expected rise and fall of tide, storm surge when tidal range may increase by up to 5m (15ft), the likely direction of the sea and the forecast changes in wind direction. The strength of cleats and rings and their fastenings should be considered carefully before deciding to secure to them. Chafe points on the warps should be protected. Rubber shock absorbers or similar devices are likely to be valuable and it is worth using short lengths of chain around rough cleats or bollards that otherwise might chafe the lines. Weight should be distributed as evenly as possible over the various breast lines and springs and, as far as is possible, one rope per mooring line should be used so that each line can be adjusted independently. Polypropylene is a good choice for shore line because it floats. This makes it much easier to take a line ashore by dinghy, or to float it downwind – perhaps with a fender

attached to increase windage. If in harbour, carrying a floating line around other boats minimises the difficulty. John Andrews carried a total of 220 metres (722ft) of 25mm 3-strand polypropylene for polar regions aboard his Oyster 47, *Suilven*, and found a number of occasions to use it with advantage. If drifting sea ice was a risk, he found the long length of rope light enough to lift above the ice and he rigged a halyard with a running loop on the shore line to facilitate this. Once one's own boat has been properly secured, consideration should be given to the mooring arrangements of adjacent vessels, as if one should break loose it could cause significant collateral effects.

Finally, the danger of flying debris should be anticipated. Flying galvanised iron roofing has been known to cut telegraph poles in two and fish boxes form common projectiles once airborne. In the tropics, flying coconuts are less comical than they sound.

In conclusion, the hazards of entering or remaining in harbour in heavy weather should not be underestimated and adherence to the suggestions given will make a safe and restful period in harbour rather more likely.

Remaining at sea in stormy seas off Chile. Photo: Onne van der Wal/Bluegreen

12 Helming Rigid Inflatable Boats in extreme weather and open seas

Hugo Montgomery-Swan

Hugo Montgomery-Swan relates his experience of helming a RIB in stormy weather on an occasion when he and a flotilla of fifteen other RIBs embarked on the 2002 circumnavigation of Ireland.

The forecast was not good for leaving Newport, County Mayo – an initially 'on the nose' north-westerly, with a wind strength of Force 7, increasing later. After some consideration, we decided to set out with the intention of reaching Killybegs, some 80 nautical miles to the north, but on the understanding that we would return to port if the conditions became too hazardous.

The Severn Class lifeboat that led the RIB flotilla out of Newport and down the waterway to the entrance of Achill Sound dwarfed our little 'ships' as we plunged along behind. The wind was fairly whipping off the land now, and the spray from the agitated waters of the lifeboat's wake flew horizontally across our craft. Even here, in sheltered waters, the scene about us was already menacing and did not bode well for the day ahead.

Soon the lifeboat cox radioed his goodbyes and set course for home at Clew Bay, and we were left to our own devices. We made our way along the winding sound before joining the rest of the fleet waiting with idling engines in the inshore waters of Blacksod Bay. It was touch and go for the big boats to clear under the road bridge, but this tricky inshore route cut off a good twenty miles of potentially difficult and exposed waters around Achill Head and we were all very grateful for the pilotage provided by our RNLI friends that had made it possible.

Now all safely mustered on the seaward side of the bridge, everyone busily set about ensuring their kit was fit, lashed down and ready for sea. It would be our last chance, for once out into the open ocean, the likelihood of being able to stop to secure gear would be remote.

We all tried to stay together as a group in the rough conditions that we encountered in the exposed fetch beyond the bridge and I was amazed at just how well my little RIB was coping. Some RIBs of this size, 6.5m (21ft), would have been throwing their heads wildly in such close-coupled, steep seas, but not ours. She ran astonishingly level and, because of this, maintained a speed that justified leading the flotilla.

As we met the waters between the heads of Inishbiggle and nearby Bunacurry, we faced the true effects of the north-westerly fetch running directly in from the Northern Atlantic. Adding to this was the concentration of tidal stream through the narrow passages that caused unusually high seas to pile in relentlessly at both Annagh and Inishbiggle. We powered on to meet the first of the big seas. It is always difficult to judge the height of waves in these situations, but suffice to say, they were easily able to accommodate the full length of the 10-metre (32.8ft) RIB running off our starboard side, as she climbed to their summits.

Icy spray smacked against our screen, running in torrents down the glass and momentarily obscuring any clear forward vision. Screen wipers would have helped but we were still very glad of the cuddy cabin, as our weather side was taking a real hammering from the driving rain and spray. To add to the difficulties of forward vision, I had to crouch over the wheel and crane my neck to get a proper view of each sea as we began to climb the face. Applying the correct amount of power was vital in order to maintain good steerage, and ensure we negotiated the crests of these waves comfortably. Of course, the bigger the wave the bigger the trough on the other side – the slide down into some of these chasms was sometimes nothing short of breathtaking. By now the size of the seas frequently required the use of reverse power to slow our descent. Surfing too wildly would be sure to result in the boat suffering an unwelcome 'stuffing', i.e. she could smack the bow into the wave beyond the trough so firmly that a wall of green water would come over the bow and the boat would stop and lose steerage way. Such an incident would immediately compromise our own boat's security and also the safety of any other members of the flotilla who might come to provide assistance. All 16 RIBs had to keep moving.

We pushed on out to the open sea beyond the complicated area of tide and overfalls. Mind you, we didn't really have a choice; turning round was not an option – it would have put all the boats at a very real risk of capsize.

Running as a pack, the flotilla continued to remain tightly grouped all the way out to the land west of Belmullet. Every now and then I would glance astern, much to the annoyance of my navigator, Jan Falkowski, who quite rightly reminded me that it was my job to look ahead. 'Never mind what's going on behind, we'll take care of that,' he shouted. He was right, of course, for just a momentary lapse of concentration could result in a breaking sea catching the boat unawares. As it happened, moments after he shouted at me I failed to steer square to a very steep sea and as we ran up its face the crest curled and burst down from above on the starboard side of the cabin – streaming down the canopy and onto

the rear deck in a cascade of freezing water. Thankfully, due to our RIB's extraordinary lateral stability, we suffered no harm – but it was a tense moment nonetheless. Thomas, my teenage son and third crewmember aboard our RIB, remained cool amidst the commotion, though I could tell by the hard-done-by look on his face that he really wanted to be behind the wheel! We pushed on as we had to although, as later weather reports confirmed, the wind in our region was by now touching Force 8.

With the seas now on our quarter we were able to push along at a surprisingly good 17 knots. One moment we would be climbing dark grey ramparts of water that occasionally replaced our view of the sky ahead before surfing at even greater speed down their long sides into the deep troughs below. But as we edged further offshore to maintain our course, the seas began to lengthen to a more typical ocean type swell. This sea state was less dangerous and, although maintaining visual contact with our buddy boats continued to be difficult, it was apparent that many of the RIBs were now getting into their stride.

All the boats and engine systems fared remarkably well that day, with no breakdowns. When talking to the crews and watching with interest how the RIBs performed in these sea states, one thing became obvious; the smaller boats very often had the advantage with their high degree of manoeuvrability and quick acceleration proving very successful in the near-gale conditions. The big RIBs, especially those fitted with turbo-charged diesel engines, were disadvantaged by the throttle response times and proved more difficult 'to place' in the difficult seas. The little RIBs were nippy, weaved a safe course and proved nimble enough to dodge the big 'curlers'.

Most of the Round Ireland RIBs were open craft, and we were very glad of the protection the soft-top cabin our RIB gave us. Without it, the amount of flying water would have been difficult to deal with, so the protection that it gave was a major safety factor as well as reducing fatigue caused by the wind and elements.

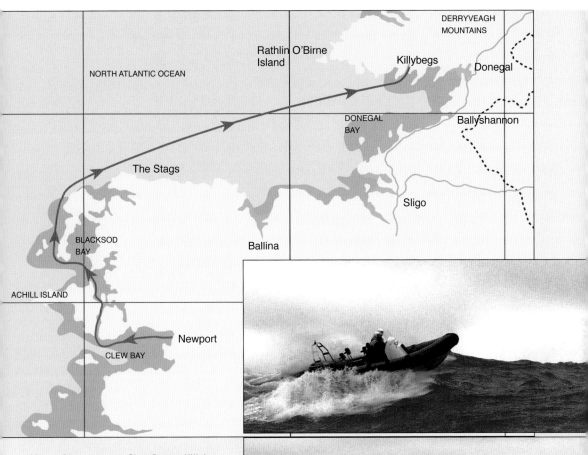

Above: Chart extract: Clew Bay to Killybegs.

Right, top: The small, outboard-powered RIBs often fared better than their larger diesel-powered counterparts. This is a Ribcraft 5.85m (19ft).

Centre: With the Stag Rocks in the background, a big sea sweeps across the path of one of the RIBs as it crests a wave.

Bottom: This Tornado outboard RIB with crew of five shows its immense stability, amidst the heavy seas. Note the relaxed nature of this RNLI crew taking part in the event.

Photos: RIB International Magazine

Report analysis

Driving and design

All the crews taking part in this leg of the Round Ireland Challenge learnt an important lesson: sheer LOA was not necessarily an advantage in these heavy sea states. In fact, the smaller RIBs with their high power to weight ratio seemed to fare better than their larger counterparts.

Whilst the larger craft at between 8.5 and 12 metres (28 and 39ft) were more able to take a sea broadside or even a breaking wave thanks to their greater tonnage, they invariably featured turbo-charged diesels, which caused them to suffer from 'turbo lag'. This mechanically delayed throttle response meant that the helmsmen of these larger craft were unable to respond quickly enough to the more dangerous seas that confronted them; they lacked the powerboat's greatest attribute – immediate power. Once the force/power advantage is reduced, to the point it is not available in sufficient measure, even a RIB with its low central point of gravity can be compromised in certain sea states. The smaller RIBs rarely came close to being compromised thanks to their nimbleness. Nearly all the RIBs between 5.8 and 7.5 metres (19 and 24.6ft) were outboard powered, with horsepower ranging from 150hp to 250hp. Agility is the RIB's trademark and with a responsive throttle, a well-found RIB should be able to both dodge and run from a dangerous sea, even when the cox is on passage and steering to a compass course. A policy of yield and adjust should be adopted under such circumstances. Contrary to many people's imagination, seas move very quickly in heavy weather, and often in more than one direction, so reaction time on the part of the helmsman and the motor he is controlling is absolutely paramount. But one word of caution, rapid helm adjustments, and particularly in short steep seas can encourage the propeller to cavitate – or spin in its own pocket of air. The correct choice of propeller is paramount when it comes to operating in adverse sea states. In most rough water instances a slightly lesser pitched prop is

required to ensure quick throttle response, but also the number and type of blades the propeller features is important too. One of my favourite rough water propellers is stainless steel and five-bladed. The stainless steel construction ensures near zero flexing, plus coupled to the shape and number of blades it features, results in a propeller that is almost immune to cavitation – the enemy of quick throttle helming.

A good helmsman or powerboat cox will use his engine's power to great advantage – one moment hitting the throttle to the stops, the next, snapping the engine into neutral to let a dangerous sea pass by. He will also need to gently feather the throttle to nurse his craft over a crest to prevent it from flying wildly off the top of the wave – before then powering up again to lift the vessel's bow in readiness for the next sea directly ahead. The use of trim requires a skilful understanding of the boat and the sea state it is operating in. Correct use of trim will allow the boat to operate to its optimum and thus even affect fuel consumption – which may be a matter of growing concern on a long haul in worsening weather. But in adverse seas it is quite possible that the cox will be constantly adjusting the angle of trim; trimming the nose right down in an effort to literally pin it to the water's surface as a steep sea is climbed, before quickly trimming out again on the downhill slide into the trough, in order to raise the bow of the vessel before it negotiates the sea ahead. Ballast tanks are often employed in larger RIBs. These allow water to be collected into a holding tank within the vessel's bow which can then be dumped by means of a release system controlled at the helm. This form of trim device, as in the case of trim tabs, is useful because, unlike trimming in the leg of an engine with its spinning propeller, the craft can be trimmed or balanced without the unwanted effects of prop torque. Very often, a powered craft will heel horribly to port, landing on the flat of its chine in the process when fully trimmed via engine leg alone. Even if a boat does not possess ballast tanks and the like, a great deal can be achieved by giving careful attention to where and how ancillary kit and items such as dry bags are stowed. In head seas strap as much down as possible in the forepeak, or alternatively when running in following seas, transfer this kit into the stern. It really makes a difference. Electrically controlled trim tabs can also transform a boat's performance in steep head seas or when running in a strong crosswind. Both tabs can be employed to mechanically force the vessel's bow down to the face of waves or independently used to correct lateral heel.

Whether due to poor use of trim or some other misjudgment, if a cox does get it wrong with the result that the RIB flies off the crest in an ungainly fashion, the advantage of a RIB, with its inflatable sponson design, is that its high degree of lateral stability is usually more than capable of saving the day. RIBs are very forgiving beasts after all and in general the golden rule is always, 'when in doubt power on'. Further to this, if a sea is negotiated with too much speed and the boat does fly, once again, try to re-enter water with some power on, in order not to land with a sudden stop, with all the dangers to crew that may present. So, if it is judged that the boat has really taken off, a quick shut down of the throttle in mid-air will help negate an over-revving of the engines before opening the throttle wide once more just prior to the prop re-entering the water again. Of course, as we have already said, successful helming takes skill, feeling, a sense of rhythm and, in the instance just described, split second timing as well.

In a previous experience of running before a gale in a 7.5 metre (24.6ft) RIB off Cape Wrath, in order to prevent the boat surfing at too great a speed down into the deep trough of a following sea (where she might well stuff her bow) it was necessary for us to slam the throttle hard astern in order to brake the RIB's descent. Such tactics can be employed with great effect as long as one has plenty of power/ acceleration response at one's fingertips, though the loads on the transmission can be quite intense of course – so *if* you do feel the need to employ this 'hard astern' method, do so calmly and smoothly. Power is the RIB's

great asset, so, understanding how and when to employ it is critical in testing conditions. Without acceleration/definite forward motion, the sea will quickly take charge and determine your outcome for you.

In addition to the use of throttle in the manner described, in very large seas where one is running before a gale, or even when crossing a dangerous bar, a wise and safe tactic can be to literally sit on the back of a wave, positioning the boat just behind the crest as it progresses forward. When the sea breaks or dissipates, its force is released forward or downwards well clear of the RIB. Upon this occurring the cox should then simply advance to ride piggyback up onto the next sea and repeat the procedure all over again. I will just say that whilst this tactic can be most effective in affording one the means of making good speed in dangerous seas, it is nonetheless imperative to keep a strict watch astern to ensure the following sea, which no doubt is being destabilised by the boat's wake, does not itself break and overtake one. I have, though, employed this tactic to both cross bars with seas running to a height of at least 8 metres or to gain additional depth beneath the hull when crossing sand bars where there has been a real risk of running aground or 'grounding out' in the trough of the wave.

Still on the matter of engines, if it has been decided that the right form of power for a RIB is an inboard/stern-drive diesel installation, it is really important to ensure that it is properly installed, protected and the structure of the hull along with the engine mountings, are strong enough to take it. On one occasion, when running off La Corbiere in an 8-metre (26ft) Italian-built RIB on Jersey's west coast in a Force 6 head sea/wind against tide, we suddenly suffered a broken engine mount. Its diesel engine, which as a result of the broken mount, now lay crooked within the engine bay, started to suffer and very quickly the crew had to adapt their helming to lessen the likelihood of yet further damage. This was difficult given the conditions, as much power was needed to climb the steep, white capped, tide induced, and curling seas. Poor installation caused this gear failure and led to the crew being endangered. It also resulted in a wrecked engine by the time a safe haven was found in one of the local islands.

In cases where the boat is diesel powered, it is vital that the engine compartment is watertight and secure, and that all breathers are located well above the top edge of the tubes, so even if the boat is swamped, the engine will remain unaffected. Frequently 'water-tight' hatches are not as watertight as they should be, so it's worth checking them out. And, remember, however watertight the hatch might be, it is vital in adverse conditions to ensure all external hatches remain firmly closed. Cabins should also have watertight doors and adequate drains leading to bilge pumps, as should cockpits on RIBs designed for offshore use.

Of course, it is particularly vital that a diesel inboard engine housing is designed in such a way as to ensure that no water can get inside even if the vessel is swamped from tube to tube. If a big sea sweeps right over the boat, or if the boat buries its nose in the foot of a trough at speed, the weight of water charging down the length of the craft will easily amount to several tons. The force of this can take out screens; smash consoles and even lift the crew clean out of their jockey seats. (In one instance, when ribbing solo, mid-channel, 56km (35 miles) offshore, I had the misfortune of the entire boat suddenly disappearing beneath the water's surface. The RIB, a 4.8 metre (15.7ft) with 50hp (a craft in which we successfully circumnavigated the British Isles), stuffed itself very badly indeed in a following sea. I can remember looking up and seeing the top of the helm console beneath the water and the sun shining down through its surface! But I have never yet found any modern outboard to suffer adversely from a swamping, such as the engine experienced in this mid-channel incident. (The RNLI of course not only immersion-proof the outboards on their RIB fleet for normal work, but also to protect them in the case of a capsize.) Today's marine outboard technology is highly suited to the environment in which it is designed to operate. Being immensely

reliable, robust and efficient, these modern engine systems, both 4-stroke and 2-stroke, have changed beyond all recognition in recent years. This is why so many commercial and offshore operators often favour outboard power over the inboard alternative.

However, if the worst happens and total power is lost through engine malfunction, as long as the vessel's essential components such as battery and electrics are not earthed by sea water, then in extreme conditions it has been known for steps to be taken to actually encourage the swamping or flooding of a deck on an open RIB. The intention being to reduce the central point of gravity yet further and cause the boat to sit even lower in the water. As powered craft of this type tend to lie with their stern quarter to the seas, the more they wallow with reduced windage, greater weight and lowered central gravity, the less likely they are to be capsized in very steep seas. Despite many attempts, I have never found a drogue to be particularly useful to a stationary RIB in heavy seas. On the other hand a parachute sea anchor with the line over the bow can work well, well enough to steady the boat sufficiently for the engine to be worked upon if necessary. In terms of RIBs, a drogue would rarely be deployed over the stern in the instance of crossing a bar because, once again, a RIB's main line of defence lies in the use of its throttle. Powering up onto the back of a wave is a much better option than a device that holds the boat's stern true to the waves at the expense of it being swamped clean over the transom.

Fit out

Though one may not associate a vessel's fit out with the all-important factors of weight and balance, it is nonetheless crucial to consider the effects that every item has upon the vessel's well-being. The position of the RIB's batteries, how much offset should be given to the helm console and to the engine especially in an effort to counteract propulsion torque. Where is the optimum location for under deck fuel tanks? If carried, where should the reserve/donkey engine be located – up in the

A purpose-built 7.4m (24ft) Delta in the Atlantic on the west side of the Outer Hebrides in a 9-metre (29.5ft) sea. This RIB is used for transport of freight and personnel in this exposed and isolated area winter and summer. The tubular structure forward is to assist when landing on platforms. Photo: Murray MacLeod

forepeak above the anchor locker or strapped to the arch-mast on the transom's inside face? Such decisions, when correct, will not only enhance a boat's performance but may make the difference between a boat that's surefooted in all sea states and one that struggles when the going gets tough.

On Round Ireland, aboard our 6.5 metre (21.3ft) soft-top cabin RIB, it was clear that the additional weight of the forward cabin structure and the extra large helm console, balanced the boat to just the right angle of trim to allow it to perform superbly in high head seas. Furthermore, when climbing up the face of a wave, just before breaking through the crest, we were able to use the boat's forward weight to our advantage. This was achieved by half closing the throttle abruptly just at the point of breakthrough, and allowing the boat's inertia to let it fall forward so the bow punched *through* the wave crest as opposed to 'skimming' up and over it. If the RIB had suffered from being bow light, such a technique would never have been possible. Thanks to the high bow sheer and good forward buoyancy/lift in her hull, she was also able to recover very ably in the deep troughs.

When considering the fit out of a RIB, it is imperative to consider the likely ultimate use to which it will be put. Offshore 'ribbing' necessitates sufficiently large through-transom

155

Meticulous attention to every detail is essential when preparing a RIB for use in rough sea states. Seen here, an 8m (26ft) Delta in storm swells off the Isle of Lewis. Photo: Murray MacLeod of Seatrek

deck scuppers, for example. Water entering the deck must be able to drain quickly back through these scupper points by the simple application of forward power. If water cannot be ejected quickly and efficiently, then the resulting payload of trapped seawater on deck will burden the boat to the point of it being as manoeuverable as a holed battleship! Whilst electric bilge pumps are a useful addition, they should never replace a natural means of draining off water through scuppers. Many commercial craft, such as the RNLI's Atlantic Class, have open transoms and the deck is sufficiently above the waterline so as not to require any fixed scuppering.

Offshore venturers should also consider as great a duplication of systems as possible; besides a fixed radio and GPS it is good practice to carry hand-held back-ups and a good supply of batteries. The carrying of a full-blown fixed EPIRB plus PLBs for each crewmember will save lives. I have firsthand experience of this. But whilst on the subject of fixed equipment, remember that the seas always do their utmost to un-fix it! Fixings for offshore use need to be somewhat better than those on a RIB whose only use will be on fine Sunday afternoon jaunts round the bay with the family. Prior to a testing passage, some mariners will further secure brackets with duct tape to stop gradual loosening.

The ergonomics relating to such items as the console screen in an open RIB which, without a stainless steel grab rail to guard its leading edge, can be as lethal as a knife at one's throat, or the positioning of the throttle in relation to the helm seat and the wheel, are important factors to consider. Good positioning is not only highly relevant to comfort of course, but also enables one to drive the boat to its optimum. GPS brackets, VHF antennas and lashing cleats are all vulnerable items that invariably fail in adverse sea states, and though relatively small bits of kit, they all have the potential to divert a helmsman's attention away from the job in hand – the next sea!

Giving attention to detail when rigging and maintaining a craft will pay dividends out at sea. Preventative maintenance is essential but should be used in conjunction with trial runs of emergency equipment. For example, it would be easier to have a rehearsed drill for rigging an auxiliary engine rather than doing it for the first time in a heavy sea when things have already gone badly wrong.

If all these factors are considered in advance and the skills relating to their use are developed progressively in the 'field', then, when foul and angry seas are met with, it will be all the more possible to yield and adjust, to keep a level head and keep the advantage.

A final thought for RIB drivers is that the helmsman should drive in a sympathetic manner, which reflects consideration, not only for the well-being of the vessel but also the crew. Even in rough conditions, little will be gained if the helmsman has the attitude that the sea needs to be *fought*. It is better to try to accommodate the angry moods of the sea. Whilst positive helming is essential, too heavy a hand on the throttle will likely lead to gear or component failure and cause possible injury to the crew. At the very least, the latter will become fatigued and even unnerved. A good cox therefore, will constantly seek to reassure his crew both by the manner in which he drives as well as by conversing with them, and enquiring how they are feeling from time to time, throughout the passage. 'Pee' breaks, food breaks and suitable liquid intake stops, not only allow a moment to refresh and restore one's strength, but also give an opportunity to build morale, communicate and re-appraise. Amid a bleak situation, a smile and even a joke shared are as important to human well-being and survival as anything I know.

13 Handling powerboats in rough seas

Dag Pike

The shape of powerboat hulls is generally very different from that of sailboats and apart from a few notable examples they tend to be less seaworthy. This means that in rough sea conditions a powerboat will have to be nursed much more carefully and the speed of progress can be quite critical to survival. Initially, methods of handling displacement craft at speeds of below 10 knots will be covered. Whilst the displacement hull is primarily built to operate at these speeds, in a planing boat low-speed operation tends to be a secondary consideration, so the particular problems of handling planing vessels at slow speeds in stormy seas will be covered in a later section.

Rough seas are considered to be those in which the throttles cannot be left set and the boat left to take its course. Instead speed has to be reduced or throttles operated continuously to negotiate the boat through the waves. Much depends on the size and construction of the vessel as to what might be considered to be rough conditions, but in general these will be seas generated by winds of Force 6 and upward.

Displacement craft

Head seas

When operating in a head sea the main thing to do with a displacement hull is to find a speed at which the boat proceeds comfortably. Provided the boat is strongly built, even in quite rough seas it is possible to find a speed where the boat will lift over the wave and drop down the other side without too much discomfort to the craft or the crew. Matching the speed to the conditions is the secret of operating in head seas, provided the waves have a normal gradient and a wavelength that allows the boat to operate without any excessive change in trim.

When a displacement boat is driven hard into a head sea, the bow will lift to the wave and then become unsupported as the wave crest passes aft. Then, the bow will drop to restore equilibrium before lifting once more to the next wave. The problems start in a short, steep sea when the bow may not have time to lift to the next wave, particularly as the stern will still be raised under the influence of the wave that has just passed. Reducing speed will give the boat more time to adjust to the changing wave profile and will thus help to make the motion easier.

If the vessel is driven too hard in a head sea, then there is a real danger of a wave breaking on board as the bow is forced through, rather than over, a wave. Water has surprising weight and so with solid water breaking on board in this way there is a risk of structural damage. In this situation, the most vulnerable parts of the boat are the wheelhouse windows, although having said this I have never experienced them breaking, despite seeing tons of water crashing down on many occasions. In a boat with a fine bow there is a greater risk of the bow burying itself into a head sea because it has less buoyancy.

When trying to find a comfortable speed for operating in particular conditions, it is important to ensure that sufficient speed is maintained to give steerage way. At a slow speed the response to the wheel will be slower and the bow could fall quite a way off course before the corrective action of the rudder starts to have effect. If, at this time, a wave should rise and strike against the weather bow, then the slow rudder response could mean that the boat will be knocked round, beam-on to the sea, before the corrective action is effective. In this situation, opening the throttles is one way to get a fairly immediate improvement in control, and this can bring the boat back on course quickly without any rapid increase in momentum. The safe minimum speed to maintain steerage way will vary from boat to boat and with wavelength, height and steepness but it is unlikely to be less than 3 knots and will be more with craft which have small rudders. The risk of being knocked off course is greatest with a breaking wave where the water is actually travelling towards the boat, as this exerts a considerable force on the bow.

If the sea conditions reach the point where the boat has to be forced hard in order to maintain steerageway in deteriorating conditions, then the time has come to start nursing the boat over the waves. This is when the throttle can be used to good effect. By opening the throttle as the wave approaches, the bow of the boat will lift and a burst of engine power will also improve the steering effect. As the bow lifts to the wave, the throttle should be eased off before the bow punches through the crest. Easing the throttle will then cause the bow to drop slightly, thus reducing the tendency for it to fall heavily into the trough. As the next wave approaches it is time to be ready to open the throttles again.

By using this throttling technique, reasonably comfortable progress can be made to windward. There will be better control of the boat, and if a larger-than-normal wave comes along the person at the helm will be better prepared. However, this type of operation does require considerable concentration, because there is always the risk of being caught out

of step by the irregularity of the waves and the larger-than-normal wave. This need for concentration can be very tiring and the right level of concentration can only be maintained for around an hour or so.

Beam seas

Going with the wind and sea on the beam in moderate seas has the disadvantage of discomfort, due to the heavy rolling which is likely to occur. In these conditions, full speed can generally be used on a displacement boat without any real problems arising, because the boat is lifting bodily on the waves and the bow and stern have little movement in relation to each other. However, occasionally the boat drops off the edge of a fairly steep wave front, which can be both uncomfortable and a little frightening so, as the beam seas start to get rougher, more care has to be taken.

Keeping the sea on the beam exposes a large area of boat to the approaching waves and in stormy seas this can make the craft vulnerable. The transition from what is an uncomfortable beam sea to a dangerous one will depend a great deal on the type and characteristics of the craft, but once the waves have started to break then, again, more care has to be taken.

There are two main problems with beam seas. First, as the waves become steeper, the boat will try to adjust to the tilted surface of the sea and, consequently, will heel to quite a large angle. This in itself is not too serious, provided the range of stability of the boat is adequate, but it has to be remembered that the wind will also be pressing on the windward side of the boat, tending to increase the angle of the heel. The second problem is more serious and occurs when breaking waves are encountered. This means that the surface of the water is moving bodily to leeward and can exert very great pressures on the windward side of the vessel. The pressures are resisted by the still water on the lee side of the hull, which produces a heeling moment, which could develop to the point where the boat will capsize. There is also the risk of seas breaking on board, because many displacement boats tend to have reduced freeboard amidships. These breaking seas could fill a cockpit or other deck openings which makes the predicament worse, so that there will come a time when operating in a beam sea is not the optimum course.

Fortunately, a wave rarely breaks along a long front, but tends to do so in patches so that, with anticipation, it is possible to avoid breaking waves in beam seas. This means watching the sea ahead carefully and anticipating which part of the wave crest is going to break. Then it is necessary to reduce speed to let the wave break in front of the boat, or turn into or away from the wind so that the boat passes either behind or in front of the breaking crest. Even in moderate breaking seas, life can be made a lot more comfortable on board by this method of avoiding the largest of the waves and steering round the less friendly looking crests. In moderate seas there is not too much to worry about if things go wrong, but once the seas start to break then the stakes become higher and it is necessary to be much more cautious.

If, in a beam sea, a situation occurs where a wave that is about to break is bearing down on the boat and it is too late to reduce speed, then there are three options: the course can be maintained, hoping that the boat will cope; the boat can be headed into the wave; or the boat can be steered away from it. A lot will depend on the type and capabilities of the boat, but the best action would normally be to turn away from the wave, because this has the advantage of not only buying time, but will also reduce the impact of the wave on the boat which is then moving away from the wave. The breaking crest often rolls only a limited way to leeward and it can be possible to escape the breaking water altogether by this action. If it is decided to turn away from a breaking wave in this fashion, then the throttles should be opened wide, both to get the maximum steering effect and also to keep the distance from the breaking crest as large as possible. If the opposite course of action is chosen and the boat is headed into the wave, then reducing speed will probably be necessary to reduce the impact of the wave.

A point to notice when in a beam sea is that a wave will often be seen on the quarter starting to break. It may seem lucky to be always in front of these breaking crests, but they are, in fact, caused by the wash of the boat combining with the approaching wave to create an unstable wave that consequently breaks when otherwise it would not have done so. Such seas seem to have little force in them.

Following seas

Running before a heavy following sea has the reputation of being the seaman's nightmare, conjuring up visions of broaching, capsizing or being swamped. Much of this fear stems from sailing boats, where running before a sea may be the only action left under extreme conditions. There is no doubt that running before a following sea has its dangers, but provided they are recognised, they can be compensated for and the dangers can be minimised.

At first glance, it would appear that running before a sea and travelling in the same direction as the wind and sea would be a far safer course to take than battling against the waves. However, the rudder controls a boat and it needs a good flow of water to be effective. If the water flow is reduced or even reversed because of an overtaking breaking wave, then there will be much less control of the craft, or control could be lost altogether, and it is this factor which presents the major hazard in a following sea. An average open sea wave will be travelling at somewhere between two and three times the speed of the average displacement boat so the wave will take some time to pass the boat.

When the crest of the wave is approaching the stern, this face of the wave is the steepest part and the bow will be pointing downwards towards the trough. In this position, gravity will exert a downward pull on the boat; combining with the thrust from the propeller leading to the boat gaining increased forward motion down the wave slope. Similarly when the boat is on the back of the wave with the

The throttle setting is the key to heading straight into the sea. Find a comfortable level, which is tolerable for the crew, and then keep clear of the breakers. The photographs in this chapter were taken at the entrance to Cork Harbour in a southeasterly gale. All the craft shown in this series were built by Safehaven Marine and were designed by Frank Kowalski who, in many cases, was at the wheel. Photo: Safehaven Marine

bow pointing upwards, it is, to all intents and purposes, going uphill and the speed will be correspondingly reduced. These involuntary increases and decreases in speed can be controlled to a degree by opening and closing the throttle as the circumstances dictate and, unless the waves are breaking, it should be possible to retain adequate control over the boat. But beware of closing the throttle completely as steering control can be lost.

In a breaking wave, the surface water is moving forwards in the direction of travel of the wave at a speed slightly in excess of the speed of the wave. This forward movement of the breaking crest is transient, starting as the wave crest becomes unstable and ending when the wave has reached stability again and stopped breaking. The behaviour of a boat in a breaking following sea will depend, to a certain extent, on the position of the boat in relation to the crest as it breaks and on the design of the vessel itself.

If the wave rises up and starts to break immediately astern of the boat, then there is a real danger that the breaking crest will fall on to the craft. This is more likely to be a problem with the type of heavy breaking wave found when a current or tidal stream opposes the waves. One thing in favour of the boat at this stage is that the downward angle of the boat on the forward surface of the wave will help to increase the speed of the craft, and might even enable it to accelerate away sufficiently to escape the breaking crest. If not, the crest, in falling, will accelerate and take the boat with it, which will also help to increase the momentum, particularly if the boat has a large transom stern, which faces the oncoming rush of water. With a double-ended boat, also known as canoe stern, the theory is that the pointed stern divides the oncoming water and allows it to pass safely along each side of the boat.

A craft which is accelerating under the combined influences of the rush of breaking water at the stern and the downward slope of the face of the wave would probably be alright if the boat could just keep accelerating in this way. As the rush of water lifts the stern the

time comes when the bow of the boat starts to bury into the next wave ahead. This means that the bow starts to act as a pivot and also starts to put up considerable resistance to the forward rush. It is at this point that the risk of broaching occurs, with the bow trying to stop and the stern trying to swing to one side or the other under the influence of the rush of water. This strong turning effect can turn the boat broadside on in the classical broaching situation. Once broadside on the sea, the turning moment reduces, but is then replaced by a capsizing moment similar to that of a beam sea. Even if the boat escapes this particular situation, it could well find itself vulnerable to the next wave that comes along, because it is unlikely that it will have recovered in time and achieved the steerageway necessary to cope with the situation.

A deep-draft vessel with its rudder well immersed should still retain steerage control in this following breaking sea situation, whereas the shallow-draft boat could be much more vulnerable. Apart from shallow-water breaking waves, the actual depth of the breaking crest can be quite shallow, rarely more than a metre, so the deep rudder will be in more stable water below and remain effective. The hull design of the boat will also have a bearing on its behaviour, and a boat with a sharply angled forefoot is likely to create a pivot point more readily than one with a cutaway forefoot. A transom stern also makes the boat more vulnerable because of its resistance to the breaking crest.

In this situation, with a breaking wave approaching at the stern, there is not a great deal that can be done, other than trying to keep the boat absolutely square on to the sea for as long as possible and opening the throttle wide. This will demand concentration and hard work with the wheel, although the rudder could become virtually ineffective in these conditions. As a general rule, the throttle should be opened as wide as possible to try to run from the breaking wave or at least reduce its impact, and to retain steerage control for as long as possible. This will also have the effect of lifting the bow to a certain extent and with

At near displacement speeds it is necessary to keep the bow up as a wave approaches using a burst of high engine power. This will also improve steering control. Photo: Safehaven Marine

the increasing speed it will also help to reduce the impact of the wave at the stern.

When the breaking wave crest is overtaking the boat the waterflow past the boat may be reversed. In theory this means that the rudder on a shallow draft boat should work in reverse but I have never had the courage to try this in rough following seas because the consequences of getting it wrong could be severe.

When running before a following sea that may be large, but is not breaking, full throttle should be used to maintain steering control. Try to keep pace with the waves as far as possible, although on a displacement boat the waves will be overtaking. In these conditions it may be noticed that the waves astern are starting to break, but this is again usually the influence of the wash of the boat combining with the crest, which causes it to break. This can be a significant problem when crossing a

harbour bar in a following sea, and I have seen quite harmless looking waves suddenly rear up astern in this situation. It seems that the extra disturbance caused by the progress of the boat is enough to turn the waves into an unstable form. In theory these breaking waves that are assisted by the wash from the boat should not cause any problems, although they present a frightening picture when looking astern.

When running in front of a moderate following sea that is not breaking, there can still be a considerable change in the stability of the craft as a wave passes underneath. In this case any tendency of the boat to roll is more noticeable than in a head sea because the wave takes longer to pass under the vessel, giving it longer to adapt to the angles of the different faces of the waves. When the crest of the wave is passing underneath, the boat suddenly feels rather unstable. This is due to the fact that because the boat is only supported amidships, rather than over its whole length, her stability is considerably reduced. This is a fairly transient situation and stability is rapidly restored as the wave passes. But if running at a speed close to that of the wave, this period of instability could last for longer, and it might be sensible to consider reducing speed to allow the wave crests to pass more quickly and thus reduce these periods of instability.

One problem found on many boats when operating in a following sea is that the visibility astern is not as good as it might be. It helps a great deal to have a good view astern and on each quarter as well, but many boats lack this facility.

With a well-found vessel, running before a heavy following sea can be a very exciting experience. I have travelled down the Irish Sea in a 14.5m (48ft) lifeboat on a wild night when the wind was blowing up to Force 10. The first hour or two were quite frightening while we became used to the conditions, but once we had gained confidence that the boat was adequate for the job, we could revel in the excitement of rushing like an express train down the face of a wave, or so it seemed, and then watching out through the windows in the top of the wheelhouse for the next wave approaching from astern. I think an unnecessary dread of following seas has been built up amongst the small-boat fraternity, but one needs a sound boat before taking chances in a following sea, or indeed in any rough sea, and concentration is vital.

In conditions where the sea is starting to become rough when running before it, a quite dangerous condition can build up because one is unaware of just how bad things are getting and because, to a certain extent, the boat is running in harmony with the sea. The lack of impact of the waves in a following sea can lull one into a false sense of security. Thus it is a sensible precaution to stop every now and again, turn round, and head into the sea, just to see what conditions are really like. It might be frightening to realise just how the waves are building up, but it is better to be frightened in this way than to be caught out unawares.

Planing boats

If operating a planing boat at displacement speeds, then the boat can be more vulnerable than would be the case with a displacement boat in the same conditions. A planing boat is not running at its optimum at displacement speeds, both in terms of hull shape and of control.

In terms of hull shape, planing boats tend to have fine bows and full sterns, which is not a happy combination in rough seas. At the bow there can be a lack of freeboard when off the plane, or if the boat has a reverse deck sheer. This, combined with a fine bow, gives a lack of buoyancy in this area, which can mean the bow buries itself readily into both a head sea and a following sea. The craft is also much lighter and probably more affected by wind, so that it may be more difficult to maintain steerage way at low speeds in a planing boat because the bow will tend to fly off to one side or the other. This situation will be exaggerated because the rudders are always smaller on fast boats and are therefore less effective at slow speeds. On vessels fitted with outboards or stern drives, where the propeller thrust is used for steering, good steering can usually be maintained at low speeds.

A delicate hand will be needed on the throttles at displacement speeds because a small movement of the throttle can produce quite a large variation in the speed. However, this effect can be used to good effect when it is necessary to nurse the boat through the waves. The throttle will need to be used a lot more on planing boats in rough seas with a short burst on the throttle being used to help maintain heading and to help lift the bow to approaching waves. A marked lifting and dropping of the bow can be noticed when the throttle is opened or closed.

The tactics of operating a planing boat in rough conditions can often mean that, rather than reducing speed when operating in a head sea, one should look for an alternative heading for the boat on which it can still be operated at higher speeds. For instance, whereas a planing vessel may well have to slow right down in a

Above: It should be possible to turn and accelerate away from breaking waves in a planing boat. Photo: Safehaven Marine

Below: Much concentration is required when steering through beam seas to find the flat water between breaking crests. Photo: Safehaven Marine

head sea, it can still maintain good speed in beam seas or in following seas particularly, and this could well be a safer course to take, rather than running the boat at displacement speeds on the original course. Much will depend on the destination and what the options are, but high speed in a following sea will often be safer than for a displacement boat operating in the same conditions, because the high speed increases the ability of the helmsman to dictate his position with respect to the waves.

Most long-distance cruisers are of the displacement type because this is where fuel economy for long distances is achieved. However, an increasing number of semi-displacement long distance cruisers are appearing. Most of them are trawler yachts of one type or another but some planing, deep-vee boats are able to achieve respectable ranges for cruising. The big difference between these types and displacement hulls is the influence of the dynamic stability on the performance. The dynamic stability created by the forward motion of the hull helps to stabilise the hull at speed, but a much greater response to the throttle will be noticed, not only in the speed of the hull but also in its trim angle. This change in trim angle can be used to good effect to help progress in rough seas and it can even be effective at quite low speeds down to those found on displacement hulls.

Indeed, it would be fair to say that the primary means of control in semi-displacement and planing hulls is the throttle. By varying the propeller thrust with the throttle there is the ability to raise or lower the bow, but the throttle also has a vital role to play in the speed at which the boat impacts with approaching waves. This speed of approach, to a certain extent, determines whether the boat will fly off the top of a wave or not. Although it looks photographically spectacular when a boat does this, it is not an efficient means of progress. Every time the boat flies or even partially flies off a wave the propeller is losing its bite on the water, but more importantly, it puts an enormous stress on the boat, the machinery and the crew. When we were setting a record round Britain a few years ago in a 15m (50ft)

deep-vee, we made it a rule that the hull should never leave the water. In this way we felt we might be able to cope with standing up in a fast boat for 44 hours.

Few cruising boats are likely to attempt such heroics, but the same rule applies. If bad weather is encountered, particularly head seas, then careful throttle control is vital to give the boat as gentle a ride as possible, but this doesn't necessarily mean that one has to come down to displacement speeds. In many cases the bow should be kept up to reduce the chance of water coming over the foredeck and one can use the change of trim that usually occurs at around 12–15 knots when the hull tries to climb over its own bow wave, to keep the bow up.

Unless the sea gets too rough, it is possible with a deep-vee hull to get it up and running so that it stays virtually at a level trim despite the impact of the waves that try to upset the trim. Much will depend on the wave size, but if the boat is trimmed properly it can run virtually across the top of the waves with the control of the trim of the boat being exercised solely by the use of the throttle. The biggest problem with this is actually getting the vessel up into this situation, and it does mean that several waves have to be negotiated rather uncomfortably as the boat builds up speed. The boat will level out once at high speed.

Getting a craft trimmed in this way is a real joy and the boat really sings as it flies along. It requires careful setting up, using the power trim – i.e. the capability of altering the line of thrust of the propeller in a vertical plane by adjustment of the trim of an outboard engine – when available, the flaps and then, finally, the throttle to keep the balance, as passing waves have varying influences on the hull. When the boat is up and running in this way, it is possible to make very rapid progress to windward even though the waves can be quite large. It does require some degree of courage to take the bull by the horns and get the boat up into a situation where one can take advantage of this, but this is not just a technique for use on smaller sports cruisers. When I was delivering the world's first large deep-vee hull from Britain to Greece we managed to get it up and running in this way when the mistral started to kick up a nasty sea in the Mediterranean. The boat was a 30m (85ft) patrol boat for the Greek Navy and the choices were to wallow at displacement speeds for a long night at sea or try the high-speed technique to make harbour in a couple of hours in the rapidly freshening wind. This is probably a technique to use when running for shelter rather than something to do for general cruising. It needs a strong boat and it is not likely to be effective on semi-displacement craft.

When running like this concentration is needed, because there is always the risk that a bigger wave than normal will come along and upset the delicate balance of the boat. A good throttle man will read the waves and concentrate very closely on each one as it approaches, adjusting the throttle almost by instinct as the craft meets the wave, so that the bow slices through the top without the wave imparting too much lift, allowing the boat to continue on an almost even keel. With the Greek boat it took a fair amount of courage to wind the boat up and open the throttles and we suffered a few nasty bangs as we hit the first two or three waves, but soon after the boat really got up on top and, with the trim tabs down, away we went, travelling at close to 30 knots in conditions which I would never have thought possible for a boat of this size.

One of the major ingredients for success when running a planing boat in rough seas is to use the throttle very delicately. The tendency, when a larger wave is seen approaching, is to bring the throttle right back to reduce the impact between wave and boat. But this will bring the boat off the plane, the bow will drop and there is every chance that the larger wave will come curling down the deck as the bow buries into it, rather than the boat riding over it. In most cases only a slight reduction of the throttle setting will be needed to adjust to the approaching wave. This will not change the trim of the boat too dramatically and it will be found that much better progress can be made. This is one of the reasons why I favour throttle controls separate from the gear lever, because then you have a much wider range of throttle movement which allows for the more sensitive control necessary for this type of driving.

Head seas

We have already covered most of the aspects of head sea handling when talking about using the throttle. Getting the boat up and running on the tops of the waves may have limited application and those with a cruising boat, which tend to be less well designed to cope with the heavy impact which can result if things get out of hand, are not likely to take the risk. It is also unlikely on a cruising craft that the necessary level of concentration can be maintained for any length of time, and very often the visibility from the steering position is not good enough for the waves to be easily read. Reflections in the windscreen, and even the windscreen itself, if it has been sprayed with water, can greatly reduce the ability to read the waves ahead.

In these conditions, one is more likely to find a throttle setting at which the boat runs comfortably and let the boat do the work. In moderate seas good progress is often made in this way and certainly if on a long passage, this technique takes a lot of the tension out of driving and makes for a comfortable life. In moderate conditions it may be possible to set the autopilot and have a relatively gentle cruise, but always in a planing boat it pays to remember the wide variety of shapes and sizes of waves that can be met at sea. If the throttle is set in this way, then the speed at which the boat is travelling must leave an adequate margin for the boat to ride comfortably over larger than normal waves, without danger or too much discomfort.

If conditions start to deteriorate there will be an instinctive tendency to ease back on the throttle, because the motion of the boat will soon indicate that things are being pushed too hard. Fortunately, with most modern fast cruising craft, the weak point in the boat (and the one that generally starts to complain first) is the crew itself, and this is a good safety factor. If the motion starts to get uncomfortable for the crew, then the boat is probably being pushed too hard and by easing back the throttle a more comfortable speed should be found.

When conditions get to the point where it is difficult to find a comfortable speed and still keep the boat on the plane, then there are two options. The first is to ease back and come off the plane and operate the boat in the displacement mode, but the low freeboard at the bow of most planing boats does not always make this a comfortable option. Nevertheless if there are any doubts about driving or concentration capabilities, then this is probably the wise course of action to adopt. The main secret of fast boat driving into a head sea is to match the speed of the craft to the conditions, and the throttle is the main control to work with. Obviously, there will be a benefit from adjusting the trim tabs to help keep the bow down when on the plane and normally if a reduced speed has been chosen, it will almost certainly be necessary to bring in the power trim if it is fitted, which will also help to balance the boat to the conditions.

The other option open is to alter course. Even a 20° alteration can make a significant difference to the way the boat behaves. Altering course off the wind may take the boat away from the direct course to the destination but it will have the effect of extending the wavelength, which in turn reduces the wave gradient, which in turn will give a more comfortable ride. Experimentation will be necessary to find the best amount to alter course. There may be times when it is necessary to turn up into a big wave and reduce speed, or turn away and open the throttles to escape from the section of a wave which is breaking. But 'tacking' in this way can be a very effective tactic in rough conditions.

Beam seas

A planing craft in beam seas can be quite an exhilarating ride, but if rapid progress is required in waves on the beam then again much concentration will be needed. Even in beam seas it is necessary to read the waves

ahead all the time, otherwise there will be some unpleasant moments. If the waves came in a regular pattern, then it would simply be a question of the boat lifting over the wave as it passed underneath and dropping down into the trough in a nice rhythmical way. However, waves are far from regular and when in a beam sea this becomes most apparent. It can happen that a wave suddenly presents what appears to be a near vertical face as the boat approaches, and then equally quickly that wave seems to disappear and the boat drops into a trough. The boat can suffer some quite heavy impacts dropping off waves in this way, but much of this can be avoided if the steering and throttle controls are used to good effect.

Watch the waves in a beam sea and it will be noticed that some are considerably higher than others, some having gentle gradients, others having steep gradients and with varying peaks and troughs. Very rarely is there a long wave front. It is quite easy to see where the flatter areas of sea are and by using the throttle and steering one can often steer around the worst of the waves, which tend to form in localised peaks. It is surprising how comfortable a ride can be achieved if the boat is driven in this way but it does require a lot of concentration and a sensitive hand on the throttle and steering. It is often difficult to get good steering control in these conditions because only one hand is available on the steering wheel. And it can pay to concentrate on just one of these controls, normally the steering wheel, so that this can be really used to good effect, leaving the throttle setting at a speed that is comfortable for the conditions.

In taking evasive action from threatening wave crests with the wind on the beam, the boat will steer off the wind much more easily than trying to alter course towards it, so turning away will be the common way to alter course. Having said that, when steering off the wind, the waves are still effectively coming from ahead, so it may be necessary to steer further off to actually miss a particular wave. By steering into the wind, on the other hand, one will get a better chance to let the wave pass across the bow and run into the smoother water behind.

A comfortable ride is achieved in beam seas by steering round the wave peaks.
Photo: Safehaven Marine

Every wave is different and a quick assessment is required for each one. A point to remember here, as far as navigation is concerned, is that if one is frequently turning off course in the same direction, the course made good can be a long way off from the intended course.

Even when the wind is not exactly on the beam, and a course 30–40° from the wind is steered, the same technique of driving the boat across or round the lower parts of the wave can be adopted to make good progress. These are tactics that can be adopted even in quite rough seas, but as the seas get rougher the consequences of making a mistake become greater and concentration needs to be yet harder. It can be a very exhilarating ride, but it is necessary to be aware of the risks that are being taken and the consequences of getting out of step with the waves.

Mention needs to be made of the way in which fast boats, particularly those of the deep-vee type, heel under the influence of the rudders. This is most pronounced when the wind is on the beam. Obviously, if there are trim tabs fitted to the vessel, then the boat can be levelled up so that it runs true. But even then, if steering to avoid the worst of the seas, turning whichever way will cause the boat to heel. This is one of the primary causes of an uncomfortable ride in a beam sea because the hull may land on the flat of the vee rather than the apex. The only way to avoid this is to use the steering gently so that the effect on the transverse trim is minimised.

Following seas

Running before a following sea in a powerboat can be equally exciting. Not only is it possible sometimes to employ full throttle in this situation, but also it may be felt that it can be done with comparative safety, because the speed of encounter with the waves is much slower than with a head sea. The speed at which the waves travel is determined by their wave length, so that smaller waves will be travelling at 12–15 knots and the larger waves, perhaps those generated by a Force 5–6 wind, may be travelling at between 15 and 20 knots. In coastal waters waves travelling at more than 20 knots are unlikely to be found unless, of course, there is a swell running where the wavelength can be considerably longer and the wave travels faster accordingly. But swell tends to have a very gentle gradient, which is unlikely to impinge on progress. With a moderate-speed planing boat, there should be the potential to overtake following sea waves, possibly even travelling at twice the speed of the waves, so that the period of encounter allows the boat to recover from each wave in turn without any dramatic change of attitude of trim (see photo page 132).

With boats capable of speeds up to around 30 knots, it is often possible to simply set the throttle and let the boat take its course whilst still making rapid speed downwind. Much will depend on the size of the waves and their speed of travel. One of the problems is that, as the craft climbs up the back of the wave it tends to lose speed because it is, in effect, climbing uphill. Then when it gets to the crest it tends to sit there for a moment until enough of the bow projects over the steeper leeward face of the wave to cause it to drop with a quite sudden change of trim. This all tends to happen in slow motion. Relatively speaking, with the boat on the crest of the wave travelling little faster than the wave itself, there is a marked change in trim as the boat drops down the leeward face of the wave, and at the same time suddenly accelerates. This acceleration is under the impetus of the throttle and of gravity. In rough conditions, and depending a great deal on the speed and type of the boat and the speed of the waves, the bow of the vessel can be found to be burying itself quite heavily into the next wave in front as it rushes down the downhill slope. Certainly, with a boat with a full bow, the impact of the boat into the wave can be quite harsh, giving a very uncomfortable motion.

There are two remedies in this situation if it becomes uncomfortable, which is likely if the wind and waves start to increase. First, if there is the power to increase speed, this will have the effect of reducing the time that the boat spends on the crest of the wave, thus reducing the dramatic change of trim at the crest. Second, if there is not the potential to increase speed, it can be reduced so that the boat will tend to ride with the bow on the upward slope of the wave, virtually keeping pace with the wave. If the wave should disappear in front or break, then the throttles can be opened and the boat will accelerate over it. This will give a slower and more comfortable ride, and is the tactic to adopt if the sea conditions start to rise to the point where it is felt that the boat ought to be nursed. Sitting on the back of the wave in this fashion also requires a fair degree of concentration and a bigger wave may come up behind which could well be travelling faster than the boat. In this case there is the potential to have a broaching situation, unless the problem is recognised and action taken to accelerate away.

In rough conditions, say Force 7 or upwards, running in a following sea in a planing boat can be one of the safest means of progress, provided of course that the vessel underneath is reliable and sound. Rapid progress can still be made in this direction, at least travelling roughly at the speed of the waves, simply by sitting on the back of a wave and waiting for that wave to collapse or break before driving onwards. It is not really a wise tactic to adopt if there is a long way to travel because the person at the helm will soon get tired and lose concentration. As already stated several times, concentration is the name of the game because in a rough sea the safety margins get smaller and mistakes can soon cause trouble.

The same technique can be used when entering harbour where there is breaking surf on the bar and the boat has to be driven in through this with the wind and sea astern. In many situations, such as a harbour entrance, it could prove dangerous for a displacement boat because of the risk of broaching and losing control as the waves overtake. In a planing boat there is more freedom to dictate position in relation to the waves, and here the boat can be kept riding on the back of a wave while heading in. If the wave breaks, then it should be driven over to place the boat on the back of the next wave in front and so on until

A quartering sea can be comfortable at high speed in a planing hull, but watch that the bows do not bury themselves in the wave ahead. Photo: Safehaven Marine

through the area of breaking waves. It requires nerve, concentration and good visibility, and this is not the time when one can afford to have anything go wrong with the boat, but it is feasible way of running an inlet.

In following seas one problem that can be encountered is a certain loss of stability, particularly when travelling at lower planing speeds, say around 18 or 20 knots. Here the dynamic stability of the hull, generated by the boat moving through the water, will be much less and it will be further reduced if the boat is in breaking waves where the water is moving ahead. This loss of stability will be found most noticeable when the boat passes through the crest of a wave where the inherent stability of the hull is also reduced. It can cause the boat to lean over, so that if the boat does fly off a wave it could land very heavily on the flat of the vee of the hull. Whilst such a loss of stability is not likely to be dangerous to the point of capsize, it can make handling the boat more difficult. If this sort of instability is felt

to be developing, once again it is a question of using the throttles at the right time to increase the dynamic response to get the bow up as one comes through the crest of the wave. Instability will be apparent by the rolling of the boat and by sloppiness in the steering. As so often with a high-speed craft, when this situation seems to be occurring the solution is to put on more power rather than to close the throttles.

At slower speeds in following seas the trim tabs will generally want to be kept up in order to give the bow as much lift as possible so that the bow doesn't drop off as the waves are overtaken. At these slower speeds the power trim should be brought in, if it is fitted, for the same reason. Both of these controls have less effect at slower speeds anyway.

In planing and semi-displacement boats it is not possible to relax in rough seas in the way that one might with a displacement boat. The boats tend to be more lightly built so that they are less resistant to wave impact. Even by slowing down to displacement speed the best solution will not always be found, particularly if the bow drops in a trough at the same time, as will certainly happen with a fully planing hull. Semi-displacement hulls tend to be better because they have a fuller bow.

The need for concentration has been constantly mentioned in faster boats but this can become a problem at night when it can be difficult to see what the waves are doing. This is the time to set the boat on the most comfortable and least demanding course, irrespective of destination. Again a lot will depend on the conditions, but somewhere with the sea about 30–45° on the bow is likely to give the best ride running at reduced speed, with the reserve to cope with those larger than average waves when they are spotted.

Coping with extremes

When conditions turn really bad, the best place to be is in harbour. However, it can sometimes be more dangerous to try to enter harbour than to stay out at sea. Some of the worst sea conditions can be found in harbour entrances, so the first decision that has to be made when bad weather arrives is whether to stay out at sea or whether to make for harbour. It is never an easy decision because the thought of harbour always seems so attractive, but before heading for harbour consider the conditions in the entrance, particularly if the harbour lies downwind and is wide open to the wind and sea. The worst conditions of the voyage can be just on arrival given that adverse weather may extend the time at sea.

Speed is the first thing to consider when out at sea. Speed, comfort and stress are directly related and a slower speed can solve many problems when bad weather is encountered. However, speed should not be reduced to the point that steerage way is lost, otherwise the boat becomes vulnerable to breaking waves. Unless steering control is maintained the desired heading will be lost and that could bring as much trouble as going too fast. If the sea builds up to the point where the situation is worrying then it is time to look at what

resources there are to cope. When things get really bad then it is time to go into a survival mode with the object of weathering the storm until things improve.

There are no magic solutions in these situations and the decisions will be based to a large degree on the type of vessel, the nature of the conditions, and personal experience and ability to cope. In these extreme conditions, lifeboats are expected to cope and to have something left to help others in trouble. A lesson can be taken from lifeboats and the way they operate, but it has to be remembered that much of the safety of lifeboats in rough seas is determined long before they actually put to sea. The boats are strongly built, their equipment is sound and the crews are well trained and fit. These are all prerequisites for survival in bad conditions. But there is always the risk of being caught out, and the prudent sailor will make some mental as well as practical preparations for this by ensuring that both he, his crew and his craft are in good condition before putting to sea.

When caught out in worsening conditions, the first thing to do is to make an assessment of the situation. What are the weak points in the boat and its equipment? Is the crew fit for the task ahead? Where is the nearest shelter and safety? The first concern should be with the boat and where the weak and vulnerable points might lie. If there are large areas of glass in the bridge windows it is wise not to push the boat into a head sea. If there is a deep rear cockpit, the risk of a sea breaking over the stern in a following sea should be avoided.

On the machinery side there could be concerns about the amount of fuel remaining. Also the reliability of the engines, and auxiliary systems such as the electrics must be considered. In rough seas it only needs a small failure which, in itself, may not be too serious but which can start off a chain reaction of events that can lead to disaster. I remember coming across a boat at sea which was on fire in rough conditions, a pretty serious situation that had started because of a steering failure! The steering was a wire and pulley system and the wire frayed and then finally broke.

Given time, such a condition would not have been too difficult to fix, but without steering the boat turned broadside on and was rolling very heavily. This made it difficult to effect the repair and, much more seriously, the rolling set the poorly secured battery sliding about, which eventually broke the main battery cable. The short circuit that resulted started a fire and the single occupant was lucky to get out alive. This may be an exceptional case, but any failure in the boat or its systems can escalate and add to the worries. When assessing the situation it is important to take all factors into account, and if unhappy with any of them then it is time to go into survival mode.

Methods of heaving-to in a powerboat tend to require the boat to be driven, which means that long hours have to be spent at the controls. There are alternatives, and one is simply to close the boat down and leave her to her own devices. I don't think this would be my choice, but I know of several cases where powerboats left to drift have come through unscathed. The problem is that we tend to hear about the ones that made it rather than those that simply disappeared without trace.

Even when one is very tired, keeping some semblance of control is better than just letting the boat drift. With nothing to do, there is a tendency to give up mentally and that is not a good state of mind for survival. It might be possible to get away with it in a strong displacement vessel, but in a light planing boat the chances would not be so good.

One solution is to drive the boat on a course that seems sympathetic to the boat and the sea, but the good skipper tries to keep something up his sleeve. There are the traditional methods of coping with rough seas, such as using drogues, sea anchors (Chapter 7) and oil (Chapter 15). The use of this equipment may often be talked about, but few modern skippers have the experience of using this equipment and fewer still have used them for survival. They are certainly not the solution to all the problems as often portrayed, but they are worthy of consideration if only to know when to reject them.

The universally proclaimed panacea for all desperate situations at sea is that of spreading oil on troubled waters. There is no doubt that the correct type of oil used under certain circumstances can have a beneficial effect,

An Interceptor 42, powered by two 426hp diesels, off Toa Mor, West Loch Roag, used for transport of freight and personnel, often to St Kilda, all through the year. Photo: Murray MacLeod

Going downwind is the most comfortable direction for a planing hull, but dynamic stability can be lost on the wave crests. Photo: Safehaven Marine

but this is limited and miracles must not be expected. The recommended oil is unrefined fish oil, normally supplied as 'storm oil'.

It is rare to find a boat carrying oil for the specific purpose of spreading it on the water, so that when the need for it arises, the only oil likely to be available is either lubricating oil or diesel oil. Diesel oil is almost useless, but lubricating oil will have some effect. It is less viscous than the optimum and it will spread readily on the water, but its effect in reducing the breaking of waves will be less than the recommended fish oil. On balance, though, I do not think much of the idea of using oil mainly because everything will get coated in the oil and that can increase the risk of personal injury, something you can do without in this survival situation.

Drogues, sea anchors and oil can be some of the weapons available to help cope with extreme conditions, but the best weapon of all is a fit crew who think about what they are doing and how they are doing it. In a slow displacement boat the best approach is to drive the boat at slow speed, probably head to the sea or just off the bow. In a planing boat the best solution may be running before the waves

provided that the boat has enough speed to travel faster than the waves. Failing this, turn and point the strongest part of the boat, the bow, into or close into the waves and *just* maintain steerageway to reduce the stresses as much as possible. Preparation is another important weapon, but there is not much to be done about that at sea except batten down and make sure everything is well secured.

Survival in extreme conditions will be a mental as much as a physical challenge so it is necessary to guard against tiredness and stress. When one is tired everything seems to be too much trouble and there is a tendency to let things take their course. Having crew who can alternate routines and take charge is a huge bonus in these situations, and getting whatever rest possible will help survival. There is no magic formula here, and most reactions will be guided by instinct. The most important thing to guard against in survival conditions is a failure in the boat. Failures can escalate in a way that that puts a boat on the road to disaster. Preventing failures is something that is best done before leaving harbour and a well maintained boat is good protection when survival conditions are encountered in a powerboat.

14 Multihull tactics in heavy weather

Mark Orr

When the first edition of this book was published in 1967 multihulls were on the fringe of the sport, at an experimental stage in their development, with designers and adventurers pushing the boundaries of what multihulls could do. James Wharram's transatlantic voyage in 1956, and Derek Kelsall's Transatlantic in 1964 and Round Britain adventures in 1966 gave significant examples of early progress, but were countered by yachts breaking up or capsizing that gave the impression of an experimental concept in the early stages of development.

Nearly 50 years later multihulls are raced in the America's Cup, hold virtually all global speed records and have circled the globe fully crewed in under 46 days and singlehanded in 57 days 13 hours; less time than that first transatlantic multihull voyage.

This has all been made possible by materials technology, computers, experience and passion. The technology from the superb racing multihulls we now see has trickled down into cruising boats. Multihulls have been transformed to a position where they are a respected and reliable option for anyone who might be looking to race, cruise or embark on a long distance voyage.

There are so many different types of multihull available, with such a wide range of uses that it would be hard to prescribe for the handling of all in heavy weather. Not surprisingly the handling of a lightweight racing trimaran will differ considerably to that of a heavier cruising catamaran.

However, there are common features that apply to all multihulls: they are generally lightweight, their stability is provided by their beam, and they have shallow draft, though some will have small unballasted stub keels that provide directional stability and protect rudders and propellers.

In heavy weather a catamaran's motion will vary depending on its design. However, beam gives it great stability so there is minimal rolling. There is likely to be more pitching when going to windward than a comparable monohull and a catamaran's relatively little mass means that the frequency of pitching will be quicker.

Their buoyant bows cause multihulls to go over, rather than through, the waves. At a given speed, generally speaking, a multihull ride will be more comfortable than a monohull's. However, due to their relative light weight, generous sail areas and windage, multihulls can be hard to slow down when sailing off the wind or downwind.

On catamarans there are generally large working areas, whereas on a trimaran, unless it is also fitted with trampolines, the working areas are usually limited to the central hull. As a result they are therefore equivalent to that of a similar sized monohull.

In heavy weather a multihull's speed, light weight and stability are key factors that can be used to advantage. However, there are actions that consistently threaten survival in heavy weather.

Banque Populaire V, *skippered by Loick Peyron, circled the globe in 45 days, 13 hours, 42 minutes and 53 seconds in 2012.* Photo: B Stichelbaut/BPCE

Structure

Multihulls have increased in popularity as reliability has improved. Designers and builders have successfully taken what has worked on the racecourse, and engineered it into cruising structures. Even the most modest cruising multihull will usually be designed to accept high point and torsional loads. The structure will be light but strong and will often use complex woven fibreglass, carbon or Kevlar laminates to achieve this. Its engineering will include a high safety margin. However, attempts to modify it, by cutting holes in bulkheads to fit heating for example, or removing structure to modify interior accommodation, can compromise strength. If making any major changes do check if this is wise with the designer!

Modern materials may seem reasonably easy to repair but often require professional support to do so effectively. Damage must be properly repaired to ensure long-term reliability. For example, a high tech composite craft will require high tech composite repairs.

All multihulls should be fitted with escape hatches. They should be fitted in either the hull sides or the bridgedeck. They must be large enough to allow a fully clothed crewmember to go through, and be able to be opened from both sides. A robust deck hatch is often used but the escape hatch must be sited away from areas of wave impact such as hull sides forward of the bridgedeck. They must be sited in a position that is above the inverted waterline so opening the hatch does not allow water to flood into the boat. Lifelines should also be securely attached to the underside of the boat so that the crew can clip on to the relative security of the upturned hulls. Painting the bridgedeck, rudders and daggerboards in high visibility paint is a sensible precaution.

Overloading

The space available on any cruising catamaran often tempts owners to overload them. Loading should not exceed the designer or manufacturer's recommendation, but a useful guide is that loading should not exceed one-third of the weight when the craft was built (in other words, when empty). Overloading affects speed, places additional load on the structure and reduces the height between the bridgedeck/beams and the waves, thus increasing pounding and the likelihood of damage through wave impact.

Weight should always be kept out of the ends of the hulls to reduce pitching and to ensure that the bows and sterns lift easily over waves. Thus weight should be concentrated around the centre of the boat, and, in a catamaran, it should be evenly balanced between the two hulls.

In extreme conditions multihulls rely on being able to side slip when hit by a big wave. The more weight a multihull carries the greater the inertia to be overcome by the wave and therefore the greater the likelihood of damage.

Windage

Whilst most trimarans are designed for speed, many catamarans, even of modest length, boast full standing headroom on the bridgedeck. Either lowering the bridgedeck floor or increasing roof height achieves this, but a compromise between the two is usually the result. The consequence is increased windage and the possibility of increased wave pounding.

In heavy weather the greater the windage, the less the windward performance. Multihull owners have a tendency to add biminis, sail covers, dinghies on davits, which all increase windage unless they are stowed away. So in strong winds greater leeway is likely than in more modest winds which will affect the upwind strategy to be taken if beating off a lee shore.

Maintenance

Multihulls generally have more equipment than the equivalent monohull. If not properly maintained then there is more to go wrong. Poor maintenance of engine and electrical systems will usually ensure that when an item is needed most, it will let you down. Make sure that these systems are accessible so maintenance is encouraged rather than ignored! Rigging and sails will be tested most in heavy weather, so highly loaded components, such as halyards, rigging, furling systems and sails should be routinely checked or replaced e.g. standing rigging, like any other sailing vessel, should be changed at least every 10 years.

Preparation for heavy weather

Weather information

All skippers of craft sailing offshore or ocean voyaging must have a reliable source of weather information and be aware of how to analyse it. The onset of heavy weather should rarely be a surprise. The prudent sailor will analyse the weather information available and plan accordingly. With sufficient warning a multihull should have time to use its speed to sail away from the worst of the weather in an approaching depression and, if sea room permits, position itself to receive least risk from lee shores, rocks, shoals, shipping lanes and suchlike.

Deck preparation

There is much that a crew can do to prevent damage from breaking waves and to reduce windage. All moveable deck gear should be stripped off and stowed securely below. Biminis and spray hoods should be removed, dinghies deflated and stowed in lockers. Sail covers and stack packs removed or lashed down, windsurfers stowed or stored flat, etc.

Consideration should be given to crew movement around the boat. Nowadays, multihull cockpits are large and should have some rope lifelines set up at the mid point, for example, to prevent crew being thrown too far by the sudden motion of the boat. On deck, in addition to lifelines to which safety harness strops can be attached, there should be jackstays to enable movement from side decks to the mast, or forward onto the trampolines or foredeck.

The blocks and ropes for sea anchors or drogues should be set up for immediate use. These drag devices should be checked and stowed in deck lockers for easy access.

All ocean voyaging multihulls should have storm boards for large saloon windows and smaller boards for port lights or hatches in the hulls. These are usually 6mm plywood with a strongback and butterfly nuts to enable the plywood to cover the damaged window or port light. With the plywood placed over the outside of the damaged saloon window or portlight the strongback should be tightened against the boats' structure with the butterfly nut. Waterproofing can be improved with thick neoprene, perhaps from an old wetsuit, being placed between the plywood and the hole it is sealing. The trend toward vertical saloon windows and large hull portlights make the carriage of storm boards more critical.

Storm sails

Compared to trimarans, catamarans rarely have a particularly tight forestay due to lack of bow structure. Consequently forestay sag is likely to increase as the wind builds, and in turn windward performance will deteriorate, particularly if the part-furled headsail has a poor shape. In both cases a backstay may not be fitted because the roach of the mainsail is too large and the forestay can only be made taut by tensioning the mainsheet. Generally foresails have a reasonably high centre of effort that often increases as the sail is reduced, which is exactly the opposite of what is needed.

Two options exist. The first is to replace the working headsail, before the storm is evident, with a flatter cut storm sail, which can be reduced in area without furling through having slab reefs. As the wind increases the slabs are taken in, reducing sail area while keeping the centre of effort low.

The second option is to have an inner forestay attached to a separate strong point or alternatively a high load lashing around the front beam, which can be tensioned using a bottle screw or Highfield lever. The storm sail can then be attached with hanks and reefed as described above.

Few multihulls carry storm trysails, usually relying on a deep fourth reef. This is acceptable provided that the reef is truly deep, and equivalent in area to that of a storm trysail by being no more that 15 per cent of the total mainsail area. The reefing line must be rigged as part of storm preparation and a strop used to ensure that the reef tack can be brought down to the gooseneck when required.

Multihull storm sails needs to be very strongly built, as with little heel to dissipate the load, the head, clew and tack have to absorb the impact of a gust. Moreover sails have to withstand the flogging that often occurs in heavy weather. Once the reef has been set, it is essential to have a rope lashing (earing) between the clew of the mainsail and the boom to help absorb some of the load, and to provide a backup should chafe cause the reefing line to fail. If not fitted with a rigid boom vang or other means of supporting the boom the topping lift can be attached to the head of the mainsail to provide backup in the event of chafe causing the main halyard to fail. If at some point the mainsail is not required the boom should, if possible, be lowered to the deck, supported with fenders, and be well lashed down. The reduction in windage will be significant. The redundant main halyard and topping lift can then be used to support the mast should one of the cap shrouds fail.

Crew preparation

It is essential that crew eat, drink and sleep to maintain their alertness and, happily, the stability of a multihull means that the weather will have to be exceptionally bad to prevent

Multihulls have to be strongly and carefully designed and built to withstand the huge stresses of travelling at speed in heavy weather. Photo: Thierry Martinez

preparation of food and drink. A multihull with a bridgedeck cabin is the ideal place in which to rest, as it is light and airy, close to the helmsman, and reasonably stable. It is very important to keep crew briefed and active so that they know what is going on and feel that they are playing their part.

If the saloon is large and open then rope lifelines should be set up to assist crew movement but also to restrain if a crewmember falls over.

Sailing to windward in heavy weather

There are times when a lee shore, proximity to a shipping lane, or the avoidance of even heavier weather makes sailing to windward necessary. Sailing to windward in heavy weather is wet, uncomfortable and can be testing for the helmsperson and the crew. Good waterproof clothing is even more essential than for monohulls.

Progress will be greatly influenced by the wave height and sea state. A general rule is to point up as the crest of the wave is approached and to bear away once the crest has passed. This technique should enable reasonable progress to be made to windward under shortened sail, but it is important to have sufficient sail power to drive over waves and not be pushed aside by them. If this means carrying more sail than would be prudent, then running the leeward engine, or if necessary both, usually at slow speed, will serve to ensure progress is maintained. Engine power can be varied with wave conditions.

If there are strong gusts the helm should head up in the gusts rather than bear away to avoid the boat rapidly accelerating and generating higher apparent winds speeds than are desirable for the sail area set and the desired course.

When it is necessary to tack there should be no hesitation in backing the headsail to ensure that the boat comes round. It will be necessary to bear away, whilst sheeting in, to build boat

179

Above: A headsail without barber hauler

Below: Headsail fitted with barber hauler
Photos: Woods Designs

mainsail sheet manned by a crewmember who can ensure the boat is not overpowered in the gybe when the stern passes though the wind by releasing the main sheet as necessary.

A boat with daggerboards should only keep the windward board down. Use of the leeward board may provide too much lateral resistance and will prevent the boat slipping sideways should the boat be hit by a large wave, which could expose the boat to the risk of wave damage or even capsizing.

When sailing to windward the load on the windward shrouds will be large whilst the leeward shrouds may become loose enough to shake around as the boat rises over the waves. Shock cord should be used to restrict this movement and avoid fatigue with the risk of a failure when the shroud becomes loaded.

In strong winds, sails need to be sheeted as flat as possible and it is important to ensure that the slot between the headsail and the mainsail is even. This can be hard to achieve with a furling headsail whose poor furled shape, combined with forestay sag, may cause there to be a lot of twist in the sail and decrease the sheeting angle. Correct adjustment of the genoa sheet car is essential to maintain a good sail shape. It may also be necessary to use a barber hauler on the headsail sheet to pull the clew to leeward to open the slot as shown left.

Sailing to windward places a lot of load on equipment so it is necessary to conduct frequent visual inspections to ensure that gear remains in the right place, rigging is secure, shackle pins are in place and that chafe is being managed. A checklist will remove the need for a tired crewmember having to remember everything. The checklist also engenders confidence that all that can be done is being done. This, along with regular briefing, feeding and sleeping will keep a crew efficient and morale high.

Sailing on a reach

Sailing free but not downwind can be exhilarating in a fresh breeze with even the most modest cruiser. These are the most favourable of multihull conditions. However, wave height

speed before coming back onto the wind. If there are doubts about the ability to tack in the prevailing wave conditions, the engine should be used to drive the boat through the wind. If without an engine, a moment has to be found between large waves to gybe round. The gybe should be done quickly with the

Team Philips, *Pete Goss' 36m (120ft) catamaran, running downwind. Note the breaking cross-sea. This particularly dangerous type of wave tends to run across the existing wave set at a random rate, representing the remaining effect of the previous front that has already passed through.*
Photo: Phil Aikenhead

and shape will dictate the safe speed at which to sail. The more confused the sea, and the steeper the waves the greater the restraint required. On this point of sail a greater safety margin is required, as an increase in wind or a change in sea state can turn being 'under control' to being on the 'edge of control'. Small increases in true wind will mean that apparent wind has increased further and this should be monitored and sail changes made early.

When sailing free there is always the option to bear away or to point up a little to avoid a large or breaking wave. Indeed with multihull speed available, a good helmsman will be able to pick the easiest path through the waves.

At night, unless there is plenty of phosphorescence, it is much harder to steer through the waves, and the prudent option is to slow down by reefing. It is also psychologically more comfortable. Sailing free in a fresh wind will mean rapid progress but it is usually noisy below deck and wet and uncomfortable above deck. The boat will be hit by waves, sometimes going through wave tops, so that deck hatches, windows and portlights will be vulnerable.

Crew morale will need to be maintained through frequent rotation of helmsman, making sure that ample food is eaten regularly, lots of fluid is imbibed and rest is taken whenever possible.

Sailing downwind

There may come a time when reaching is no longer safe as wave fronts have become too steep, or the sea conditions have become too confused. The decision may be taken to sail downwind if sea room allows it. Indeed it may suit the destination. Downwind a multihull will have plenty of stability and can sail quickly and reasonably comfortably, usually with the wind over the quarter, but rarely completely downwind, as there is a great speed advantage to have both headsail and mainsail filled on the same side.

Downwind sailing can be exciting, as multihulls, being light, will tend to surf in the right conditions. There is therefore a balance to be struck between exhilaration and safety. At speed, particularly when surfing, the rudders may cavitate and control can be lost. The only remedy is to slow down.

Small increases in the apparent wind can mask significant increases in true wind and an unwary or tired helmsman may not appreciate the significance. If, for whatever reason, the boat stops, it is then exposed to the true wind. If it has to go upwind, perhaps to reduce sail, the boat will be sailing in the true wind plus boat speed. In either case the crew will now find themselves with too much sail area for the conditions, and the stability of the boat will be tested unless immediate action is taken to reduce sail. A useful rule of thumb is only to sail downwind with the sail area that is appropriate for making to windward in the same conditions and use the wind speed of the gusts, and not the lulls.

In these conditions, when it is essential to reef, prior fitting of reefing downhauls, attached to the tack of each reefing point enables the halyard winch to be used to pull the tack of each reef down to the gooseneck. If the mainsail slides 'stick' against the mast track under batten load then pump the mainsail to momentarily relieve the compression load of the batten.

If wave conditions increase then the boat may start 'running over' waves, which will increase the pounding on the bridgedeck. In some cases this may require a boat to slow down. Indeed in one race I have been in this has caused an escape hatch to burst, with obvious dangers. If reducing sail cannot slow the boat then other tactics need to be employed.

Slowing when sailing downwind

There are many means of slowing down and their effectiveness needs to be practised by the crew prior to their use in a real situation. It is often very difficult to control the speed of downwind sailing in heavy weather as the stability of a multihull encourages the crew to keep too much sail area, and windage alone can drive the boat fast downwind. The main cause of a capsize is digging in a hull or float as an indirect result of sailing too fast for the sea state. Moving weight aft and to windward

will help prevent the bows driving in the waves, but prior to this point being reached the crew need to slow the boat by reefing and, when no sail is left, by towing warps or a drogue. This will apply when it is necessary to reduce progress toward a lee shore or to allow crew to rest.

The simplest method is to tow long ropes, for example mooring warps. These can be as many as there are available. Their efficiency in slowing the boat can be increased by tying knots in the ropes and by weighing down the ropes with anchor chain. Indeed anchors can be towed at the end of the rope to increase drag. However, the more drag created, the greater the load on the attachment point and the harder it is to recover all the gear.

Some prefer creating a large loop with both ends of the rope attached to the boat. However, if sailing quickly downwind, the rope will need to be weighted to prevent the acceleration of the boat pulling the rope out of the water and the rope bouncing on the top of the waves until the boat slows down again – quite the opposite of what it was deployed to do.

A more efficient means of slowing progress will be a purpose built drogue. These are canvas or solid plastic devices often attached to between 5 and 10m (16.4 and 32.8ft) of chain, specifically designed for slowing vessels. They work by choking the rate at which water flows through the cone, or a series of vanes, or a large number of droguelets and are more fully described in the chapter on drogues and parachute sea anchors (Chapter 7). The load induced is considerable and drogues are an effective means of slowing a boat's rate of progress downwind. In particular they keep the stern and the rudders immersed, and prevent a multihull sailing so fast that severe cavitation at the rudders causes a loss of control. They can turn a boat sailing on the edge of control to being once again in control and allow safe progress to be made downwind in the desired direction. The attachment points must be purposely built in order to be strong enough to take the load created by a drogue.

It is important to adjust the rode length as wave conditions change. The drogue needs to sit at least 1.5 waves behind the boat, so that it sits in a trough as the towing craft sits on the top of a wave. A steady pull is essential so if the wavelength changes so that the drogue starts to sit on a crest it will be necessary to adjust the length to prevent the rapid acceleration of the boat forcing the drogue out of the water to bounce down the wave front. The use of a series drogue does help to avoid this as the long warps are deployed with multiple small cones (over 120 for an average sized multihull) with a sinker weight at their end so the drag effect occurs down the warp's length rather than relying on one submerged device to apply the desired braking force.

If a drogue fails to slow the boat sufficiently then it will need to be supplemented with warps. If that is not sufficient then it will be necessary to find a means to stop.

Stopping

There are three recognised methods of stopping. Whatever the method the key moment will be when coming head to wind to enable the boat to take any seas over the bow. Coming head to wind must be made with regard to the sea conditions with the minimal sail area to ensure sufficient speed for control. In most cases a quick turn between waves is better than taking too long. Use of the engine to make the turn is recommended.

Parachute sea anchors

These are described at length elsewhere in Chapter 7. As a rule multihulls require a sea anchor equivalent to 1.5 times the overall length of a monohull, so a 12m (40ft) multihull will require one appropriate for an 18m (60ft) monohull. This is to allow for the additional windage and snatch loads that a multihull will place upon it. Once deployed the 'parachute' opens and the boat is anchored to the ocean and should drift with the tides or currents. Downwind drift is significantly reduced, and in all but the most severe of conditions multihulls will lie comfortably to a sea anchor.

Figure 14.1 *Typical plastic drogue – the vanes choke the water movement through the drogue, increasing the drag. It should always be used with a length of chain to ensure it stays beneath the surface of the water.*

To provide directional stability and to help spread the load, the sea anchor rode should be attached to a bridle mounted on the outer hulls of a catamaran or trimaran. The length of the bridle lines needs to be adjustable so it is preferable to lead the lines back to mooring cleats perhaps using spinnaker sheet blocks to feed the bridle lines cleanly onto them. Alternatively lead the bridle lines back to the cockpit genoa or spinnaker sheet winches so that the bridle can be easily adjusted without too much manual effort. The bridle lines should be tied onto the rode with a rolling hitch and the rode led through the anchor roller to the anchor windlass, if fitted, or to the anchor cleat as a back up.

The sea anchor requires a substantial rode, as a guide the same diameter as anchor warp, ideally attached to a swivelling shackle at the end of the bridle. A lot of warp is required, approximately 20 times the height of the waves.

A multiplait rope is ideal as a rode as it resists the twisting loads that the sea anchor will place on it. For this reason cheaper hawser-laid warp is not recommended, as it tends to tie itself into knots as the sea anchor twists under load. Most cruisers will combine anchor warps and their chain with spinnaker sheets to ensure sufficient length.

The chain inserted mid length will provide some load absorption, relieving snatch loads on the boat. This chain should be mid length as placing it too close to the sea anchor will pull the sea anchor down too low in the water which in turn will pull the boat's bow down. The sea anchor float has to be large, much larger than a typical fender, if it is going to have any effect on lifting the parachute, and is important for keeping the sea anchor at a set depth beneath the water.

Launching the parachute sea anchor or drogue

Unless kept in a deployment bag, the parachute sea anchor should be wetted before deployment to prevent it inflating in the wind before it is put in the water. The yacht should be rounded up into the wind and sea, and the sea anchor deployed over the windward bow to allow the multihull to drift back without fouling the sea anchor. As the multihull drifts downwind, the rode should be paid out under control, and use of a winch is advisable as the loads can be significant. Steady paying out of the rode is essential as the tension created helps to deploy the parachute, whereas surges of warp will cause the parachute to collapse and possibly tangle.

The object is to have the sea anchor deployed in the water beneath the crest two wavelengths away from the boat. Once deployed, attach the bridle to the rode using a rolling hitch, and check that the parachute has pulled the bows around into the sea. If not, adjust the bridle. Relieve all possible chafe points.

Once everything has been checked, if the boat has daggerboards, these should now be part lowered as these will provide directional stability and stop the boat yawing around the bridle. Rudders should be rigidly locked on the centreline or lifted to prevent damage.

Launching a sea anchor is not the end of the story. Loads on the structure will be considerable and all lines and equipment must be frequently checked to ensure that chafe is prevented. With the boat 'anchored' waves may now break against the boat with an awful surging noise that preludes a wave strike. Crew need to be briefed that this is normal and survivable, but storm boards should be fitted if waves start hitting the saloon windows. Generally waves will tend to roll under the bridgedeck with little more than spray hitting saloon windows. If wave strikes are too powerful or the snatch loads too great, more rode should be let out if it is available. If this is still not enough, then lower a weight down the rode. On one occasion I deployed a padlocked

Figure 14.2 *The drogue should sit about 1.5 waves behind the boat, and when sea conditions change it is important to lengthen or reduce the rode.*

tool box down the warp as everything else, including the anchor, had been used.

Once the sea conditions allow the crew to start sailing again, it will be necessary to recover the sea anchor so that it can be used again. A trip line and float (an anchor tripping line and hi-vis buoy is ideal) should have been fitted to the crown of the anchor to hold the parachute at a suitable depth. It enables the crew to see where the parachute is and adjust the length of the rode to ensure the sea anchor is two wavelengths away and assist recovery.

Recover the rode whilst motoring gently towards the float. As the sea anchor is approached, slow down, and take care that the sea anchor does not go under the boat. Retrieve the tripping line, and then recover the sea anchor using one of its shrouds, which will cause the anchor to collapse. Wash the sea anchor in fresh water at the next opportunity, to prevent the salt crystals rotting the anchor. It is better to keep the sea anchor wet rather than allow it to dry out prior to being rinsed in fresh water.

It can be difficult to recover a sea anchor, particularly if sailing shorthanded or with a tired crew. There are a number of cases when the crew has decided to recover what they can and cut the parachute and its rode adrift with their consequent loss.

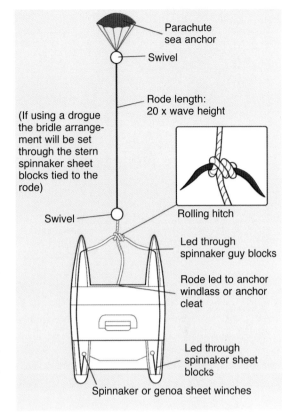

Figure 14.3 *The ideal bridle arrangement using spinnaker sheet and guy blocks to lead the bridle lines back to cockpit sheet winches, enabling adjustments to the bridle to be more easily and safely made.*

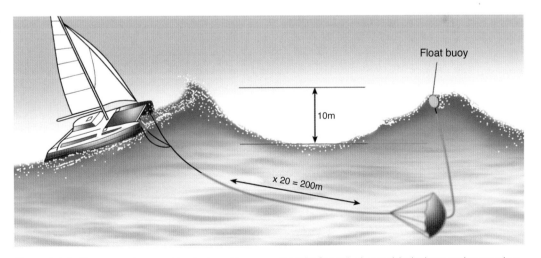

Figure 14.4 *The sea anchor must be deployed two wavelengths from the boat with the boat and sea anchor moving together up and down the wave. As a guide, the rode length needs to be 20 times the height of the wave.*

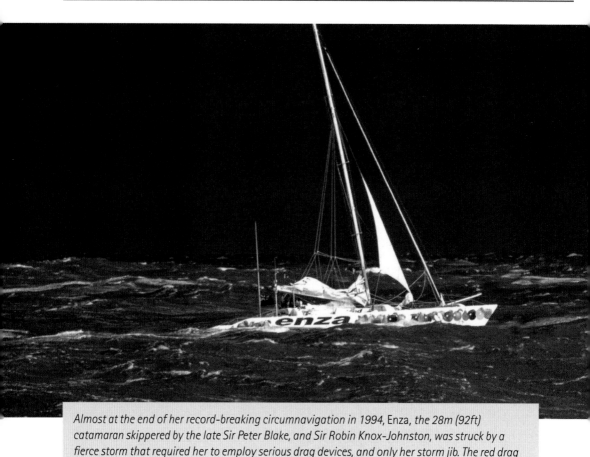

Almost at the end of her record-breaking circumnavigation in 1994, Enza, the 28m (92ft) catamaran skippered by the late Sir Peter Blake, and Sir Robin Knox-Johnston, was struck by a fierce storm that required her to employ serious drag devices, and only her storm jib. The red drag device lines can be seen extending from the stern. Photo: PPL

Heaving-to

This is a commonly used tactic, popular with the older multihulls, which have less windage than current production designs. Heaving-to means that the helm is turned and lashed so that the boat is trying to round up into the wind. As the foresail is aback (sheeted on the wrong side) and the mainsail is set normally, the boat cannot tack. Most multihulls will alternate between sailing on a reach, then accelerate, be driven by the rudder angle to sail to windward, stall and then drift slowly back to sailing on a reach. They make slow progress upwind and therefore do not drift downwind. This is a good tactic as the boat is continually moving, is not losing ground downwind and is not tethered to the ocean and therefore not resisting breaking waves. However, it is not advisable in extreme conditions as the boat can be pushed downwind by a breaking wave, at which point the mainsail and headsail will fill and accelerate. A compromise is to lower the mainsail and set a small headsail but lash the helm to windward so that the same effect applies. Even if knocked well off the wind, the helm will always drive the boat quickly upwind.

This tactic is generally effective in most heavy weather conditions. However, if the boat is frequently being pushed astern either as a result of a wave strike or a steep wave front, then the load placed on the rudders can be considerable and damage is likely. The crew should try more sail area to increase forward motion, or if this is not feasible then turn downwind or lie to a sea anchor.

Lying a'hull

This means lowering all sails and drifting under bare poles at the mercy of the wind and the waves. A multihull will generally sit beam on to the seas, where it will be uncomfortable, as waves will break against the structure forcing the boat downwind. In exceptional circumstances waves will lift the windward hull and the crest breaks beneath the bridgedeck and against the leeward hull, forcing the boat to surf beam on until the trough is reached when the same cycle may start again. Not a happy situation.

A particular danger is that with no forward motion or sea anchor to hold the bows into the sea, a breaking wave may force the multihull to surf backwards. This places a huge load on the rudders causing possible damage to them but may also force the leeward stern to dig into the water possibly prompting a diagonal capsize.

Lighter craft with daggerboards and rudders raised fare better when lying a'hull as they present little lateral resistance, indeed they may sail downwind at between 45 and 60° to the sea. In this case the motion, though still uncomfortable, is much kinder as the waves are taken along the length of the boat whereas heavier craft will be lying broadside on giving the feeling of being at the mercy of the sea. If sea room allows and the breaking waves are infrequent this can be a useful tactic, even though the downwind drift will be considerable. Lying a'hull is ideal for temporary repairs but has many disadvantages over long periods.

Capsize

The worst that can happen in heavy weather is capsizing. It is a terrible event but should not result in the loss of the crew or the yacht, provided that escape hatches are fitted, and the crew are trained for this situation. A good grab bag is essential and should be accessible whichever way the boat lies and contain: handheld radio, flares, telephone, emergency food, whistles, emergency blankets, etc. A capsized multihull becomes a stable raft in which the crew can survive inside the hulls or, at worst, survive between the upturned hulls.

With no fixed ballast and buoyancy compartments in the bows and sterns, multihulls will tend to sit high in the water, and, provided the hull is not punctured, the

Ten people hung on to the capsized catamaran Paragon *waiting for help off Lana'i, Hawaii.*
Photo: Sonny Rivera/Honolulu Advertiser

safest place for the crew is inside the upturned hull sheltered from the wind and the waves. There are many reports of an inventive and resourceful crew living for extended periods in their upturned hulls until rescue arrives. Careful preparation and thought should go into planning life after a capsize, which is one of the very worst events that can happen to a multihull and its crew. Frequently testing that escape hatches open and close and are not likely to be blocked in the event of a capsize is essential. Placing handholds, emergency supplies and clothing above the inverted water level will enable the crew to survive inside the hulls. Emergency floor lighting should be fitted which, of course, becomes overhead lighting after a capsize. If the hull interior is inhabitable hand holds, jackstays and the right safety clothing will enable the crew to survive on or between the upturned hull even though they are exposed to the weather and the sea. Daggerboards should be capable of being locked into position so that they can be used to assist crew in climbing onto the top of the inverted hull and out of the water.

The upturned multihull, particularly if the bridgedeck, rudders and daggerboards are painted orange, will be more easily spotted by emergency services than a fragile and vulnerable liferaft, which should only be used as the very last resort.

Conclusion

Heavy weather should be expected and prepared for. It should be approached with confidence gained through prior preparation and knowledge of the options available. Multihulls do require different handling to monohulls in heavy weather, though many of the matters discussed elsewhere in this book are relevant to whatever hull form is chosen. Their inherent advantages of speed, light weight, stability and shallow draft are advantages that dictate the tactics deployed by the crew in preparing for and handling their boats through heavy weather. Regrettably, overloading can compromise much of this.

Unless a crew on their own boat has tested equipment required to tackle heavy weather the equipment is of little use. A well prepared boat and crew will survive all that the weather can throw.

15 Monohull storm tactics

Peter Bruce

Military officers are fond of saying that few plans survive first contact with the enemy and the same may be said for the plans of the crew of a small vessel encountering heavy weather for the first time. All plans have to be flexible. Unexpected events are likely to occur, the weather forecast is often a simplified overview, and peoples' behaviour may be unpredictable after prolonged exposure to blinding spray, fear, cold temperature, wearying noise and violent motion. One can be fairly sure, however, that crews, boats and equipment that have done well in previous storms will do so again. If drag devices are involved it may need some hard work to set up the chosen tactic but do not try to fight the storm, try to accommodate the weather whilst making the crew and boat as comfortable as possible. Try to keep everyone safe, warm, fed and having had adequate sleep.

Regardless of the expected wind strength, there are courses of action that can be taken before the weather takes control that can much reduce the chances of disaster. Vessels should be placed to avoid lee shores, shoal water, currents, tidal races, headlands and areas marked on charts as having overfalls.

Once the storm has struck, while a vessel is likely to remain afloat, however uncomfortable the conditions the crew should neither seek nor accept offers of rescue from another vessel, nor take to the liferaft without very good reason, for to do so may incur graver risks than enduring the storm. One should also be very cautious about taking a tow in a seaway.

Few modern craft have adequate strong points for towing even when the master of the towing vessel has the ability, patience and skill to maintain a low enough speed.

Apart from these recommendations there is no universally applicable advice to be offered. There is no one simple remedy. If only there was. Every skipper should plan suitable tactics, carefully taking into account the characteristics of his boat, and be prepared to adopt them in good time. Some courses of action are, of course, heavily committing, and once decided upon are hard to change.

In this concluding chapter of Part 1 a summary will be made of the various tactics available to the skipper of a mono-hulled sailing boat in heavy weather.

Drag devices, both drogues and parachutes, have established their worth and can be counted as important additional options for coping with heavy weather, but are not the only option. The tactics that are described in this chapter have been employed in one or more of the accounts of heavy weather in this book and their effectiveness in actual circumstances can best be judged by referring to them. It is not possible to specify the exact wind strength when the various options can be recommended due to the number of variables involved. The size of the craft is of relevance and, in storms, big is usually advantageous. But other factors count heavily too, such as the nature of the seas, the design and strength of boat, and the size and strength of the crew. In broad terms, this chapter covers courses

This is a most unusual and amazing photograph, as Jérôme was not to know, as he took it, whether his boat was to be capsized through 360°, and whether he would be able to continue to cling on to the rigging as his boat was knocked over by the breaking wave. As it is, the boat has been flung about 75° onto her starboard side. Photo: Jérôme Poncet

of action to consider when the wind speed exceeds Force 9, to Force 10 and above.

It is evident from Adlard Coles' own modestly written accounts that he was skilful at choosing the moment to shorten sail. As he advocates, this should be undertaken in advance of immediate necessity, despite a natural reluctance to do so in the hope that the weather may show an improvement. Unless having a junk rig, the longer sail reduction is deferred, the harder it is to carry out, and the greater the risk of damage meantime. Incidentally this applies to all heavy weather tactics, in that resolute decisions are best made before a situation becomes desperate. Likewise, some serious problems are often best dealt with as soon as they occur.

An example of a serious problem rightly *not* dealt with straightaway was when *Uhuru*'s davits collapsed under the weight of water in the dinghy after a big following sea had broken over the boat. The result was that the

dinghy was draped over the stern along with a tangle of cordage and covers. Steve Powell chose to ignore the dinghy situation, rightly believing other matters were of higher priority (Chapter 25).

When bad weather is approaching, most people, very sensibly, make for a safe harbour or, while conditions allow, make maximum distance from the storm path. However, once caught out in a storm there is much to be said for enduring it rather than continuing to run for shelter, as breaking waves in shallow water can be far more of a hazard than the open sea. Besides, if entry into harbour becomes unwise or impossible, the loss of sea room may be irrevocable.

When beset by a storm, the human objective is to remain as safe and as comfortable as possible. As far as the boat is concerned, the aim is to avoid sinking, being rolled over, pitch-poled or otherwise suffering damage to hull, rig and sails. As Adlard Coles says, the wind dictates the amount of sail that can be carried and can also cause loss of sails, rigging or mast, but it is the breaking seas that do the more dangerous damage to hull and superstructure. There is great energy bound up within a wave, and major forces are at work when a breaking sea strikes a boat. A boat can also be picked up by a breaking sea and accelerated to an alarming speed. A moment later the boat may be flung into the still water in the trough of the wave where she will stop almost instantly. It is at this point that serious damage to crew and boat is likely to occur. Clearly, it is desirable to avoid breaking waves but, if this is not possible, then the waves should be taken within about 20° of either the bow or the stern. Before the days of self-draining cockpits, being pooped, i.e. a wave breaking over the stern, was a major hazard to yachtsmen. It is now less of a problem, but remains a danger to boats open at the stern, to

yachts with unusually large cockpits, or with low sills at the companionway that require washboards or doors in place to prevent a sea sweeping down below.

Sailing 50° to the wind

As increasingly severe weather overtakes a craft, a seaman's instinct encourages him to continue to maintain his approximate course whilst reducing sail appropriately. When the destination is to windward and the crew has the determination to press on, perhaps under one or more storm sails despite the uncomfortable motion, this is commendable and, incidentally, is a policy that has won many races. The helmsman's technique is to close reach across the troughs, then head up into the waves and bear away hard on the top to avoid a slam. Likewise, when reaching, the

Bernard Stamm and crew broad reaching off the Lizard in February 2001. The determination of top single-minded racing sailors is borne out by this photograph, which shows his yacht carrying maximum sensible sail in a winter storm. Photo: Thierry Martinez

helmsman will luff into the wave crests and bear away in the troughs. Every wave may need different treatment: a steep wave about to break, or already breaking, will need to be taken head on followed by bearing away hard to re-gather speed and to avoid a slam, while a gentle sloped wave will need no change of course at all. Judgement is needed, as on the one hand there is a danger of capsize should the boat be caught at an angle to a breaking sea, whereas on the other hand the boat can be stopped by heading straight into a breaking sea and then thrown backwards onto her rudder. Light craft are more likely to suffer the latter fate but are also most responsive. In this case, keeping speed on can best be achieved by giving a last minute luff into an unavoidable breaking wave. If having to contend with such breaking waves head on consideration should be given to the use of the engine to help drive the boat through the crest and to give control in the troughs.

The crew will be heartened if continuing in the desired direction and hand steering – unlike heaving-to or lying a'hull – does provide an opportunity to avoid breaking waves. The tactic was adopted in the 1994 by the crew of *Sula II*, a 13.7m (45ft) cutter (Chapter 19) who sailed close-hauled under trysail through the Queen's Birthday Storm. Also by Ed Psaltis, skipper of the overall winner of the tempestuous 1998 Sydney–Hobart Race (see Chapter 3) who sailed through the storm under storm jib alone. The technique seems particularly appropriate in daylight for beamy IMS racing yachts with low underwater lateral area and low range of stability. To paraphrase Ed Psaltis, 'Having speed and acceleration gives manoeuvrability to steer through big and confused seas. It is possible to position the yacht best for each wave as it comes, or steer around it. Without speed, acceleration and manoeuvrability, a boat is a sitting duck to large waves.'

It is significant that comfortable majority of the yachts in this race reported that they fared best when sailing about 15° off close hauled rather than running before the wind when a number of yachts had severe problems. There were other instances of yachts employing a trysail on its own to sail just off-the-wind successfully, such as *Berrimilla* (Chapter 3) and the 9m (31ft) Farr-designed *Bin Rouge.*

Sailing 50° to the wind was also a technique adopted by the J46 *Cielita* as described in Chapter 26. The three experienced crew encountered unforecast very severe weather off Greenland in July 2005 with wind speeds of 55–65 knots, gusting 70 knots. They had tried running under storm jib but after two severe broaches they changed tactics and sailed just off the wind much as Ed Psaltis did. For two days under the small flat-cut storm jib, 45° to the wind, they found the J46 was well-balanced and easy to sail. To deal with occasional breaking waves it was necessary to bear off to gain speed, which had been lost in the nearly windless troughs, and then head straight into them to avoid being rolled. Luckily there was enough light to spot the breaking crests at night. Charles Welch, one of the crew of physicians, said that they set great store by the nature of their small flat-cut storm jib and the use of ski goggles, without which looking to windward for breaking waves would have been impossible.

Sailing just off the wind under either a storm jib or trysail on its own is a primary storm tactic which has shown to be entirely satisfactory in utmost extreme conditions, so long as the sails are small enough and the crew can continue to helm competently.

Heaving-to

Uhuru, an Oyster 62, hove-to successfully off the Falklands in March 2012 in Force 10 (see Chapter 25). *Sabre*, a 10.4m (34ft) steel cutter with a crew of two, was one of the few centre-stage yachts that survived the June 1994 Queen's Birthday storm virtually undamaged. She sailed through the eye of the storm and undoubtedly endured as bad conditions as any without any rolls or knockdowns. Her crew commented afterwards: 'Our boat is prepared with very rough conditions in mind and, lying hove-to, has proved herself on several occasions.'

Bernard Stamm, now single-handed, hove-to whilst adjustments are made to the steering system. Notice the wave breaking upwind of the bow but not in the area of the slick.
Photo: Thierry Martinez

When it comes on to blow it is better to heave-to early rather than late and indications that the time is ripe usually come from the helm. If control is becoming difficult and the helm is feeling spongy as a result of water aeration, it is time to heave-to. One can often find a good area of water just behind a wave that has recently broken or, failing that, just try to find a calm patch. At night, breaking waves can be heard and sometimes the phosphorescence can be seen.

One can heave-to either by backing a small headsail or storm jib, or by tacking and leaving the jib sheet made up, accompanied by a mainsail appropriately reefed for the conditions, or a trysail. The helm should be secured with heavy shock cord or rope so as to hold the boat's bow towards the wind, and adjustments then made to the sheets and the helm until the boat is at her most comfortable. At this point she will probably be moving gently forward at a knot or less and, hopefully, not much more to leeward. The lower the speed the more the boat will be protected by the slick left to windward resulting from the sideways drift of the hull. There will be no benefit from the slick if the boat is moving forward faster than perhaps 1 knot, as the slick is left behind where it serves no useful purpose. It may help to take in a further reef in the mainsail or furl the headsail, or both, to achieve the balance necessary to keep the boat about 50° from the wind direction with minimal forward speed.

Some yachts will lie closer to the wind and this is advantageous if waves are breaking. If hove-to for many hours shipping should be alerted and it will pay to put something suitable, such as hosepipe, between the sheet and the shroud to reduce chafe. Otherwise try to find the fairest lead possible. Yachts with two masts have more options and every boat will be different, so experimentation is always necessary. The amount of leeway will much depend on the boat's underwater lateral area, and modern yachts with slim keels can make swift progress downwind. It is highly desirable to heave-to on the tack that gives the smallest angle to the waves.

The increase in comfort that can be derived from heaving-to in a seaway has to be experienced to be believed. Noise and motion are promptly much reduced and there is no longer a need for a helmsman, though it is important to check for chafe. Thus heaving-to is a good expedient to adopt, not only in heavy weather but also for having a meal in comfort or when an uncertain pilotage situation demands time for thought. It is wise not to try to back an overlapping headsail in order to heave-to, as there is a high chance of bursting the sail on the spreaders.

It is possible that the boat will inadvertently tack as a result of wave action when hove-to and, if so, the boat has to be brought back to the previous condition as soon as possible to avoid the chance of being rolled. Once hove-to again perhaps try a little less tension on the mainsheet, or set the helm to point the boat a little more to leeward.

Storm jibs, deep-reefed mainsails or trysails are sometimes best employed on their own. Given the choice, it may be better to heave-to setting a deep-reefed mainsail or trysail on its own rather than a storm jib on its own (see Sydney–Hobart Race of 1998, Chapter 3). The optimum sail is usually a matter most affected by the qualities of a particular boat. For example cutters or slutters with significant windage from their rolled headsails may not ever need to set a backed jib.

It is relevant to quote Alan Webb who used to have a 13.7m (45ft) heavy displacement steel yacht called *Supertramp*. He now owns a quicker, much lighter and more lively cold-moulded 10.7m (35ft) yacht designed by Laurie Davidson called *Supertramp II* with a fin keel and a skeg-hung rudder. She draws 1.78m (5ft 10in) and weighs only 5,000kg (5 tons). Incidentally she has a separate track for her trysail. Alan Webb writes:

IN HEAVY WEATHER SAILING these two yachts responded very differently. With the heavy displacement *Supertramp*, the tactic in extreme conditions was to run under bare pole as long as sea conditions allowed and as a last resort to lay a'hull and take the pounding. In the lighter boat I found the only strategy in survival storms is to turn up into the wind with the trysail sheeted in hard and the helm lashed to bring the boat to windward. The yacht then travels up the waves and lies on the peak of the wave so that her forward momentum carries her through the breaking crest and prevents her from being knocked down heavily. In this lighter vessel, to continue to run in heavy conditions would surely mean a pitch pole or capsize. Initially I tried this tactic in the first 40 knot easterly I encountered in the lighter vessel to test the theory of John Sanders, the famous West Australian sailor who completed three non-stop solo circumnavigations. I found it worked well then but I never anticipated risking this strategy in survival conditions. Yet as luck would have it, I was already hove-to under trysail when I was hit by what I believe was a hurricane. This, the strongest storm I encountered, was at only 34° 35' South, 3° 32' East, in the South Atlantic en route from Recife, Brazil to Cape Town, South Africa on 1 November 2005. It happened so fast that I had no choice but to leave the trysail in place, and anyway it was working well in these extreme conditions when the violence of the squalls was comparable to the williwaws I had experienced in the Cape Horn region.

The wind was ESE 25–30 knots to start off with. I was pounding into it getting nowhere, except being pushed too far north, so I hove-to under trysail. I slept for two hours and awoke just before dawn to find the barometer had plummeted. At 0730 the wind backed northeast 45–50 knots with violent squalls. I stayed hove-to under trysail. At 1000 the wind went southwest like a hurricane. I estimated it was blowing 80 knots with torrential rain. The sea was a total white out. I couldn't see anything for the blizzard of rain and spray. The yacht under trysail was laid over to 60° with water streaming over the decks. This lasted two hours when the storm moderated to 60 knots increasing to 70–80 knots in the squalls. The waves reached 9m (30ft) with the top 1.2m (4ft) being torn-off white spume. The yacht was pointing high, climbing the waves, making 3 knots to windward. These conditions prevailed until 0100 when the wind decreased to 40 knots with stronger squalls.

I am certain that to attempt to run in those conditions in a light boat of 5 tons would have meant certain capsize due to the violence of the squalls and the state of the seas. The wind was so strong it stretched the trysail, and I had to have it re-cut in Cape Town.

Alan Webb's experience is of much interest to owners of light yachts that, as a rule, are difficult to stabilise in stormy conditions. It is noteworthy that the trysail was sheeted flat and that *Supertramp II* has a skeg-hung rudder. With the helm lashed to bring her up to windward she would come up to 25° off the wind in very strong gusts of 70 knots plus, but then would fall off again to about 40°. She never once tacked. A concern is that, if the boat was doing 3 knots, she would have sailed clear of her protective slick, but it seems that *Supertramp II* needed the speed to carry the boat through the breaking crests.

A deeply reefed mainsail can work as well as a trysail but should not be considered an unqualified alternative to a trysail as mainsails can tear and cannot work efficiently if the boom or gooseneck has broken. Thus a trysail should be carried as it can be used with or without the boom. If reaching or fetching, the sail will work well without the boom, which will be less of a hazard to the crew. If it is necessary to run dead before the wind, two headsails boomed out on either side may be preferable to running with a deep-reefed mainsail or trysail and storm jib, depending on the boat.

Traditional remedies often best suit traditional boats. When hove-to a yacht should lie about 50° to the wind, but unfortunately not all fin keeled yachts will heave-to untended in a sea, probably because they lack underwater lateral area. In particular, light-displacement yachts with slim high-aspect ratio keels may not stay at a constant angle to the wind and can dance about whilst making great speed to leeward. The problem with such boats is that when it seems advisable to slow right down, they won't. Heaving-to is a time-honoured and seamanlike tactic to employ in moderate to severe conditions, and owners of many craft may need no other. However, owners of some modern yachts (though it seems not *Supertramp II*) may find that heaving-to can become neither comfortable nor safe, and there is always the chance that any yacht lying hove-to can be caught heavily beam-on by a large breaking cross sea.

Lying a'hull

If heaving-to seems no longer sensible it may be tempting to resort to lying a'hull, i.e. taking off all sail, lashing the helm – usually slightly to leeward – closing all hatches securely, and letting nature take her course. The ease with which types of yacht will lie a'hull is variable.

Broadly speaking, old-fashioned narrow-beam heavy-displacement yachts often lie a'hull well, whilst light-displacement beamy yachts often do not. Harry Whale lay a'hull off Ushant aboard *Muddle Thru* in the great English Channel storm of 1987. It is a tactic employed by many yachtsmen – and not always of dire necessity.

In a sufficient force of wind the windage of the mast alone provides stability, like a steadying sail, and the turbulence caused by the yacht's drift may reduce the chances of waves breaking to windward. As an illustration of a vessel's ability to look after itself during a storm, one may recall that most of the vessels abandoned in the 1979 Fastnet Race were later found bobbing about in the swell, and some with hatches left open.

Unfortunately, while lying a'hull may seem relatively comfortable, often more so than other tactics, it gives a false sense of security. The problem again is that the boat is vulnerable to breaking waves from broadside on and, to paraphrase Andrew Claughton in Chapter 2, 'breaking waves do not have to be very big to roll any sort of small craft right over, whatever her hull features'. The consequences of a roll-over can be most dramatic down below – more so than one might imagine – and the chances of the mast being lost are high. This occurrence, apart from the obvious effect on mobility, can lead to all kinds of immediate problems – not the least of these is that the lack of damping effect of the mast, without which a yacht's roll inertia is halved, results in quicker and more unpleasant motion with a much-increased chance of being rolled again.

Whilst on the melancholy subject of capsize, it may be significant that several yachts have been rolled over just as a storm seems to have abated. Examples are Bill King in *Galway Blazer* in 1968, *Sayula II* in the first Whitbread Round the World Race in 1973, Michael Richey in *Jester* in 1986, and the Swan 46 at sea in the October 1987 storm, described in Chapter 17. This is a phenomenon called 'overshoot', for which Professor Sheldon Bacon provides the explanation in Chapter 9. Another contributory factor may be the shift of wind direction as a front goes through, when the effect of two wave trains crossing at an angle is known to produce regions of extreme wave height where the seas may break heavily. Having pointed out the dangers of lying a'hull, to try to put matters into perspective it should be mentioned that world girdlers such as Alec Rose, Nicholas Davies and Alan and Kathy Webb, albeit with heavy-displacement boats, have found the practice of lying a'hull satisfactory for weathering gales during their world circumnavigations.

For such solidly built vessels it is quite a rare event to encounter the sort of weather that does not allow lying a'hull without a high risk of capsize, but there are enough examples in this book of yachts being rolled over while lying a'hull to show that the tactic, sooner or later, may lead to being rolled all the way through 360°. For this to happen a craft has to be caught broadside on just as a wave breaks, so luck plays a strong part, but this is not a risk worth taking.

Use of engine

Nowadays the diesel engine is a generally reliable item of equipment that can be used to good effect when managing under sail would be difficult, such as entering and leaving a berth. The old-fashioned view that for a yacht skipper 'to use an engine is unseamanlike' may have been based upon more than just prejudice, for early auxiliary engines were not always dependable whilst running, nor easy to start, and it was wise not to encourage over-reliance on them. Moreover, the high chance of catching a rope round the propeller in a stressful situation is well known.

An engine is often used to help a yacht sail to windward in strong winds and may lose lubricating oil suction at the consequential high angle of heel. This angle is a useful fact to gather from the manufacturer. The risk can be minimised by having the oil level filled to the top mark.

There is a remarkable difference in propulsive power when an engine has a reduction gearbox with a commensurate big propeller and when not. A two-bladed folding propeller and an engine with no reduction gearbox, as often used by racing yachts, will start to cavitate and not usually provide much propulsion into the wind above Force 5. A three-bladed propeller, whether folding or not, is a big improvement on a two-bladed propeller whilst a three-bladed propeller with a 2:1 reduction gearbox will usually enable a yacht to motor into a gale. An impressive example was in the 1994 Queen's Birthday Storm (Chapter 19) when *Por Vida*, a 13m (43ft) Westsail ketch, used her engine fitted with a 3:1 reduction ratio transmission and a 56cm (22in) propeller to motor successfully into the storm for its duration, albeit with a trysail up as well, just off the wind.

The competent use of an engine was demonstrated by Alain Catherineau in the 1979 Fastnet when he rescued the crew of *Griffin* from a liferaft after their boat had sunk. One is not always able to make directly into the sea under auxiliary engine or tack through the wind in storm conditions but, bearing in mind that even a bare pole will provide some aerodynamic lift, it may be possible to make across the seas to windward. There may often be circumstances when it will be safer to 'heave-to under engine' rather than lie a'hull, especially when running before a storm is not possible due to a lee shore. In this case the use of an engine, either in combination with sails or without, may be highly desirable. It should not be forgotten that skippers of power craft have no option but to 'heave-to under engine'. An advantage when using the engine is that the flow past the rudder is increased, giving improved manoeuvrability and, if confronted with an oncoming breaking wave, power can be increased to drive the boat through.

When running before the sea it may be significant that the old-fashioned British lifeboat with a top speed of 8 knots could not always be handled confidently without the use of a drogue in combination with the engines. Coxswains of modern lifeboats, with a speed of 18 knots, find they have no such trouble as they can power their way clear of breaking seas. Bearing in mind the opening sentence of this chapter, which suggests that flexibility may be necessary when facing severe weather, yachtsmen should regard the use of an engine as another string to their bow, and be ready to use it when the situation justifies, after carefully checking for ropes over the side.

Running before the seas

There is nothing new about the tactic of letting a vessel run freely before the sea, when sea room permits. Apparent wind is reduced, motion is more comfortable, and the risk of being rolled becomes less likely than when lying a'hull. When considering extreme conditions, running with full directional control is important to avoid the breakers and keep the stern at the optimum angle to the waves to avoid broaching. This is not easy, especially at night, though experienced racing dinghy helmsmen and surfers may have an advantage. In a confused sea, usually the result of a big change of wind direction after a front has gone through, waves can come from unexpected quarters, necessitating a quick response from the helmsman and boat. The speed of the boat has to lie within a range necessary to achieve good control. If speed is too slow, the boat does not respond quickly enough, and if too fast, especially in darkness, the helmsman may not be able to react in time to avoid burying the bow in the wave ahead at the bottom of the trough, pitch-poling or a broach, all of which can have serious repercussions. By heading across 20 to 40°, rather than down the wave, 'stuffing' the bow can be avoided whilst the risk of broaching increases, so the course selected is a matter of fine judgment. Before there is insufficient margin between the two evils a means must be found to slow the boat down. A particular feature of the infamous 1979 Fastnet was the confused cross seas, and in *Eclipse*, the top Admiral's Cup yacht and winner of Class 2, we successfully employed a crewman seated at the forward end of the cockpit, looking aft, whose duty it was to call the direction of the next breaking wave.

Some craft undoubtedly handle better than others when running before the seas and it might be easy to assume that displacement is the controlling factor. The situation is not so clear cut, with a combination of design factors such as the degree of balance of the ends affecting the issue, as described by the late Olin Stephens in Chapter 1. In any case an overly low-geared wheel is a considerable disadvantage. The corollary is that, in the case of a high-geared wheel or a tiller, some large degree of physical strength is likely to be needed on the helm. It is worth mentioning that vane self-steering is particularly effective in strong winds, and can be invaluable for shorthanded crews in heavy weather who should leave the vane to cope in order to save their strength for possible future issues. It will help to ease the load of the self-steering gear if the sails and helm are set up for optimum balance. As described by Alex Whitworth in Chapter 24, the 10m (33ft) *Berrimilla* ran under a bare pole and her vane self-steering through a storm where the wind speed peaked at 84 knots. The boat steered a course of 15° either side of dead downwind.

The professional crews of yachts in the Volvo Round the World Race and the like, find exhilaration in the downwind 'sleigh-rides' through the southern oceans under as much sail as they can carry. Their technique is to luff across the trough to maintain speed, then to bear away almost square to the wave, just as the crest arrives, to encourage the boat to surf down the wave. It is similar to methods used by dinghy sailors and Malibu board surfers and requires some skill, strength and a great deal of concentration, especially when carrying full sail. Such crews will have perhaps more than a handful of expert racing helmsmen to share the steering task, whereas the average cruising boat may not have more than one, for whom the task of steering, without self-steering, may become extremely wearisome after a few hours. Thus the average cruising yacht should only run before the seas whist it is safe and comfortable to do so. Some vessels have come to grief by pursuing this tactic for too long, though a most successful passage when running before a storm was made by Michel and Jacqueline Hennebert, the crew of a shallow draft French Garcia 52. Caught north of Japan by a vicious low coming out of Siberia they sheeted the staysail centrally, raised the centreboard, lowered the daggerboard just forward of the rudder and went below. The autopilot steered them as they ran before over 80 knots of wind. The large cockpit was often full and Michel Hennebert said that he thought that if they had tried to slow down they might well have been rolled. They averaged between 10 and 18 knots for three days, never touching either the autopilot or staysail sheets. They subsequently found out that three nearby yachts and a fishing boat had been lost.

Only light, directionally stable yachts would be suitable for this bold procedure which is similar to taking a powerboat at full planing speed down sea in stormy weather (see Chapter 13). By travelling at about the same speed as the waves their effect is much less. Keeping weight out of the ends is always desirable, and particularly out of the bow if running before the sea at speed.

Running with warps

As already mentioned, it is important to try to find an appropriate speed for good steering when running before a storm. Towing warps as a means of keeping the stern to the seas, while flattening the breakers behind and helping to reduce the yacht's speed to a desirable level, may sound archaic to some but it is a technique still used by experienced seamen, particularly in shorthanded situations.

Firstly, warps, having more than one use, are usually available, easy to stow and uncomplicated. Furthermore, one can control the length of rope paid out to ensure a steady pull. Too short a warp and breaking crests can carry it forward so that there is at times no retarding force at all. A long warp, unlike a single drogue, can span a whole wavelength so making the pull more constant but warps just intended for securing alongside, even when attached to each other, will seldom be long enough to span an ocean wave.

Thus for ocean passages one should be looking at a length of 122m (400ft) or more. Even experienced warp-users relate the ease with which warps can tangle when being paid out in the sort of conditions when they can help. Thus preparation and care are necessary in their deployment.

After two severe knockdowns while lying a'hull, Ernest and Val Haigh tied together 183m (600ft) of heavy line and trailed it astern. The improvement was immediate.
Photo: Ernest and Val Haigh

When Sir Robin Knox-Johnston encountered heavy weather in the southern oceans when undertaking the first non-stop world circumnavigation he put out 183m (600ft) of 5cm (2in) circumference warp in the form of a bight, lashed the helm tightly amidships, and went to his bunk. He says:

THE WARP HELD THE HEAVILY BUILT *Suhaili* firmly stern-to the waves. She lay very comfortably, regardless of the wave height, in forces of at least 12 on the Beaufort scale when the sea was white with spindrift. *Suhaili* drifted downwind at an average of about 2 knots in big stuff and strong blows with only a storm jib set right forward, sheeted tight amidships. If she tended to yaw, the force on the jib increased the more she came round, tending to push her back downwind. *Suhaili* has a Norwegian style canoe-type stern, and this meant that there was no great resistance to the waves as they rolled past, they were just divided. The warp stretched quite a lot in surges, but that was to be expected. Had I been able to get the warps out in 1989, I am

sure that we would have been all right, and I am intending to make a couple of rope reels, which I shall hang from the deckhead in the fo'c'sle, so in future I can lead the warps directly over the stern if I need them in a hurry.

Bernard Moitessier's experience with warps during a survival storm in the South Pacific in 1965–6 is often quoted. The 12.2m (40ft) yacht *Joshua* was towing 'five long hawsers varying in length from 30.5m (100ft) to 91.4m (300ft), with iron ballast attached and supplemented by a heavy net used for loading ships'. At the onset of the storm it seems possible that this arrangement was successful, but once the wave height and length reached a certain point, the yacht failed to respond to the wheel, and the warps did not prevent her from surfing down the crests. Not finding these circumstances satisfactory, eventually Moitessier cut the warps, whereupon he found himself in a much more comfortable situation.

Dr David Lewis, returning from the USA after the 1960 single-handed Transatlantic

Race, recounts a similar experience. He had been running under staysail alone, but after the sheet fairlead had pulled out of the deck with the increasing wind strength, he lowered the sail and streamed 36.6m (120ft) of warp in a bight. At once, he says, his boat became unmanageable, and even when he did succeed in steering down the seas, the breaking waves would carry the warp alongside. Similar difficulties were experienced in the 1979 Fastnet Race.

The apparent anomaly regarding use of warps is explained in Tony Marchaj's book entitled *Seaworthiness: The Forgotten Factor* (published by Adlard Coles Nautical). In a fast growing sea, wave height increases more quickly than wavelength, producing especially steep seas. As waves develop in size there will be a time when their wavelength is twice a given boat's length. At this point the bow will arrive in the trough just as the stern is at the top of the crest. With steep enough seas as a result of the fast-growing effect, one can see that there may be a tendency for the boat in this attitude to topple, i.e. pitch-pole or broach, especially as the water particles driven by the orbital action within a wave will be moving forward at the crest of the wave, reducing the effectiveness of the rudder.

When a boat has been designed with the rudder placed well aft, the control situation may be further aggravated as a result of 'ventilation', a term used to describe the situation when the rudder may be lifted partly out of the water or its efficiency reduced by aeration.

Moreover, if a yacht is overtaken by a breaking wave the water flow upon which the rudder relies can be reversed. In very short steep seas, when a boat could topple and when the rudder may be less effective than usual, many yachtsmen have felt that they would benefit from the use of some drag device to prevent their vessel broaching or pitch-poling.

Tony Marchaj suggests that when the wavelength has had time to develop further there will be a need for less drag and more speed to evade breaking crests and awkward cross-seas in the troughs; hence a need to

discard the use of warps as the wave system matures. Nevertheless, this does not explain why those such as David Lewis and Bernard Moitessier had control difficulties with warps streamed after seas had had ample time to grow and others did not.

The explanation seems to lie in the length and height of waves compared with the length of warp used. If Bernard Moitessier used warps of up to only 91.4m (300ft) in seas of wavelength 152–171m (500–560ft), as he says, one could expect, through the orbital movement within a wave, his warps to be ineffective at times. Likewise, allowing for the bight, David Lewis' warp only extended 18.3m (60ft) in waves that he estimated to be 46m (150ft) in length.

After disposing of his warps Moitessier found that it was an advantage to luff a little at the arrival of each wave crest to take the sea 15–20° on the quarter. He was now in the same situation as the Webbs in *Supertramp* (Chapter 16) and using the same tactics. These two are not alone in preferring to run free with the seas slightly on the quarter. Not only does it reduce the chances of pitch-poling, but also – like a surfer – by steering across the waves one may be able to avoid the worst of the breaking crests. When the face of the wave is exceptionally steep there will be a very fine balance between pitch-poling and broaching and in this case the helmsman may have to weave his boat down the wave to optimise the situation.

The experience of Bernard Moitessier and others leads one to the view that to avoid being pitch-poled, rolled over or being pooped, boat speed must be kept at a level to give directional stability at all times. Of course, once huge seas have had the time to develop, it is usually in the troughs of the waves that problems occur. Here the boat's speed is no longer being helped by gravity, and the shelter of the adjacent wave crest may reduce wind strength. In the trough of a wave, the need for directional stability remains as vital as elsewhere and it may be necessary to luff to maintain speed.

Thus warp drag has to be adjusted, or enough sail has to be set, to take the craft safely through the troughs accepting that, at other times, even with warps streamed, this

A view of the Southern Ocean by Les Powles. He estimates the wave height to have been 18.3m (60ft). Photo: Les Powles

may mean that a boat could be surfing at what may seem to be an unnatural rate. Some boats, like *Suhaili*, may be directionally stable when towing warps with helm lashed; others may demand someone on the helm.

An auxiliary engine can possibly provide the additional drive needed to achieve good steering control in the troughs. To illustrate this point there follows an extract from an account by Richard Clifford when cruising off Ireland in his Warrior 35, *Warrior Shamaal*, in August 1979. As luck would have it, he found himself alone in the Celtic Sea in the midst of the infamous Fastnet storm of 1979. It may be of note that it was not his first storm encounter.

I DROPPED OFF MY CREW IN GLENGARIFF on 13 August and sailed gently down Bantry Bay, then headed south-west out into the Atlantic. At 0400 the next morning the wind was too much for the storm jib, so I handed it and lay a'hull. Very soon afterwards *Warrior Shamaal* was knocked flat by a large breaking wave. I grabbed a bucket and bailed, found the bilge pump and pumped, and fought my way to the wheel to try to get the boat to run downwind, but she would

not come round. The next extra large wave again filled the cockpit and the saloon to just above the cabin sole. When we came back on an even keel I noticed that the liferaft was floating in its container beside the boat, the bilge pump handle had gone and the anchor had come out of its well on the foredeck. The immediate problem was to stay afloat, so I rushed below, got the heads bilge pump handle, and put the washboards in position. Still *Warrior Shamaal* would not run downwind and yet another wave bowled the boat over, filling the cockpit and pouring water below. By this time the liferaft had inflated itself and broken adrift.

I was not prepared to set my 9.1sq m (98sq ft) storm jib as it would have been too big: my 4.6sq m (50sq ft) spitfire jib was in my garage! So I started my 15hp auxiliary engine and with this ticking over in gear I was able to keep the stern into the wind with an occasional burst of full throttle after my concentration had lapsed.

Suddenly we were at the top of an extra big wave. *Warrior Shamaal* hung at the top then plunged forward in a horrifying nose-down attitude. Her bows plunged into the trough and

I fully expected to continue on down, or the stern to flip over, pitch-poling the yacht. With a shudder we pulled out of the dive and rushed on with the next mountainous wave.

Tactics had to be changed again, so between waves I passed a mooring line from one cockpit winch aft around the self-steering, and back into the cockpit. My 91m (300ft) warp is coiled and seized with sailmaker's twine every 18.3–21m (60–70ft) to avoid tangles. I attached the end of this onto the mooring line and paid out each coil until the whole bight of rope was more or less floating astern. Still running ahead on the engine and towing the bight, I experienced no further problems.

In this account we not only have an engine being used to good effect, but we again see that lying a'hull is not a satisfactory tactic in extreme conditions. Furthermore, we see that warps were thought to be necessary to avoid broaching or pitch-poling during the period when the seas were developing rapidly in height and steepness. It is noteworthy that experienced ocean sailors take care with their trailing warp stowage, flaking the line in figure-of-eights and lashing the coils at intervals.

On balance it appears that warps streamed astern on their own can work well in extreme storms so long as the warp arrangement is long enough to span a whole wavelength of the seas. The shorter the warps are in relation to the wavelength, the lower the proportion of time when the warps are providing effective drag. Consequently a collection of short warps may slow a boat down below the speed necessary to steer, or for the boat to steer herself, yet they may provide insufficient drag to prevent wild surfing when the orbital movement within the wave is moving in the same direction as the boat.

Having established that a long length of warp can be one form of desirable equipment for heavy weather, it is worth quoting from Michael Richey's experiences in July 1981. He was returning to the UK from Bermuda in the famous 7.6m (25ft) Folkboat *Jester* when he was overtaken by a fierce storm from the south-south-west. He writes:

HOW TO HANDLE A BOAT in extreme conditions is a matter for judgement and much will depend upon one's knowledge of how the boat behaves. Perhaps there are no hard and fast rules. In *Jester* I have never felt the need to tow warps, although I have often run before gales. Now, under self-steering, we were surfing down the slopes of heavy seas and the tops were beginning to fall off. My fear was that she might bury her head and pitch-pole. It seemed essential to slow the boat down. I carried on board a 5kg (11lb) Bruce anchor as a kedge, and since the Bruce is reputed to be hydrodynamically stable I reckoned it should tow like a paravane. Accordingly I streamed the anchor over the starboard quarter, on some 23m (75ft) of line, taking the end – with some difficulty, as one must crawl out to it – to the cleat. This immediately slowed the boat down to about half her speed and kept the stern nicely into the seas, preventing her from slewing about. So we spent the night of 9–10 July, the storm rising in violence and with a general situation of discomfort, but *Jester* well under control.

This report encourages an alternative to the use of very long warps during a storm.

Using drogues

Warps have several disadvantages. The warp, or series of warps knotted together, may need to be very long to provide enough drag and also to bridge a whole wavelength. Not every yacht carries enough line and, even if it does, the crew may not have the will and patience to deploy a long length of rope in bad weather and, when the storm is over, there is the dreary task of bringing the line back on board.

Much the same effect as that of a warp can be achieved by using a line in conjunction with a weighted drogue. A good drogue will provide the same drag as hundreds of feet of rope and can also provide strong resistance when the boat is tending to go too fast and disproportionately less when the boat slows down and is in danger of losing steerage way. Additionally, a suitably weighted drogue will operate clear of surface effects. Given the choice, a drogue is much more efficient but allows less scope for fine tuning and is more committing, as it is even more difficult to heave in than a long warp. Fuller details are in Chapter 7.

A disadvantage of any form of effective drogue is that it will hold the stern aggressively into the seas, increasing the chances of the boat being pooped. Centre-cockpit vessels are to be preferred when using drogues and aft cockpit boats may need washboards in place, and hatch reinforcement. Small bore cockpit drains, often fitted to older boats, may need to be increased in capacity.

It may be necessary to steer when using a normal drogue, but some vessels will be steered by an autopilot and a few others, particularly long-keeled yachts, will steer themselves with the helm lashed. As in the case of warps, there may come a point as waves mature when a drogue will give more hindrance than help and the boat is better off without. Alternatively, waves may develop so much that there is a risk that the yacht may pitch-pole, as happened to *Silver Shadow* in the Queen's Birthday storm of 1994 (Chapter 19). If the boat is of a type that does not heave-to comfortably, and there is a danger of pitch-poling, the options are to motor into the sea, deploy a parachute sea anchor or set a *Series Drogue*.

The Series Drogue was invented by a distinguished aeronautical engineer, the late Don Jordan, after the 1979 Fastnet Race, to provide an effective drogue for small vessels caught out in a storm. It consists of a hundred or more small fabric cones attached to a rope of about 100 metres (328ft) in length. Although the device has been around for a long time it has taken some time to become established because it is an elaborate appliance to manufacture and it may not be obvious why it should work so well. However, more and more people who have used it in exceptionally

severe weather speak very highly of it. Not only does it hold the stern into the sea without the need for a helmsman, its action appears remarkably gentle and effective. A further enhancement is to use the Series Drogue with a bridle that can be adjusted to give a small angle off dead downwind which gives a further improvement in comfort. The time was when one had to make one's own Jordan Series Drogue but not anymore. One can now purchase the whole sea anchor, or just the cones which can be attached to one's own line.

Using parachute sea anchors

If running before a storm, perhaps using a drogue or warps, a point may be anticipated when the vessel is in danger of being pitch-poled, a lee shore is becoming an issue, or the crew is too exhausted to continue to steer. Another remedy in these circumstances is to deploy a parachute sea anchor. The advantage of a correctly deployed parachute is that it will hold a yacht bows-on to the seas, so when struck by a breaking wave she will not be rolled or pitch-poled, however large that wave may be.

Of course it is not necessary for the situation to become desperate before deploying a parachute sea anchor, and it will be much easier to set it up before the storm breaks. For success a number of conditions have to be met. The parachute has to be the correct size and strong enough; the parachute line has to be the right length, of the correct diameter and well protected from chafe. Moreover, all the components of the system, including the securing points on the boat, have to be strong enough to take the considerable load. Some people do not achieve a good deployment at their first attempt, loss of the parachute through abrasion is quite common and recovery can sometimes be difficult.

One variation, developed by the remarkable couple Lin and Larry Pardey on lying head-to-wind and sea on a parachute sea anchor, is to set up the parachute line at an angle to the seas using a snatch block on a strong pendant line led from the parachute line to a position aft. With a trysail or deep-reefed mainsail set, the boat is protected from breaking waves by the slick from her sideways drift and can be much more comfortable than when the parachute is directly over the bow. This method may take time to perfect and the technique appears to be most suitable for long-keeled yachts less than 12.2m (40ft), such as the Pardeys' own yacht *Taleisin*. More information is to be found in Chapters 7, 19, and 20.

Using oil

There has never been any doubt that oil on troubled waters provides a calming influence. Scientists attribute the mechanism to something called the 'Marangoni Effect'. A point also only of academic interest is that a film of vegetable oil, which has a higher elasticity, is said to work better than a film of mineral oil. However, there are precious few recent records of small craft using oil of any sort to their benefit during severe weather. It may be significant that whereas British lifeboats were fitted with a small tank of 'wave subduing oil' – a vegetable oil called Garnet 46 – the oil was seldom used, and modern lifeboats no longer carry it. We have the instance of HMS *Birmingham* using oil in the 1987 English Channel storm to assist a vessel in distress (Chapter 17). The captain had good reason to use it and the opportunity to study its effectiveness; in this case the oil could be seen to be working, but the problem was to position it so as to be useful. There is no doubt that oil can be a lifesaver in the right place though slipperiness through oil on deck is most unwelcome. Oil is best dispensed by pouring into the galley sink or pumping it out of the heads.

Final thoughts

A feature of many storm experiences is that crews are often forced to work through a variety of tactics as conditions worsen beyond their previous experience and it becomes obvious that something different has to be done. Instinct and improvisation come to one's aid, but we can be sure that skippers who deserve to come off best are those who have the resolve to keep on top of the situation, who have chosen and thoroughly prepared their vessels and crews for heavy weather and, when necessary, have alternative measures in mind.

This book illustrates that there is no one answer to survival in heavy weather and there is a great deal that can be done to optimise one's chances. In summary, it is good to reef early, good to avoid breaking waves and good to locate the boat away from obvious hostile waters where most breaking waves occur. Given enough people able to helm, it is good to sail 15 per cent off the wind under storm jib or trysail. It is bad to run for shelter without careful thought. Heaving-to is good and lying a'hull bad. Running before the sea with a suitable drogue and towing long lines has some merit, as does lying to a parachute sea anchor, particularly when sea room is limited. Again, given enough people able to helm, using the engine can be good, and finally, using a Jordan Series Drogue appears to have considerable worth and few disadvantages. At the same time one must not forget Adlard Coles' words: 'No yacht, however sound, and no crew, however experienced, is immune from the dangers of the sea.'

PART TWO

Storm Experiences

Short accounts of weather phenomena, 1983–1997

Peter Bruce

When Adlard Coles started to write *Heavy Weather Sailing* in the 1960s he drew mainly from his own experiences because there were not many recorded accounts from small craft caught out in very severe weather at that time, and the number of ocean going yachts then was tiny compared with today. Besides, when small craft were overtaken by extremely rough weather, there was often a scarcity of information from which comparisons could be made.

Corroborative weather information was not easily available and accurate anemometers were seldom fitted in yachts, so good information was probably lost through sailors not having enough solid facts on which to hang their account. Adlard Coles' collection of storm stories, based on such corroborative information as could be found, gave the background to the thinking of 50 years ago or more. Knowledge of meteorology has moved on and so has instrumentation, so it is now much easier to quantify heavy weather than it was then.

Continuing with Adlard Coles' own practice, a collection of brief accounts of heavy weather is given in this chapter, together with occurrences such as the effects of thunderstorms and waterspouts. These latter events, which are often short-lived, can be as life threatening as any normal storm.

Bill Cooper has an account of an extraordinary experience in the Bermuda triangle aboard his 17.7m (58ft) steel ketch *Fare Well* in June 1982. He, his disabled wife Laurel and a lady friend Nora had sailed from Bermuda heading for New England when they heard on the radio that Hurricane Alberta was coming their way. The forecast gave conditions in which 'elderly gentlefolk should not be at sea' but they had nowhere else to go. Having made relatively light work of the hurricane, happily quite distant, something totally unexpected and sinister then took place.

BY THE EVENING OF 19 JUNE we were hove-to under storm jib and very close-reefed mainsail. Our wind was averaging 40 knots with the gusts going well off the clock. I think the seas were about 4.6m (15ft). These conditions persisted all night; the average wind not rising much but the seas built up a bit, and I estimated 6m (20ft) in the morning watch. Each broadside wave shot a little jet of cold water through the perished rubber sealing of the deckhouse window onto the protesting form of Laurel in the stand-by berth. Otherwise all was dry and sound below. The yacht was behaving very well indeed. The decks were awash most of the time, but the high poop had only spray, and the cockpit, which is really a sheltered area at deck level, had received no green sea, but enough itinerant slosh to justify one storm board in the hatchway.

The storm centre was then reported to be in position 41°N, 66°W, some 170 miles away to the northwest, and probably the closest we came to it. Our position was based on DR, of course, for we had seen no sunshine for some time.

I had got the mizzen half-way up when I heard, rather than saw, what looked like a wall of very heavy rain approaching. In a second or two it arrived, rain of unbelievable intensity. I had been glad of our cockpit shelter, but it was of no help against this sort of rain, when even the splashes wet everything. Then the wind arrived before I had time even to move. It came across the few yards of water I could see, blowing the waves flat. It hit us an almost solid blow, and we were flung over to starboard; how far I cannot say for there was no point of reference, but certainly more than 90°, and I fell onto the starboard bench at the limit of my lifeline. While we were over, a sea broke and swept us, wresting the boom from the gallows, parting lashing and gaskets.

I scrambled up as the ship righted. The mizzen blew out. The main boom shook like a slipper in a puppy's mouth and, with a loud report, the 14oz (397g) main split and blew to shreds. The genoa, which had been rolled up, stretched in the wind and, without the core turning, allowed a few feet to unroll; the clew then blew out. My oilskin was ripped open; all buttons gone and the zip pulled apart.

As I tried to gather myself to deal with matters, I felt all the power to move leave me. I stood holding the leather-covered wheel feeling strangely euphoric as if being drawn steadily upward off my feet. The feeling went on and on as if time had stopped, and I could not breathe, though my lungs were full. I could not move at all.

Then the lightning struck. Instantly, tension disappeared. The whole space around the yacht seemed to be glowing but I had absolutely no sense of time. I was aware of Nora appearing in the hatch followed by Laurel, looking very white. Both had been rudely propelled from their bunks when the gust had heeled us over, and all the above had taken place as they scrambled to the deck, say 20 or 30 seconds. Laurel describes me as standing motionless at the wheel, mouth wide open, with water streaming down me as if I were standing under a waterfall. I had to be roused to move. Presumably I was in a state of shock.

Bill and Laurel Cooper's Fare Well, *which was thought to have encountered a waterspout at night.* Photo: Bill Cooper

A feature of these violent and fast moving storms is that the advanced semi-circle has strong winds over a much greater radius. Behind the storm the radius was only 50 miles and conditions soon started to improve. The sea was slow to give up, but the wind moderated quite quickly. We tacked when reasonably sure the storm had passed, and headed 290°T, leaving our reduced sail up for the night.

When I took over the watch at 0400 on 20 June the wind had eased to force 4, but the seas were still considerable, though not dangerous. We rolled badly, and the main was not filling properly. I furled it, and decided to set the genoa and mizzen to get some way and stability. It was very dark, and raining heavily. There had been a couple of thunderstorms during the night producing moderate squalls: there was thunder about at that time, but nothing exciting.

The ladies turned to, and gradually I joined in, largely doing as I was told. Together we tamed the main boom, which had broken its gooseneck. When it was safely in the gallows we bundled together the collection of streamers that had been a mainsail. The mizzen was grappled in. The genoa was more of a problem. The sheets had slackened as the clew pulled out, and had tied themselves into a spaghetti knot so tight we could neither furl the sail, nor get it down its extrusion core. I did not fancy my chances half-way up the forestay at that time so we let it go.

There was big trouble in the engine room, and compass deviation went from zero to 90°W then slowly to 25°W, which only came to light through logging the direction of the swell. But what was it, apart from the lightning that struck the ketch at 0430 that morning? Bill Cooper now thinks that he encountered a waterspout. Presumably, it would have been the lightning strike that caused the magnetic anomaly. Details of the mechanism of tornados/waterspouts will be found in Chapter 8. Whilst it is too simplistic to describe a waterspout as a tornado at sea, there are many similarities.

A yacht race off Australia in 1983 will long be remembered for the loss of four yachtsmen who were drowned when their yachts sank. This was the JOG Tasman Cup on 15 April 1983 with a 44-mile overnight course from Sydney Harbour, south along the exposed coastline to a buoy off Port Hacking, and back. The forecast was for 20–30 knot south to south-west winds as well as southeasterly swell, giving a beat down to Port Hacking. It seems that the wind that materialized was much as forecast, but it created a secondary swell across the one from the southeast. In addition, there was a south-going current running offshore – locally known as the 'set' – and the whole combination created steep breaking waves.

The first yacht to run into trouble was the *Montego Bay*, a Hood 23 production boat with an experienced crew. After falling heavily off several waves she was found to be making water. The crew decided to abandon the race but, in spite of some spirited work with a bucket, the boat sank rather quickly. Just before this happened, they had succeeded in firing two flares but had obtained no acknowledgement from their Mayday transmission and were too late to reach their lifejackets in the cockpit locker. There seems to have been some confusion in the crew of the two boats of the fleet that saw the flares, as to whether there was a genuine emergency, and it was not until three hours later that a yacht returning to Sydney after abandoning the race happened to find two of *Montego Bay*'s crew in the water, and raised the alarm. Two more of the crew were picked up half an hour later, but a fifth man was never found.

Meanwhile another yacht of the same size, the Farr 727 *Waikikamukau* with a crew of four, had also sunk. She had been capsized by a particularly large breaking wave, and with no washboards in place, she had filled rapidly through her main companionway. The crew was attached to the boat with their safety harnesses, and one of them was unable to detach his safety harness before the stern of the yacht submerged and he was drowned. Another crewman had great difficulty in kicking off his sea boots which were hampering his ability to swim. None of the crew was wearing lifejackets, and the horseshoe lifebuoy stowed in the stern sheets of *Waikikamukau* had gone down with her. The three remaining crew quickly separated in the heavy seas and darkness.

In the end, there was only one survivor, who had to swim for ten hours before being picked up by a passing fishing boat. He reported that both helicopters and rescue craft, who were still looking for the fifth man from the *Montego Bay*, had repeatedly passed close by him, but had failed to spot him or hear his cries. He was spotted by someone who was leaning over the side of a fishing boat being seasick.

But for the warmth of the water, no one would ever have known what had happened to the two yachts and their crews, and there were several hard lessons to be learnt from the tragedy. The importance of lifejackets is clearly one of them.

Another is the necessity of having washboards (or storm boards) in place in the main hatchway in big, breaking seas. Compliance with current regulations would probably have saved the lives of some or all of those lost. The World Sailing regulations for category 3 races stipulate, for example, that lifejackets must have a light, and be worn between sunset and sunrise; safety lines must have a snaphook at each end.

There are dramatic local changes in the weather from good to bad that are seldom forecast, and sometimes are over so quickly that those who were not there often doubt their severity. They could account for a number of losses of vessels without trace in what seemed to have been benign conditions. For example, the British barque *Marques* was racing from Bermuda to Nova Scotia in 1984. At about 0800 she was 129km (80 miles) north of Bermuda in moderate weather when a hurricane force wind hit the ship 'out of the blue'. She capsized and only those on deck survived, the remainder being trapped below. One of the explanations was that she was hit by a microburst, a localised down draught associated with a thunderstorm that struck at an angle of 45°. Thunderstorms were about that morning, though the *Marques* was apparently not particularly close.

A less distressing event took place in the South Pacific in February 1985 when an experienced Australian couple, Alan and Kathy Webb, with their 16-year-old daughter, Portia, were overtaken by a survival storm. Their heavily built 13.7m (45ft) steel cutter *Supertramp*, in which her owners had great confidence, had been designed for world cruising with a moderate fin keel, a skeg hung rudder and immense strength.

They arrived in the Roaring Forties with Easter Island 724km (450 miles) to the west and Chile some 2,250km (1,400 miles) to the east (40° 20' S, 101° 37' W) to be confronted by a plummeting barometer and 80-knot winds that continued for 36 hours. The self-steering soon broke and Alan Webb was left to steer for the duration as *Supertramp* ran under bare pole in winds they estimated at Force

12. Huge breaking seas developed, aggravated and confused by squalls. The Webbs make a practice of lying a'hull with the wheel lashed to windward in gales but in this instance Kathy Webb says it would have been impossible to heave-to as they would certainly have been capsized. Alan comments:

WHEN RUNNING DOWN waves of this extreme height, *Supertramp* developed too much speed, but by surfing down them at an angle, I found I could remain high on the crest and also take speed off the yacht. It was vital to keep her on top of the first tier, high upon the shoulder of the wave, by steering about 20° across its face rather than let the boat slip into the trough. We still stood a chance of being rolled over, but a slow roll-over would do much less damage than being pitch-poled at speed.

The Webbs have since wondered if they might have used their storm jib in the lulls to give steerageway, but conclude that their bare pole speed seldom dropped below four knots; for the rest of the time any sail would have been too much. Perhaps a drogue/engine combination may have helped?

Several other interesting points came from the experience. Firstly, Alan Webb felt his beach surfing experience was helpful in negotiating the breaking seas. He was also assisted by the fact that *Supertramp* was extremely controllable under bare pole, and could even be gybed when lying a'hull. Another good feature of the boat was her centre cockpit with 10in (25cm) coamings and large diameter drain holes. Alan Webb now has a smaller light displacement yacht and his comparisons with the two contrasting types can be found in Chapter 15.

Harry Franks had a slightly similar tornado cum waterspout experience to Bill Cooper in 1997 off Ushant in the 11.6m (38ft) Morgan Giles wooden sloop *Matawa*:

WE WERE COMING TO THE END of our summer cruise in *Matawa*, celebrating her 50th birthday that year. After a quiet night a little way up the river Elorn attached to a convenient buoy, we had taken the ebb out of the Rade du Brest and were heading for Ushant.

The wind was light and on our beam from the north and we were intermittently sailing and motoring, wanting to make Ushant in good time for a run ashore that evening. A few showers were threatened and there was some thunder about, but it looked like an uneventful sail as we passed Pierres Noir South Cardinal and headed for Pierres Vertes buoy. I was on the helm and the rest of the crew were variously loitering below, navigating, sleeping, reading etc. We had the engine on to help us to windward as the land breeze that had helped us out of the Rade had given way to the forecast northerly. To starboard the rather jagged rocks of Les Pierres Noir were coming and going in the poor visibility but we were well clear of them and to leeward.

I was idly wondering what the likelihood of a lightning strike on our metal mast was as the thunder rolled around us when suddenly 'BANG', over we went as a massive gust hit us. For a moment I had that frightening feeling, remembered from dinghy sailing in times past, that we were going to go right over as I hung on desperately to avoid being pitched over the lee rail. Thankfully, *Matawa* did the right thing and slowly came into the wind, giving me the chance to check sheets. Down below, Henry on the windward bunk had been thrown across onto Michael junior on the leeward one and Tim, in the forepeak, was sure we were going to capsize. With the wind came torrential rain and much reduced visibility and we were now, it seemed to me, being driven towards the rocks.

Fortunately Mike senior had recovered from the initial shock quickly, thrown oilskins on and was soon on deck. The first priority was to lower the foresail and this we soon managed though, as I checked away the foresheet, I had a glimpse of the comprehensive shredding of the sail, fortunately not a new one. We were still out of control and the wind seemed to be turning us around like a top, the sea flat but stirred by driven wavelets. By this time Tim was also on deck and we had hands to lower the main; those rocks looming in the mind closer by the

Matawa is a traditional 11.6m x 2.7m x 1.8m (38ft x 9ft x 6ft) yacht designed by Morgan Giles and built of plywood by Cardnell Bros in 1947.
Photo: Peter Bruce

second as we were driven onwards. Down came the main and I finally began to feel that I had some control, thankful that the engine was still on. I steered due south as gradually the wind subsided and the rain eased off from its frantic pelting. Soon, and with much relief, the rocks appeared still to north of us – I half expected us to have been driven past them! Fifteen minutes later we had the main up again, soon after that the number 2 genoa, and we were able to get back on our old course.

One hour later we were at anchor in Lampaul. We did however notice that one or two other boats had their oilskins out to dry which reassured us that we had not been hallucinating. The whole episode had only lasted half an hour at the most.

In retrospect, I suspect that we had experienced a tornado-cum-waterspout. This is surely why I had the impression of being driven at will through all points of the compass while we reduced sail. What warning had we had of such an 'event'? The navigator says that he had noticed the sky going dark; but obviously not dramatically enough to mention it to me. I suspect that I had not noticed it because I was wearing dark glasses. More important was our mind set; we had had two weeks of calms and light airs and, perhaps out of ignorance, associated thunderstorms with drenching rain and calm wind. I shall know better for the future. Fortunately, the only damage was to the sail, because that sort of experience really tests the seaworthiness of a yacht, not only the rigging but how well things have been secured above and below decks after weeks when the most extreme motion we had experienced was the wash of passing trawlers.

This alarming experience is again notable for the sudden arrival in thundery weather of storm force wind, accompanied by unusually heavy rain. It was noteworthy that *Matawa* was out of control and being turned by the wind like a top.

Sandy Gilbert, with *Magnum Opus* in the Mediterranean, sailing between Majorca and Minorca, tells a story of how, with a distant thunderstorm in sight, his boat was hit by a squall of tremendous violence, later accompanied by hail, which ripped to shreds the only sail that was left set. The boat would not respond to the helm and was circling. A catamaran's crew in the same situation not far away reported that they had also spun round and round. In one yacht nearby, a man went overboard, and in another the main sheet would not release under its load and the fabric of the mainsail had to be cut to prevent a capsize. Of quite a large number of yachts in the area, almost all reported an initial severe knockdown.

The event is similar to Harry Franks' tornado cum waterspout, in that the wind arrived with remarkable suddenness and strength, boats were spun round, and it was all over in half an hour. The forecast of easterly Force 4 would not have accounted for such strong winds, estimated to have been Force 12, and the explanation seems to have been that the thunderstorm

Thundery squall. White breaking seas can be seen under the right hand cloud, indicating that the squall has much wind as well as rain. The presence of a strong wind in a squall is rarely so obvious.
Photo: Christian Février/Bluegreen

brought about a precipitation down draught, a microburst, which turned into a tornado.

Finally there is another account of a large US cruising yacht in the Bahamas torn from her berth when hit by a waterspout, breaking off two marina piles in the process. The owner, who said the noise was like an underground train at speed, saw a motor bicycle lifted into the air from the jetty, and when last seen it was ascending at an angle of 45°. His steel foredeck ventilator weighing 91kg (200lb) was found half a mile away.

Accounts of vessels being hit by waterspouts, which can be between 15–46m (50–150ft) in diameter, are rare, though waterspouts are known to have caused great damage when they have come ashore. It is rare but not unknown for a waterspout to form in the early morning as happened to *Fare Well*.

Clearly thunderstorms (even when distant), tornadoes and waterspouts at sea can be dangerous and should be avoided if possible. The noise of thunder, anvil-shaped clouds combined with dark low-level cloud or an actual waterspout may be as much warning as one may ever have. The good seaman should adopt practices that will withstand sudden adverse weather and be ready for an intense squall whenever thunder is about.

The events described in this chapter, in most cases, were not expected and the crews were operating from their normal level of preparation.

The harrowing story of the JOG Tasman Cup is, perhaps, the most instructive. The yachts that sank were close to land, close to other yachts, and experiencing rather less heavy weather than in most of the accounts in this book. Chances to save the situation were missed. Accidents often result when insufficiently strong action is taken in the early stages of an adverse situation. We need to remember Admiral Nimitz's words about precautions at

A vertical waterspout, though sometimes they are curved or even in the form of a spiral.
Photo: NOAA/Dr Joseph Golden

the beginning of Chapter 6, 'The time for taking all measures for a ship's safety is while able to do so'. We need to ask ourselves whether we can be sure that, in the same circumstances, our own standards of seamanship would have prevented loss of life. For example, why was it that other yachts did not respond to the distress flares from the *Montego Bay*? Aboard *Montego Bay*, in the rush of activity, would we have had the presence of mind to say firmly 'it's time to put on lifejackets, boys' before it was too late? Would we, in *Waikikamukau*, have insisted upon washboards being fitted in the companionway?

Assuming some fundamental error has occurred, will our remedies that are required as a result do the job? As Chay Blyth so rightly says: 'Hope for the best: but prepare for the worst.'

17 Channel storm of 1987

Peter Bruce

There were several small vessels at sea during the great storm of October 1987, but with massive destruction ashore dominating the news, both on the north coast of France and the south coast of Britain, little was heard about them. The intense small depression brought winds of over 100 knots to the English Channel area, and though the wind speed was of hurricane strength, it is wrong to describe the event as a hurricane, as it was by the UK media. It was a storm, albeit a truly violent one, but not a tropical revolving storm.

October is late in the year for leisure sailing, but the sea water temperature is still warm; so there are still a few sailors who go out for pleasure at this time. Moreover, delivery trips continue all through the year, and the Joint Service Sailing Centre yachts, based at Gosport, have a long season. Thus, with manageable conditions during the day, and without a warning of ultra-severe weather made manifest in the forecast, it was not surprising that several yachts were still out at sea on the night of Thursday 15 October. A small fleet of warships from Portland naval base were also at sea for the opposite reason. In very strong winds, ships at anchor can drag onto the shore even in Portland Harbour, and as a result of a timely warning from the senior meterological officer there, Lieutenant Commander Peter Braley, who had made his own interpretation of the impending weather, the Portland fleet was ordered to sea.

Five descriptions from the sailing vessels at sea in the storm are related in this chapter, to give a wide cross-section of experiences; but before the accounts from the sea, there follows a meteorological report by Peter Braley.

Meteorology

AS EARLY AS THE WEEKEND of 10–11 October 1987, the Meteorological Office at Bracknell had been forecasting severe weather on the following Thursday and Friday.

At midnight on Tuesday 13 October, the depression in question was centred near 50°N 47°W, off Newfoundland, tracking east. It was expected to deepen progressively by midnight on Thursday 15 October, after which explosive deepening was predicted, with storm force winds expected in the South Western Approaches during Thursday, and moving up Channel and into the North Sea overnight. The prediction was reinforced and updated at 1545 on Wednesday 14 October, when the low had begun to move rapidly east. The storm warning suggested that the centre could be expected to be 150nm north-west of Cape Finisterre by 0600 on Thursday 15 October, with winds in its southern quadrant expected to reach storm force 10 up to 200nm from the centre. The low was then predicted to curve north-north-east to bring south-west storm force winds to the east Channel and southern North Sea areas late on 15 October.

The development became noticeable to meteorological authorities throughout Western Europe after midnight on 14–15 October. At that time, an elongated trough was located over a distance of some 500nm westwards from Cape Finisterre with two apparently distinct depression centres – one 983hPa (mb) just north-west of Coruña, the other about 986hPa (mb) near 43°N 19°W, some 450nm further west. A strong pressure gradient existed on the warm southern side of the frontal trough, but with a slack gradient on the cold side. Noticeable potential temperature differences across this front were apparent from the few available observations, suggesting a sharp differential between the polar maritime and tropical maritime air masses. By midday on 15 October this broad surface trough lay from Brittany across Finisterre, and pressure in the trough was falling markedly. By 1800 the axis of the surface and upper troughs had extended north-east, bringing the frontal feature across the Channel and into southern England. The two centres were still apparent, one over Ushant, and the other now more vigorous centre of 963hPa (mb) near 45.5°N 8.5°W. Surface pressure continued to fall within the trough but, more significantly, marked rises in pressure had occurred over the previous six hours both south-west of the main centre and astern of the cold front, with corresponding increases in wind speed. At about 2100, a signal was received at Portland from the forecaster in RFA Engadine in the north Biscay area, drawing attention to the sudden falls in pressure in his vicinity, thus suggesting explosive deepening of the Biscay centre. The signal also remarked upon the pronounced cross-sea and swell conditions. Soon afterwards the centre passed close to Engadine and winds rose rapidly in strength, occasionally to exceed 90 knots.

By 2100 the depression centre had tightened considerably and begun to move rapidly north-east at about 40 knots to deepen to about 960hPa (mb) in the extreme south of sea area Plymouth. The trend continued towards midnight when a centre was indicated just south of the Eddystone with a central pressure nearing 952hPa (mb). Notably, this feature was now a single, definable centre. A clear and fairly accurate track became discernible,

making short-term forecasting and timing somewhat simpler and more certain. These, together with surface analyses, demonstrated the exceptional pressure gradients now developing in a narrow swath to the south and east of the centre, with surface gusts exceeding 100 knots in exposed locations.

During the next six hours the centre of the depression moved in a north-easterly direction across England after crossing the coast between Charmouth and Lyme Regis at about 0215. By 0500 on 16 October it had reached Lincolnshire and the occlusion had swung rapidly across southern England. Very marked rising pressure tendencies were widespread in the three hours from 0300 to 0600 as the depression filled: for example, +25.5hPa (mb) at Portland. This later rise has now been established, by a comfortable margin, as the greatest three-hourly pressure change ever to be recorded in the UK.

Retrospective examination of meteorological records has been extensive, but it may be of interest to draw attention to a few facts:

1 The band of strongest gusts, with isolated maxima over 100 knots, extended across the Channel areas from north-west France in a band some 145km (90 miles) wide, parallel to the track of the depression centre.

2 Gusts of 70 knots or more were reported for a period of three to four consecutive hours, during which time the wind veered from 180° to 230°.

3 A double-peaked wind speed region apparently occurred over central southern England and the adjacent Channel coast. The first was associated with winds from 170° and 190°; the latter from a direction of around 230° – the peaks being at around 0200 and 0500 respectively.

4 A separate area of strong northerly winds affected Cornwall and North Devon from 2300 on 15 October until about 0200 on 16 October.

5 The strongest gust over the UK was recorded at Gorleston (Norfolk): 106 knots at 0424.

Over 20 other gusts in excess of 90 knots were recorded between 0400 and 0715. A higher gust was estimated at 119 knots at a station near Quimper on the Biscay coast, while a gust measuring 117 knots occurred at 0030 at Granville on the south-west corner of the Cherbourg peninsula.

6 The passage of the cold front heralded the onset of the really strong winds at the surface. It was the strength of mean wind speeds that was noteworthy, rather than individual gusts.

7 The pressure falls ahead of the advancing depression were large but not remarkable, yet the subsequent rises in pressure appear to have been exceptional. Large areas of south England experienced rises in excess of 8hPa (mb) per hour.

8 While very marked, short and steep seas built up in the Channel, recorders show that no remarkable storm surge followed and no pronounced swell developed due to the short duration and small size of the maximum windfield.

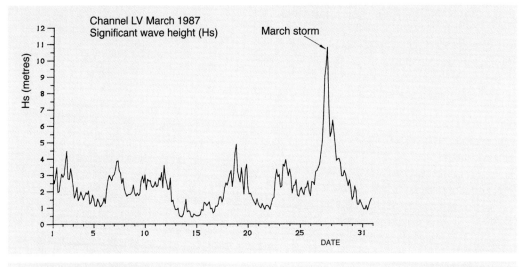

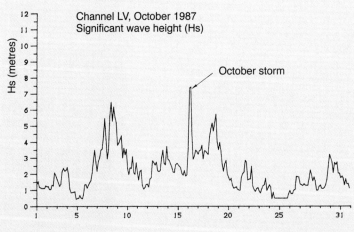

Figure 17.1 *The charts show two months of wave data recorded at the Channel lightvessel in 1987. This includes the very severe storm of October, and also the one in March of the same year. Though the intense, fast-moving system of October 1987 caused havoc on land, it was not around long enough to create exceptionally high waves, unlike the very large depression of the March storm.*

A Sadler 34 off Ushant

The first sea account comes from a new shoal-draft Sadler 34 called *Muddle Thru*. She had been bought by a Canadian, Allan McLaughlan, who had come over to Poole in Dorset, England, from Ontario with two other Canadians, Harry Whale and Bill Bedell, both of long sailing experience, to take delivery of his boat and sail for the Caribbean.

They set out on 13 October 1987, but progress towards Ushant was very slow due to strong head winds, and the boat was 'caught out' 60 miles to the north of Ushant in the 100–120 knot winds of 15–16 October. The persistence of *Muddle Thru*'s crew was enhanced by the fear that VAT might have to be paid on the boat if she was to return to the UK. After the great storm, another gale came, and this time the boat was rolled through 360°. The effects of the capsize, which included a broken lower shroud, caused Harry Whale, the skipper, to head back to Falmouth, where, incidentally, HM Customs took a benevolent VAT view in the circumstances. Harry Whale kept a log of events by speaking into a tape recorder, and it is his account of the storm that follows:

WINDS INCREASED TO FORCE 9 from the west-south-west during 14 October; and though close-hauled and carrying only a deep triple reefed mainsail, we made fairly good progress in almost the right direction. To keep a proper lookout was difficult because one could never be sure in the dark if we were looking towards the horizon or merely into yet another big wave. Certainly we did see many ships and made every effort to stay well clear, believing that under the prevailing conditions we were probably invisible, despite the radar reflector on the mast.

By about 0300 on 15 October the wind had abated enough for us to add some foresail to the sailplan and, after experimenting with the furling genoa, we rigged the detachable headstay and hanked on a small flat jib. The rest of the day was spent in heavy rain, crashing along into Force 7 wind, heading south-west by south. In the afternoon the wind ceased quite suddenly

and, after an hour or so, came in from the opposite direction, north-east. It then rapidly built up to Force 7 again. Under jib only we were soon making splendid time directly towards our destination with a following wind, but meeting the waves that were still coming from south-west. Some waves we seemed to jump over and others we went through; nevertheless, it was good finally to be able to make our course at a respectable speed. Suddenly the turn at Ushant didn't seem so far away.

The run continued until 2100 when the wind died completely for half an hour. It then came in from the south, quickly built up, and veered to the south-west. By midnight we had taken off all sail and were lying a'hull. On the tape I said 'we are in a shocking blow'. Having experimented with the helm and the wind vane steering, I finally came to the conclusion that the boat took the best attitude to wind and waves when left to its own devices with the wheel lashed amidships and the wind vane disconnected. I feel sure this was largely due to the sprayhood and its considerable windage, which had the effect of keeping the bow into the weather.

Having seen several east-bound ships I was concerned about traffic in the area. We had heard the traffic controller at Ushant speaking to another vessel on VHF radio. I called to inform him that we were lying a'hull and virtually at the mercy of wind and sea, so suggested a securité call to vessels in the vicinity. This he did very obligingly, giving our position, estimated drift and course. He also told me that his wind gauge indicated wind speed ranging from 100 to 120, and that he was concerned for the safety of his radar. I did not think to ask if the wind speed given was in nautical miles, statute miles or kilometres per hour. It seems now that they were knots. Psychologically I think all of us on board felt better for the exchange, especially when he called an hour or so later for an update on our position. I provided this, and mentioned that we had noticed two or three west-bound ships passing to the north of us. I was impressed by the fact that he wanted to know how our position was obtained. By now we were starting to hear parts of one-sided conversations on the

VHF and realized that something pretty major was going on by the number of distress calls, including a Mayday from a yacht in a French port. Two other conversations I remember involved one vessel that had been driven hard aground, and another that had lost its steering.

Generally, our little boat seemed to be handling things very well, although the noise of the wind and the waves breaking over the vessel was extreme and the motion quite erratic. Occasionally the boat would seem to get temporarily turned broadside onto the waves and a great thumping one would hit her full on the beam. The furling jib was tightly wound about its stay, the small hank-on jib tightly lashed to the toe rail, and the mainsail lashed to the boom. A small part of the mainsail got free and proceeded to thrash so wildly that I felt sure the sail would end in tatters, and possibly even strain the rigging. Having determined that the loose part of the sail was below the second reefing point and therefore most of the sail should survive, I decided to let it flog rather than risk a man or two overboard trying to retie it to the boom, which would involve working around the sprayhood where the holding was least secure. As it turned out, the sail fared well, though the battens were lost.

The three of us remained fully dressed in foul weather gear and harnesses; we spent our time below with just a brief check on deck every 15 to 20 minutes. With so much water constantly coming onboard the boat, one had to be careful about the timing when opening and closing the main hatch.

Eventually, at about 0730 on 16 October, the wind abated sufficiently to start sailing again. We had gingerly worked our way up to a double-reefed main and small jib by 1400, and even had glorious sunshine for three hours. We were visited by some dolphins, and though still on a dead beat, we generally felt very fortunate to be in such good overall conditions as we listened to the radio telling of the damage done during the night both at sea and ashore. At 1600 more gale warnings were broadcast – force 8 going to force 9 from the south-west. For the

next 13 hours we made good course of west-north-west at an average speed of 3¼ knots.

During 17 October the wind direction varied from south-west to west-south-west and we tacked accordingly, always mindful of giving Ushant a wide berth. By 2200 we were again down to bare pole in a raging gale, this time with mainsail lashed very tightly to the boom and the outboard end of the boom lowered and lashed to the toe rail. Once again I experimented with the wind vane steering and various positions of the helm, but came to the same conclusion as before – to lash the wheel amidships and allow the boat to take care of itself. From our perspective the main wave pattern was from the south-west; however, we seemed to be constantly under attack from quite unpredictable waves from the south-east and north-west. Some of these seemed to be not so much waves as just great eruptions of water, happening without rhyme or reason.

As before, we huddled below fully dressed in foul weather gear and harness trying to catnap, with a check on deck every 15 to 20 minutes. I suppose this continued for three or four hours. I was lying down in the starboard bunk and had dozed off nicely when suddenly I realized I was airborne and on my way across the cabin, easily clearing the lee cloth and table en route. I came up short against the other side of the boat on top of Bill. As I scrambled around trying to extricate myself I remember enquiring after Al, who had been using the quarter berth. He spoke up from underneath me saying that he was OK. He had given up the quarter berth and rigged himself an accommodation on top of some cans of water we had lashed into place in the U of the dinette settee and was wedged between Bill and the folding table. About this time I heard 'we're upside down, boys' from Bill in a quite conversational voice – indeed, almost a mumble.

By use of the two full-height teak pillars that the Sadler has in the vicinity of the galley and chart table, I was able to heave myself over the galley sink and, by the time the boat was completely inverted, I was standing on the deckhead holding onto a pillar with each hand, facing forward, with my back to the engine compartment and the main hatch boards.

The exact sequence of events and time involved is of course very uncertain, but I do have a vivid recollection of standing there and being aware that the noise and motion had ceased, other than the sound of water rushing in through various small openings; I was expecting at any moment to be struck from behind by the hatch boards collapsing inwards under the pressure. It was as well that Bill had insisted that the cockpit locker lids be well secured.

As the boat continued its roll-over I remained clinging to the pillars, negotiating them rather like climbing a large two-rung ladder that is being rotated. As the boat resumed its normal upright position several impressions struck me; one was the resumption of the old noise and motion, another was the additional sound of water sloshing back and forth; and the most disturbing was what I can only describe as a 'wobbly' feeling about the boat. Several explanations flashed through my mind, the first being that maybe we had sustained some sort of a longitudinal hull fracture – yet there didn't seem to be much water coming in. Then I wondered if the keel had loosened, but discounted this thought on the grounds that surely it would have gone entirely or not at all, and since we seemed to be remaining right way up, the keel must still be in place. The only possibility was that the hull was being wrenched around by a loose rig.

My first resolve was to try the diesel engine. This would enable us to run the electric bilge and shower pumps, and also provide motive power should we need it. When we tried the switches we got the whistle of the Calor gas alarm. We waited for some time and it didn't stop. Because the alarm had acted strangely on another occasion, and because we had always been careful to turn off the supply, I felt sure this was a false alarm, at least as far as the Calor gas was concerned. We turned off the alarm and gave the engine a try. It started. Now to check the rig.

Getting on deck to investigate was no easy matter. The sprayhood, with its stainless steel framework, was crushed down over the main sliding hatch and the hatch boards. Eventually Bill and I both got through, and discovered with the help of a small torch that the port lower shroud was loose. Bill bravely went forward and took a jib halyard one turn around the mast and attached it to a stanchion base near the chain plate. He then did the same within the main halyard so that we now had the two halyards running from the spreader roots to the stanchion base. From the cockpit we did our best to sweat up these halyards, no easy matter without winch handles, which had left their pockets during the roll-over. Having thus more or less stabilized the rig, we proceeded to haul inboard sheets, halyards, and other odds and ends all hanging over the port side of the cockpit.

Below, Al had been doing his best to assist the bailing process by trying to pour water into the sink with a saucepan. The outlet was not very big and sometimes, because the motion was so violent, the water was flung back at him before it had a chance to drain away. However, we certainly seemed to be holding our own because the water level was not much above the cabin sole. Bearing in mind that a large part of the volume of the bilge was taken up by canned food and built-in flotation material, the actual volume of water aboard could not have been great.

We found that the shower pump was not operating, and only one of the interior lights was working. All of the electronics except the satnav had ceased to function, ie radios, windspeed and direction, log, speedometer and depth sounder. Our spectacles, charts, dividers, hand compass, torches and spare winch handles seemed to have vanished into the heap of sodden mattresses, tools, clothing and sundry other items.

I decided that the prudent course of action was to make for Falmouth. I thought of Moitessier and Vito Dumas, who advocated that the best way to survive in heavy breaking waves was to sail with them at good speed.

Because I had stared at the chart for so many hours before the incident, I knew the course was about 050°. Before shoving the gear shift into

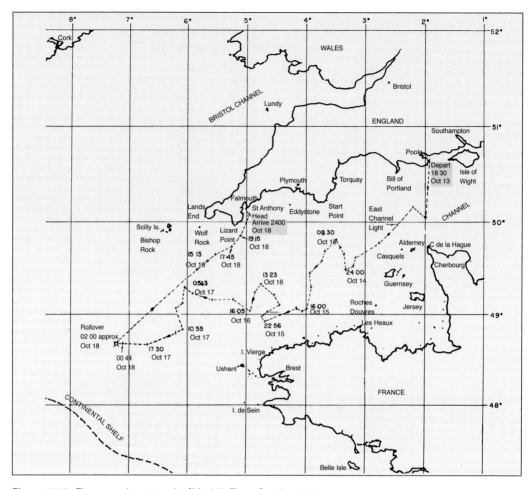

Figure 17.2 *The approximate track of* Muddle Thru, *October 1987.*

forward I tied a huge knot in the furling line of the jib, gauged to stop at the fairlead. Thus about 1.8m (6ft) of it and no more could be let out in a hurry by one man, should the engine stall and force us into taking a chance on the rig.

We were off on the wildest sleigh ride of my entire sailing career. In the cockpit it was impossible to hear the engine over the roar of the wind and water, and there were no gauges of any kind to indicate rpm or boat speed. The main compass seemed to be working, though a little sluggishly. It was strictly seat of the pants stuff, aided sometimes by the vibration of the engine and propeller through the soles of the feet. The boat was completely overwhelmed on several occasions, leaving the helmsman

spluttering and gasping for breath. It was the blackest of nights, and I remember thinking it would be so much better once daylight arrived.

When daylight did finally arrive I wished it had remained dark. It was an impressive scene, huge steep breaking waves everywhere and the air filled with water, either rain or spume. At one point some dolphins came along to join in the fun. Like young skiers on a mogul run they cavorted and frolicked around us, frequently leaping right out of the advancing face of the waves. Never did I feel so out of my element as I cowered at the wheel, tired and afraid, while admiring their wonderful performance. About the time I was beginning to worry about fatigue and hypothermia, Bill squeezed his way out of the hatch and offered to take over. This was a great relief to me, first, because I needed the break, and second, it meant that Bill was now endorsing my strategy of heading for Falmouth, albeit tacitly. I am sure he was originally not in favour.

Later, Al also came up to be initiated and join the watch roster. Time and again it would seem she was about to broach, and be rolled over in a breaking crest; yet at the last minute a little extra power would straighten her out and away we'd go, surfing down yet another huge wave, only immediately to worry that the bow could bury and cause a pitch-pole. Bill was to tell me much later that, at one point when he was steering, the boat did a complete 360° turn (horizontally this time); she seemed, he said, to sail close around a great pinnacle of water, with a cliff face on one side of the boat and a precipice on the other.

About 1900 in the failing light, the loom of the Lizard light showed 10 miles to the north-north-west. The satnav had done a splendid

job for us. Now, without tidal information or depth sounder, came the task of piloting our way the remaining 20 or so miles to the harbour. As it turned out, everything went well: and the wind and waves even abated a little as we came into the lee of Manacle Point and the Manacle rocks. The limited information we had on board showed the harbour entrance and not much else. We shot through the entrance, did a sharp left turn, and suddenly all was tranquil, relatively speaking anyway.

A Swan 46 in the Bay of Biscay

Had *Muddle Thru* made Ushant and into the Bay of Biscay, she would not have had a much easier time, as can be appreciated from another drama going on 346km (215 miles) south-south-west of Ushant. On the morning of 15 October a Swan 46 fitted with a Scheel keel, on passage to Spain, hove-to

This Bay of Biscay roller is to be reckoned with if approaching anywhere near this long lee shore. As it was in the October 1987 storm, waves, though high, never had time to develop to extremes.
Photo: Yvan Zedda/Bluegreen

in wind speeds shown on the yacht's Brookes & Gatehouse anemometer of, at times, over 85 knots. Apart from periodic lookouts, the crew of four remained below, where it was dry. At 1800, without warning, the boat rolled quickly to port through 360°. Floorboards, and everything stored under them, flew through the boat. The yacht's owner, who was standing in the main cabin after returning from a lookout on deck, broke a shoulder. The mast broke at deck level, probably due to a lower shroud failure.

The mast remained attached to the boat by her intact rigging and, without suitable cutting devices on board to cope with rod rigging, the crew were unable to cut it free. Around 2000 the mast broke at two other points and started to pound against the hull. At this juncture the owner decided to ask for outside assistance, and an EPIRB was activated. The Swan 46 was 'localised' in 45 minutes, and a Japanese freighter appeared on the scene at 0100 in the morning of 16 October. The freighter launched a boat, but this soon capsized; so the yacht, with her engine still working, was asked to go alongside. While the crew were disembarking, the yacht was smashed several times against the freighter's hull, and at one point she surfed down a wave and struck the freighter at full speed with her bow. Though the EPIRB was heard for an hour afterwards and hatches were left closed, the yacht was never found.

A significant point in this episode was the difficulty experienced in detaching the mast. Bolt croppers will not cope with heavy rod rigging: only hydraulic cutters or other special tools will do the job.

Rescue seen from a destroyer bridge off Portland Bill

But for the seamanship of the rescuers, another craft might have been lost that night. The story is a little bizarre, and is best told by the captain of HMS *Birmingham*: Cdr Roy Clare (later Admiral) a most experienced yachtsman. The vessel was a gas-turbine powered destroyer, carrying a Lynx helicopter on board:

HMS *BIRMINGHAM* was operating 7 miles south-west of Portland Bill, turning endless circles on the calibration range. At about 1800 on 15 October my navigator showed me the latest Mufax weather chart, with isobars tightly packed over the Brest peninsula. I commented that I was glad we weren't farther south, and forgot about the weather. We did not see Michael Fish, the weather forecaster, on TV that evening.

At about 0115 I was nearly thrown out of my bunk by an unusually heavy roll. I called the officer of the watch on the intercom to find out what he was up to; he answered at once, saying that the weather had suddenly freshened and that he had just heard a call on VHF for help from a yacht... would I come to the bridge?

I quickly established that the yacht was in touch with Portland Coastguard. Her position was some 29km (18 miles) south of me, about 39km (24 miles) from the Bill. Our weather conditions were wind: south-south-west Force 8–9; visibility 9.7km (6 miles), less in drizzle. We set off on a course of about 200° at 22 knots; this was the maximum we could do in the prevailing conditions. We pitched heavily in the steep seas, but there was only a modest swell and we did not thump at all.

Meanwhile the yacht transmitted frequently on VHF, using Channel 67, as directed by the Coastguard. I put an experienced yachtsman on the circuit to give an informed point of contact. We started an incident log book, told the naval operations room we were proceeding to assist, kept in touch with the Coastguard, established that the Royal Fleet Auxiliary tanker *Black Rover* was also in the area, and made basic preparations on board for search and rescue. Flying was out of the question; the sea state was worsening rapidly and the wind limits for helicopter operations would have been exceeded unless we had been heading out of the wind at some speed. This was clearly undesirable; in any case, the ship's Lynx helicopter was not equipped

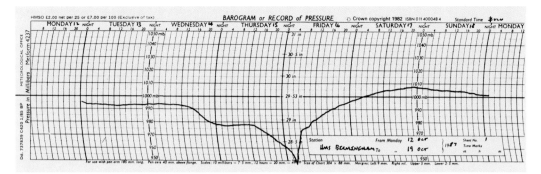

Figure 17.3 *The barograph trace from HMS* Birmingham *recorded during the October 1987 storm whilst standing by a distressed multihull south of Portland Bill. Note the rising pressure, which at +25.5hPa (mb) in three hours, comfortably exceeded any UK pressure change over the same period ever to be recorded.*

for night search and rescue over a small object like a yacht, so it would only have been able to aid the search, not the rescue. Ashore, the coastguards decided that the Weymouth lifeboat should be called out. I do not know whether the shore-based search and rescue helicopter was considered; in my view, it would have been of very marginal value in those conditions. In the event, search was not necessary; location was straightforward, aided by a reasonable position report in the first instance, and by continuous VHF transmissions from the yacht, which were DF'd by the Coastguard stations at Portland Bill and Berry Head to give a cross bearing fix.

By 0150 we had established that the yacht was a cruising multihull of 12m (40ft) length. The vessel was in no immediate danger of foundering, had sustained no damage, and was managing to make way across the wind at about 4 knots on a westerly course apparently bound for Ushant. The crew sounded terrified; they were pleading to be taken off their craft, urging rescuers to hurry before dire things happened. It seemed that there had been a difference of opinion as to whether to continue or turn back. The yacht was said to be shaking violently in the gusts and the voice was convinced that each moment was to be his last. In the background of each transmission, it had to be admitted, there was a fearful noise of wind in rigging and crashing waves. We did our best to reassure and console the yacht, keeping the crew informed of our progress.

By 0215 we were down to about 15 knots. The sea state was rising high, the wind gusting 75 knots. Visibility was down to a mile or two. *Black Rover* and *Birmingham* arrived on the scene at about the same time – 0245 approximately. Between us we manoeuvred to windward of the yacht, whose lights were clearly visible in the driving spray.

Black Rover kept pace with the catamaran and provided a solid breakwater; I manoeuvred *Birmingham* between the two, pumping light oil from my bilges to take the edge off the sea. The yacht crew reported that our combined efforts gave them an easier ride; how much of this was due to oil and how much simply to our lee I don't know. Derek Sergeant, the lifeboat coxswain, said he thought the oil helped, but none of us felt it was a conclusively valuable contribution. I believe that the yacht was moving too fast to make maximum use of my slick; with hindsight it might have been more effective if laid to leeward and ahead of the yacht, to allow the craft to pass through the relative calm. That the oil calmed the water was not in doubt as we could see its effectiveness in the searchlight beams: placing it where the yacht (and, subsequently, the lifeboat) could benefit was more tricky.

The craft continued to make progress to the west-north-west as the wind increased to 90 knots. My anemometer would not register above this speed, but it was clear from the roar in my own masts and aerials that the wind was still rising. There were long periods, while I lay virtually a'hull, rolling violently, keeping pace with the yacht, when the anemometer needle lay hard against the stops, and the note in the wind continued to rise steadily and unbelievably higher. On the bridge of *Birmingham* I think most of us were too busy to marvel at the strength of the storm. The ship rolled nearly 45° at times, her stabilizers unable to operate as designed at these very low speeds. I used the bridge throttle controls myself as if they were Morse controls on a speed boat, using high power on each shaft, alternately ahead and astern, keeping the ship close – but not too close – to the yacht. This seamanship was as nothing compared with that in Black Rover; she had a single shaft, variable pitch screw, and has a generally heavier and more ponderous hull. Yet she stayed in position and coped very well indeed.

Shortly after 0320, with no warning whatsoever, the wind swung from 180–190°, 95 knots plus, to 270–280°, 95 knots plus. This was remarkable for all sorts of reasons, not least of which was that the sea flattened out for a while. 'Confused' is too elementary a word; the sea was gob-smacked, as one of my sailors put it! The catamaran at this point began to head north-north-east, maintaining a beam wind and a speed of about 4 knots. The crew of the yacht continued to plead periodically with me to take them off. I pointed out that since they were in no immediate danger they were better off where they were. I was about 4,800 tons of crushing death if I closed with them in those conditions, and I was not about to put my rigid-hulled inflatable in the water in those seas.

Meanwhile, the Weymouth lifeboat approached steadily from the north-north-east. They had a heavy time of it, and it was to their undying credit that they arrived so quickly, at about 0420, to set about rescuing the crew of the catamaran. For the ensuing hour we in *Birmingham* had the privilege to be spectators as the Arun class vessel manoeuvred repeatedly alongside the yacht. We closed in to about 183m (600ft) from the scene to provide the best lee. The sea was beginning to

build steadily from the west. The dramatic wind shift was followed by two hours of unabated fury: the sea became very angry indeed by 0530 when the lifeboat completed her last approach, with, incidentally, no damage on either side. By then the wind was 260°, 80–100 knots, with possibly stronger gusts. The seas were confused and steep with a very heavy Atlantic swell. The female member of the yacht crew had been invited to cross to the Arun first, but she was in fact the last to go, showing some courage. The skipper elected to stay on board and drove his yacht to shelter in Weymouth with resolution, though nearly coming to grief on the Shambles in the process. Once in the lee of Portland Bill, at about 0800, I used the rigid-hulled inflatable to transfer an experienced yachtsman to assist the yacht into harbour.

A Contessa 32 in the Solent

Meanwhile, not far away, a Joint Services Sailing Centre Contessa 32 called *Explorer* was on passage from Poole, Dorset, to Gosport in Hampshire on the last day of an RYA coastal skippers' course. The instructor and skipper was Ray Williams, but the story is told by one of the crew, Martin Bowdler, due to take his examination the next day:

WE INTENDED TO MAKE THIS a lazy passage, adding a few night hours to our week's trip. Therefore when we heard the shipping forecast at 1750, we knew we would have a lively sail. The general synopsis gave gale warnings for most sea areas, and for Wight it was cyclonic, becoming west to south-west Force 7 to the severe gale Force 9, decreasing to 6 later.

We cast off from the Town Quay at Poole around 1845. Our course had already been planned and plotted on the charts. All the sails were sorted out for quick access, in case the conditions strengthened. Anything that could crash around was secured or put away and our harnesses were fitted once more. Though in the week we had many a soaking, we all still had at least one dry shirt at the ready to don if we were to have another wet trip. All other clothes were stowed away. One important aspect that we did not remember was to fill our thermos and make lots of sandwiches for the passage.

When we cast off, the sea and sky gave no indication of the waves and wind to come. The sky was watery; dark – yes; forbidding – no. The course planned was a very simple one: from Poole Fairway across Christchurch Bay to Bridge Buoy, through the Needles Channel to the Solent and thence to Gosport.

At Poole fairway we had one slab in the main and the No 1 genoa set. The weather sharpened to Force 6 from the west-south-west, and a well-rehearsed sail change to the working jib was executed. Our thoughts of this passage had not been to push ourselves, therefore our sail changes were always one step ahead.

By the time we were crossing Christchurch Ledge this routine was overtaken by events. The wind picked up to what we imagined to be around Force 8 or more, which caused the crests of the waves to froth up and turn into heavy spume. By then we had three slabs in the main and the storm jib set. We were surprised how suddenly it had become very dark; this was not your average cloudy sky at night. The wind continued to pick up; and as a result the sea was gathering strength and height. We had been able to pick out the lights of Bournemouth and Highcliffe continuously, but this became more difficult with the spume and the deepening of the troughs.

Our navigation became an increasingly odious task. As the seas increased, so too did the emergence of a pattern of rogue waves. These would hit us on our quarter and happily break on the cockpit and coachroof. Every so often, one of these would be much larger than the others. We had the hatch shut and the washboards in except for the top one, but these larger rogues had enough force to slide the hatch forward and completely drench the navigator and chart table. I had just finished my stint at the helm and, as part of the rotation of crewing, found myself down below navigating. At last I had a chance to change my sodden

shirt. This done, I felt so much better. However, the first of the larger rogues swamped the boat. I know this because much of it came down my drier and warmer neck and the chart table was awash. As I appeared in the hatch this caused much amusement to the crew, who had already taken the brunt of the wave.

We found that we could be prepared for the normal series of waves by continually weaving along them to avoid the breaking crests. We could feel the normal pattern, as the boat began to lift, and whoever was at the helm would play the waves, riding through them as they broke at their crests. A Contessa may be a most forgiving boat, but in these waters we had to play her firmly, constantly dumping and tightening the main. The motion gave us the overall effect of cork-screwing through the water.

However, the rogues were different, in so much as we could not see them coming until the last possible moment – too late. One of the crew, armed with a torch, was detailed to watch for these rogues. Not a very satisfactory task as he would be certain for a head-on soaking. This was one of the jobs no one really enjoyed, but certainly amused the rest of the crew.

Our crew rotation proved valuable in these conditions, due to the various physical tasks on the boat. No one person could continue on a particular job for a long stretch, as certain jobs required more exertion or concentration than others.

The most spectacular seas were off the Shingles where the large waves piled up on meeting the shallows. White waves resulting from this could be made out, although the visibility was limited, while the crashing noise was almost deafening. We had the impression that we were much nearer to the Shingles than we actually were. The seas around us were very steep, broken, erratic and white. This made steering difficult, as our rudder would be as much out of the water as in. We did notice we were being blown down towards the Shingles, and had to harden up to allow for our considerable leeway. For about the next hour the heel of the boat was such that her cabin windows were almost constantly under water. When we bore away there was a moment when *Explorer* would drunkenly come upright, only to fall over again in the next gust. One of the crew found it all a bit overwhelming and he had to retire to the cabin, where he spent the rest of the trip. I cannot say that we were all scared, because there was so much to check on. Having said that, we were apprehensive off the Shingles.

The sails and rigging were being put under a great deal of strain, so the general appearance of the sails, hanks, reefing lines and sheets had to be checked so as to pre-empt any sort of accident. This was a hazardous job, but one that was enjoyable.

Explorer was fairly bucking around and very wet at the bow. But with a lifeline to prevent one being lost overboard, the job felt like a fairground ride.

By the time we had passed Hurst Castle, the wind became increasingly local under the lee shore of the island. The seas had lessened, so while navigating I tried to take the opportunity to make a sandwich for the crew. However, odd omnidirectional gusts threw *Explorer* around; the same can be said of my attempts below – but we were all grateful for something to eat, even if crude, wet and very salty. Past Yarmouth this freak condition lessened. The wind had not yet reached its full force, even though it was screaming through the rigging. The barometer was still falling at an extraordinary rate.

People have often asked why we did not make for shelter to somewhere like Yarmouth; the simple answer being that we seemed to be safer on the water than making for land, and we had our appointment with the examiners the next day at Gosport. However, passing close by Cowes, we did have a small twinge as we could see all the various lights on. The thought of a whisky in the warm, talking about the storm, was not lost upon me.

Past Prince Consort buoy we put our final slab in the main. This did little to affect our speed, some 6½ knots. At just before midnight we came out of the lee of the island and were once again in the full force of the storm. This was an interesting experience as the change of conditions was so quick. From the very loud wind we had experienced in the lee of the island, the wind now roared. *Explorer* could be felt groaning under the strain, while rapid easing of all the sheets did little to improve the slamming of the boat. We fairly hurtled towards Gilkicker Point.

The 0030 shipping forecast was now nearer the mark. Wight was 'south-westerly gale Force 8 to storm Force 10, decreasing Force 6 to gale Force 8'. The storm Force 10 surprised us, but accounted for the noise and strong conditions.

Normally we might have taken the inshore small boat channel between Gilkicker Point and Portsmouth, but to give a greater margin for error we took the Swashway route. When the moment came to turn towards the harbour entrance we tacked rather than gybed as far to windward as possible. On the new course our angle of heel was markedly increased, such that the cabin windows were constantly awash, and we noticed that we were making a good deal of leeway towards the beach. We were able to make a large allowance in our course for the leeway and, thankfully, no extra tacks were needed to get inside the harbour entrance.

Once we came within the protection of Fort Blockhouse, *Explorer* immediately came upright and we seemed to stop. Our handkerchief representation of sails was dropped and secured. It was just after 0100 and we had made our destination in good time, though, ironically, when day dawned our examiners had to call off the tests due to the weather, being blocked in their homes by fallen trees.

A Hallberg Rassy 42 in the North Sea

At much the same time some more heavy weather sailing was being experienced in the North Sea. In this case the account is by Jeff Taylor who, with two crew, was delivering a new Hallberg Rassy 42 from her builders in

Sweden to Southampton. This was a trip he had done many times before in all weather conditions:

AFTER A TROUBLE-FREE trip across the North Sea, we called into Lowestoft on the morning of Thursday 15 October to fill up with diesel. With a forecast of south to south-west Force 4–5 for Thames and Dover, but a wind from the east to south-east of 5 to 10 knots, we departed at approximately 1400 and made good progress motorsailing at 7 knots for the first three to four hours. The 1750 shipping forecast was the first indication that there might be a strong south or south-west wind on the way. At this time we were just north of east from Harwich, with a light south-east wind, making good progress motorsailing with full sail. I looked at all the options and decided to carry on, with the intention of going in to Ramsgate should the wind pick up later, as forecast. After all, even if the wind should increase to Force 8 from the south-south-west, it was nothing that we could not cope with, as we were in a well-found boat in which I had utmost confidence.

The wind gradually increased from the south and by midnight was approximately 20 to 25 knots. We were by now motorsailing with no genoa and one reef in the main. Our position at the time was 8 miles west-south-west of the Galloper light buoy and the tide was about to turn with us. The sea was starting to build up from the south. I heard a gale warning on the VHF just before midnight; the forecast was for gale Force 9 from the south-west, imminent. I was firming up my plans to make for Ramsgate as we were only 38km (21 miles) away, and obviously something was going to happen. The wind steadily increased up to south-west 30 to 35 knots, with the sea becoming quite rough and uncomfortable. It was enhanced by the now south-going tide. There was a lot of water over the decks at this stage, and our boat speed was down to 4 knots.

At about 0130 on Friday morning I was on watch when George popped his head out of the hatch; he told me there had just been a storm Force 10 given for Thames and Dover. By

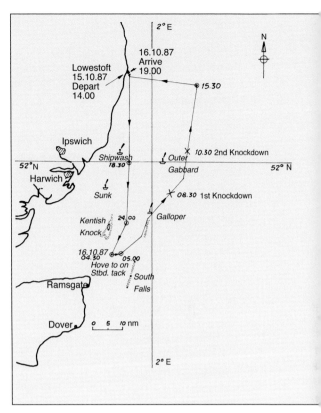

Figure 17.4 *The track chart of the Hallberg Rassy 42 during the October 1987 storm.*

this time I was starting to get nervous about the situation, so I asked George to make sure everything down below was well stowed and to prepare for some very heavy weather. The next gale warning came at about 0330 and forecast south-west violent storm 11, imminent.

The wind was still only 35 knots and we were making about 4 knots towards Ramsgate; but it was obvious that we were not going to arrive before the gale.

At 0430 the wind suddenly increased to 60 knots. I decided to heave-to on the starboard tack and stand out to sea. This presented me with a bit of a problem as we had no storm jib or trysail on board. In the end I found that with no sail up, the helm lashed to weather and the engine running ahead at about 1,200rpm, the yacht lay with the wind about 60° off the starboard bow and was reasonably comfortable in the circumstances. We were 19km (12 miles) north-east of Ramsgate at this stage. The seas were getting very big with breaking crests and spray everywhere; we started to get laid over on our beam ends as the boat rose up the face of the waves and over the tops. Visibility was down to about half a mile.

At 0500 the wind had increased further and we were approximately 22.5km (14 miles) north-east from Ramsgate. Our radar, which worked well throughout, showed a lot of shipping in the vicinity; so I was very keen to get outside the North Falls banks, and decided to run off into deeper water. We were running downwind in generally a north-easterly direction, using our faithful Decca for navigation. The sea continued to rise and became very steep, with every crest breaking. Flying spume filled the air, reducing visibility to nil.

It became increasingly difficult to steer, due to our speed; but it was essential to keep the boat dead down the face of the waves in order to avoid a broach. I felt we really should have had a sea anchor out, but we had nothing suitable on board to rig one with, and I thought it too dangerous to let anyone out of the cockpit.

We suffered our first knockdown at approximately 0830. As we surfed down a very steep wave the boat started shearing off to port, and I was unable to correct this. The wave then broke on top of us, knocking the boat down to about 90°. The boat righted herself very quickly, and the only problem left was a cockpit full of water; but this drained away rapidly. The seas were continuing to get worse. I had sailed in winds as high as we were experiencing, but I had never encountered seas as severe and dangerous. Previously I had always been in very deep water which made the seas long, unlike these very steep short waves that were being caused by the shallow waters of the North Sea.

The storm was at its peak around 1030, which was when we suffered our second knockdown. This happened in the same way as the first one, but was far more severe. We were covered by a solid wall of water that seemed to pin us down below the horizontal with a suddenness that was quite alarming. When we came upright we noticed the liferaft, complete with its stainless steel cradle which had been attached to the deck, had been washed over the side. The liferaft, having by now inflated itself, was being towed astern by the painter. Our sprayhood had been turned inside out and the lifebuoy washed over the side. The water in the cockpit had seeped through the sides of the washboards, soaking the VHF radio and rendering it inoperable. Then the liferaft broke adrift and I started to feel very vulnerable, as without a liferaft or VHF radio, I realized that we were very much alone.

The storm started to abate around midday when the average wind speed dropped to approximately 40 knots; but there was still a very fierce sea running. In comparison to the average wind speed of 70 knots that we had sustained over a period of about half an hour, with gusts up to 95 knots (as recorded on the Brookes & Gatehouse equipment), it was relatively quiet. The sea had died down enough by 1530 for us to set some sail and confidently turn the boat beam-on to the seas. We headed in a westerly direction for Lowestoft, from whence we had come. We were approximately 40km (25 miles) east of the port, and arrived at 1900 where three very tired and relieved yachtsmen were glad to get ashore.

As a professional delivery skipper, sailing approximately 24,140km (15,000 miles) a year offshore, it is easy to become complacent. I felt that I had a lot of experience interpreting the UK shipping forecasts, with the time delays that one normally gets prior to a severe gale.

In this case I was wrong about the weather, and perhaps could have got some shelter in Harwich. In retrospect, this may not have been a good idea, as there was much damage to yachts in this part of England. Certainly I feel that when we turned and ran, this was the only and correct decision to make.

An experience such as we had brings home the fact that we are all human and that one must always have utmost respect for the sea. There was no doubt in my mind that if I had been in a less seaworthy boat we could have been in serious trouble.

COMMENT

Peter Braley modestly describes the meteorology of the Great Channel storm of October 1987 as seen from the old naval base at Portland. As a result of his recommendation to the Portland Admiral (which put his professional reputation at risk, as his view was not supported in other meteorological quarters, cf Michael Fish), the Portland naval fleet was ordered to sea. This must have been an un-popular action just before the weekend, but evidently the Admiral did not ignore the bringer of bad news. No doubt he found Peter Braley's case logical, and consequently made a tough, but – as it turned out – correct decision. In this case a potential disaster was averted.

Muddle Thru's brave story provides much interest. First, one has to say that mid-October is getting rather late in the sailing season to embark upon Atlantic crossings via the Bay of Biscay. Having elected to go, one would urge caution to those planning to leave in strong head winds. One should try to look beyond the pressure of tight schedules when making a decision to sail in unsettled weather.

In the worst part of the storm, *Muddle Thru* was left to lie a'hull with the windage of her sprayhood pushing her bow into the wind. We can be sure that the wind speed was over 100 knots, and yet she survived. Only later was she rolled through 360° while lying a'hull in the next gale. Apparently the sprayhood was not enough to keep her bow to wind. Of course it is not the high wind speed, as such, that is dangerous to yachts that lie a'hull, it is the breaking waves that develop as a result. Sooner or later, it seems, a yacht lying a'hull in breaking seas will be inverted, whereupon the mast will often be lost. In this case the mast would have been lost but for Bill's brave and timely action.

The wisdom of keeping cockpit locker lids firmly closed is apparent from this account. Should one open when a yacht is badly knocked down, she will fill and sink rapidly.

The matter of the lost winch handles bears comment. Both cockpit winch handles were lost when *Muddle Thru* capsized, and in case of this eventuality, spares should always be kept below.

With *Muddle Thru*'s mast damaged by the roll, it was necessary to use the engine, and it was noteworthy that by increasing power, and therefore the water flow over the rudder blade, broaching was avoided. It is assumed that the lee cloths were the standard ones provided but, as often happens, the boat builders had probably not allowed sufficiently for the extreme hull movement to be expected in a severe storm when lee cloths need to be deep and strong enough to contain a person when hurled in any direction. Harry was lucky not to have been injured when he flew out of his bunk (see Chapter 6).

The Swan 46 story shows that 360° rolls are not confined to yachts of under 12m (40ft). The Swan is described as having been hove-to, but it is not known what sails she had hoisted and at what angle she was lying to the wind. It seems possible that she was caught beam-on, or nearly so, just as a wave broke. The situation was aggravated by a severe injury to the skipper and the fact that the floorboards were not secured and everything stored under them 'flew through the boat'. It is a time-honoured practice to stow tins of food under the cabin sole, but owners of ocean-going yachts have to weigh the consequences should their boat be unlucky enough to be rolled. The solution may be to assemble groups of tins that constitute a meal, tape them together and mark them, make a stowage plan so that each meal's whereabouts is known, and screw down the floorboards or use special fastenings, so that the floorboards will stay in place in an inversion, yet can easily be removed.

The rescue by the Japanese container ship sounds most hazardous, and underlines the difficulty that ships experience when trying to rescue yacht crews.

The catamaran rescue is more revealing of human qualities than anything. The skipper was clearly a determined man and may have been right in considering his multihull to be in little danger. However, when the wind increased to hurricane strength he must have had some special reason for not choosing to go to a safe refuge, especially when Weymouth was at hand. Heavy weather is something a crew should work up to by going out in successively stronger winds and bigger waves. Whatever was going on in this case, it does not look as if the crew was familiar enough with rough conditions to warrant an overnight passage in October in fierce storm conditions.

The story of the bold participants of the coastal skipper's course in their Contessa 32 reinforces the reputation that this design has for good sea-keeping qualities. To have navigated the dangerous Needles Passage at night in such conditions calls for a good deal of luck and skill. Generally it seems that the crew was keen, strong and cheerful. With such a crew, a good skipper can work miracles. Some would say that Ray Williams did just that, though perhaps the seas had not had time to build up to be really dangerous, when the Needles Passage could have become impassable.

Jeff Taylor's courageous account of his delivery trip with a new Hallberg Rassy 42 is an example of how quickly conditions can change. It must have been difficult to imagine in a light south-easterly that the wind would be blowing like fury in the opposite direction in a few hours. As luck would have it, his chosen port of refuge was to windward, ie the worst case.

At least Jeff Taylor had a sound engine and did not have to make to windward to avoid a lee shore. Without a trysail, storm jib and then VHF, he would have been in worse trouble. He does not say whether he was carrying flares.

Regarding his liferaft, this is yet one more instance of a raft lost overboard from its deck stowage, as frequently seems to happen. It has taken too long for designers to plan for integral storage of liferafts. There may be an occasional eventuality when a deck-stowed liferaft is an advantage, as for example in Chapter 6, but more often than not it may suffer from exposure and not inflate when required or, as happened in this case, be driven overboard by the force of a breaking wave. On balance, it does seem best to stow liferafts in a dry dedicated cockpit storage, or below.

18 Storm winds, storm lessons

Lin and Larry Pardey

'Was it as rough as you imagined it would be?' people ask about our east to west rounding of Cape Horn. Yes, it was rough. But on reflection, though *Taleisin*, our 9m (29ft 7in) cutter encountered headwinds topping 60 knots near the Straits of LeMaire and even stronger when we reached the Pacific and battled the Roaring Forties, with seas topping 15m (50ft), the situation felt less threatening than the out-of-season storm which caught us unexpectedly near Australia's Great Barrier Reef. The severity of the seas we encountered, driven into stunning steepness by storm force winds blowing against two to three knots of current plus the threat of coral reefs less than 100 miles to leeward, made heaving-to, assisted by a parachute anchor, our only option. This storm forced the closure of all ports along the eastern coast of Australia from Sydney to Brisbane for three days and also caused the loss of three lives, five fishing boats and two yachts. Two fully laden container ships each lay within sight of us for over 13 hours, held by their engines at slow, facing the tumbling breaking seas effectively hove-to, just as we were. We have never before, nor since, seen ships lying hove-to.

For three days we beat to windward, using every wind shift, as we tried to complete the last leg of our fight south towards the Tasman Sea and clear of Australia's Great Barrier Reef. We had just spent the southern hemisphere winter of 1988 exploring as far north as Townsville. For a month we had been working south through the islands, hoping to catch the light northerly winds shown on the pilot charts for the month of October. Fair winds had failed to materialize. Instead we had fresh headwinds and frustrating sailing. Anchorages that should have offered pleasant havens were rolly and uncomfortable. It was 3 November by the time we reached Rosslyn Bay, just south of Yeppoon and 150 miles from the open sea. We were concerned about getting clear of the tropics before the beginning of the cyclone season[1]; we had to short tack along a shoal and island studded route using navigation aids designed for motorized vessels, which tend to stick to the centre of the main channels.

Three days after reaching Rosslyn Bay we woke to a forecast of 10 to 15 knot north-easterlies for 72 hours followed by a south-easterly shift ahead of a frontal system with squalls to 25 knots; winds were due to shift to the northeast following the passage of the front. We backed up the coastal weather report with a phone call to Brisbane Airport. Mike S, meteorological officer for air traffic control, warned me the forecast squalls might reach 35 knots for a short while. 'Haven't had a cyclone form in the Tasman before the

---

[1] The Australian Bureau of Meteorology statistics show the majority of cyclones affect this area between mid December and early April, but show occasional tropical depressions reaching the Barrier Reef area as early as mid November.

middle of December in the ten years I've been in this job,' Mike added. 'Let's set sail,' said Larry, 'It's only 250 miles to Mooloolaba, and with this forecast we should get in before the front. If not, 35 knots of wind isn't the end of the world.'

Only a few hours of northerly winds materialized. Then the headwinds returned. But our determination to reach our New Zealand Christmas rendezvous, plus unsettled conditions in each of the potential anchorages we checked along our route, kept us doggedly sailing onward instead of diverting to Bundaberg, the only all-weather anchorage in the area. After 65 hours of beating, we were clear of the Great Barrier Reef, beam-reaching with a fresh northerly and I was already picturing the next evening in port at Mooloolaba, now only 161km (100 miles) south of us. The most recent forecast did agree with Mike, that within the next few hours we could expect south-easterly gusts to 35, possibly 40 knots as the front passed by our position.

At 0330 light rain, occasional flashes of lightning plus a sudden increase in the wind that shifted quickly to the south, encouraged me to lower the big jib and secure it in the jib net. Just for comfort, I reefed the mainsail, set the staysail and kept *Taleisin* sailing close-hauled on the offshore tack, though we could have lain south-west towards Mooloolaba. Why not err on the side of prudence and gain more sea-room? Two hours later we were becalmed 80.5km (50 miles) off the coast. Flashes of lightning showed a low, cigar-shaped band of clouds rolling towards us. That's when I decided to remove the jib from the forestay. The sea was almost flat with a low undulating swell as the first hint of daylight highlighted the approaching front. I was wearing nothing but my foul-weather jacket as I sat on the cabin-top enjoying the play of lightning behind the approaching clouds. Enjoyment faded quickly with the first gust of the frontal system.

Taleisin heeled until her cabin portlights were awash. For the first time ever, as I crawled

forward to pull down first the staysail and then the reefed mainsail, I found I had to hold my breath and, like a swimmer, turn to leeward to gulp in air free of wind-driven rain and salt spray. Hailstones felt like buckshot as they hit my bare bottom. With both sails lashed down securely the boat still lay heeled about 15°, beam-on to the wind. I was just starting to pull the storm trysail up when I felt Larry alongside me. 'Want me to do that?' he yelled. 'I'm okay, get the windvane cover[2] down before it blows apart,' I answered. 'Get down below, you're soaked,' Larry called when I came into the cockpit to sheet the trysail in to hold *Taleisin* closer to the wind so she lay hove-to. 'I can take over. This is a hell of a lot more than 35 or 40 knots of wind.'

I gratefully went below, shaking with cold but also eager to catch the updated 0600 weather report. It wasn't what I wanted to hear – a storm-warning effective immediately, small vessels were advised to return to port. A ridge of high pressure lying just off the Queensland coast. An area of low pressure intensifying and remaining stationary in the Coral Sea. Reports were of gusts to 85 knots, sustained winds to 65 knots. Wind decreasing to 45 knots by noon.

Soon after, Larry climbed through the hatch in a cascade of rain and spray; he offered to wipe down my back and broke out laughing. 'You should see your bum; it's full of red polka dots, looks like you've been peppered by buckshot,' Larry said. Then he asked me to dig out the components of the combination hatch protector cum sprayhood we use when we head offshore and I realized we'd screwed up. With the favourable forecast, the relatively short and coastal nature of our voyage, we hadn't bothered to set the boat up for going to sea. A pile of books and tumble of bedding lay on the cabin sole, unrestrained by their seagoing lee cloth. The hatch protector/ sprayhood and other parts of our heavy weather offshore gear were in their in-port storage area right forward next to the chain

---

[2] The vane on *Taleisin*'s self-steering gear is a lightweight wooden structure with a removable Dacron cover.

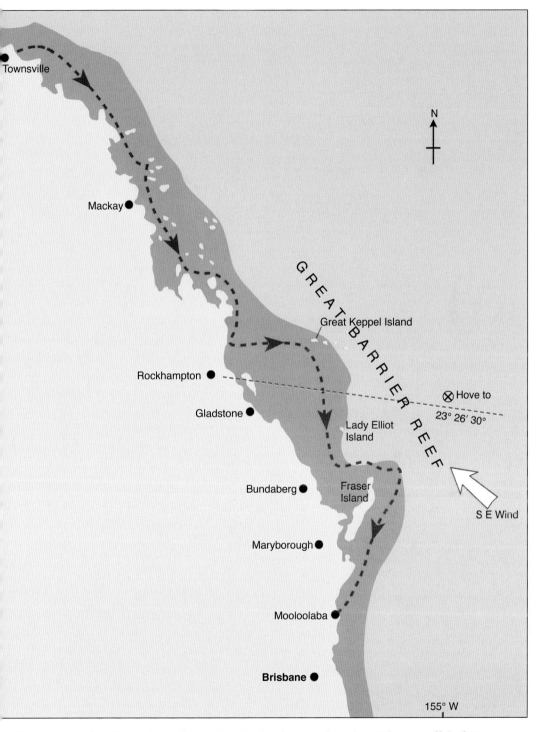

Taleisin's *route from Townsville to Mooloolaba showing the area where she was hove-to off the Great Barrier Reef.*

Taleisin *in ocean-going guise. Note the shoulder high lifelines.* Photo: John Roberson

locker. Preparations that took about half an hour in port would now be a time-consuming struggle that left us feeling less organized, less competent, less prepared.

Larry stayed on deck once he finally got the dodger and storm gear[3] in place, watching the way *Taleisin* lay, adjusting the shock cords restraining her tiller and estimating her drift. Over the next hour the seas began to build. Heavy spray began pelting the cabin sides on a regular basis. Then Larry called down, 'How many miles between us and the nearest reefs?'

'Nearest one is about 90 miles north of us, but the Aussie current is going south. It should help counter any drift. Now the front is past us the wind should ease in three or four hours.'

'F....ing forecasts haven't been right in months. I want to slow down her drift just in case this wind has slowed down the current,' Larry yelled. 'Seas are damn steep and her head's falling off in between the gusts. I think it's time to get out the para-anchor.' I stuck my head

outside for the first time in an hour as I passed him the gear. The rain had stopped but the situation was definitely not improving. How high were the seas? They definitely were not as high as those we encountered near Cape Horn, but never have I seen steeper nor more closely spaced seas, driven by wind-against-current into pipeline-like breakers through which we could see the green colour more usually associated with waves along a sandy shore. The most awe-inspiring aspect of these tumbling breaking seas was the way they seemed to crumble as they hit the slick that *Taleisin* was forming as she slid slowly to leeward. Port and starboard of the slick, the crests broke into roaring cascades that could have poured tons of green water onto us.

We worked together setting the para-anchor, a 3.6m (12ft) diameter surplus military Bureau of Ordinance parachute (a Bu-Ord). Larry led the spare anchor rode through a 5cm (2in) diameter snatch block secured to

---

[3] This includes the hatch protector/spray hood; shoulder high lifelines, extra rope handrails on the cabintop, plus covers for the forward hawse pipe.

Taleisin's bow fitting back over the lifelines to where I held the para-anchor. He attached it to the para-anchor's swivel then put another 5cm (2in) diameter snatch block onto the rode and rigged a bridle line which he led through the windward, amidships fairlead in *Taleisin*'s bulwark and back to the sheet winch, leaving the line just long enough so the bridle block was near the forward shroud. Together we slid the parachute itself down the windward side of the hull.

As soon as it was about 15m (50ft) from the hull, the chute filled. Larry gradually let out more scope until we could see the chute lying two crests to windward of us. The effect was immediate. *Taleisin* lay with her bow about 50° from the wind, all signs of forward motion gone and a swirling slick forming to windward of her, her leeward motion cut to less than a knot through the water. Because we'd been lying hove-to, steadied by the trysail while we worked, it was not extremely difficult to work on deck, though having to fight to keep from sliding around, and effectively help Larry, had been tiring. I went below to heat soup for Larry while he added chafing gear to each line and also jammed cockpit cushions between the tiller and taffrail knees to absorb some of the shock loading on the rudder. It was soon after this that Larry yelled down, 'Take a look out here; this is something I have never seen before!' Just to starboard of us, within a mile, lay two container ships, heading into the wind, hove-to, battling the storm just as we were. They stayed in sight for all that day and into the long night that followed.

Over the next hours, seasickness kept me in the leeward bunk most of the time. I did not have the will to clean up the fallen gear that cluttered the cabin sole. Instead I shoved each new escapee in with the rest of the mess in the forward cabin. This mess, plus the reports

I began hearing on the radio, did nothing to make the situation seem better. Within 161km (100 miles) of us, a massive air search was on for three fishermen we had come to know in Rosslyn Bay. They had headed off when we did, to work near Kepple Island. Now they had sent a Mayday from a position that put them only 64km (40 miles) upwind of the maze of the reefs lying to the north. Within 10 hours of the first blasts of that front, another search effort was being reported: *Marymuffin*, a 22m (72ft) maxi that had been a well-known racer under the name of *Ragamuffin*, had called for assistance. Her skipper had tried to outrun the front and reach the anchorage inside the ring of coral that is Lady Elliott Reef. There is a narrow entrance through the coral. But we later learned the anchorage turned into a hellhole for the five boats seeking refuge there when the waves went right over the windward side of the reef. Unfortunately for *Marymuffin*, the storm force winds set her 24km (15 miles) north of her route. To clear the edge of the reef, she headed closer to the wind only to suffer a knockdown with the mast in the water, which left crew and boat injured, engine non-functioning and mainsail slides jammed in the track so the crew could neither reef nor take down the sail. Now she was in danger of foundering on the very reef her skipper had tried to reach for protection.[4]

When Larry did not come below promptly after his latest hourly gear check I dragged myself out of the bunk and found him lying over the taffrail cursing. Another oversight had been escalated by the storm into a gear-threatening situation. When we first hove-to earlier in the day, Larry had pulled in the taffrail log spinner and its 15m (50ft) of braided 5mm (³⁄₁₆in) line and tucked it behind the windward cockpit coaming. Now the occasional wave, rolling along the deck, had washed the spinner

---

[4] Radio reports over the next hours added to the drama of the storm as we followed the rescue efforts. A large ferry was able to reach *Marymuffin* in time to tow her clear of the reef and escort her into Bundaburg.

The air search for the crew of the sunken fishing boat went on for almost two days. Their over-turned aluminium tin tender was spotted, surrounded by large sharks, dozens of miles from the Mayday position. Only one of the crew managed to survive, by clinging to the tender.

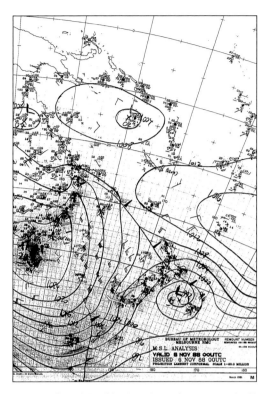
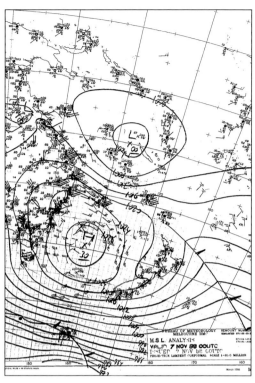

Above, left to right: Weather charts from 6, 7 and 8 November 1988.

and line overboard. The bucking of the boat had crocheted the line into an ever tightening web which had almost immobilized the trim tab. Larry was worried that the strain could damage the self-steering vane. It took us over an hour to finally cut away the last bits of our taffrail log spinner line to free the trim tab.

Each six-hourly update of the forecast added hours to the expected length of the storm. The reported wind speed for Fraser Island Lighthouse, approximately 89km (55 miles) from our position, was 60 knots. By dark we'd almost come to accept the motion, the roar of cresting seas to port and starboard of our slick, the splats of foam against the topsides. Larry and I stayed prone most of the time, taking turns to doze off and also taking turns going on deck every hour to ease the main para-anchor rode about a foot (about 0.35m).

Just before midnight, an exceptionally loud snap woke Larry. The permanent preventer line attached to the rudder, which keeps the rudder

from going over far enough to endanger the pintles, had chafed through. There was no way to rig new preventer lines. To ease some of the shock-loading, Larry added two extra lengths of heavy-duty shock cord to the inboard end of the tiller. He sounded pretty discouraged as he listed the toll that the past 18 hours had taken on our gear. His most careful use of anti-chafing gear had not prevented wear on the 16mm (⅝in) anchor rode holding the para-anchor. The shock cords holding the tiller were wearing through the woven coverings at the rate of one shock cord every three hours. 'We've got a spare anchor rode and if this doesn't start to let up by morning I want to use it,' he commented. 'Lin, why don't you put up the lee cloth just in case.'

He was using the windward pilot berth and lee cloth. I did not see a reason to put my lee cloth up since I was in the leeward berth lying against the pillow-padded hull. Besides, I am a bit claustrophobic and hate the closed in feeling it gives. Just before dawn another

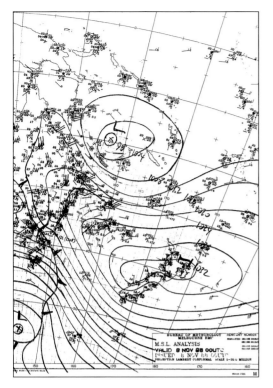

screaming squall line roared down on us. Larry was quickly suited up and on deck. I remember dozing off. Then I was levitating, grabbing desperately for anything to hold as I heard the snapping rattle of the storm trysail, the loud roar of a breaking wave crest. I flew clear of the bunk as *Taleisin* tacked through the eye of the wind to come to a sudden halt, heeled sharply to starboard. All the breath flew out of me as my chest hit the bronze table support stanchion, then I hit the cabin sole, my teeth slammed against the ice chest so hard I was sure they would be knocked loose. As I slowly pulled my face clear of the woodwork, *Taleisin* lurched sharply one more time, I felt something hit my head with a sharp but not terribly painful blow and warm liquid began running through my hair and across my face. I couldn't restrain the tears as I gingerly felt my head. I did not feel any sense of relief when I realized the liquid was coffee not blood; instead I was downright angry.

A wave breaks ahead of Taleisin. Photo: Lin and Larry Pardey

My hair was now covered in coffee grounds from the pot I had meant to secure more tightly the last time I had been on watch. To make matters worse, as I sat up and gingerly touched ribs that were badly bruised if not broken, I noticed the deep gouge the flying coffee pot had cut into the otherwise perfect varnished teak of the ice box facing. Just inches from that gash were a second set of dents, the exact shape of my front teeth. By now I had time to realize that no water had found its way into the boat and Larry had not called for urgent assistance, so that meant *Taleisin* was still riding safely. But I could hear him winching and working with the lines that held the para-anchor. Chagrined and guilty at having ignored Larry's warning to use the lee cloth, I had most of the coffee grounds out of my hair before he opened the hatch and said, 'Everything okay down there? I think the damn parachute is too big. We came up over a big wave, *Taleisin* headed close to the wind. The chute didn't seem to give at all and pulled us over onto port tack. The rode is under the bobstay and if we don't get her back on the starboard tack it's going to chafe through.'

The hardest part of the task was getting into my foul weather gear. By the time I got on deck Larry had eased the bridle line and *Taleisin* lay head-to-wind, ranging first 10 or 15° onto port tack, then tacking through the eye of the wind onto starboard. I got into position at the sheet winch in the cockpit. Larry waited until *Taleisin* tacked over onto starboard, then he quickly paid out about 6 or 9m (20 or 30ft) of rode and as quickly as I could, I winched in the slack of the bridle line. *Taleisin*'s head paid off as soon as the full strain came back onto the rode and bridle and she again lay on starboard tack.

After two days of lying to the para-anchor, the wind eased below storm force, the seas began to crumble instead of breaking, and sprays of spindrift no longer swept the deck. Only then did I show Larry the bands of bruises crossing my abdomen and lower chest. In a way I wish I'd waited. Now he wanted to get underway immediately and begin beating south towards medical attention. But I convinced

him the motion of sailing onward in these conditions would be more uncomfortable for me than the motion we were experiencing as we lay hove-to. By late afternoon the winds had dropped to gale force, the seas had lengthened and, with the latest forecast predicting another frontal system crossing our area within the next 36 hours, Larry and I prepared to retrieve the para-anchor.

I gingerly worked with him, for by this time I wanted more than anything to be in port, on an unmoving boat with a long hot shower, medical assistance and lots of time to rest. We use a barebones para-anchor set up, no floats, no trip line, no weights. We also have no engine to let us motor towards the chute and ease the strain on the anchor rode. But retrieval, though it took two hours to accomplish, was relatively easy in spite of the strong winds. Larry removed the pennant line and block and *Taleisin* immediately laid head-to-wind. Just after each wave crest passed, the strain on the rode eased. Then Larry was able to winch in about 6ft (1.8m) of rode. I sat on the deck box next to the mast tailing the line and each time *Taleisin* began rising on the next wave I put two turns on a mast cleat to hold the strain. Six feet at a time, we got closer to the parachute. When the swivel for the chute lay just at our bow, Larry snagged one of the shroud lines with the boathook. Then he began pulling the shroud line in by hand. The water spilled out, within two or three minutes the chute collapsed, and he had it on board. As he secured the mass of the anchor rode against the windward bulwark we found almost 3m (10ft) of the anchor rode, the portion that had been riding in the snatch block at the bow, was chafed with almost 10 per cent of its diameter chewed away.

I was too exhausted to sail onward that evening so we lay hove-to under just the trysail until daybreak. Then we began close reaching towards the coast, storm trysail and staysail set in 35 to 45 knot winds while I lay on the pillow-padded cabin sole. Our landfall confirmed Larry's concerns, and the sights he'd taken the afternoon before. The storm had caused the south-going current to stall. We had been set 48km (30 miles) north during

Taleisin *lying a'try before the parachute sea anchor was deployed. Though waves break immediately ahead and astern, the turbulent water created by her hull and keel making leeway prevents waves breaking to windward most effectively.* Photo: Lin and Larry Pardey

the 2½ days we lay hove-to and only 97km (60 miles) had separated us from the almost certain destruction of those just submerged coral reefs.

The lessons we learned or which were reinforced during that storm:

1. Seeking refuge by running back to a marginal anchorage can be far less safe than getting sea room and staying at sea.

2. We knew we would be out in the open ocean for 161km (100 miles). If we had prepared the boat for an offshore passage, nothing would have got loose inside or on deck.

3. Lee cloths are not just for keeping someone in the windward bunk, they are there to keep all crew safe in all bunks.

4. Heaving-to, assisted by a para-anchor, cuts down drift. (In our case our drift was reduced to less than a knot once the chute was set, compared to 1.3 to 1.5 knots with just the trysail.)

5. The motion while lying in the hove-to position 50° off the wind with the trysail steadying us was far more comfortable than lying directly to the wind as we did while Larry prepared to retrieve the para-anchor.

6. Having too large a para-anchor can be a mistake. Compared to the 2.4m (8ft) chute we'd always used previously on 7.4m (24ft 4in) 5-ton *Seraffyn*, the 3.6m (12ft) diameter chute on *Taleisin* held more than twice the volume of water and exerted tremendous pressure on the rode, the fairleads and blocks. The larger loads meant more stretching, more shock loads, more chafe. Unfortunately, deciding what size parachute to use as a sea-anchor is not something that can be done with any mathematical or engineering certainty. But from this experience and from discussions with many sailors who have used similar gear, we have come to feel that manufacturers are leading sailors to err on the large size.

We used those lessons well as we voyaged onward: downsizing to a smaller 2.4m (8ft) diameter para-anchor, upsizing to a 10cm (4in) diameter snatch block to help reduce chafe on the main rode, making our sea-going heavy weather gear easier to get to, improving and strengthening our rudder stop system, adding extra heavy weather hand holds below and above decks, and using weather forecasts and pilot chart information as guidelines instead of gospel. Probably just as important, I came to trust *Taleisin* and myself to competently handle heavy weather, which let us eventually choose to sail from the Atlantic to the Pacific by way of Cape Horn with better preparations and far more confidence.

COMMENT

It is easy to understand the Pardeys' mindset when they set off from Rosslyn Bay. They were racing to get south to be clear of the cyclone area and to meet their Christmas rendezvous after a long period of unexpected adverse winds: just the scenario to be caught out in an unforecast tempest. Instinctively and wisely they sought sea room rather than shelter when the storm struck.

Those who ply tidal waters when a stiff wind is against a strong stream will be familiar with close-packed, steep, breaking waves, often emitting a modest roar. The Pardeys experienced this situation on a grand ocean scale and it hardly needs to be said that such conditions are extremely dangerous. Larry rightly places much value in the smoothing slick created by his para-anchor and hull. There is no doubt that such a slick will inhibit breaking waves. The skill is to have the boat placed in a position to take advantage of it and the Pardey method of heaving-to can achieve this objective handsomely. If hove-to under sail the protection of the slick can only be experienced if the boat is virtually stopped, so slowing right down must be the objective.

It was interesting that *Taleisin* tacked by herself in a squall. Once a self-tack occurs the whole Pardey para-anchor system becomes defunct and subject to heavy chafe. When trying out the Pardey method in moderate conditions aboard a Naiad 39 it was found that the boat did tend to tack herself, suggesting that experimentation is necessary to find a stable arrangement. The loads are colossal and it was noteworthy that Larry decided to double the size of his snatch block on the rode from 5 to 10cm (2 to 4in).

Lin candidly describes how she failed to set up her lee cloth on the leeward bunk and paid the consequences, which could have been even more serious. If the watch on deck manages to find an opportunity to rig the missing lee cloth while the off-watch crew slumbers, it is a noble deed. Even better is to rig all lee cloths at sea as a routine whenever the wind reaches Force 5–6.

This honestly told tale of an unexpected storm by one of the most respected sailing couples the world has ever known is most instructional. Lin and Larry Pardey find themselves in a situation where bad weather was much more severe and prolonged than expected, and they deal with it using their well-tried methods.

One can only but admire them.

19 The Queen's Birthday storm of 1994

Peter Bruce

Every year between November and April some 500 cruising boats avoid the south-west Pacific cyclone season by sailing to New Zealand for the summer. As it is customary to return to the tropical Pacific islands from New Zealand after the cyclone season, and before the New Zealand winter, the Island Cruising Association organizes a cruise in company starting around the end of May, an event called the Auckland–Tonga Regatta.

It was widely believed that the date finally selected in 1994 coincided with a perfect weather window. About 80 yachts were heading happily north-east at this time, either as part of the regatta, or on independent passages with a similar strategy in mind.

After the bulk of the fleet had left, a number of late starters were caught in the path of an unexpected storm of extraordinary ferocity and duration. Large breaking seas over-whelmed many of these yachts. One yacht was lost with her crew of three, two people aboard other yachts received severe injuries, and seven yachts were abandoned. Another yacht suffered a fire when electrical circuits shorted after a knockdown.

This storm is often called the Queen's Birthday storm, as it started during the annual New Zealand holiday to mark this event. Alternatively it is also called the June 'Bomb' in recognition of the meteorological term used to describe the explosive manner in which some depressions can develop. It has some parallels with another fierce storm that had occurred at the same time of year in 1983, when some

yachts were returning to Auckland after a race to Suva. On that occasion eight lives were lost. The situation was also similar in some respects to the 1979 Fastnet Race in that a group of yachts was caught out in unforecast hurricane force winds, although the 1994 Pacific storm lasted rather longer. A notable difference was that in the Fastnet the fleet was composed of racing yachts with racing crews, whereas in the Pacific storm the fleet was mainly cruising yachts with cruising crews and, in some cases, children.

Search and rescue was conducted by five ships and one patrol aircraft. The rescues have been well recorded and make dramatic reading. Much can be learnt from Kim Taylor's *1994 Pacific Storm Survey*; from Tony Farrington's *Rogue Storm*; from Commander Larry Robbins' report as seen from the bridge of the principal rescue ship, HMNZS *Monowai*; from a television documentary; and from the New Zealand Maritime Safety Authority's report. An especially valuable feature of Kim Taylor's *Pacific Storm Survey* was his inclusion of the yachts that were in the direct path of the storm, but which did not seek outside assistance. Media attention leans heavily towards casualties, yet we can probably learn more from those who did not need help.

The fact that a number of different craft were caught out in the same storm has allowed comparisons to be made that might not otherwise be so reliable, and this chapter endeavours to recount the strengths and weaknesses exposed by the storm and any lessons that can be gleaned. The emphasis in

241

Heavy Weather Sailing is on prevention rather than cure, and little attempt will be made to comment upon rescue or matters of legislation that arose as a result of the storm. The aim is to identify those actions that will give justifiable confidence to a crew, rather than have them look to making a Mayday call on the SSB radio or the activation of the EPIRB, notwithstanding that these appliances are well worth their place aboard as a last resort.

The yachts, in the order mentioned in the text, are as follows:

Silver Shadow	12.8m	(42ft)	Craddock-designed sloop, 4 crew
Pilot	9.8m	(32ft)	Colin Archer cutter, 2 crew
Arosa	10.6m	(35ft)	Lotus sloop, 4 crew
Sabre	10.4m	(34ft)	Ganley steel cutter, 2 crew
Destiny	13.7m	(45ft)	Norseman 447, 2 crew
Ramtha	11.6m	(38ft)	Simpson catamaran sloop, 2 crew
St Leger	12.5m	(41ft)	GRP cutter, 2 crew
Sophia	9.8m	(32ft)	Thistle cutter, 2 crew
Quartermaster	12.2m	(40ft)	Paul Whiting sloop, 3 crew
Mary T	12.2m	(40ft)	Cheoy Lee yawl, 4 crew
Waikiwi II	12.2m	(40ft)	Les Rolfe sloop, 4 crew
Heartlight	12.2m	(40ft)	Catalac catamaran sloop, 4 crew
Sula II	13.7m	(45ft)	Clark-designed cutter, 5 crew
Por Vida	13.1m	(43ft)	Westsail ketch, 2 crew
Hippo's Camp	13.1m	(43ft)	Morgan cutter, 2 crew, 2 children
Kiwi Dream	10.7m	(35ft)	Ganley sloop, 2 crew
Swanhaven	14.6m	(48ft)	Roberts ketch

Preparation

This storm showed that there is no substitute for knowing how one's boat will react in really bad weather when using a variety of tactics. For example, one owner said that 'he lacked familiarity with how to heave the boat to. That's the one area where I don't know whether I did her justice.' If an owner knows that his boat will lie comfortably hove-to, he will save a lot of energy by having found this out beforehand. Alternatively, if an owner knows that his boat always takes on volumes of water from somewhere or other in rough weather then although there would be no reduction in pumping, there will be significant reduction in *stress*. However, a survival storm is not the time to experiment with heavy weather tactics. It is too dangerous, exhausting and worrying.

When *Silver Shadow* had the misfortune to be knocked down and then rolled, her crew was able to note that few items had broken loose. They attributed this to the double latches that they had fitted to lockers and the care with which everything had been stowed before leaving harbour. The instrument sensor plug that was blown out of its tube into the inside of the boat illustrates the force in the wave that caused their first knockdown. When she came to be rolled through 360°, her floorboards and floor locker tops came out, but that was a lot less than might have happened. When the rescue aircraft asked how serious their predicament was on a scale of 1 to 5, the answer was 2. Overall, one gains the impression of a well-prepared boat, and a competent, courageous and resourceful crew.

It has to be said that not all the yachts that suffered heavy knockdowns or rolls gave the impression of being as well secured for sea as *Silver Shadow*. In particular, the frozen contents of freezers were a common hazard. Being struck by 'aerobatic frozen chickens' rather than the 'aerobatic batteries' encountered in the 1979 Fastnet might be regarded as an improvement, but this too may probably be avoided by spending 20 minutes putting a sliding bolt, or whatever, on the freezer door. There was a 24 volt battery in one yacht that came loose, releasing battery acid and breaking a portlight. The same boat, which had been prepared for a five-year cruise, also had to contend with the spillage of diesel fuel and a two-year supply of flour. One yacht suffered from flying pot plants. When one's boat is one's home, it is understandable that such items come on board, but it might be suggested that if they are to come to sea such items as pot plants must have a proper sea stowage made for them – for example, a bracket within a locker with a restraining arrangement to prevent the plant escaping from the pot even if the boat is inverted. The same applies to another yacht's vagrant sewing machine.

Chaos resulting from a 360° roll is dramatically reduced if a yacht has been systematically prepared for this eventuality before departure. The Royal Navy and other navies make a religion of 'securing for sea', the practice of fastening or enclosing every object that could possibly break loose in a heavy sea before leaving harbour. However, those who have been brought up properly in this respect may agree that teaching a crew, especially those who operate the galley, to secure for sea is difficult without the heavy hand of naval discipline. Nor does the average human seem to learn quickly by experience, especially the slightly reluctant sailor.

Few yachts are built with 360° rolls in mind. It must be appreciated that standard production craft are seldom, if ever, 'ocean-passage' seaworthy when new. For example, positive locking arrangements are required for horizontal locker doors, chart table lids and floorboards; in short, anything kept in place by the force of gravity. It behoves owners contemplating ocean voyages to spend considerable resources in preparing a vessel properly in order to warrant the expression 'roll-over ready'. As it is time-consuming to make proper brackets for pot plants, sewing machines and all other potentially hazardous items of equipment, one should take advantage of any suitable purpose-made brackets.

Seasickness was a problem for some, though with all the high drama not much about it was reported. One yacht's crew tried seasickness pills in the Queen's Birthday storm for the first time. The pills apparently caused an adverse reaction worse than the seasickness, suggesting that the best time to try out new remedies is in less demanding times.

Crew experience

There has been no suggestion that difficulties arose because crews lacked seagoing experience. Very severe storms are, thankfully, rare in the sailing seasons, which raises the question as to whether the crews who requested help were experienced enough to cope in such conditions – a different matter to sailing even 80,500km (50,000 miles) in normal weather. One skipper who lost his yacht said, 'We certainly had enough experience on board for normal sailing, but we didn't have experienced people for those extreme storm conditions; if we'd had three people who could steer in 14m (46ft) seas, maybe it would be a different story now.' There is little information on this question, and anyhow a survey on this matter would be hard to quantify. It could be argued that those who have great skills in avoiding bad weather may sometimes be the least prepared for it if caught out.

Some crews comprised simply a couple, and others had six or seven on board. There were examples of tremendous feats of endurance, as in the 1979 Fastnet, when boats had only one helmsperson confident and strong enough for the conditions. In this particular storm it would have needed super-human endurance to carry on steering for two or three days. The skipper of *Pilot* said, 'If we'd had just one other strong healthy crew member, I don't think that we would have abandoned.' One of the yachts that came through the storm unscathed, but not without difficulty, the 10.6m (35ft) Lotus sloop *Arosa*, was steered by hand for the duration. *Arosa* was one of the smaller and lighter yachts in the storm, so she could be expected to be lively. Such yachts do not tend to heave-to comfortably, and clearly the owners felt that four capable crew were essential for them to cope with drogues and, no doubt, steering in heavy weather. Aboard one boat the crew had never hand steered at sea, and had to learn when their autopilot gave up. Thus, bearing in mind that auto-pilots and self-steering gear often become unequal to the task sooner or later, one may conclude that one should have a crew strong enough to continue to hand steer a boat competently in all weather conditions, unless one has been able to prove that the vessel can be left in some way so that she will look after herself.

Ideally one should have a second-in-command on board who is ready, willing and experienced enough to take over should the skipper be incapacitated, as happened to *Destiny*. When the crew consists of only a man and his wife they should exchange roles from time to time so both are familiar with all aspects of handling the boat. Practising for 'man overboard' is more important than for 'woman overboard' as, generally speaking, a man is the more likely to fall over the side and a woman is less practised in recovery.

Crew endurance

Fatigue is one of the biggest enemies of the small-boat sailor. Thus one of the fundamentals of coping with storms is the conservation of energy. There is little doubt that some of the yachts were abandoned simply because their crews were over-stressed and utterly exhausted. After the first 24 hours of storm conditions, few

of these crews, understandably, were able to do much to help themselves. Yet the 10.4m (34ft) Ganley steel cutter *Sabre*, with a crew of only two on board, encountered as severe weather as any, and passed through the eye of the storm without any serious problems, hove-to under deep-reefed main. Comments made by the crew after the storm, drawn from Kim Taylor's report, are illuminating: 'The confidence of previous heavy weather experience tended to reduce stress. Practise well beforehand to identify any weakness. We lay on the floor and attempted to rest. Consumption of liquids and high-energy foods is important. Our small opening ports are modified to take an outside storm window. Our boat is prepared with very rough weather conditions in mind and, lying hove-to, has proved herself on many occasions.' One has the impression of sailors who were mentally and physically prepared for whatever the sea could do. They did not need to experiment to try to find the most comfortable way to ride the storm and, owing to confidence in their preparations and their robust craft, they could conserve their energy and cope for as long as was necessary.

Less confident and less heavy-weather conditioned crews may have used up energy dealing with matters that should have been dealt with before going to sea. It is important to make a careful selection of priorities. Certain irritating things should have been dealt with at another time. They were not, and everyone has to force their minds to ignore them. It can be more important to avoid the risk of injury and husband one's strength for life-threatening situations that usually have to be dealt with straightaway. Not only does the workload sometimes have to be kept to essentials for survival, it also may have to be spread evenly, rather than have one over-motivated person do it all.

Even when all the crew are in their bunks, for example, a crew should stay in watches if possible, so they take it in turns to worry about what might be going on up top. In dire straits, notwithstanding collision risks, a skipper should be prepared to order his crew to stay in their bunks with as much force as he may use on other occasions to have them leave their bunks.

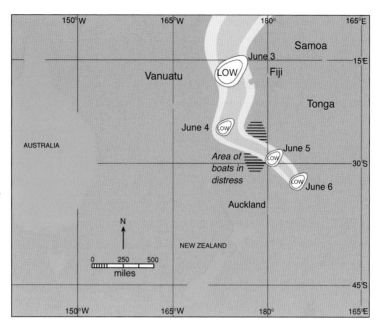

Figure 19.1 *The path of the Queen's Birthday storm cut across the route of yachts taking part in the Auckland–Tonga Regatta, and forecasts were not entirely helpful as to both the strength of wind and the direction the storm was to take. The predicted 40–50 knots became 75 knots in the event, and instead of taking the anticipated south-easterly course, the storm first veered to the south.*

Design issues

A fundamental of coping with heavy weather might be thought to be the size and design of the craft. In this respect, all the hulls stood up pretty well. One catamaran suffered a cracked hull and there were broken windows of all sizes; otherwise, there were very few structural problems. In terms of length, beam, stability and displacement there did not seem to be any particular reason why some boats were rolled and others not. Factors such as a vessel's aspect to the breaking waves and luck seemed to be more relevant. Yachts that were lying a'hull were prone to join the '360° Club' as one might expect, but not in the case of the Robert Perry-designed 13.7m (45ft) Norseman 447 cutter *Destiny*. She seemed to have been overtaken by an extreme wave that pitch-poled her, and it is hard to see what her crew could have done to avoid their predicament. Likewise *Pilot*, a 9.8m (32ft) Colin Archer cutter, was running under control with bare pole when she was pooped by a wave that carried away her heavy-section mast. One can only pity the plight of the crews of the dismasted yachts. Without the windage of mast and rigging it was found that the boats simply did not lie

to drag devices, rigged either from the bow or stern, and thus they adopted disastrous beam-on-to-the-seas attitudes. Only aboard *Pilot* was the broken mast cleared away and then the boat steered by hand down the seas. Again, without a mast this could be done only with difficulty, but she experienced no knockdowns, and running before the seas seemed infinitely preferable to lying a'hull. One must not forget, though, that yachts seldom seem to sink if left to their own devices. Of the eight or nine yachts abandoned, four (*Destiny*, *Ramtha*, *Silver Shadow* and *Sophia*) were found later either afloat or aground somewhere.

Only one vessel appears to have sunk as a direct result of the storm, and her family crew was tragically lost too. This was *Quartermaster*, a 12.2m (40ft) Paul Whiting sloop, advertised as being designed for serious cruising, but of lighter displacement than most offshore cruising yachts of her size. During the onset of the storm the owner had been in regular contact with the Kerikeri shore radio station, and from just before midnight on 4 June he reported the first of a series of bad knockdowns and the fact that his wife had been injured. Two hours and 18 minutes later the third 'hard knockdown' was reported. The boat and her crew appeared to be in serious trouble, though no flooding was mentioned. This was the last call that was heard. *Quartermaster*'s EPIRB was activated another two hours and 36 minutes after that, and at 1745 on 6 June, a day and a half later, *Quartermaster*'s transmitting EPIRB was found lashed to her eight-man liferaft. Examination showed that the liferaft canister had been smashed, probably by the mast, and some or all of the crew had been aboard the liferaft until a wave had, presumably, washed the occupants out. One can only speculate what might have happened after the owner's last radio message. *Quartermaster* could, for example, just possibly have been sunk by a whale-strike, or collision with a semi-submerged container; however, the most likely explanation is that she was sunk by breaking waves.

Apart from this awful and harrowing misfortune, no other yacht was abandoned because she was actually sinking. One of the yachts, thought by her crew to be in immediate danger of foundering due to the battering of the hull by a section of her broken mast, was spotted afloat some months later and then found after yet more months high and dry on a distant reef. In all cases, with the possible exception of *Quartermaster*, the boats' hulls appeared to withstand the conditions better than the crew.

Standing rigging did not break, but mast tubes did not usually withstand a full 360° roll, as they also had not in the 1979 Fastnet. There is a case for looking again at the derided 'tree trunks' of the past, bearing in mind that mast failure is catastrophic for a sailing boat. Apart from the additional strength, a heavier mast section will bring about an increase in inertia that will reduce the chances of being rolled in the first place.

Steering arrangements were another weak point, as they were in the 1979 Fastnet. *Ramtha*, a 11.6m (38ft) sloop-rigged catamaran designed by Roger Simpson, had a steering failure before the storm and again during the storm. Her crew was not new to stormy weather but, apart from severe discomfort, they were having control problems, as well as

near-capsizes. With the survey ship HMNZS *Monowai* close by, they had talked about being taken off, but when their steering failed again at the height of the storm the decision was made to abandon ship. *Mary T*, a 12.2m (40ft) Cheoy Lee offshore yawl, also reported steering problems at one time, and the 12.8m (42ft) Craddock-designed sloop *Silver Shadow* was found to have an uncontrollable rudder when the crew tried to motor her. In the 1979 Fastnet the numbers of steering failures were increased by the fact that many rudders from a particular designer had been changed to an inadequate carbon-fibre construction. Others failed by simply not being strong enough. One has the feeling that, owing to the additional complication of having two rudders to operate from one wheel, catamarans' steering systems need to be particularly well engineered. This seems obvious, but one does not know the extent to which, in order to keep prices competitive, the person in control of the specification has thought in terms of the average yacht that, arguably, will never encounter a survival storm. It may not be relevant to say so here, but there are brilliant naval architects who are not such good engineers. Design and construction of the steering gear and adjacent hull structure of ocean-going yachts should allow generous safety margins.

A notable similarity with the Fastnet was leakage from cockpit locker hatches after the cockpit had been filled. At one point *Mary T*'s crew found that water was coming in faster than it could be pumped out. It was some time before it was realized that the leak was from the cockpit locker lids. Builders seldom fit watertight seals to cockpit locker lids; indeed, sometimes glassfibre mouldings are constructed so that making a watertight seal can be very difficult. Nonetheless, as cockpits can be filled frequently in heavy weather and remain filled owing to small-diameter drains, it is important that locker lids can be positively clipped in the closed position and adapted, as necessary, to make a watertight seal when closed. Undersized cockpit drains were a problem for *Destiny* as well as for *Mary T*. Pumps also gave problems in at least two yachts. *Mary T* had three pumps

Ramtha *and her crew before the rescue. Wind speed at this time was 55 knots average, gusting to 70 or more according to HMNZS* Monowai's *instruments. Significant wave height was 10m (33ft).* Photo: POAHS Lindsay Turvey RNZN

operable from on deck, but her crew regretted that they did not have a manual pump that could be worked from down below.

Cabin windows are often a risk to watertight integrity and, through breakage or deformation, became matters of concern in this particular storm. The leeward windows of the 13.4m (44ft) Les Rolfe-designed sloop *Waikiwi II* did not have storm boards and were broken. Big windows, such as those of many catamarans, caused big worries. An anonymous catamaran owner cited his big windows as the principal danger during the storm. To make a series of large windows requires much of the sides of the coachroof to be cut out. This can normally be expected to reduce the strength of the coachroof and hence its ability to withstand a plunging wave. It may be relevant to note that *Quartermaster*, built as a dedicated cruising yacht, had four

comparatively large windows on each side of the coachroof, and her skipper had registered concern about them before contact was lost, though there is no evidence that they caused the loss of the yacht. *Ramtha*, a 11.6m (38ft) sloop-rigged catamaran designed by Roger Simpson, sensibly had storm covers for her large windows. So did *Heartlight*, a 12.5m (41ft) Catalac sloop-rigged catamaran designed by Tom Lack, but one of them was ripped off by a wave. Moreover, the smaller portlight windows let in water when they flexed.

It is significant that none of the three catamarans in the storm area capsized, even though two of them lay a'hull for periods. However, two of the catamaran crews abandoned their vessels. Their accounts did not lend much confidence to the seaworthiness of catamarans, as opposed to monohulls, in the extreme conditions they experienced.

One catamaran crew was at one moment standing on the side windows. Capsize, with its dire consequences for non-self-righting craft, came very close to both *Ramtha* and *Heartlight*.

A serious problem, and not a new one, was injuries sustained when crew were flung out of their bunks. Coming out of one's bunk in this Pacific storm, either intentionally or unintentionally, increased the risk of bodily injury acutely. For example, Peter O'Neil, owner of *Silver Shadow*, was brewing up at the galley when his shoulder was broken. In *Mary T*, sailbags were brought into the saloon and successfully used as buffers. Thus for one not importantly occupied, a bunk is a very sensible place to be and really good lee cloths become of tremendous consequence.

Of all the interior appurtenances ever supplied to a yacht, few need as much careful thought as the lee cloths. *Destiny*'s lee cloths failed before she was pitch-poled, and one therefore assumes they were not strong enough. If the maximum possible forces at work in a storm are taken into account it will probably be found that few standard lee cloths are strong enough for the job. When told that people fell out of their bunks, one is curious to know how strong and deep the lee cloths were – probably not strong enough or deep enough. It is possible to design a lee cloth that is held down at the outboard side of the bunk, which is next to impossible to come out of unintentionally. In so doing it may be necessary to provide additional handholds around the bunk, a quick release system for the upper body end, and greater material strength than the norm. The skipper of *Sula II* suggested that strongpoints should be fitted down below and safety harnesses worn in bunks.

Tactics

Regarding tactics and drag devices, as in the 1979 Fastnet, there was no obvious procedure that could be guaranteed to work for everyone. Two yachts were rolled when lying a'hull, and most other yachts did their best to avoid this situation.

It is noteworthy that more boats found comfort and safety heading into the seas than the more popular tactic of running before them. Heaving-to under sail or engine was successful for all the yachts that tried it. A fourth reefing slab in the mainsail and an inner forestay was often an advantage when hove-to. The 10.4m (34ft) steel yacht *Sabre*, as we have already seen, remained hove-to under deep-reefed mainsail for the duration of the storm without any significant problems. *Por Vida*, a 13.1m (43ft) Westsail ketch, motor-sailed under trysail almost straight into the wind and sea at two-thirds throttle. She lost her storm jib and anchor from the pulpit, which carried away the hawse pipe leaving a hole to be plugged. Otherwise she had no problems. The 13.1m (43ft) Morgan-designed cutter *Hippo's Camp* spent part of the storm hove-to under storm jib, with her helm lashed to steer to weather. She used her engine in the windless eye of the storm to motor 'around' the waves, but later found the wind blew the boat flat under her storm jib. Then she lay successfully to a plastic drogue, though it is not clear whether this was led over the bow or the stern. *Kiwi Dream*, a 10.7m (35ft) steel Ganley sloop, successfully hove-to under a backed scrap of headsail and deep-reefed main, and *Swanhaven*, a 14.6m (48ft) Roberts ketch, hove-to successfully within the area of the strongest wind. Finally, *Sula II*, a 13.7m (45ft) Clark-designed cutter of 12 tons, was sailed close-hauled under trysail and her speed maintained at 3 or 4 knots by feathering into the wind. The effect of feathering took speed down to a comfortable level and brought the bow closer into the wind than would have been achieved by heaving-to. She experienced no rolls or knockdowns, but might be considered outside the strongest wind area. Kim Taylor points out, interestingly, that all these vessels were in the moderate or heavy displacement category.

It was disappointing to an analyst that the two yachts carrying parachute anchors did not deploy them, but their reasons were understandable. By the time they had come to realize that it was parachute anchor time, conditions had become very risky for working on deck. In the moderate conditions just prior to the storm, *Ramtha*, the catamaran, had spent a night lying to a sea anchor on a 91m (300ft) warp from her bows, but in the morning the sea anchor was found hanging vertically rather than holding her into the wind and sea. For some reason the sea anchor could not be tripped and, as there was only a twosome on board, winching it in proved very heavy work. Consequently, it was cut loose and abandoned. The catamaran *Heartlight* did have a 5.5m (18ft) Para-Tech parachute on board, but the skipper felt that a drogue was more suitable in the extreme conditions prevailing due to varying angles of the seas. Only when the drogue line fouled his propellers was the parachute deployed. Not finding it an advantage, the skipper said he would have cut it adrift had it not been his desire to remain in one place so he could be found more easily.

After *Silver Shadow* had been dismasted and later rolled, her crew managed, much to their credit, to release their broken mast and, following various experiments, lay from the bow a sea anchor made from a No 4 genoa. Then they rigged a jury mizzen sail which was enough to hold the yacht into the seas some of the time, and which seemed to help to prevent further capsizes.

A variety of drag devices was used over the stern, either warps, warps and chains, or drogues. Six yachts were either rolled or knocked down when trailing drag devices, two of them while being hand steered and four when not. The 12.5m (41ft) cutter *St Leger* was the most successful. Her crew deployed a Galerider on 76m (250ft) polypropylene while under vane steering. Though the boat steered well and the speed was comfortable, the line went slack when the boat was in the troughs and it was found necessary to shorten the line to 24–27m (80–90ft). For the next 60 hours with winds over 60 knots the drogue remained stable and effective. *Destiny* towed a Sea Squid drogue using 61m (200ft) of line and 3.7m (12ft) of 10mm (⅜in) chain that proved to be very satisfactory at first. With hand steering dead downwind, the drogue kept *Destiny* at a 'comfortable' speed of 3–8 knots, but as

conditions became worse the drogue broke out from the surface on two occasions, allowing the boat speed to become dangerously fast. They felt with hindsight that a longer line was necessary, but one could also imagine that more weight of chain could have helped. As it happened, *Destiny* was pitch-poled in spite of her drogue. *Quartermaster* was probably towing drogues, and was under engine and autopilot when she was last heard of in an attempt 'to get seas to come in over the back quarter' which 'seemed to be working'. *Silver Shadow* was running under storm jib and autohelm when she was struck by a breaking wave, 30° more towards the port beam than the usual seas, and this brought down her mast. At least four yachts were neither rolled nor knocked down when on autohelm or vane steering.

These records, once again, may not indicate anything very strongly, but there seems to be more than a tendency in favour of hand steering. For example, *Pilot*'s skipper felt that he would have been able to avoid the 360° roll if he had been hand steering, and *Waikiwi II*'s skipper wished he'd had more storm-skilled helmsmen. *St Leger*'s skipper felt that the quick reaction of a helmsman was essential to avoid a broach. An experienced sailor at the helm is influenced by what he can see or hear coming at him. He is influenced by speed, acceleration, angle of heel and waveform. On the other hand, the automatic helm has no anticipation and is merely influenced by the angle off course, which may occur too quickly to make any difference at critical times. Thus it could well be that the hand-steered yacht is safest, provided that the helmsman is alert, strong and competent for the task. This was also a finding from the 1979 Fastnet.

A useful point made by several skippers was that, when lightly crewed, only one tactic might be feasible. Once a severe storm has developed, one may be stuck with whatever tactic was chosen first. This point underlines the case for experimentation in moderate conditions.

One wonders how much crews are influenced when choosing their tactics by the direction in which they happen to be already going. It is easier to carry on along roughly the course one had originally intended than not. It requires a very definite decision to change course from going into the sea to running away from it, and a yet more bold and confident decision to turn into the wind and sea having been running away. In this storm the quickest route out of it was the same direction as the fleet was heading. Thus those on the western side of the storm track tended to run with the wind astern and those on the eastern side were more inclined to head into it.

As noted above, perhaps one of the most significant aspects of the storm was the surprisingly high number of problems encountered by yachts running before the sea compared to those heading into it. On the face of it, the time-honoured technique of 'heaving-to' under sail appears to have been the safest tactic for moderate- or heavy-displacement yachts. On the other hand, modern, lightly constructed yachts do not always heave-to comfortably under sail, as *Arosa*'s crew decided. Many are too lively, make too much leeway, and do not 'look after themselves' as traditional yachts do, so an alternative has to be found. Running before the seas with a Series Drogue may be the solution. It was also noteworthy that sailing into the wind under trysail worked well for *Sula II*, and *Por Vida* successfully relied on her trysail and on her engine, fitted with a 3:1 reduction ratio, to drive close into the wind and waves.

Liferafts

During rescues, hand-held VHFs were useful on board. A waterproof hand-held VHF will be even more useful if a crew is forced into a liferaft. Several crews were tempted to inflate their liferaft as a precautionary action. *Waikiwi II* had two on board, and one of these was inflated in case of immediate need. After four hours it was 'blown to bits' and eventually was torn away. *Destiny*'s only liferaft was also inflated and lost when the painter parted. Two other liferafts were ripped from their deck mountings and were later found inflated and,

presumably, some considerable distance from where they had been lost.

These events suggest that one should keep the liferaft in its container, stowed until required in a purpose-made deck locker or down below in an easily accessible position, and rely on regular maintenance to ensure it does inflate when really needed. One should note that *Quartermaster* carried an eight-man liferaft and a crew of only three. Liferafts are designed to perform best with their full complement weighing them down, and it could be that the *Quartermaster* crew was lost because of this. It would be normal for an owner to have a liferaft for the maximum number of crew he is likely to have on board. However, some liferaft vendors advise that it is preferable to have one person too many in the liferaft rather than one too few; this suggests that the size should be for one person less than the likely minimum crew. Short of hiring a liferaft for the appropriate number each time crew size changes (an unappealing solution), the owner is left in an unfortunate dilemma. Larger craft often have two four-man or two six-man liferafts; this is a tidy, if rather expensive, solution to the problem. Alternatively one supposes, if at all possible, an oversize liferaft should be ballasted with whatever sensible means comes to hand.

A point well made by Kim Taylor in his *Storm Survey* is that the crews who asked to be taken off were in more danger during the transfer than at any other time. Besides, they were putting other lives at risk. Another key point is that, once abandoned, the boat may be considered a hazard and deliberately sunk. So, as in the past, everything points to staying with the boat and keeping her afloat as long as possible.

Useful equipment

Apart from the invaluable EPIRB, useful miscellaneous items of equipment cited were: strobe lights, ski goggles, cyclume sticks, hot water bottles, wetsuits and cyclists' helmets. Commander Larry Robbins, commanding officer of HMNZS *Monowai*, mentioned that *Mary T*'s strobe light was very, very effective. He makes the point that the strobe is much more visible than standard navigation lights and, as it can't be mistaken for prescribed lights, the strobe could become a useful safety aid, as with aircraft. Pilots say that the powerful strobes of commercial aircraft can be seen at distances up to 64km (40 miles), and they have to switch them off on the ground to avoid dazzling everyone. Perhaps when the entire crew is stormbound down below would be a good time to switch on a strobe.

Anyone who has tried to look to windward from a small craft in Force 10, both with or without goggles, will vouch for their value. Goggles have become standard equipment in the BT Global Challenge, the race around the world the wrong way. As Alby Burgin said after Cyclone Emily, 'If I'd held my head up the wind and water would have cut my eyes out.' Cyclume sticks provide a source of light when everything electrical has failed. Could this ever happen? Given bad enough conditions and the hostility of salt water to all things electrical, the answer has to be yes.

Even in the relatively warm waters in which the storm originated, hypothermia was a problem. Dampness works its way into the insulating layers, reducing their efficiency, and forced inaction does nothing to keep the body warm. One can become uncomfortably cold even on the equator if one has no protection from heavy rain. *Pilot* had a hot-water bottle on board, and this came in handy when Greg Forbes started

Australians Bill and Robyn Forbes, both aged 53, being hauled aboard HMNZS Monowai *from their 11.6m (38ft) catamaran* Ramtha. Photo: POAHS Lindsay Turvey RNZN

Silver Shadow *from HMNZS* Monowai *as her four crew were taken off.* Photo: POAHS Lindsay Turvey RNZN

suffering from hypothermia. *Mary T*'s crew found space blankets good for keeping warm in the damp conditions. A wetsuit can often be worth a place on board. For example, Bill and Robyn Forbes wore wetsuits when they were hauled aboard HMNZS *Monowai*. Apart from using a wetsuit for leisure diving, it can be used, for example, when clearing a fouled propeller.

A wetsuit's survival capabilities are illustrated by a story of many years ago, when a fishing boat capsized at night in a winter storm some miles off Iceland. No one else realized what had happened until one of the crew, who was wearing a wetsuit top, fetched up alive on the beach. He was the only survivor. Drysuits have now become cheaper, easier to put on, and can be made of breathable fabric. Consequently, they are worthy of consideration, but probably more

worthy are the survival suits that are coming onto the market. Sailing people are not likely to invest in clothing that may only be used once, so survival suits that have a dual purpose are the ones likely to be best value.

As for cyclists' helmets, one can see the virtue of head protection in almost any sport. The 'Boombanger Club' can be even more disastrous than the '360° Club' and a helmet could be a major benefit. However, most people feel self-conscious about wearing helmets aboard a boat, so not everybody will be seen wearing one, but this attitude could change in time.

External support

Nine yachts, which ranged from 9.8–13.7m (32–45ft), put out Mayday calls. All except one of these was fully equipped with safety equipment, and all had either reasonably experienced or very experienced crews. Most of the crews that were rescued had actuated their EPIRBs. Not only can a 406MHz EPIRB alert shore authorities of a Mayday, it will identify the boat and give its position. Then, when rescuers are within a few miles, they can home in on the EPIRB's transmissions. This equipment, *from a rescue point of view*, could be called the outstanding device of the event. New Zealanders will remember the story of *Rose Noelle*, a catamaran bound for Tonga in 1979 at exactly the same time of year. She capsized in a storm, eluded the search, and drifted with her crew for five months before going ashore on Great Barrier Island. The event makes a good case for the 406MHz EPIRB, though it has to be said that *Rose Noelle* was carrying an older-type EPIRB, but this was not heard.

Judging by the recordings of the radio conversations, many boats used Kerikeri shore radio – incidentally now closed down – for meteorological advice. As the storm developed some leaned heavily on the radio station for comfort and the general support that was readily given. Indeed, Jon and Maureen Cullen, who used to provide their service as a hobby, managed to stay on the air for the duration of the storm. While SSB is a superb product of the technological age, and the Cullens provide a wonderful service – especially during this storm – ideally one will not want to depend too much upon advice from someone who is not present and therefore cannot be expected to appraise the situation fully. It can be argued that the ability to talk to those ashore, and the existence of an EPIRB on board, could possibly divert attention from the primary task in severe weather and to give a false sense of security. One cannot pass responsibility on to someone else over the radio. Nor, equally, should one give up trying to take control of the situation just because the EPIRB has been activated. On the arrival of a rescuer it must require a lot of courage to announce that help is no longer required. Such decisions need finely balanced judgement, not easily found in an over-tired, over-stressed mind. Nevertheless, assuming one does decide to do without help and lives to tell the tale, it should be remembered that one can always show one's gratitude properly and explain the circumstances to the would-be rescuer at a later date. A good seaman will understand entirely and may be glad not to have to attempt a difficult rescue.

Another form of a false sense of security can be given by the presence of other friendly yachts in the vicinity. While there are circumstances where this situation can be of advantage, in a violent storm, there is little chance of assistance from other small craft. Crews have to cultivate a sensible level of self-reliance.

Finale

One might be disappointed, but one should not be surprised to find that, once again, there was no obvious panacea, no one piece of equipment or single tactic identifiable that would have enabled all the yachts to lie quietly for the duration of this storm while their crews slept.

So we are left with the conclusion that to survive a rare and tremendous storm like the tropical depression of June 1994 one must have some fundamentals right, such as tactics proven for each individual yacht as a result of experiments with a strong crew on a daysail. One must also put into effect many detailed preparations for prolonged bad weather. Once caught out in a severe storm one must avoid becoming over-tired and over-stressed, and ruthlessly separate 'nice-to-have' actions from those upon which survival is likely to depend.

It does seem that more boats did well heading into the sea, either by heaving-to, or sailing or motoring into the wind.

20

A winter storm off the south-west coast of Australia

Deborah Schutz

A letter to the Australian magazine Cruising Helmsman, *seeking accounts of the use of parachute sea anchors in severe storms, led to Deborah Schutz's description of how* Prisana II *rode out sustained winds of hurricane strength off Perth. The story shows whether a parachute sea anchor is capable of doing its business when it really comes on to blow.*

*P*risana II is a glassfibre ketch. She is a Tayana Surprise 45 measuring 13.7m (45ft) with two equal-height masts, both with in-mast furling. Her draft is 2.1m (7ft), displacement 13 tons, beam 4.1m (13.5ft), and her ballast 5 tons. She has a fin keel, a skeg rudder and a hydraulic autopilot-to-quadrant-wheel cable steering.

We departed from Adelaide, South Australia, in early July 1996 with six people on board. These were Steve (the skipper and my partner), myself and our son Ben (seven years old at the time), and our long-time friends Trevor, Sam and Patrick. Steve has sailed for most of his life. Ben and I have been sailing for the six years since Steve and his father purchased *Prisana II*. Trevor had considerable sailing experience and was mechanically minded (like Steve). Sam had sailed previously, but Patrick had no previous sailing experience. Our plan was to cruise the Western Australian coastline and offshore islands for six months. We expected the Great Australian Bight would test us – especially as

it was the middle of a southern winter. I had visited the Bureau of Meteorology a couple of weeks before we left and was warned that we were about to cross one of the worst seas in the world for storms.

With this in mind, we decided to set up our 5.5m (18ft) Bass Strait 18 Para.Anchor, manufactured by Para.Anchors, Australia in Sale, Victoria,* before we left port. The parachute anchor – with an 18mm (¾in) stainless steel swivel – was shackled to the rode which was 125m (410ft) of 18mm (¾in), three-strand nylon contained in a deployment bag. The other end of the rode was shackled to a 12mm (½in) chain link welded to the ship's main anchor that is stowed on the bow in a custom-made stem fitting. To give added security, the anchor was held by a 10mm (⅜in) Ronstan rigging screw, secured to a 10mm (⅜in) stainless steel plate bolted under the windlass. Winch and plate were fastened by six 10mm (⅜in) stainless steel studs. Both the fixing point to the anchor and to the plate were backed up by secondary systems. A slack chain from the nylon rode was attached to a 16mm (⅝in) stainless steel bolt passing through the anchor cheeks, and another short length of chain was secured between the anchor shackle and the 10mm (⅜in) plate bolted under the windlass. We used a partial trip line – two floats and two 15m (49ft) lines with swivels (see Fig 20.1).

Fortunately we crossed the Bight within a high-pressure system. After eight days, we

---

* This sea anchor was incorrectly described as a Para-Tech anchor in previous editions.

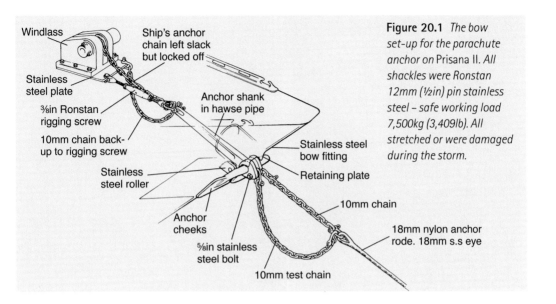

Windlass

Ship's anchor
chain left slack
but locked off

Stainless
steel plate

⅜in Ronstan
rigging screw

10mm chain back-
up to rigging screw

Anchor shank
in hawse pipe

Stainless
steel roller

Stainless steel
bow fitting

Retaining plate

Anchor
cheeks

⅝in stainless
steel bolt

10mm chain

18mm nylon anchor
rode. 18mm s.s eye

10mm test chain

Figure 20.1 *The bow set-up for the parachute anchor on Prisana II. All shackles were Ronstan 12mm (½in) pin stainless steel – safe working load 7,500kg (3,409lb). All stretched or were damaged during the storm.*

sighted Cape Leeuwin, the south-western-most point of mainland Australia and one of the world's great navigational landmarks. A wide berth is required to round the Cape, as immediately west and north of the lighthouse lies an extensive area of reefs. The area is known for rogue breaking waves and strong tides. We encountered choppy seas, much large shipping and a falling barometer. Winds increased up to 30 knots from the north. As the day progressed we headed farther out to sea while the weather deteriorated. During the night, gusts reached 40–45 knots as we beat into a westerly, by now 129km (80 miles) out from Cape Leeuwin.

Near nightfall on Sunday 14 July we were almost abeam of Cape Naturaliste. Our weatherfax showed a complex low was fast approaching. Growing darkness, our position, the unfamiliar coastline and the wind direction (a 40 knot north-north-east) meant that it was inadvisable to look for an anchorage. We had already considered using our sea anchor, but owing to the number of ships in the vicinity we decided to keep going. We reduced sail, expecting the winds to swing south-west with the approaching front, which we would use to get us to Fremantle. We were wrong! Throughout the night, Mother Nature un-leashed a storm of unrelenting fury, with the

wind increasing to 50 knots from the north-north-east with large seas, leaving us little choice but to head out to sea.

At first light on Monday 15 July we came about. Perth Radio issued another gale warning. The barometer read 996hPa (mb) and was falling. By evening, the wind had become a strong westerly, the barometer now read 990hPa (mb), though the sea had moderated. As the night progressed, squalls reached 60 knots and lightning could be seen behind us as we sailed in a northerly direction. Eventually the anemometer was off the scale at over 65 knots and the seas were rising dramatically. At approximately 0300 a huge wall of white water knocked us over to starboard. The helmsman (thankfully harnessed) was chest-height in water, and our masts were horizontal in the sea. Ben and I were asleep below and we were both flung out of our bunks.

Steve, Sam and Trevor deployed the sea anchor, using a flying set. Even in the dark, this was relatively easy. Deployment simply involved reaching from the safety of the cockpit to the rode deployment bag, unlacing the top, removing the end of the rode, and shackling it to the parachute anchor. Trip line and float buoys were fed overboard, followed by the parachute anchor in its deployment bag. Within about 30 seconds, we had taken up all

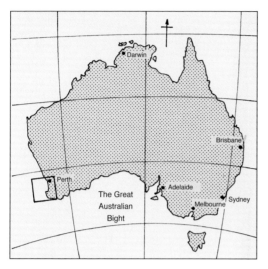
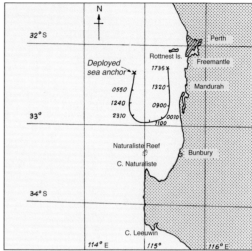

Figure 20.2 *Track of* Prisana II *during the storm, July 1996.*

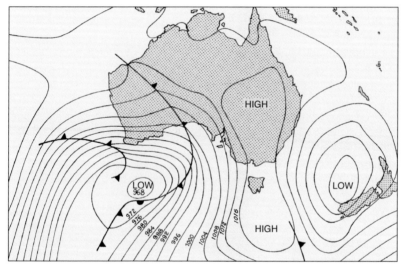

Figure 20.3
Weatherfax chart for 17 July 1996 showing the deep low south of Cape Leeuwin and the packed isobars between the two.

the rode and were gently pulled head-to-wind, allowing us to furl the sails entirely. They were to remain furled for the rest of the storm. Then we put an 18mm (¾in) bridle line on the rode, with a view to lying to the parachute at an angle in the manner described by Larry and Lin Pardey, but the bridle broke almost as soon as it was tensioned. So we gave up that idea and contented ourselves with leaving the rode to lead straight out over the bow. After that it was all crew below with hatches battened. At this point we were 30nm to the west of Rottnest Island.

During the morning of Tuesday 16 July I ventured into the cockpit and was immediately awestruck. The seas were incredibly huge. I soon retreated below, after taking a couple of photos. I later found out the seas were reported to be 11m (36ft) on top of a 9m (30ft) swell – a total of around 20m (64ft). When the parachute rode emerged as it spanned a trough, it sliced through the water like a knife, and one could see massive tension come on it as *Prisana* surged forward and back with the waves. A lot of white water was being swept from the tops of the swell, with large rolling crests of white

Prisana II *is a sturdy Tayana Surprise 45.* Photo: Deborah Schutz

water underneath. Prisana took many loads of white water across the deck, and even some green water. The conditions were such that it would have been foolhardy to be anywhere on deck. We used a safety harness when visiting the cockpit, otherwise almost all of our time was spent down below.

At that time we felt that we had plenty of sea room as we drifted in a southerly direction in the Leeuwin current on a west wind for 24 hours. This current runs southward down the Continental Shelf from Indonesia, bringing masses of warm water. It begins flowing around April each year through until October, and seldom moves faster than 1 knot in a band approximately 50km (31 miles) wide. Throughout the storm our drift rate averaged 0.9 knots. The parachute anchor held us while the winds screamed at over 70 knots. The noise was incredible! We rolled heavily from gunwale to gunwale and it appeared that we yawed about 45° on one side to 35° on the other. Occasionally, we felt the rode become slack as the bow paid off somewhere over 45°,

then there would be a tremendous jerk as the rode became taut again. This may have been due to rogue waves coming in on a different angle, but we believed that it was because the boat yawed a lot and surged on the huge swell. It was hard to tell from down below.

Steve awoke at dawn on Wednesday 17 July to see a ship on our stern, only 1.3km (0.8 miles) away. We tried to make contact using VHF, and an Australian vessel promptly answered, but he was 6 miles away. He informed us that the other vessel was a foreign ship, along with mentioning that he didn't envy us one bit. For 15 long minutes, we tried to make contact. We were losing sight of the whole ship (approximately 125m (400ft) long with an extensive bridge structure) behind the seas. Finally, a man's voice responded in broken English causing us a minor panic. He didn't seem eager to alter his course, telling us he had no ballast and that he couldn't even see us. We managed to persuade him to alter course a little and, after ensuring that he could see our spotlight, we saw him pass 0.4nm away on our radar.

The parachute sea anchor is taking the strain during the storm while the crew take to their bunks.
Photo: Deborah Schutz

We had drifted almost as far south as Bunbury when we began to drift east and believed we were in an eddy of the Leeuwin current. We appeared to have been caught up in a typical anticlockwise flow that took us inshore and then northwards along the coast.

The weather remained unchanged. All day long the winds continued to blow over 70 knots. We heard that a large cargo ship had just lost 30 containers off Cape Leeuwin. The Adelaide media reported that a cyclone had hit Perth.

By Thursday 18 July conditions were moderating, the wind was now down to 50 knots and the barometer slowly began to rise; the seas were still large and getting steeper with shallowing depth as we crept closer to the coast. Concerned about running out of sea room late in the afternoon, we decided to retrieve the parachute anchor. This wasn't easy. Noise from the wind and sea made it difficult to hear the skipper's instructions from the helm to the bow. Trying to use the engine to pick up the recovery float, we fouled the rode on the propeller. When

we finally retrieved the parachute anchor, we found two large well-frayed holes in two separate panels between the vent hole and the skirt. We have no doubts about the manufacture or design of the parachute, nor do we believe that it was snagged during recovery, so it is probable that the holes were caused by flotsam. By the time we set a course for Rottnest Island the wind was down to 30–40 knots, which felt like a gentle breeze.

Around 1030 on Friday 19 July we motored into the Fremantle Sailing Club, grateful that we had decided to buy a parachute anchor. With it we were able to ride out and survive the storm with our bow held into the seas. During the storm, Bunbury and Fremantle Harbours were closed and the harbourmaster at Fremantle said they were the largest seas he could ever remember. Rottnest Island, 19km (12 miles) off the coast of Fremantle, had holidaymakers stranded there for three days as the ferries were unable to make the crossing. When he docked at Fremantle on 19 July the captain of the ship that had lost 30 containers off Cape Leeuwin

Sam heading for Perth after the storm. The steering was damaged but still functioning.
Photo: Deborah Schutz

said, 'In all my time, I've never seen seas like those.' In addition to the unusually strong winds, what the weather bureau in Perth described as a rare winter tornado, which had formed at high altitude somewhere around where *Prisana* was on the night of 15 July, had struck south Perth with 200km/h (108 knot) winds.

We spent the following three to four weeks in Fremantle repairing *Prisana*. She had suffered quite some damage. The rudder shaft had been twisted, the forward bulkhead damaged, and four stanchions had been ripped from the deck, to name but a few of her problems.

During the storm both our primary systems to take the load of the rode at the bow had failed. The Ronstan rigging screw had broken, stripping eight turns of thread, and the chain/link welded to the ship's anchor had torn off. Thankfully, in both systems, the back-up held but, when the rigging screw broke, the anchor was free to smash around, which caused some damage to our stainless steel bow fitting. We also found that our 125m (410ft) of 18mm (¾in) rope had stretched an extra 20m (66ft).

Prisana's rudder shaft had about a 15° twist in the 50mm (2in) diameter 316-grade stainless steel shaft at the point where the quadrant is fixed. It definitely wasn't twisted before the deployment of the parachute anchor. The rudder lashings holding the rudder on the centreline at the quadrant had broken twice during the storm. We managed to hold it, third time lucky, on spare 18mm (¾in) nylon anchor rode. The forward bulkhead was damaged, mostly due to a design fault rather than the conditions.

To the question, 'Did the sea anchor save the boat?' the answer is, 'Absolutely!' In the conditions we were caught in, we believe that having the parachute anchor set up before departure was crucial to its safe and easy deployment. Had we not had it (an awful thought) we would probably have tried to find shelter behind Rottnest Island by sailing on a broad-reach, possibly dragging warps as we were not carrying a drogue. I believe our chances of surviving had we done so would have been extremely slim.

COMMENT

It seems that *Prisana II* must have experienced hurricane strength winds for about 48 hours. That she survived in the way she did brings credit to her crew and their parachute sea anchor. It is one of the most testing accounts of a parachute sea anchor deployment, and goes to show that a parachute can work in very extreme weather. It is significant that the parachute sea anchor was set up before the yacht left harbour, in anticipation of bad weather.

The parachute system appears to have been taken to its limit. The canopy was damaged, the rode stretched, and the primary method of securing the parachute line at the boat end failed, possibly during recovery as the damage was not in a stressed part.

As is normal, the parachute did not give a comfortable ride: *Prisana* rolled from gunwale to gunwale and yawed about 80°. Then there was the time when the parachute line would become slack and then take up with a jerk. Having two masts, *Prisana* had more windage aft than a sloop and therefore just about managed without a riding sail at the stern. It is probable that she would not have yawed as much, nor would the parachute line have snatched, had one been used. The Pardey method of lying to a parachute, which was conceived to improve comfort, was tried without success in that the bridle line broke. This is not surprising due to the huge loads the bridle line has to take when the vessel is as big as *Prisana*.

It is noteworthy to find that *Prisana* was in danger from other shipping. A lookout in a yacht in storm conditions cannot easily look to windward without eye protection. Even then, spume can obscure visibility almost entirely. Looking from most enclosed bridges of ships in a storm does not improve visible range by much. The windows are continuously spattered with spray that blurs the view entirely between sweeps of the wiper. Only just after the wiper has passed is there a split second of good vision before the window blurs over again. This allows a brief view in one narrow direction. Radar is not much help either, as a yacht's echo may well be completely lost in the wave returns. Thus there is no better chance that a yacht will see a ship than vice versa. Salvation comes in the form of an automatic identification system (AIS) and VHF. It is wise to make a regular Sécurité call, giving position and circumstances.

At the start of the storm it was commendable that the skipper, Steve, did not try to run for shelter towards the hazardous lee shore. It is noteworthy that two crew were thrown out of their bunks, suggesting inadequate lee-cloths, that verbal communication was difficult on deck and that, on recovery of the rode, it fouled the propeller.

Did the parachute save the boat? We don't know what would have happened if the crew had been forced to adopt other storm tactics, but at least we do know that by using the parachute the crew of *Prisana II* survived to tell the tale.

21

Black Velvet's bothersome return from Iceland

Ewen Southby-Tailyour

It was July 2001. The mountaineers had flown back to Iceland from Greenland. I had hoped to deliver them to Scoresbysund in Greenland, then support and collect them from their expedition, but that is not what happened. The *storis*, or sea ice, of summer 2001 had been too thick for *Black Velvet*, my Tradewind 35, a 12-ton gaff cutter even though she had been strengthened for ice.

The subsequent climbing in Iceland had been testing, but the mountaineers' greatest concern was a six-day trek to get help if necessary. Neither they, nor *Black Velvet*, had long-range communications and nor had we wanted them; our collective view was, and remains, that there is far too much reliance on outside help and advice these days and achievements are diminished for that. Conversely, long-range communications would not have prevented our eventual situation, but at least I could have had a weather report and known that the end was not in sight!

The one mountaineer who elected to sail back to Plymouth in England was Dave Wilkie, a strong man but with no sailing experience; he was a crocodile breeder in Australia and crocodile hunter in East Africa. I warned him that just because it was the return journey, there was no guarantee that it would be easy. As a climber he was well aware that 'down-

climbing' to base camp can produce the greatest dangers. As far as a yacht is concerned, after a two-month expedition in hard weather, unsurveyed waters and with no shore support, gear is probably worn, spares are running out, the engine and associated mechanics – including steering gear – need servicing. There is also a certain relaxation, as all eyes focus on the homecoming.

Black Velvet racing off Cowes. Photo: Patrick Roach

Black Velvet *showing her traditional underwater profile.* Photo: Ewen Southby-Tailyour

We sailed on 24 July with a fine forecast that should have taken us a good way towards the north-west Irish coast where, after six days or so, I had planned to telephone home via a coast radio station with our, very approximate, ETA in Plymouth. Thank goodness the Irish have not closed down this safety facility. If I had known what the weather was actually going to do, I would either have delayed sailing or headed due west from Reykjavik in order to give me maximum sea room over an arc of 270°.

About 193km (120 miles) south of Heimaey the wind starting backing to the south before we had cleared either end of Iceland. I altered course southeastwards but after only 32km (20 miles) the wind continued backing to the southeast so we started sailing as fast as we could to the west; but only for another 32km (20 miles) as the wind then veered back to the south. We now headed north-east (not an ideal course but, in theory, a safe one) to get clear of that end of Iceland instead; any closer to the wind in those confused seas and the

bluff-bowed heavy *Black Velvet* would stop in the water. The Reykjanes headland and the associated shoals that stretch for 72.4km (45 miles) south-west were a constant worry as we could not afford to be embayed between them and Heimaey. However, after another 30 or so kilometres (20 miles) the wind increased dramatically. After handing the log, we ran north trailing four warps in a very heavy, breaking sea.

I had two very long warps carried for mooring to the shore; these certainly stretched back over two wave formations. Two other warps were streamed in bights and, in extremis, I planned to ask Dave if we could use his precious climbing ropes, knowing that they would, of course, then have had to be written off.

To begin with we had enough sea room (177km/110 miles) as I did not believe the wind would stay in any one direction for long – as had already been demonstrated. After about 64km (40 miles) I was planning to see if we could make Heimaey but steering under warps is not a precise art and, with the seas that

Black Velvet's *trysail has been set as a sea anchor.* Photo: Ewen Southby-Tailyour

were running at the time, I doubted that under storm sails we could have made a safe landfall.

Eventually the wind not only moderated but it also shifted to the west again, and for a brief period we were making a course towards Stornoway – albeit with some danger to the upper deck gear. In nearly 24 hours we managed only 13km (8 miles) over the ground thanks to the steep seas, a fickle wind, *Black Velvet*'s heavy displacement and short waterline length.

Then, at 0730 on 29 July and following a sharp rise after low pressure (lowest – 994hPa mb), the wind backed to the south again and this time increased to an average of 55 knots with powerful gusts on top of that. The seas were far too dangerous to do anything other than face them with our bows and so a makeshift sea anchor was rapidly made out of the trysail. Because of its asymmetric shape we could not get this to open like a parachute and so it was, effectively, never more than 'semi-inflated'. There does not seem, in practical terms, any substitute for the real

thing and if we had had the real thing we might have stopped in the water; on the other hand while the 2 knots we were making to the north did not help the 'lee-shore aspect' they did help to take some of the sting out of the breakers – aided, of course, by the presence on the near surface of the sail itself.

When we started this exercise we were almost exactly 96.6km (60 miles) south of Iceland's southern coast and 'aiming' for a point about 40km (25 miles) east of Heimaey. Unable to reduce this 'leeway' to less than two knots I considered what other options were open to me and the only solution I could come up with would be by courtesy of the Almighty! Any wind shift now had to allow us to sail over 60° either side of our downwind track: an angle of 135° that was opening quickly. On the other hand, at that moment, we could not, with safety, have sailed either side of our track by about 20° due to the steepness of the seas.

No matter what we threw over the bows we could not reduce our drift. In the deeper troughs, *Black Velvet*'s bows would pay off

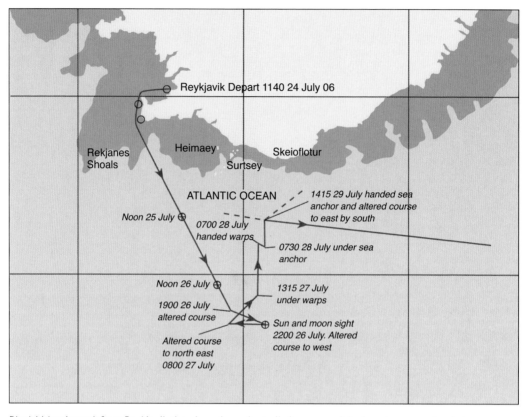

Black Velvet's track from Reykjavik showing where she trailed warps and deployed a sea anchor in heavy breaking seas. The dotted lines represent courses drawn to clear land.

by about 70° and then, as she began sliding backwards down the forward edge of an approaching wave, the sea anchor would bite and usually – but only just in time – bring the bows back to face the breaking crests. Sometimes this did not happen on cue, causing me real concern that we would be rolled to port. For much of this time the whole port side up to the mast was under water. It was too dangerous to be on deck because a breaking sea had removed much of the cockpit gear, including an inflatable dan-buoy. I had lashed the helm hard to starboard, hoisted the storm jib up the windward running back-stay (with a Spanish-reef in it to reduce the sail area – but it made little difference to our weather-cocking and was really only more windage), and went below.

As time moved on and Iceland moved closer I had few plans left to guarantee our eventual survival. Although we were not in distress, clearly we were going to be in about 30 hours' time so I began putting out an 'all stations' call every 30 minutes. Not, I hasten to add, to ask for help but merely to seek a weather forecast.

For seven anxious hours we waited for a wind shift while watching every slightest variation on the barometer – and for seven hours no one answered our calls.

As we approached the land and, thus, I hoped, within communications range of somebody, I was prepared to set off the EPIRB and transmit a Mayday. When beaching became inevitable I intended lowering two of the three anchors, but not to their full scope in order to be able to pay out more cable if they found the bottom. The seas were, of course, horrendous otherwise we might have tried sailing across them; seas would be building up even more as the water shoaled. I doubted that the anchors would be of any value at all but had to keep my mind active.

With only 72.4km (45 miles) to go to the lee shore, a wind-shift did occur and, conveniently, through almost 120° towards the northwest. With it also came a marked reduction in wind speed. Nevertheless, I allowed one more hour of precious sea room to be lost before deciding to haul in the sea anchor and everything else that was streaming from the bow. With the heavy weather jib (and extra worries about the bowsprit), no stays'l and three reefs in the main, we managed to claw to the east slowly. As the seas became more confused but less dramatic we were able to make a course of east-by-south. It was not comfortable nor was it entirely free from the possibility of being rolled but it was preferable to beaching. We could have headed slightly further south but I wanted to get as much easting under our keel as possible. Two days later we were at last east of the eastern end of Iceland and thus, if necessary, with sea room all the way to the Arctic ice.

It had taken us eight days to clear the island and instead of arriving home three weeks before my son's wedding we arrived with five days to spare. We had been less than 24 hours from being wrecked on a rockbound lee shore, so we were glad to arrive at all.

COMMENT

Even with ever improving computers and skill it should be accepted that weather forecasting is not an exact science. Therefore it should be expected that the weather could occasionally be other than as forecast. Taking the argument further, it should be expected that the wind will occasionally be completely opposite in both strength and direction to that forecast. Ewen Southby-Tailyour is too experienced a seaman to put too much reliance on his forecast, yet he came close to annihilation in a sound and sturdy sea boat in just these circumstances.

It is sometimes jokingly said that 'Gentlemen do not go to windward', but sailors would be unwise to assume that they never need to go to windward. Modern yacht design is often influenced by the racing requirement of excellent windward ability, but Ewen Southby-Tailyour's attractive heavily built gaff rigged yacht is probably not in the first league when making upwind. *Black Velvet* was built to be bomb proof and ice proof. It is debatable whether the wind strength

Black Velvet *trailed four warps in heavy breaking seas.* Photo: Safehaven Marine

given in this account was such that no craft of *Black Velvet*'s size could have made much ground to weather.

The best remedy if having a vessel with below average windward capability would have been an effective sea anchor. A correctly constructed, appropriately sized, parachute sea anchor will usually reduce drift to less than 1 knot, so Ewen Southby-Tailyour's attempt to make an ad hoc sea anchor from a trysail was the right tactic to adopt, although a sail with more equal length of sides could have been preferable. Makeshift sea anchors have been made out of sails that, if sufficiently large and strong, are almost as effective as commercially available, purpose-made parachute sea anchors. However, a sail-formed sea anchor needs to have rigging lines that are both long enough and of the correct disposition for the sail to fill and remain stable. The lines should be equidistant from the centre of effort, which can be found by bisecting the angles at each attachment point. Clearly this is best done before the situation has become desperate (see Chapter 7). Once a sea anchor has been deployed it is neither easy nor wise to try to recover the system until the weather has abated, so it has to work first time. Indeed the only time to experiment is in moderate weather in a non-threatening situation.

With gift of hindsight, Ewen Southby-Tailyour was remiss in not adequately testing out his makeshift arrangements beforehand, especially with a vessel with not-so-good heavy weather windward capability. Had he done so he might have established the lengths of rigging line on his trysail, or other sail, that worked efficiently. In all other respects he did all that could be done. Indeed he applied a cool and logical approach to a most difficult situation. Nevertheless, his experience should be a salutary lesson to those whose yachts simply do not even have suitable sails to go to windward or the means to hoist them, and have given little thought – apart from unwisely assuming that their engine will be effective in a storm force seaway – as to how they would deal with a lee shore situation should it come on to blow from an unexpected direction.

22 The loss of *Reliance AC*

Richard Heath

I left my family home in Romsey, Hampshire UK in December 2003 to join a delivery crew who were to take a new 15m (49ft) yacht from Les Sables d'Olonne, a fishing port and holiday resort on the North Biscay coast in France, to St Lucia in the West Indies. I was 23 and had been sailing for five years. The yacht, *Reliance AC*, was a Jeanneau Sun Odyssey 494. She had just been built and launched at Les Sables d'Olonne, and was specifically designed for the charter business. She was of light displacement with a relatively low draft and had a pleasantly spacious interior. She carried a low rig and just two sails: a mainsail with two reefing points, and a furling genoa. She was also equipped with a 75hp Volvo diesel engine along with a three-bladed propeller.

Our skipper was Alasdair Crawford, a Scotsman from Kirkcudbrightshire. At 24, he was already an experienced yachtsman with over 80,500km (50,000 miles) under sail to his credit, including five transatlantic crossings. Alasdair and I met for the first time just before Christmas 2003 on the ferry journey across to France. Once we arrived at Les Sables d'Olonne we spent a week preparing the yacht for our voyage. Much of this work involved laboriously taping plastic sheeting over the newly varnished surfaces, so protecting them from damage; mousing all the shackles, and putting anti-chafe material on the rigging. As might be expected of a new boat destined for charter in the West Indies, *Reliance AC* was short of equipment, and Alasdair used some of his lump sum payment to buy crucial items for

the delivery such as charts, an EPIRB and hand-held red flares. He also had his own hand-held Garmin GPS for navigation, and a sextant.

After Christmas, Kasper (Mick) Dieperink, from Bussum near Amsterdam in the Netherlands, joined the crew. Although only aged 17, he, too, was an experienced sailor and the three of us were all qualified Yachtsmasters. We would have had a fourth crew member (a Spaniard) on board when we left Les Sables d'Olonne, but his oilskins had been delayed in the Christmas post so we arranged that he would join us at La Coruña, the first planned port of call after our south-westerly course towards the Spanish peninsula. Given fair winds, we expected this initial passage to take three days and, once Mick arrived after Christmas, we were waiting for a window in the weather to leave. We were all very keen to sail south to warmer climes as soon as possible.

On 27 December it seemed that a weather window had appeared. The daily synoptic chart posted in the marina office window showed the pressure to be 1,006hPa (mb), with loosely spaced isobars across the Bay of Biscay. The nearest 'low' was just east of the Orkney Islands, and it seemed reasonable to expect that a ridge of high pressure was heading our way from the 'high' over the Azores. However, the French verbal forecast was not quite so benign. It was offering SE Force 6–7, veering NW. The weather that day at Les Sables d'Olonne was warm, dry and sunny with 15 knots of breeze from the SW. There was a moderate swell and although the forecast suggested an uncomfortable first

267

night, there might be in winter an even longer wait for better weather conditions. We decided to leave at midday.

Mick and I had every confidence in our skipper and, indeed, some confidence in the size of our vessel. We were not to know that a revised French forecast was issued at 1300, one hour after we had sailed, giving SW veering NW Force 8–9, nor did we have a long wave radio on board that would enable us to receive BBC Shipping Forecasts, which were predicting much the same thing for Biscay. None of us spoke French so we were unable to use the French radio forecasts or understand the VHF radio warning when we were at sea, which announced an imminent storm.

We left the harbour, in good conditions, with two reefed slabs in the mainsail but we soon took these out and made reasonable progress on a course slightly north of west. This heading took us between the Rochbonne Plateau and the Ile d'Yeu. We were sailing to windward, which was not the yacht's best point

of sailing as she did not sail very close to the wind, nor did she seem fast or responsive. The swell built up steadily and after two hours the wind increased, gradually at first, and then quite dramatically. We put two reefs back in the mainsail and furled the genoa down to just a scrap of baggy and ineffective sail as it had entirely lost its aerofoil shape.

The wind increased to 45–55 knots, with some much greater gusts. I saw the anemometer register 58 knots in a gust and Mick saw it reach 85 knots. Waves built up on the ever-increasing swell and broke over the boat with water pouring down below through the main hatch. We were knocked down twice. The yacht was not easy to handle in these conditions, as without a possible third reef in the mainsail, we were over-canvassed. Then one of the new genoa sheets parted and we had little alternative but to furl the genoa entirely. We all felt seasick.

At about 1800 Alasdair decided that we should turn back for Les Sables d'Olonne. A position was plotted using Alasdair's

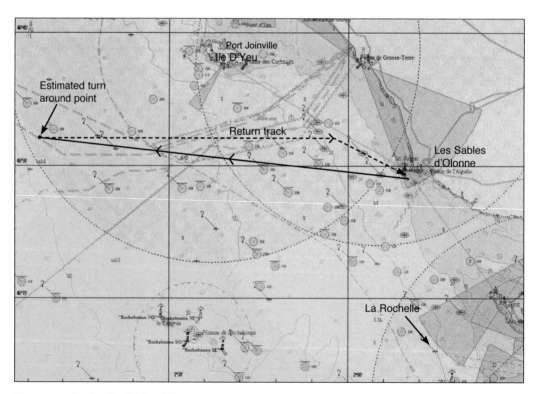

The passage back to Les Sables d'Olonne.

handheld Garmin GPS and a course laid off, but inaccurately, as we made a landfall somewhat north of our destination. I was off watch during much of the passage back to Les Sables d'Olonne but I do remember hearing the engine being started. When I came on deck I took over the navigation while Alasdair remained on the helm. Visibility was quite good between rain showers, but when we were in the troughs of the huge waves we could not see any lights, making their identification difficult. I felt sure that we identified the lights of Petite Barge and Nouch Sud buoys correctly, as we left them close to port and I put a fix on the chart from the GPS. However, I did not read in the almanac that the south-western approach channel should not be used in bad weather as waves break over the Barre Marine even in moderate seas. The lights of the town were showing clearly but I did not pick out the leading lights at Potence. After heading in on the town lights our course should have altered to port towards the harbour entrance for which

there were fixed red leading lights. I never saw those but I did see a red flashing light, which was marked on the chart at the end of the harbour wall. We headed for that. By then the waves were much bigger than I had ever experienced, and on this new course they were approaching from the port beam. Suddenly, an even bigger breaking wave was heard and, at the last moment, seen. This huge wave lifted the boat and rolled her over, breaking the mast off in the process.

Our safety harnesses dragged us all underwater. Mick told me later that he had cut his harness with a shark knife that he kept strapped to his leg, then disentangled a rope wrapped around his feet and finally surfaced. That rope helped him to stay close to *Reliance AC*. When another wave came the boat was rolled upright again and Mick was able to climb aboard as the partially waterlogged boat rolled towards him. While still submerged I tried to inflate my lifejacket and detach my safety harness. Something finally gave way

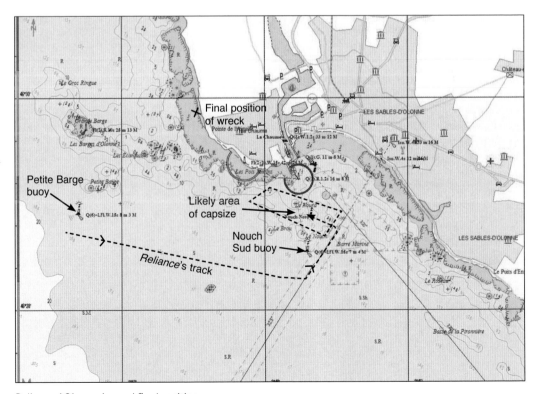

Reliance AC's capsize and final position.

The French Search and Rescue helicopter searching for survivors on the night of the storm. The flash of La Grande Barge lighthouse can be seen over Reliance AC. *Photo: Jacques Archambaud*

and I arrived at the surface after about a minute without a lifejacket and having swallowed much seawater. Later it was revealed that a clip on my lifejacket had failed. Alasdair was nearby in the sea and full of reassurance. He had not lost his lifejacket as, I was to discover later, the clip on his safety harness had failed, which had been holding him underwater.

At this point the partly submerged boat was already 100m (328ft) away. I was astonished and dismayed to see how far away she had drifted from us in so short a time. We swam backstroke towards her, coming within about 15m (50ft), close enough to shout to Mick onboard, over the noise of the wind and waves. Alasdair told Mick to set off the EPIRB and the red flares. We saw Mick ignite one of the red flares that Alasdair had bought, and at the same time he activated the EPIRB. Alasdair was still most encouraging, and positive that we would come through the ordeal, but the boat drifted faster than we could swim and we soon lost sight of her. After hitting the rocks for the first time, *Reliance AC* lost her keel, but remained upright and continued to be carried over the rocks towards the shore. Alerted by the EPIRB, in due course brave Frenchmen from the local search and rescue team, led by Monsieur Vincent Castin, wearing flippers and

diving suits, swam out to *Reliance AC* and persuaded Mick to swim ashore with them. The time was 0247 and the wind was NW 45 knots.

At some time after we lost sight of *Reliance AC*, I thought that I could see a rescue boat to seaward, searching for us. Later I heard that the sea temperature was 11°C. Alasdair and I clung together for warmth, with waves breaking over us continuously, hoping that the rescue boat would come our way. But this boat may well have been an illusion, as I did not see her again. I could, however, see a fixed red light on the shore and decided to swim for this while helping Alasdair, who was now showing signs of acute hypothermia. The few words that he did utter were very slurred. We lost contact in the breaking waves but eventually both of us reached the shore. At this stage we had been in the sea for about an hour, and I was almost totally exhausted, having had to finally drag Alasdair through the waves to the shore. Alasdair then stopped breathing and I did not have the strength to pull him out of the water. I gave him mouth-to-mouth resuscitation on the beach but soon gave up, feeling that our predicament was so desperate that I had to go and find help. I put Alasdair on a rock with his head out of the water and then I crawled, and then staggered, up the beach. There was no sign of anybody ashore, but I managed to break into a deserted house at a beach caravan site and found some blankets. I peeled off my oilskins, wrapped the blankets around myself and sank into a coma.

At 0800 the next morning, I woke up and went to look for Alasdair but I could not find him. I then made my way towards the marina office, obtaining a lift from an uncomprehending driver. At the marina office, I learned that *Reliance AC* had been found on the shore and that Mick was alive and well. Alasdair, tragically, had been found dead on the beach.

COMMENT

This harrowing story poignantly illustrates the acute difficulty and danger of trying to reach an unfamiliar port in safety, on a lee shore and in a storm.

The results were tragic, but much can be learnt from the event. The Maritime Accident Investigation Branch's finding was that a yacht equipped for cruising in the Caribbean would not necessarily be equipped with items needed only on the delivery voyage. UK yachts that are used in sailing schools, or for charter, have to comply with Maritime and Coastguard Agency Codes of Practice, whereas none of the safety measures apply for delivery trips. The most hazardous part of this voyage was in the first few hundred miles. A concession to safety was the provision of a liferaft, and the flares and an EPIRB supplied by the delivery skipper, Alasdair Crawford, himself. Attention was drawn to the lack of a long wave radio, a storm jib and a trysail. The final suggestion was that it probably would have been safer to stay at sea.

Following the Maritime Accident Investigation Branch's very reasonable findings, there are other relevant matters to consider.

Should *Reliance AC* have left Les Sables d'Olonne when she did? With the gift of hindsight, obviously not. After the week of preparation, probably 'harbour sickness' – a form of crew boredom brought about by having a boat and going nowhere – was taking effect. Sailors' minds need to be sharply focussed at times, for example when entering a strange port at night. The same minds may need to be re-focussed, or de-focussed, when they have been concentrating for too long on the pressing need for departure. A suitable diversion may have to be introduced, perhaps a visit to a local point of interest, such as a castle or a museum. The important objective is to break the 'bent-on-leaving' mindset. When Drake was allegedly determined to finish his game of bowls before taking on the Spanish Armada, his action may have been intended to prevent a disorganized mad rush to sea by his fleet.

Pleasant though the weather on the morning of 27 December was, just acceptable though the French verbal forecast may have seemed, and as encouraging though the synoptic chart appeared, there was a good case for waiting a day for the wind to come round to the north-west, giving a reach to La Coruña rather than 'one uncomfortable night' at sea with the wind from ahead. This would have given a chance for the ridge of high pressure to assert itself, if that is what it was going to do. The synoptic chart did not tie up with the forecast and that, in itself, was grounds for caution. When under pressure to leave, there is a temptation to grasp any favourable indication, and ignore unfavourable information. One is reminded of the autumn Biscay storm of September 1993, described in an earlier edition, when a remote favourable Danish forecast was preferred to the other far less optimistic and more local information, with calamitous consequences.

Actually, 27 December would have been a good day to go to sea to try out the new boat and new crew that had never sailed together before. It might have given some bones to a retreat strategy, in the event of things going wrong later, by revealing the two different lines of approach to the harbour entrance, and exposing the disadvantage of having no navigational information displayed on deck. A two-hour outing might have exposed the strengths and weaknesses of each of the crew that otherwise had to be measured by their ability in harbour. It might have exposed how well the yacht went to windward and the nature of her handling qualities in a blow. Charter yachts are often fitted with shallow draft, inefficient keels and *Reliance AC* was one such.

The crew, having failed to obtain every possible weather forecast, though BBC long wave transmissions are obtainable clearly but faintly at Les Sables d'Olonne, was caught in a decidedly difficult situation when the storm came. As with many yachts, *Reliance AC* was not supplied with sails that were suitable to make to windward in a blow, and the crew had few resources on board to fall back upon. So what else could they have done rather than run for Les Sables d'Olonne? The well-furled genoa was clearly useless to windward, and if it had been used on the starboard tack and if the other sheet had failed, which it clearly might have done, the whole sail might have unfurled. In the prevailing wind strength the full sail would have probably torn itself to ribbons before long, but whatever happened, the task of lowering and bringing the sail below, torn or not, would have been fraught with difficulty and danger. Three men would not have been enough to hold on to the sail and, had they tried, there would have been an unacceptable risk of losing one or more crewmen overboard. It is probable that they could not have hove-to successfully with a mainsail that could not be reduced below the double reefed state. We read, also, how difficult the big yacht was to handle as the wind freshened.

The crew did not have the materials for any sort of drag device, and the lee shore of Ile d'Yeu was only 32km (20 miles) away. They might have considered taking shelter behind Ile d'Yeu. Port Joinville is on the eastern side of the island, and offered a sheltered approach. At low water on 27 December there was enough depth above chart datum for the harbour to have been accessible for *Reliance AC* at any state of the tide. However, had they been unable to make to windward from the lee side of Ile d'Yeu, another nasty lee shore of the French coast lay not far away, and the approach to Port Joinville at night would not have been easy. Even so Port Joinville would have been a better option than Les Sables d'Olonne. La Rochelle, some 60 miles away, with its tricky approach and shallow entry, would have been a less attractive option than Port Joinville, but again certainly better than Les Sables d'Olonne. Generally the mainland French coast of the Bay of Biscay is one long dangerous lee shore, so the lee shores of the offshore islands have their uses in westerly storms. Port Joinville would have served well though Alasdair's decision was almost certainly influenced by lack of large-scale charts.

Lying a'hull is dangerous. Without the swell, the wave height would not have had time to grow to more than 2 metres or 6.6ft (see Chapter 9). But the swell had built up as the day had worn on, and the combination of swell and wind-developed waves would have been big enough to roll the boat unless the bow was held into the sea.

What about using the diesel engine? *Reliance AC* had a 75hp Volvo with a fixed three-bladed propeller. Having taken down the mainsail and lashed it thoroughly to the boom, the crew could have used the powerful engine to keep the bow into the sea until the storm was over. It would have been a long, wet and cold night, but not life threatening. Heaving-to under engine is a perfectly valid option while the engine is working and while there is fuel in the tank. The tactic is much used by fishermen who, by virtue of their job, are often caught out in storms. They call it 'dodging'. As it turned out, the weather had moderated to a manageable NW Force 5 by the morning. They could have rehoisted their two-slabbed mainsail and, given calmer seas, might later have had a chance to re-reeve the genoa sheet, enabling them to continue on to La Coruña in relatively good shape and on schedule.

The wreck of Reliance AC *well up the beach on the morning after the storm, having lost mast, keel and rudder. Her single remaining genoa sheet can be seen. The Grand Barge lighthouse is on the horizon above the bow.* Photo: Jacques Archambaud

Accepting that Les Sables d'Olonne was not a wise port to return to in the circumstances, what actually went wrong during the approach? Richard, who was doing the navigation, felt reasonably confident that he had identified the Nouch Sud buoy, but from that moment on matters are not entirely clear. The fact of the matter was that Richard was trying to find the entrance of a harbour surrounded by shoal water in the most difficult possible circumstances: at night, towards low tide with an onshore gale blowing and against a confusing background of town lights. Since navigation was of vital importance at this stage, Alasdair should have handed the helm over to Mick. Richard should have been plotting the boat's position from down below using the hand-held GPS, and should have been reading the almanac carefully, and Alasdair should have been the one to interpret Richard's information against the lights he could see on deck and pass instructions to Mick at the helm. It is customary for the skipper to take the helm on entering and leaving harbour, and with good reason, but in the prevailing circumstances and when a navigational mistake was the most likely and potentially disastrous occurrence, Richard needed help with the navigation. The skipper should be involved with the most difficult decisions and be in a position to check data for himself. Had the skipper handed over the helm to Mick there would have been more time to plan the entry into Les Sables d'Olonne, which could have been made easier by some key GPS waypoints to guide them in.

Having passed the Nouch Sud buoy, a red flashing light was spotted and they steered for it assuming it was the red light on the port-hand entrance pier. Even if it had been the correct light and they were on the chosen approach bearing, with the large waves on the beam it is quite possible that the boat would have been rolled, as entry from the south-west is only recommended in calm weather due to the presence of breaking waves on the Barre Marine. However, the green light on the starboard-hand pier which has the same intensity as the red light on the port-hand pier was not observed, nor were the leading lights at La Chaume seen, which should have been in the same direction and which have lights of greater intensity. Moreover, the flashing red light that the crew was steering for was not the ultra-quick flashing light described in the almanac as being on the port mole.

The only other red flashing light, and the one that most nearly matches Richard's description, has a characteristic of two flashes every ten seconds, and that was the Grande Barge lighthouse offshore to the northwest. It has a range of 27km (17 miles) and was less than 4km (2.5 miles) away. The course to the Grande Barge would have been 15° different from a course to the harbour entrance lights. In the circumstances, a tired crew could have overlooked such a discrepancy. The consequence of heading for the Grande Barge was that *Reliance AC* would have passed over the dangerous shoal bank of Le Nouch, or possibly Le Noura. Unless she had hit one of the odd rocks, there would have been three or four metres below her keel in calm conditions but, in the prevailing stormy conditions, rather less in the troughs of the waves. The tidal stream that would have been flowing nearly south-west at this point, combined with the shallow water, would have caused the waves to build up massively and to break. In these conditions, a sailing vessel would almost inevitably have been rolled and lost her mast on the seabed. Plotting back from where *Reliance AC* went ashore, allowing for the north-west-going tide and her drift rate, which we know was faster than a man can swim in rough water, it does seem probable that she was heading for the wrong light.

After the capsize, Mick's ability to remove his safety harness which was holding him underwater was much helped by having a knife at hand, and one is reminded of the old adage 'Every good seaman always carries a knife'. All three of the crew had difficulty in releasing their safety harnesses, and one is reminded of the sinking of *Waikikamukau* (see Chapter 17), when a member of the crew went down with the yacht because he was unable to release his safety harness. Safety harnesses must have a clip at both ends, and the old tradition of carrying a readily accessible knife remains valid.

Whilst agreeing with the Maritime Accident Investigation Branch's findings, additional conclusions are that *Reliance AC* should not have set off on passage on 27 December, and that the day would have been better used for sea trials. Having been caught out in an unexpected storm, the crew could have used the engine to keep the bow into the sea and perhaps make slow progress further offshore, or make for Port Joinville in the Isle d'Yeu. Having unwisely decided to run for Les Sables d'Olonne, they approached using a dangerous channel and then, with insufficient navigational information, they probably altered course for the wrong light, taking them to certain disaster.

It is easy to criticize with the gift of hindsight. Alasdair and his crew got it wrong, but there may be some of us, in similar circumstances, who would have done exactly the same. The account serves to reinforce the advice in Chapter 11.

23 'Bombed' in the Tasman Sea

Peter Cook

I joined *RED* in Eden on the southeast coast of Australia. She was to take us to Nelson on the northern tip of the South Island of New Zealand, some 1,770km (1,100 miles) across the Tasman Sea, known for its tempests. The owner of *RED* was Kevin Hansen from Alaska. Normally he just had his wife Beth with him, but on this first occasion in many years of cruising Beth was unable to come, so in her absence Kevin had recruited me, a yacht delivery skipper. We had met before in Tasmania.

RED is a steel cruising cutter, waterline length 14.6m (48ft) and about 20 tonne displacement, in which the Hansens have been cruising since 2000. When she was built for them in 1998, all their best ideas were put into her, gleaned from 12 years of cruising the Pacific in a Valiant 40. *RED* is a solid vessel built for serious ocean cruising and, after careful preparations in case of a stormy passage, we left Eden on 8 February 2004, expecting to take a week for the passage to Nelson. *RED* has an excellent sailing performance so we slipped along at over 7 knots with a light breeze off the port quarter. The first five days of the passage went well, with a few changes to the number of reefs as the wind went up and down.

At 1800 on Friday 13 February, Kevin and I enjoyed a meal together in the cockpit. The wind was blowing 20–25 knots from the NNE, our heading was due east and the boat was nicely settled with two reefs in the main, and the staysail set. The sea state was comfortable and our boat speed was up around 8 knots. There was about 50 per cent cloud cover with nothing unusual. Kevin went below at 1815, as we were doing three hours on and three hours off. The barometer showed 1,008hPa (mb) and we were expecting the wind to veer more to the south as a forecast shallow low passed overhead during the night.

At 1900 I was in the cockpit facing aft doing a little reading when I heard a rumble, not unlike a Boeing 747 taking off, and poked my head over the dodger to see what the noise could be. To the south I saw a huge wall of foaming swirling whiteness, like a blizzard, heading directly in our direction and it was obvious that there was a fair bit of wind about to hit us. I put the autopilot to standby, grabbed the wheel and started to turn *RED* to run off wind to lessen the impact. I was not quick enough, and the wind hit with all the force of a cyclone, *RED* gybed and was laid over to about 70° . After a couple of seconds she came upright, I got some steerage way and *RED* screamed off downwind, planing like a skiff. I could sense the force of the wind stressing the rig. There was no chance to alert Kevin, however I figured he would notice some commotion sooner or later. I remember glancing at the true wind indicator, which read 94 knots. The sound was incredible, now a close-by 747 on take off, but mingled with the scream of the wind in the rigging and a sound that I could feel in the pit of my stomach. There was no rain. I was waiting for the rig to collapse: *RED* was way over-canvassed for these conditions, and I thought at the time that something surely had to give.

That it did not indicates the integrity and generous factor of safety built into the rig of this fine yacht.

Then Kevin emerged in the companionway, wearing only his underpants, and his eyes were popping out of his head. I said to Kevin 'You had better come up as we have a bit on at the moment', which Kevin later described as the understatement of the century. Kevin quickly put on his foul weather gear and harness, and joined me in the cockpit. Just as he did so *RED* rounded up into the wind, this time staying at around 50° angle of heel with the stanchions well submerged on the lee side. She was pinned broadside to the wind, which was still blowing on the high side of 80–90 knots. It was now probably only about 10 minutes from when the first gust hit us. Kevin and I started to crawl to the foredeck to lower the staysail. The roar of the wind was incredible and the water was boiling all around us. It was not possible to look into the wind, and the spray was like being sand blasted. I have sailed a lot of offshore miles and experienced high winds before, but this was something else. I remember the struggle I had just to make it to the foredeck. Crawling forward on top of a car doing 160kph (100mph) would be a good likeness; the spray from the sea was painful against the back of my head and around the back of my ears (I was only wearing a polar fleece and my foul weather trousers and harness, as it had been such a nice evening before the blow). We finally made it to the foredeck and struggled to lower the staysail. Once down, we lashed the staysail to the lifelines. At no time was a word spoken between Kevin and myself, indeed it was pointless to try, such was the noise. Having secured the staysail I made my way to the main. Happily, the boom on *RED* is low, which makes handling the mainsail easy and safe. She is set up with Harken luff cars, which help, and she has good lazy jacks, too. Kevin had made his way back to the cockpit to secure it and retake control. Now under bare pole, Kevin was able to bear away and run off with the wind, with the result that he was steering north. The wind was still in the high

80s. We were running at over 10 knots with a fairly violent sea starting to develop. We were largely in control, though we occasionally broached.

I took the opportunity to use the video camera in spite of near darkness. We have subsequently watched the video several times and we still find that the sheer strength of the wind leaves us in awe. It was just amazing to see what Mother Nature can do without warning. While filming, Kevin asked what the wind speed was, and I swung the camera to show the wind speed at 86 knots apparent, and our boat speed at 10 knots. The boat was travelling far too fast for the conditions and the rapidly developing waves from the blow were throwing us around. It was time to trail some warps. Ready for use in each aft locker *RED* has two 91m (300ft) lengths of 14mm (½in) warp in milk crates. We took three turns around the primary headsail winches and slowly eased the warps out over each quarter. This had the effect of slowing *RED* from 8–10 knots to 4–5 knots. The warps were trailed straight out as I have found in the past that when trailing them in a bight they occasionally skip out of the water when the vessel starts to surf. With lots of sea room (we were about 644km/400 miles west of the South Island of New Zealand) we had no need to slow the boat further. At 4–5 knots we still had good water flow past the rudder and therefore the vessel steered well. We were able to activate the autopilot, which held a good, comfortable course. With the transom presented to the sea we took some water in the cockpit but with *RED*'s good storm boards, we never took any water down below.

With everything under control we went to write up our hourly log when I noticed that it was now 2125, so it had taken us around two and a half hours to recover control and settle the vessel. We were wet, cold and tired, and it was nice to be down below, insulated from the extremes of the weather. It was still blowing hard up top, however you would never know this below decks in *RED* with her comfortable motion and well-insulated hull. After five hours the wind had eased to around 60 knots, and by morning it seemed almost peaceful. We

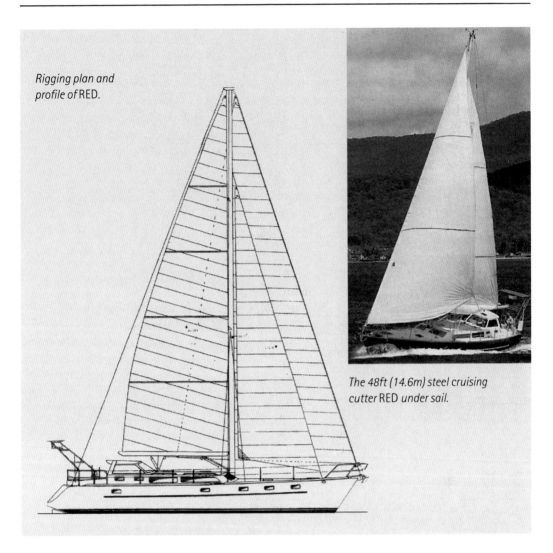

Rigging plan and profile of RED.

The 48ft (14.6m) steel cruising cutter RED *under sail.*

retrieved our warps using the winches, tidied up a little, set the headsail and set ourselves back on course. The top batten of the main had broken so we sailed the last 644km (400 miles) to New Zealand under headsail alone. But with the wind from the SE often up to 40 knots we made good progress close-hauled, sometimes under the storm jib and sometimes motor-sailing to make good our course. We arrived at Nelson at 2100 on Sunday 15 February.

Curiously we had received a weatherfax at the moment the blow hit us that showed no change in the weather we had been experiencing. Moreover, the barometer did not show any change until three hours after we were hit, but then showed that the low

had deepened from 1,008hPa (mb) to 985hPa (mb). Later we saw our depression, which we believe is described as a 'low-pressure bomb', appear on the weatherfax over our position. Twelve hours later, the weatherfax showed our low, now of 986hPa (mb), sitting over the top of the Cook Strait in New Zealand. The New Zealand weather bureau described this storm as the worst since 1976, and a 1-in-40 year storm for February, which is normally one of the most settled and fine months of the year. The weather was severe enough to stop ferries sailing the Cook Strait, close Wellington airport, create widespread flooding that shut off 18 stretches of state highway and, sadly, claimed the lives of two fishermen.

COMMENT

The unusually intense squall that hit *RED* in the Tasman Sea might appear to be rare, though one wonders how many vessels have been lost without trace as a result of a similar event. A meteorological 'bomb' is a quasi-scientific term that describes a low that rapidly intensifies, sometimes also called explosive deepening. *RED's* experience could well have occurred because she was in the '*comma-shaped*' arc in the cold air behind the cold front as described in Chapter 8 on Meteorology by Richard Ebling.

It would seem that *RED* was a sound craft to be aboard in such circumstances. She was of praiseworthy design; her steel construction, her strong rig, her warps stowed ready for trailing, her small crew of experienced seamen, Kevin Hansen and Peter Cook, all smack of a wise owner who keeps his boat and crew ready for all eventualities.

To survive such a blow, the crew has to stay on board; the boat has to be structurally strong, stiff (ie have a good righting moment) and have a rig with a large factor of safety. It is noteworthy that in a hurricane force wind on the beam, just one man could lower the double-reefed mainsail fitted with its 'good cars' and low boom.

The video shots reveal the usual photographic fact at sea in extreme winds, namely that there is too much water about at low level to catch anything in sharp relief. Moreover, darkness fell soon after the squall hit. Nevertheless, the video bears out Peter Cook's account.

Some owners continue to use the time-honoured technique of trailing warps to slow down to a comfortable speed when running under bare pole, while others use a small strong drogue for the same purpose. The advantages of the drogue are that it does not take up so much stowage space, and is cheaper to purchase and it is arguable as to whether it would have been better for *RED* to have trailed a drogue. Peter Cook has no doubt that *RED* was better off trailing her warps, and clearly the warps worked well in this case. He says that a drogue can skip out of the water, depending on the sea state and length of line; and that one cannot vary the amount of drag with a drogue – too much drag and the boat is pooped, too little and there is insufficient control. He believes that trailed lines are less vulnerable to chafe, easier to manage using primary winches, and can be staggered to change the angle the stern presents to the sea. He does not like to trail the line in the form of a loop, as the loop tends to skip the sea at times like a drogue, resulting in variable drag.

One could add to Peter Cook's remarks in favour of trailing warps, rather than using a drogue by saying that a drogue is more committing than warps. Once deployed a drogue cannot easily be recovered, and if it is necessary to cut the drogue line then a valuable line as well as the drogue is lost for ever.

24

Berrimilla braves 80-knot winds in the South Atlantic

Alex Whitworth

Designed by Peter Joubert in the mid 1960s, *Berrimilla* is a 10m (33ft) masthead sloop, solidly built of GRP in 1977 and owned by myself since 1993. She had a displacement of about seven tons in her world circumnavigation trim, and her point of vanishing stability occurs at 143°, so she is unusually stiff by modern standards. Before this account, in my term of ownership, *Berrimilla* had sailed in 13 Sydney–Hobart Races including the especially stormy 1998 race, in which she won the Performance Handicap System (PHS) class overall. She had also sailed in eight Gosford–Lord Howe Island races, again winning the PHS class in 1999.

On Boxing Day 2004, we set off for Hobart in the 2004 Sydney–Hobart Race with a crew of six, but this time with a difference. We intended to finish the race, drop off four of the crew in Hobart, turn left and sail for England via Cape Horn and the Falkland Islands. In England, we planned to race in the Two-handed division in the Fastnet race and then sail back to Sydney via the Cape of Good Hope in time to start in the 2005 Sydney–Hobart. In the event, all this was achieved.

We set off from Hobart on 10 January 2005 for the Horn with Peter Crozier, also in his 60s, as my co-skipper. All went according to plan, except for a near inversion in a storm south of New Zealand that destroyed the masthead instrument fittings and severely dented my ribs, causing an unscheduled stop in Dunedin, South Island, New Zealand, for repairs to both. We eventually rounded Cape Horn on 11 March and berthed in Port Stanley, Falkland Islands, three days later.

We left Port Stanley at 1300 on Good Friday, 25 March, after an adventurous final day in the harbour, during which a 50-knot north-easterly tried very hard to smash the boat against a big

The sturdy Berrimilla *is a Brolga 33 10m (33ft) sloop built using a very adequate number of GRP laminates. In Alex Whitworth's hands, she has competed in every Sydney–Hobart Race since he bought her from 1993 to the present date, 2007.* Photo: Alex Whitworth

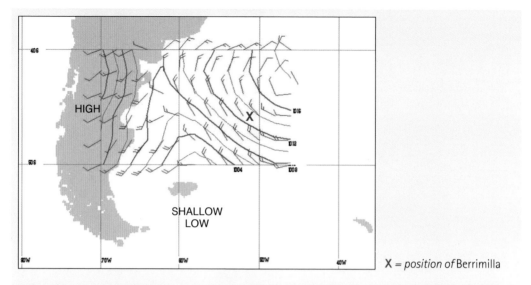

X = position of Berrimilla

Figure 24.1 *This is the GRIB forecast valid for midnight on 28/29 March. Our weather had been coming from the west and I have selected a forecast area that takes in the area to the west of our position. There is no sign of the low forming to the east.*

Richard Ebling says that with a north-westerly and from the shape of the isobars it looks as though the low was centred near to East Falkland, with a central pressure of about 1000 hPa (mb). It would have been very difficult to know what would happen next, but as the south-westerly winds behind the front are stronger than the north-westerlies ahead it would have been wise to be prepared for increasing winds.

commercial jetty. The intention after departure was to head northeast towards the more useful winds on the eastern side of the South Atlantic high and avoid the southerly current down the South American coast.

Things did not quite happen that way and on 28 March we found ourselves a long way further west than intended, sandwiched between a big high pressure system over South America and a tight low developing about 1,600km (1,000 miles) east of Montevideo.

I had pulled in the low-resolution weather file for our general area via Sailmail for midnight on 28 March (Fig 24.1), and it was not particularly startling. Indeed our actual conditions favoured optimism and

complacency. The sun was out after days of damp weather and Pete was actually wearing his shorts.

However, 24 hours later (Fig 24.2), there was a different story. We had worked out while in the South Pacific that the GRIB* weather files were reasonably accurate for predicted wind direction and barometric pressure but that it was sensible to double the predicted strength to get an idea of the actual gusts to be experienced. On that basis, Fig 24.2 predicts a south-westerly with a maximum strength of 70 knots, and this was not to be ignored. *Berrimilla* is not fast enough to go hunting for favourable weather systems and we had no option but to ride out what the weather had in store for us.

*GRIB (Graphics in Binary) files associate a specific weather datum (eg wind velocity or atmospheric pressure) with a geographic position. Because the resulting file is a collection of these points and the required forecast area can be selected precisely, the files can be kept very small and so are ideal over slow links such as Sailmail. They are transmitted as data, not text, and are reconstructed by the receiving laptop software to appear as a chart with wind arrows, predicted wind strength and pressure data embedded in them.

Figure 24.2 *24 hours later and the prediction is quite different, putting* Berrimilla *in the dangerous quadrant of the low to the east, with predicted SW winds of 35 knots. Experience told us to double the predicted wind strength and, in the event, this turned out to be an underestimate.*

Richard Ebling says that GRIB March 30 now places the deepening low some 600nm to the north-east or ENE having moved at a speed of about 25 knots, which is normal.

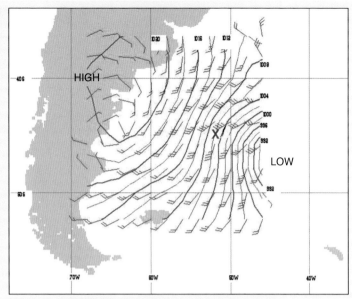

X = *position of* Berrimilla

Figure 24.3 *And another day later, the centre of the low is now 600 miles to the south-east and deepening.* Berrimilla *is in light breezes and sunshine, but still with a big south-westerly swell.*

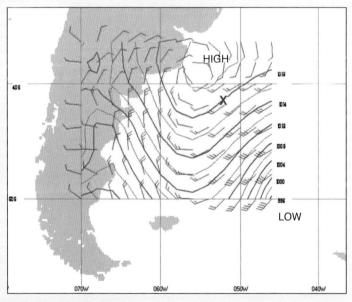

X = *position of* Berrimilla

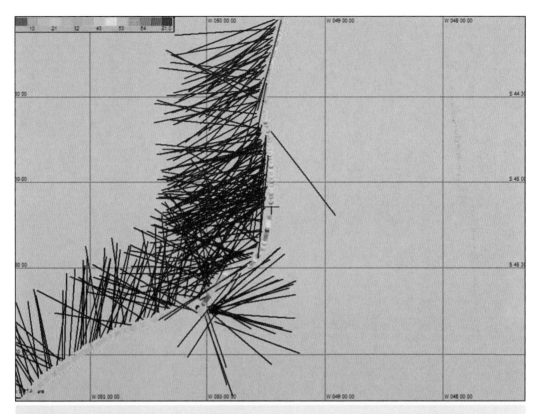

Figure 24.4 *This wind direction hedgehog figure shows* Berrimilla*'s track as a series of data points heading north-east then north during the storm; each point colour-coded for wind strength according to the colour scale at the top left corner. The orange/red dots are the 75+ knot gusts.*

The blue lines show true wind direction for each point, with the wind blowing towards the track. They are purely directional and their length is not significant. The boat is on the west side of a southern hemisphere low pressure system and the prevailing wind veers from east to south-west as the storm arrives and remains south-west to west for the duration.

Note the change in wind direction as each gust arrives. The blue lines connecting to each red datum point are about 40–60° veered from the prevailing wind.

Richard Ebling says that traditional theory has always been that in the Northern Hemisphere the wind veers in gusts, viz that the wind direction in a gust is nearer than that in the free atmosphere rather than backed to blow in towards low pressure under the effect of friction. In the southern half of the globe this of course would be reversed and so the expectation would have been for the wind to back.

Work done by Mike Brettle has shown that this is not necessarily so, but the Berrimilla *record is the first time that I have seen an instrumental plot of wind shifts experienced by a boat over open waters that were contrary to that theory.*

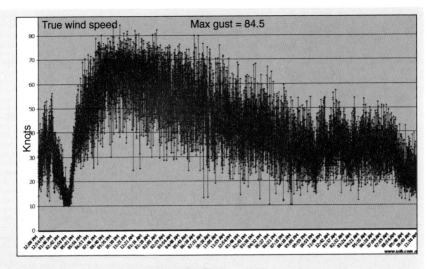

Figure 24.5 Berrimilla's *data logger for wind speed indicates how quickly a storm can arise. It also shows its typical gusty nature. Peak gusts of over 80 knots are extreme for a summer storm.*

Data from midday on 29 March to midday on 31 March. The wind drops to less than 10 knots at about 1700 on 29 March, then rises to over 80 knots by about 2200 and stays above 70 knots for the next 12 hours through the night and the next morning. Compare this with the hedgehog for the same period to see the changes in wind direction.

Pete wrote in his journal in the morning of 29 March:

WE NOW HAVE A VERY STEEP, mostly short, beam sea, which rolls the boat continuously. It has been blowing 40 knots here this morning but now that has passed through. We are left with very little wind but the sky is clear. We have had quite a lot of rain in the last 12 hours. The wind is due to go south tomorrow and blow up to 45 knots.

About three hours later he wrote:

The wind has come up quite strongly, and we have gone down from the No 4 headsail and two reefs in the mainsail to the No 5 headsail and three reefs in the mainsail. All was okay for a few hours then the wind increased to 45 knots so we decided to get rid of the main, and stay with the No 5 headsail. By the time we

got on deck to do the change, the wind was howling so we lowered both the main and the No 5 headsail, and continued downwind under bare pole.

It is now another hour later, and we are running downwind at 4–5 knots, still under bare pole, with the wind gusting to 60 knots. It is almost dark and this wind does not look like it will abate. I have entered our position of 45° 27' south and 49° 36' west in the log, just in case things get worse. This is the strongest wind we have had. The wind is now regularly above 70 knots: Alex said he just saw 82 knots.

A bit later Pete wrote:

The waves are not as bad as in the Southern Ocean. The fetch would only be 480–640km (300–400 miles) from the South American coast but, if this wind strength holds, it could produce some terrible waves later. Alex just saw 86 knots; he has stopped looking now, and is making a cup of tea to take our mind off the wind instruments. We have been hit by a few bad waves but have not yet been knocked down badly. The wind is really howling in the rigging. This is going to be a very long night and I can't see us getting much sleep.

The low intensified very quickly and the wind had risen from about 5 knots to 80+ knot gusts in about 5 hours. Fig 24.4 shows graphically the wind strength and direction on our track over 48 hours and Fig 24.5 shows the wind strength over the same period. Our Fleming self-steering gear was coping well with the wind on the quarter. There was a following south-west swell to begin with, but this came on the beam as we turned north to keep the wind abaft the beam.

At 2005 UTC on 29 March I wrote:

THOSE OF US WHO THOUGHT things would get easier this side of the Andes could not have been more wrong. Lots of wind this morning, then none, and now we are in a ferocious little storm that we were sort of expecting but at much lower strength. Quite scary at the moment – wind screaming at different levels in different bits of the rig, big waves building up, boat bare-poled, wind on the quarter as much as possible. Wind 60–80 knots in gusts, waves crashing against and across the boat. There is too much tension and noise to sleep … this is very nasty indeed. All we can do is sit it out and hope nothing breaks. It's gusting 80 knots and the waves are crashing over the boat – she's only little. Grey knuckles till it abates, and no sign of that at the moment.

In a lull a short time later I wrote:

Hi again – I'm taking a punt that it's decided to abate a bit – and I need to write a situation report as a distraction. It is still a steady 65–70 knots but the really big gusts seem to be further apart. You know things are really bad when the wind is so strong it flattens the tops off the waves and the boat has stopped rolling.

The lull did not last and later in the night I felt a change in Berrimilla's attitude and motion so I peeked out of the storm board flap with the big lantern. It was very dark, with horizontal spray, and I could see a quivering white line stretched astern from above my head. This could only be the liferaft painter, so the raft was trailing astern somewhere, and threatening to write off the self-steering or the turbine line; the turbine being an impeller on the end of a 40-metre (131ft) floating line to drive our generator.

We were both already partly dressed in wet weather trousers and thermals, so a rapid upgrade into full gear with combined lifejacket and harness was relatively easy. Both of us clipped on by reaching into the cockpit over the bottom storm board and climbed into the cockpit where we replaced and secured the top storm board immediately. The boat was rolling through a huge arc and big waves were breaking across the coachroof and decks with the cockpit continuously half full of water. The spray was blasting across in solid sheets and it was impossible to look upwind. The torch showed glimpses of reflective tape at some distance astern, sometimes high above, sometimes way below. The water-activated light on the raft was lit but mostly obscured by what turned out to be the torn canopy. The liferaft was clearly hindering the boat's progress and ability to ride the waves, but Berrimilla was coping.

The painter had snagged on the starboard secondary winch but I managed to bring it onto the primary winch and, by judging wave motion and surges, winched it in bit by bit to just off the starboard quarter. It was very heavy through being full of water, and the canopy was only barely attached. The ballast bags were, of course, full and were causing a lot of drag.

It might have been possible to keep the life-raft close under the quarter if we could have left the cockpit to attach a second line on it from a forward cleat, but it was simply not safe to do so. We decided it was probably best to let it trail aft again and assess the risk of damage – all seemed to be OK, although Berrimilla became very sluggish when raft and boat tried to move in opposite directions. I thought it unlikely that the liferaft would last the night but if it did there might be a better chance to retrieve it in daylight. I put a sharp knife within reach of the storm board flap in case we needed to get rid of the liferaft urgently, and we returned below, staying in our wet weather gear for what became a very long night indeed. The liferaft only lasted until the next big wave train, when the painter attachment tore away from the raft fabric. This was obvious from the change in motion as *Berrimilla* surged off the bigger waves. I duly reported the drifting liferaft with its *Berrimilla* identity number, on my satellite phone.

Our survey at first light revealed a badly bent stanchion, presumably caught by the liferaft capsule as it became detached, and the self-steering was still working, albeit sluggishly, with the liferaft painter wrapped around the actuator arm and paddle, as well as the turbine line of the generator. The liferaft lashings were undamaged but the pelican clip was open, with its slider jammed in the closed position.

By 1000 on the morning of 30 March, the wind was starting to abate and the barometer was rising but the waves, which were covered with flying foam and spray moving at the speed of the wind, were as big as we had seen off Cape Horn. I sent an e-mail report at 1600 to our web minder in Hobart, assessing the maximum wave height we were experiencing as about double *Berrimilla*'s mast height, which would have been nearly 30m (98ft), but this was difficult to judge with any accuracy.

Summary

We felt that the self-steering made a significant contribution to our safety by keeping the wind and waves on *Berrimilla*'s quarter and allowing us to remain below and have some minimal rest and an occasional cup of tea. Had we become beam-on to the numerous big rolling breakers, we would have had a lot more knockdowns, or worse. In an e-mail report I

emphasized the importance of having a drill or checklist for critical operations so they become instinctive. We had them for man overboard and heavy weather spinnaker drops but we did not have a drill to ensure that the laptop is always tied down and covered before leaving the nav table to go on deck. It became airborne during one of the knockdowns and its rugged frame once more preserved it from serious damage. I am writing on it now, more than a year later.

We had saved a guardrail stanchion from the Dunedin repair and we were able to fit it on 31 March, by which time the weather had become warm and sunny with a following wind. Neither of us had been hurt in this rather nasty episode and the boat was otherwise unharmed, apart from a missing spinnaker block and some seawater and disarray below. In my analysis I stressed the importance of good preparation for a storm such as we had just experienced, citing our sturdy storm boards, good harnesses and well-positioned strong points to attach them. The satellite phone had obviously been of benefit and I suggested that emergency numbers be programmed into the phone, as there is little opportunity to look them up in such circumstances. Clearly, a single pelican clip is insufficient to secure a liferaft and additional lashing is necessary with a serrated knife at hand to cut the lashing in emergency. How the clip opened remains a mystery. I am sure it was closed before the storm.

Epilogue

Sadly *Berrimilla* was rolled and lost her mast on her return from the Sydney–Hobart Race in January 2007. Whilst running under bare pole at night through the Bass Strait in winds gusting to 60 knots (according to the Met Bureau, though much higher wind strengths were also reported), accompanied by very steep and confused seas she was, without warning, caught by a breaking beam sea and was rolled. *Berrimilla* quickly righted herself, as one might expect for such a stiff design, but the mast

Berrimilla *on her way again after the storm, with the turbine line again streaming from the stern. The turbine line is 40m (131ft) and the turbine can just be seen midway between the visible end of the line and crest of the wave.* Photo: Alex Whitworth

collapsed shortly afterwards. The helmsman, Peter Crozier was thrown into the sea, held by his lifeline, and then was tossed back onto the pushpit from where he could climb back on board. The coachroof was dished inwards and holed, and the starboard aft window above the galley had been broken. The boat was flooded to about a foot above the cabin sole.

The EPIRB was actuated, though the Mayday was later cancelled by satphone. When help arrived, a tow was wisely declined as conditions were dangerous and the engine was working. *Berrimilla* made her own way to the shelter of Gabo Island, after which a water police boat towed her to Eden. She was repaired ready for the next Sydney–Hobart race.

COMMENT

It is impossible not to admire Alex Whitworth and Peter Crozier's extraordinary feat in putting a Fastnet Race between two consecutive Sydney–Hobart Races, and sailing all the way between in a 1960s 10m (33ft) design, backed only by modest resources. Their courage and determination was complemented by thorough planning and preparation, which justifies describing their voyage as an outstanding and unique achievement in the class of historic world-girdlers. Plentiful credit is also due to the designer and builder of their *Berrimilla*. The event seems to have taken the sailing world by surprise, as there is simply nothing to compare.

The storm that is described probably had the greatest wind strength of their circumnavigation, and is of particular interest as the wind speed and direction is recorded throughout. One is impressed by the rate that the wind speed increased, but also the occasional sudden and major changes in wind direction during the storm. The *Berrimilla* crew were alerted to the prospect of a storm by the GRIB file that shows a synoptic chart on the screen of their laptop. This is a most valuable facility in remote areas though the small GRIB file scale will probably not show incipient or small depressions. Other ocean voyagers have also found that the forecast wind strength needs to be doubled to obtain the strength of prolonged gusts.

Alex's and Peter's tactics were simple and effective. With ample sea room they ran before the wind under bare pole, leaving their wind vane to keep the wind and seas at a comfortable angle on the quarter. They spent most of the ferocious storm in the relative shelter and comfort of the cabin.

Short-handed yachts need to rely heavily on their wind vane, and well-designed and constructed wind vanes seem to have no upper limit to the amount of wind with which they can cope.

Regarding the loss of the liferaft, it can only be said, once again, that liferafts stowed on deck are tremendously vulnerable to major wave action. How water can bend steel is mystifying, but it does, and how deck-stowed liferafts continually carry away in heavy weather is equally mystifying but, as will be found in several places in previous editions of this book, they do. Occasionally stainless steel fastenings break and are found to have been made of 312 grade stainless steel which is not a marine grade, as 316 is, though it is usually sheer wave force that causes the problem. To avoid losing liferafts, one remedy is for designers to add a liferaft deck locker, as some do, that will ensure that the liferaft is both well protected and also available on deck at short notice. In the meantime, small craft with limited storage capacity below decks need to have enormously strong holding down arrangements which, in some cases, may entail strengthening the coach roof. The liferaft needs to be secured so effectively and cunningly that there is an apparent excess of strap, which can be quickly removed in emergency. If this latter arrangement requires a knife then this should be stowed permanently adjacent to the liferaft.

25 *Uhuru's survival storm*

Steve Powell

For those of us aboard *Uhuru*, my 19m (62ft) Oyster, the plan began to go wrong on Tuesday 29 March 2011. Whatever else I might have intended it was Antarctica and the fjords of the Chilean coast that had really been my target. Getting down to the Falklands from Uruguay had been an adventure in its own right as we slalomed between and around three quite vigorous storm centres and, although the Antarctic ice cap was the most fantastic place to visit, the passage to and from it and our rounding of Cape Horn had been in unusually benign weather conditions.

We had left Ushuaia on Tuesday 29 March and on this occasion I had as crew Chris Durham, 23, an experienced mate, and less experienced crew, David Jeffs and Fiona Sparks. We headed east down the Beagle Channel and at about 0100 on Wednesday morning, turned north through the Estrecho De Le Maire, that runs between the tip of South America and Isla De Los Estados. The winds had started building and veering north during the hours of darkness until they were coming from the northeast which made it a little uncomfortable but we plugged on not too concerned, though the forecast had predicted a short period of northerlies followed by a shift to the west with 30–35 knots and a 2.5m (8–10ft) sea running. It sounded perfect for our trip north, a little vigorous, but a good sail.

The winds stayed at 30 knots from the north and northeast until about four in the afternoon and, when standing my watch, I saw a sudden change in wind direction. I dumped the main

as quickly as I could and waited to see what was going to happen and, in all of 60 seconds, the wind backed to the west and came in on the beam at about 45 knots accompanied by freezing rain. There was a sudden change in sea state as two different wave trains fought for dominance. I had been prepared for this variation, having seen the telltale cigar shaped clouds in the west, but not the speed at which it happened.

The three crew were in surprisingly good spirits as we continued on our northerly course but, as it started to get dark, the wind increased and as the seas got bigger I started to become uncomfortable about being beam-on. We couldn't turn tail and run with the wind because we had West Falkland Island less than a hundred miles away and it presented us with a very uninviting lee shore. In these winds even with very little sail up, we would be surfing towards the rocky Falkland shores at about 10 to 12 knots so I was keen to find as much sea room as I could. I was getting really concerned, the seas had grown significantly and we were being assaulted by breaking waves hitting us abeam which risked a knockdown. Since running with the wind wasn't an option I decided to heave-to.

Heaving-to is a technique that all sailors know about but few use because either they don't really understand the process or don't trust it. To be honest, I had only ever done it in training sessions and in perfect conditions, but I was running out of options. A little before midnight, Chris and I prepared to heave-to,

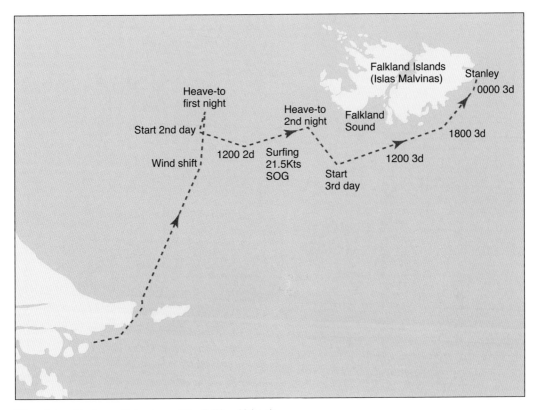

Uhuru's track between Ushuaia and the Falkland Islands.

with 6m (20ft) breaking waves and winds howling around us at a steady 40 knots, gusting to over 50 knots. It took us over half an hour but we finally got *Uhuru* what we thought was balanced using just a little main and the staysail and, although we weren't stationary, our speed was an acceptable 1–2 knots. Then we went below and closed the hatch.

It really is a remarkable sensation, sitting there in a pitch black night having a cup of tea while a severe gale raged about in the middle of the South Atlantic, still rolling quite a bit but nothing like the hammering we had been getting. I never really believed heaving-to could achieve such a desirable result, but it did, so Chris, Fiona and David set up a radar watch system between themselves, which give me a chance to get some sleep and then we all went to bed. Unfortunately, just when we thought that we'd cracked it, Mother Nature came back to teach us another lesson. About 0500 that morning and still dark outside, we were hit

by a big breaking wave on our windward side which rolled us about 70° and seawater poured in through the engine venting system, soaking our 12 volt electrics panel and blowing all the breakers. Chris and I went on deck and reset our sails, as the balance between the main and staysail was not perfect. We had started bearing away slightly on each wave, which was what we thought must have put us beam on to this wave.

When dawn came on that Thursday morning, it presented us with a truly daunting sight. The winds were still howling off the Andes from the west at 45–50 knots and the breaking seas were now running at 7.5–10.5m (25–35ft) from trough to crest, so continuing north in these conditions risked a serious knockdown. Trying to go upwind would get us a good kicking, while bearing away to the northeast risked us being blown on to the West Falklands. I decided that the only safe option was to head southeast back into the Southern

Uhuru at anchor in aptly named Thunder Bay, Antarctica. Photo: Steve Powell

Ocean, heading south of the Falklands and then, with the wind astern of us, head east to seek a safe haven in Port Stanley some 280 miles away. Once under way on a fairly steady heading it quickly became apparent that we could not rely upon the autopilot as it kept tripping out and setting off all kinds of alarms. The seas were still building and very confused because we were being subjected to the strong northerly Falklands current meeting seas from a little north of west. The bigger danger would come if, as seemed likely, the pilot lost the heading at the wrong moment and put us beam on to one of these breakers.

As the only two people onboard with any helming experience, Chris and I began the strength-sapping task of steering manually, helming one hour on and one off, while conditions just got worse with every hour that passed. The wind was gusting to 60 knots and seas were arriving as horrendous great walls of water seemingly intent on chasing us down. The significant wave height was still around 7.5–10.5m (25–35ft), but then six or seven giant waves of 13.5–15m (45–50ft) would arrive

from nowhere and, should the first one catch us wrong, it would twist *Uhuru* round hard, putting her beam on to the next giant wave that was following a few seconds later. Then the real terror began; can she be straightened out in time or is this the one that's going to poop and roll her? This went on for many hours with Chris and I continuing to rotate the helm every hour, snatching a cup of tea and a short break in between what was physically and mentally exhausting work, especially given the cold. Then the inevitable happened and a big, green, spume flecked monster wave running faster than we were and in roughly the same direction overtook us and dumped tons of water over the back of the yacht, ripping the cover from the inflatable dinghy hanging athwartships on the transom and with sufficient force to bend one of the stainless steel davit arms to which it was attached, leaving everything hanging including the crew.

We were now in the midst of what the handbooks describe as 'Storm Force 10, very high waves with overhanging crests, large patches of foam from wave crests giving sea

Chris Durham, first mate, on the helm during the storm. This distant mountain of a sea fortunately did not break. Photo: Steve Powell

a white appearance with large amounts of airborne spray reducing visibility: survival conditions.' This was turning into a very long a tiring day with no respite in sight, however the up-side was that we did set a few personal records, including the fastest boat speed ever recorded by *Uhuru* of 21.5 knots speed over ground, whilst surfing down the face of a mountainous breaker under only our double reefed headsail.

In the afternoon, the storm, which we didn't think could get much worse, got much worse. No break on the horizon, no respite, just more and more of the same, so I kept reminding everyone, myself included, that everything has to finish sometime and it's just a question of when. Chris and I were getting very tired now, and the physical effort of trying to keep *Uhuru* surfing straight down the waves and fighting against a broach was enormous. Despite our high intermittent speeds, we had covered barely a hundred miles in eleven hours for we spent as much time wallowing in the deep troughs as we did surfing at high speed down the wave face. I'd taken a fall earlier, my back and arm

were massively bruised and were aching like mad. As I couldn't risk misjudging the breakers in the dark and to bring some respite and rest, I decided once again to heave-to, and this time before darkness fell. We had drifted 17nm in 7½ hours on the first night but on the second night the winds and seas were much higher so I wasn't surprised when our SOG was 2.9kts and we drifted 38nm.

Once hove-to, the intrepid Fiona and David proved their worth by preparing a spaghetti Bolognese which we woofed up with relish and then they volunteered to take the bulk of the night watch, while Chris and I got some sleep. This time we were undisturbed which we attributed to a more satisfactory trim.

As 1 April dawned we were still 180 nautical miles from Port Stanley and the storm showed little sign of abating so with a quick bowl of nourishing cereal we were off and running again. Despite my damaged back and arm I had managed to get some sleep thanks to large doses of painkillers and we all thought it highly amusing that we should be out here on April Fools Day, a little moment of light relief as we

Chris Durham, first mate, on the helm during the storm. Photo: Steve Powell

faced what promised to be another gruelling day. Then the routine started again, hour on, hour off and every monster wave seemed to be the one that was going to end it all for us. Later that morning, with Chris on the helm, I was sitting in the cockpit having a break, when we both looked up and our hearts stopped, for coming up behind us was the biggest, scariest monster wave we had seen so far. I cannot truly explain how it felt. After all we'd been through, this wave was coming along to extinguish our adventure and we both looked at each other and simultaneously just shouted an expletive. But I should have had greater faith in *Uhuru* for as the monster caught up with us, her stern rose majestically until she was 45° bow down and we were clinging on for grim death to prevent us falling down the deck, but the wave did not break and we slid down its back side, squirreling in the turbulence. I suddenly realised that we were going to be fine, we were in a great boat, the *crème de la crème*. Nothing was going to stop us now so in some sort of primeval emotional release I shouted and got angry.

Shortly after that the first dolphins arrived, Peele dolphins, the prettiest dolphins I have ever seen, white with light blue bellies, jumping and spinning in the air as they escorted us and we were never without their escort. Occasionally, the sun broke through the cloud cover and the light illuminating the spume that was flying horizontally off the top of the breakers became the most beautiful thing I have ever seen. Power, beauty and fear, all wrapped in together. Suddenly, I was in the zone and enjoying it. For a glorious moment or two, I was king of all I surveyed.

Well my reign didn't last too long. At about eleven in the morning we got pooped for the second time, the port side davit finally gave way and the tender and motor were just hanging on one bit of rope that we had used the secure it after the earlier pooping. It was too dangerous to try and go back and put more lines around it so I just left it and, if it got any worse, we would just cut it away. We sailed on, wave after wave, fighting the helm, but all the time we had the dolphins.

It was later that afternoon that we detected the first signs of the storm losing some of its intensity and the sea state began to get more predictable. We still had the scary sets of bigger waves but they were fewer and when the winds dropped to 30–35 knots I started to relax. Now we just had to get into Port Stanley.

It came as a massive relief when I finally picked up a radar contact from Sealion Island, a rock just south of East Falkland, it was right there just where it was supposed to be, but that was the last contact we had until we were almost outside Port William, the entrance to Port Stanley Sound. We arrived safely at three o'clock on Saturday morning.

Damage from the storm after being pooped twice. Photo: Steve Powell

COMMENT

Steve Powell had joined the realms of high latitude sailors and was feeling slightly smug after pleasant and relatively unchallenging cruise around the Chilean coast, Antarctic and the Horn region. He was heading to pass inside the Falklands on his way back to temperate climes when overtaken by a fierce and prolonged storm. He had confidence in the size of his large well-found modern boat but, as the storm raged on and his electrics failed, he came to realise how vulnerable he was.

When the storm broke, he rightly felt deep respect for beam-on breaking waves and reacted prudently. Indeed his tactics were commendably seamanlike. The storm went on for three days, unusually long for summertime and, with adequate fetch, there was abundant time for large seas to develop.

It was interesting that heaving-to was adopted on two occasions, the first with slightly mixed results. The technique seems less advantageous for modern yachts in extreme conditions which are relatively lighter than their forbears, have low underwater lateral area causing tremendous leeway and are more difficult to slow right down. Steve Powell resisted the temptation to use his parachute sea anchor on the grounds that when deploying it his modest crew might have got into more, rather than less, trouble. As it turned out heaving-to was a sound tactic.

In a storm some matters must be dealt with straightaway and other matters, aggravating though they may be, are best left alone. The fact that he abandoned his davit-slung dinghy to its fate meant that he could preserve his energy and that of his mate, the only other experienced helmsman, to concentrate on what really mattered, which was to keep steering the boat through the large and dangerous breaking seas. It is questionable whether the dinghy should have been left in the davits. For ocean passages it is better to have the dinghy lashed upside down on deck or deflated and stowed below.

Regarding the problems with the autopilot, Steve had thoroughly assessed what extras he might need in polar latitudes and had the essential spares for the autopilot but it was the drenching of the 12v supply panel that caused the problem and he was at fault for failing to close off the engine ventilation when the storm came. A storm check list tuned to the individual boat is good thing to have.

The good sense, teamwork and stubborn endurance of the skipper and his small crew deserve respect. As the late Olin Stephens says in the first chapter 'once at sea, the action of the crew is what counts'.

26 A violent Arctic storm

Dr Charlie Welch

In 2002 Dr Edmund (Ned) Cabot decided that, after a lifetime of cruising between New England and Labrador, he would like to go further afield. Having retired, he set his sights on a series of summer cruises, to include Canada, Greenland, Iceland, Scotland, the Baltic, Norway and Svalbard, then eventually back to Nova Scotia via Labrador.

His choice of boat for this project was a new J46 sloop, a fin keel cruiser-racer which by then had already proven itself to be a sturdy, fast, and easily handled design. She was built in 2002 at the Johnstone yard in Rhode Island, and during construction 454kg (1,000lb) of Kevlar was added to the hull layup in case of collision with ice. Other add-ons included a watermaker, electric genoa winches, a detachable inner forestay for the storm jib, and full navigation electronics. Principal ship to shore communication was by email or satellite phone, and included weather charts.

In June 2005 *Cielita* began her summer cruise with a crew of Ned, age 63, Bob Quinlan, age 62, and myself, age 61. All three of us were physicians and fit and experienced offshore sailors.

We had a very fast trip from Labrador to Greenland, and a magical week in the stunningly beautiful fjords of southwest Greenland. After several days transiting Prins Christian Sund we departed from the Danish weather station at the eastern end on 15 July 2005, bound for Heimaey on the south coast of Iceland. On leaving Prins Christians Sund we intended to turn left and explore some of the spectacular fjords just to the north. However, the growlers and small bergs became increasingly dense and as the day grew overcast and grey it became very difficult to tell a growler from a whitecap, so we headed straight for Iceland.

The weather forecast was good for the next 48 hours but after a gorgeous day of icebergs and southerly winds, at midnight there was a sudden wind shift to NNE which rapidly built over the next four hours. By 0600 the wind was a steady 40 knots and it was clear we were in a significant gale, which was still building rapidly. We decided to prepare for the worst and, using the engine to keep head to wind, took the jib off the headfoil. As we lowered the sail it was still blowing 40 knots or so and not much wave height had developed. The sail was very wet and we were eager to be done with it, so we just flaked it as best we could and laid it on the cabin sole as bagging it looked to be pretty difficult in those conditions, and we thought it made good ballast. We had debated trying to lower it going downwind but thought better of the idea, for fear of it blowing overboard and compounding our situation or leading to injury. Then we set up our small, new, very flat North storm jib on the inner forestay, lowered and belayed the mainsail, and cleared the decks as much as possible. Raising the storm jib could not have been easier. Fortunately, during construction a short length of track was installed inboard of the regular headsail track to provide a proper sheeting angle. This coordination between

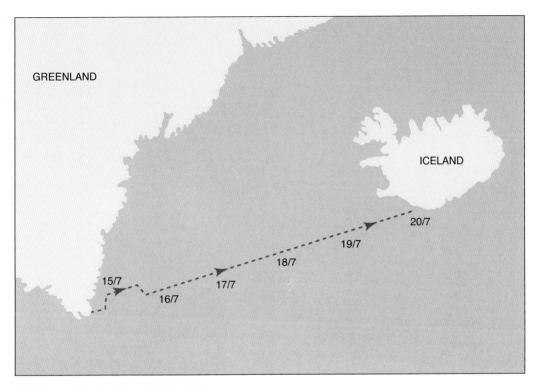

Cielita's track during the period described.

the builder and sailmaker turned out to be very important for our ability to manage this situation. The vessel was very easy to handle and quite fast under storm jib alone.

As the seas built, we tried broad reaching, having read, in *Heavy Weather Sailing*, several accounts of yachts successfully running off the wind diagonally. At first we were comfortable. However, during the next two hours the wind speed and wave height continued to build rapidly, and after four hours we broached severely twice: the second time laid *Ceilita* over horizontally.

We needed an alternative strategy. Setting our sea anchor seemed suicidal, since the waves were now 9–12m (30–40ft), very steep, and would have probably demolished a tethered vessel. At that moment we remembered the lessons of the disastrous 1998 Sydney–Hobart Race, described in *Heavy Weather Sailing*, in which the vessels that fared best in the severe conditions generally kept on sailing upwind under very short sail, often storm jib alone. So we sheeted the storm jib in flat, and headed

to windward about 45° to the wind on the port tack, coincidentally heading straight for Heimaey. Suddenly everything became much more manageable. The vessel was beautifully balanced with a slight weather helm, but very easy to steer. Even at the height of the storm, steering was easy with one finger on the wheel.

As the day progressed, the wind increased to 55–65 knots with gusts to 70, and wave height built to what we estimated was well over 12m (40ft), probably closer to 18m (60ft), but it is hard to judge accurately in those conditions. By the end of the first day the storm had reached its full force, and then continued for the next 36 hours before beginning to abate. The wave shape was very steep, but generally not breaking much. However, about every five minutes a severely breaking wave did appear with no gaps to slip through and it was essential to spot these coming, bear off to gather speed and momentum, then head straight into them as they broke over the vessel. We considered it likely that we would be rolled if we did not take these head-on, because they often buried the vessel. It does not get dark at mid-summer in the Arctic so, fortunately, the waves were easy to see at all hours from about a half mile away because of the white breaking crest. This gave us time to get some speed up though there was so little wind in the troughs so it took a while to gather any pace. The descent into these deep troughs felt like we would just keep on going down endlessly. Then the next wall of water came along.

We found that a watch system of one hour on and two hours off was about right. We began to look forward to going on watch because it was such a pleasure sailing to windward under fingertip control in those conditions: it was some of the most enjoyable sailing we had done in a lifetime of ocean racing and cruising. In these conditions it took constant effort to remain dry but it was critical, because at that latitude even a partially wet person becomes hypothermic surprisingly quickly. Keeping dry was basically a matter of close attention to tight seals around boots, wrists, and face. It was surprising how dry one could remain, although arms were the hardest to keep dry, and we had wet forearms most of the time. Ned got doused with spray early on before he was sealed up and had to go below for extended warming and dry clothes.

Below decks, things were quiet and orderly, but almost everything was wet. The communication system was soaked, and it packed up for several days, to the unease of our families ashore. Sleeping was difficult because of the extreme motion, but we were able to stay in the bunks with lee cloths. The long vertical descent between waves was stomach turning and none of us felt hungry or in the mood for cooking.

Cielita *at anchor in a fjord of southwest Greenland before setting off for Iceland.*
Photo: Charlie Welch

Bob Quinlan dressed in storm gear steering Cielita *downwind under the storm jib alone. This was before the boat started broaching and before Ned decided to bring her onto a course 45° off the wind.* Photo: Charlie Welch

Several problems we encountered were interesting. The most crucial odd piece of equipment on the vessel was ski goggles. They allowed the helmsman to look straight to windward to watch for larger breaking waves and anticipate them. Facing the wind was like being bombarded with a hail of BBs, and we could never have looked to windward adequately without this simple piece of equipment. Our voices in the cockpit were impossible to hear because of the shrieking of the wind, even if we were yelling into each other's faces. All communication on deck had to be by hand signal, and any discussions had to be conducted below decks. We left the dodger (spray hood) up, but the frame was slightly bent and, in retrospect, it probably might have been safer to lower it. We did debate this, but the shelter was so welcome that we left it up and let it take a beating. Had it broken loose it would have been a problem. The cockpit filled

completely from time to time, and an open stern would have drained more quickly.

The gale continued full force through a second day and a second night, during which a watch system of one hour at the helm and two hours below continued to work well. The vessel sailed elegantly at 45° to the wind, and when occasionally completely buried by a larger wave, would momentarily stop, shake it off, and continue on her way.

After the second stormy night the wind gradually abated and by the fourth day to a pleasant 35 knots, after which we had a beautiful sail to Heimaey. On arrival in Iceland, *Cielita* had no damage whatsoever.

It is curious how little mention there is of our storm tactic in yachting literature (with some notable exceptions), when the evidence seems to indicate that a modern yacht is usually happiest in severe conditions if sailing to windward. The evidence from the 1998

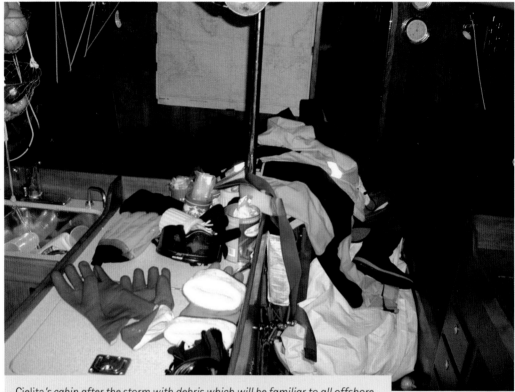

Cielita's cabin after the storm with debris which will be familiar to all offshore sailors. Note the headsail still on the floor, the pile of drinking utensils in the sink, the two pairs of ski goggles on the galley shelf and the onion on the floor which has no doubt escaped from the fruit and veg hammock.
Photo: Charlie Welch

Sydney–Hobart Race is particularly interesting when the main complaint from those who did well with this tactic is that sailmaker's tend to build maximum size storm jibs which, in extreme conditions, are too large and are not made flat enough to perform well. Our storm jib was both small and flat and this was a godsend, without which we might not have survived.

Later, on our arrival in Reykjavík, Hilmar Snorreson, the head of Icelandic Sea Safety, informed us that they were still searching for another (British) yacht in Denmark Strait which had not yet been found.

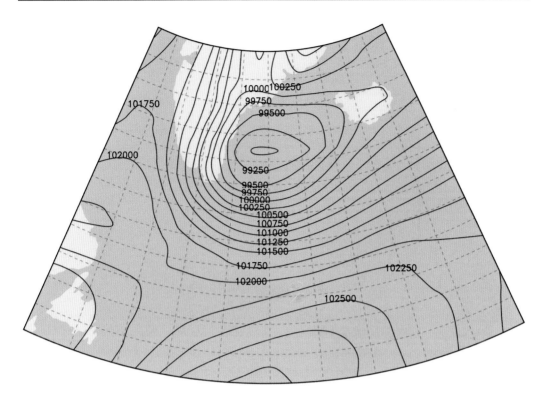

Daily mean sea level pressure for 16 July 2005, the first day of Cielita's storm. On the second day the low moved east to just south of Iceland, so Cielita was going the same way, which prolonged her exposure. Chart from: Physical Sciences Division, Earth System Research Laboratory, NOAA, Boulder, Colorado.

COMMENT

This account took place in Arctic waters but could have happened anywhere. Dr Ned Cabot – who tragically was lost overboard on his return to Newfoundland in 2012 – had gathered two tough, fit and experienced shipmates who were fellow physicians and ideal companions for when it came on to blow. Moreover Ned had been planning for seriously bad weather. In particular he specified a sensibly sized, flat storm sail and inboard sheet leads for the storm jib, a feature that makes a tremendously valuable contribution to weatherliness. He appears to have considered his heavy weather tactics carefully beforehand and he reacted robustly when the signs of a storm became apparent. When his first tactic stopped working well he sensibly switched to another. As Dr Charlie Welch, the author, and others such as Ed Psaltis, winner of the stormy 1998 Sydney–Hobart (see Chapter 3) race advocate, sailing 45° or 50° off the wind is a very sound ploy to use when there are sufficient helmspeople on board to cope. It should be noted that the storm jib was set on an inner forestay and that the outcome might not have been the same if the storm jib had been set on the main forestay.

Use of the engine to drive the boat through the breaking crests was not considered, though Charlie says that they would have been glad to use the engine for this purpose had they thought of it.

It was interesting that Ned took the trouble to take his furling headsail off the headfoil. One will never know how much this helped but one guesses that the reduction in windage would have been a big asset when the wind speed came to 50 or 60 knots or more. If the business of taking down the headsail is left rather late it will be necessary to weigh up the advantage of reducing windage with the risk of losing a crewman over the side. A compromise might be to ensure that the headsail is very tightly rolled. Another consideration is that headfoils without sails can flutter so furiously that damage may occur to rig fittings or even the mast. In this case the flopper stopper or foil saver has to be set up or a halyard has to be twisted around the mid-point of the foil and tensioned against the mast.

Looking to windward is essential for gauging the weather, watching for shipping or other solid objects and distinguishing breaking waves. Once again, goggles were found to be indispensable and every yacht should carry them.

Charlie's point about keeping dry is relevant too. In stormy weather water manages to seep into everything it can, especially going to windward, with the result that people can become very cold very quickly. Time spent ensuring seals are tight enough is time well spent. Best of all is to use 'dry suits' which are superb garments to wear in wet, cold, stormy weather.

Charlie deliberates over the matter of folding the spray hood but the protection the hood bestows is surely too valuable to warrant its removal in heavy weather though there is a good case for fitting a really sturdy spray hood in the first place.

Some very experienced owners install roll down curtains in clear spray hood quality plastic on each side of the companionway. They are secured at the bottom, in many cases, to the engine box. The curtains are edged with material and tidy away into fabric boxes when not in use. The curtains prevent water going sideways and make a tremendous contribution to keeping the interior dry either in stormy weather or when it is raining in a following wind.

Professor Sheldon Bacon, author of Chapter 9, who has spent a large fraction of his sea-going time taking measurements off Greenland and was in the same area as *Cielita* a month later comments:

'A tip jet (narrow, howling westerly gale) is formed if a westerly air stream over the Labrador Sea is obstructed by Greenland – the winds have to squeeze past Greenland at the first opportunity – Cape Farewell. Alternatively, one may find a low pressure system around Iceland has its western side obstructed by Greenland. Now the winds have to squeeze down the coast, so another type of howling gale results – a barrier wind. This is strictly parallel to the coast, and the clue in the article is that the wind is a NNE'ly. *Cielita* was unlucky enough to be hit by a summertime Greenland barrier wind!

Regarding Charlie Welch's estimates of wave height, whilst at the limit of the graph 9.6 in Chapter 9, it does show a wave height of over 14m (46ft) after a wind speed of over 50 knots for 48 hours. Thus Charlie's estimates are in the right ballpark.

It is interesting that the J46 *Cielita* became so unmanageable when running downwind whilst *Berrimilla* in similar extreme wind and seas was relatively comfortable. The explanation is that all boats handle differently. One should note the essence of Sir Robin Knox-Johnston's remark on the subject: Get to know your boat.

The late Dr Ned Cabot's preparations, planning and execution were excellent regarding the events of mid-July 2005 and he showed outstanding seamanship to bring his crew and boat through this violent storm unscathed.

Bibliography

1994 Pacific Storm Survey, Kim Taylor, Quarry Publishing 1996

All Weather Yachtsman, Peter Haward, Adlard Coles Nautical 1990

Alone Through the Roaring Forties, Vito Dumas, Adlard Coles (UK) 1960, International Marine (USA) 2004

Around the World with Ridgway, John & Marie Christine Ridgway, Heinemann, 1978

Because the Horn is There, Miles Smeeton, Grafton Books 1985

Blue Water Sailing Manual, Barry Pickthall, Adlard Coles Nautical (UK) and International Marine (USA) 2006

Cape Horn: The Logical Route, Bernard Moitessier, Adlard Coles Nautical (UK) and Sheridan House (USA) 2003

Deep Sea Sailing, Erroll Bruce, Stanley Paul 1953

Desirable and Undesirable Characteristics of Offshore Yachts, J Rousmaniere, WW Norton 1987

Drag Device Database, Victor Shane, Para-Anchors International 1998

Drogues: A Study to Improve the Safety of Sailing Yachts, Carol Hervey & Donald Jordan, Marine Technology 1988

The Eight Sailing Exploration Books, HW Tilman, Diadem Books, an imprint of Hodder & Stoughton

Fastnet Force 10, John Rousmaniere, Nautical Books 1987

Fastnet Race Enquiry Report, RORC & RYA 1979

Fatal Storm, Rob Mundle, Adlard Coles Nautical (UK), International Marine (USA) and HarperCollins (Australia) 2001

Halsey's Typhoons, Adamson & Kosco, Crown Publishers, New York 1967

Handling Small Boats in Heavy Weather, Frank Robb, Frank Robb, PO Box 1804, Cape Town, South Africa 1965

A Manual of Heavy Weather Cruising, Jeff Toghill, Adlard Coles Nautical (UK) and New Holland Publishers (Australia) 2000

Heavy Weather Cruising, Tom Cunliffe, Fernhurst Books 1996

Heavy Weather Guide, Kotsch & Henderson, US Naval Institute Press 1988

Heavy Weather Tactics Using Sea Anchors and Drogues, Earl Hinz, Adlard Coles Nautical (UK) and Paradise Cay Publications (USA) 2004

How to Cope with Storms, D von Haeften, Adlard Coles Nautical 2006

Ice Bird, David Lewis, Adlard Coles Nautical (UK) and Sheridan House (USA) 2002

My Lively Lady, Alec Rose, Adlard Coles Nautical 1988

No Law, No God, Mike Golding, Hodder & Stoughton 1994

North Atlantic, K Adlard Coles, Robert Ross 1950

Offshore, Captain J Illingworth, Adlard Coles 1963

Offshore Racing Council Special Regulations, Offshore Racing Council

Offshore Special Regulations Handbook, Alan Green, Adlard Coles Nautical 2005

The Parachute Anchoring System and Other Tactics, J Casanova, V Shane, DC Shewmon & G Macmillan, Chiodi Publishing 1985

Rogue Storm, Tony Farrington, Waterline 1995

Seaworthiness: The Forgotten Factor, CA Marchaj, Adlard Coles Nautical 1986, 2007

The Sea Anchor & Drogue Handbook, Daniel Shewmon, Inc. 100 Harbor Lake Drive, Safety Harbor, FL34695-2310 USA. Fax (813) 797 5708

Storm Tactics Handbook, Lin & Larry Pardey, Pardey Books 1995

Surviving the Storm, Steve & Linda Dashead, Beowulf Inc. 1999

This is Rough Weather Cruising, Erroll Bruce, Nautical Books 1987

Venturesome Voyages of Captain Voss, JC Voss, Grafton Books 1988

Yachting Casualties 3–8 June 1994, Maritime Safety Authority

Acknowledgements

As I have written before, *Heavy Weather Sailing* has become such a cornerstone of yachting information that it would have been a formidable task for any normal person to carry out the task single-handed. I have sought the most eminent and wise counsel that I could find to help me with the task and have had the script read by as many yachtsmen of scholarship and long experience as possible. Once again I owe much to others in the compilation of the seventh edition of *Heavy Weather Sailing*. The following have patiently given up much of their time to reading and contributing to the script:

Members of the Royal Yacht Squadron: Commodore David Hughes and Dr Nigel Reid.

Members of the Royal Cruising Club: Commander Sandy Watson – who has been closely involved in the four of my editions. David Ridout, Major General Chris Elliott, Alex Whitworth, Colonel Martin Walker, Andrew Wilkes, Hugh Marriott, Michael Derrick, Dr John Andrews, Allan Collison, Martin Thomas and David Wagstaff.

Members of the Royal Lymington Yacht Club: Mike Urwin, Michael Coombes, David Brett, Rear Admiral Kit Layman, Nick Ryley

Roger Taylor, whose high latitude experience in extraordinarily small yachts is even more remarkable than most, also read and contributed strongly.

Finally **Peter Sanders**, a sailmaker with a wide knowledge and interest who has given advice on storm sails, storm equipment and many related issues.

The first part of the book has benefited magnificently from the wealth of knowledge provided by their input. Those who have written the chapters are:

The late **Olin J Stephens II**, who must rate amongst the most admired yacht designers of the last century and whose yachts are famous for their sea-keeping qualities. Sadly he passed on in 2008.

Andrew Claughton, once from the Wolfson Unit for Marine Technology, Southampton, but now chief designer with the British America's Cup Challenge whose chapter enables comparisons to be made between design characteristics of yachts in a way that was previously only achieved by subjective means.

Matthew Sheahan, a very experienced yachtsman who writes for *Yachting World*, and used to work for a leading British mast manufacturer. Of late he has been more involved in other matters and has willingly consented to have his text updated by the well-known Harry James of The Rig Shop.

Professor Sheldon Bacon from the Southampton Oceanography Centre who has put an angle on the subject of waves which is likely to be understood by people who, like him, enjoy small boat sailing.

Dr Ed Reeves, who has written a most comprehensive guide on seasickness. He graduated from competing in International 14 foot dinghies to the equally challenging task of skippering his Olin Stephens designed yacht, a Tartan 37, to overseas destinations with just his young family on board.

Richard Ebling, a meteorologist for 41 years, who provided weather information over 20 years to the Royal Ocean Racing Club.

Hugo Montgomery-Swan, who is editor of *RIB International* and author of *Heavy Weather Powerboating*. Hugo has crossed vast areas of rough open sea in a RIB and balances this time with a love of music.

Dag Pike is one of the most respected authorities in the world on the subject of power boats and has written over 30 books on allied marine subjects. In addition to his masterly chapter on power boats, he has been extremely helpful with providing photographs of dreadfully rough seas.

Mark Orr, who has been joint editor of the magazine *Multihull* for many years, amongst other diverse pursuits.

The late Richard Clifford, who single handedly sailed half the world, and must rank among the toughest ever sailors. His skilful and courageous feats above and below sea level when a Royal Marine officer were absolutely astonishing if one is lucky enough to hear about them.

Barry Deakin, who, when at the Wolfson Marine Unit at Southampton University, brought a whole-some independent view to yacht design, especially regarding structure and stability.

I must also thank those who have enlivened and enriched the text by a major contribution from their own experiences. These are:

Lin and Larry Pardey

Lt Colonel Ewen Southby-Tailyour OBE

Alex Whitworth

Peter Cook

Deborah Schutz

Richard Heath

Steve Powell

Dr Charles Welch

I should also thank all those who sent in material for which space has not been found. Much of this material has, nevertheless, been valuable in shaping conclusions.

Last, but by no means least, my wife Sandy, for her tolerance whilst I was glued to my computer screen for months on end whilst putting the book together.

Index

Adlard Coles Nautical
An imprint of Bloomsbury Publishing Plc

50 Bedford Square
London
WC1B 3DP
UK

1385 Broadway
New York
NY 10018
USA

www.bloomsbury.com

ADLARD COLES, ADLARD COLES NAUTICAL and the Buoy logo are trademarks of
Bloomsbury Publishing Plc

First published 1967
Reprinted 1968, 1971, 1973
Second edition 1975
Third edition 1980
Reprinted 1981, 1983, 1986, 1989
Fourth edition 1991
Reprinted 1992, 1994 (twice), 1996
Fifth edition 1999
Reprinted 2001, 2003, 2006
Sixth edition 2008
Seventh edition 2016

British Library Cataloguing-in-Publication Data
A catalogue record for this book is available from the British Library.

Library of Congress Cataloguing-in-Publication data has been applied for.

ISBN: HB: 978-1-4729-2319-6
ePDF: 978-1-4729-2820-7
ePub: 978-1-4729-2819-1

2 4 6 8 10 9 7 5 3 1

Designed and typeset by Susan McIntyre
Typeset in 9.75 on 12pt Rotis Serif
Printed and bound in China by RRD Asia Printing Solutions Limited

Bloomsbury Publishing Plc makes every effort to ensure that the papers used in the manufacture
of our books are natural, recyclable products made from wood grown in well-managed forests. Our
manufacturing processes conform to the environmental regulations of the country of origin.

To find out more about our authors and books visit www.bloomsbury.com. Here you will find extracts,
author interviews, details of forthcoming events and the option to sign up for our newsletters.

Every effort has been made to contact the copyright holders of all images used within this book.
If any errors or omissions have inadvertently been made, they will be rectified in future editions
provided that written notification is made to the publishers.

Title page image: Thierry Martinez